Lecture Notes in Computer Science

Commenced Publication in 1973
Founding and Former Series Editors:
Gerhard Goos, Juris Hartmanis, and Jan van Leeuwen

Bruce Christianson   Bruno Crispo
James A. Malcolm   Michael Roe (Eds.)

Security Protocols

13th International Workshop
Cambridge, UK, April 20-22, 2005
Revised Selected Papers

 Springer

Volume Editors

Bruce Christianson
University of Hertfordshire
Computer Science Department
Hatfield AL10 9AB, UK
E-mail: b.christianson@herts.ac.uk

Bruno Crispo
Vrije Universiteit
Department of Computer Science
1081 HV Amsterdam, The Netherlands
E-mail: crispo@cs.vu.nl

James A. Malcolm
University of Hertfordshire
Computer Science Department
Hatfield AL10 9AB, UK
E-mail: j.a.malcolm@herts.ac.uk

Michael Roe
Microsoft Research Ltd.
Cambridge CB3 0FB, UK
E-mail: mroe@microsoft.com

Library of Congress Control Number: 2007940529

CR Subject Classification (1998): E.3, F.2.1-2, C.2, K.6.5, J.1, K.4.1, D.4.6

LNCS Sublibrary: SL 4 – Security and Cryptology

ISSN	0302-9743
ISBN-10	3-540-77155-7 Springer Berlin Heidelberg New York
ISBN-13	978-3-540-77155-5 Springer Berlin Heidelberg New York

Springer is a part of Springer Science+Business Media

springer.com

© Springer-Verlag Berlin Heidelberg 2007
Printed in Germany

Typesetting: Camera-ready by author, data conversion by Scientific Publishing Services, Chennai, India
Printed on acid-free paper   SPIN: 12201679   06/3180   5 4 3 2 1 0

Preface

Welcome to the Proceedings of the 13th International Security Protocols Workshop. As usual, our meeting in Cambridge was just the beginning. After that, position papers were revised (often more than once) and transcripts were circulated, discussed, and edited several times: our intention was not to produce a sterile record of who said what, but to share some promising lines of enquiry into interesting problems. Now we bring these proceedings to a wider audience so that you can join in.

Our theme this time was "The system likes you and wants to be your friend." Security is usually seen as making systems more difficult for humans to use. Might there be advantages to looking at security in the context of more general design problems? Perhaps those investigating the general properties of system design and those of us in the security community have more to say to each other than we thought.

Our thanks to Sidney Sussex College Cambridge for the use of their facilities, and to the University of Hertfordshire for lending us several of their staff.

Particular thanks to Johanna Hunt of the University of Hertfordshire for being our impresario and organizing everything, and to Lori Klimaszewska of the University of Cambridge Computing Service for transcribing the audio tapes (in which the "crash barriers" nearly prevented collisions).

The Security Protocols Workshop exists because you, the audience, participate. Once you have dived into these proceedings and have had some Eleatic thoughts, we expect to hear from you.

Bruce Christianson
Bruno Crispo
James Malcolm
Michael Roe

Previous Proceedings in This Series

The proceedings of previous International Workshops on Security Protocols have also been published by Springer as *Lecture Notes in Computer Science*, and are occasionally referred to in the text:

12th Workshop (2004), LNCS 3957, ISBN 3-540-40925-4
11th Workshop (2003), LNCS 3364, ISBN 3-540-28389-7
10th Workshop (2002), LNCS 2845, ISBN 3-540-20830-5
9th Workshop (2001), LNCS 2467, ISBN 3-540-44263-4
8th Workshop (2000), LNCS 2133, ISBN 3-540-42566-7
7th Workshop (1999), LNCS 1796, ISBN 3-540-67381-4
6th Workshop (1998), LNCS 1550, ISBN 3-540-65663-4
5th Workshop (1997), LNCS 1361, ISBN 3-540-64040-1
4th Workshop (1996), LNCS 1189, ISBN 3-540-63494-5

Table of Contents

The System Likes You
(Transcript of Discussion)

Bruce Christianson

Every year we have a theme and it's always difficult to ignore the theme if you don't know what it is, so there's a tradition that somebody spends five minutes at the beginning telling you what the theme is so that you can ignore it.

The theme this year is "the system likes you and wants to be your friend". The thinking behind this is that there might be advantages to looking at security in the context of more general design problems, and that those investigating the general properties of system design and those of us in the security community might have more to say to each other than we currently seem to.

We are all used to the idea that we design systems to have certain properties that we want them to have. In the security community we want to design systems also to not have certain properties (or to have certain *anti-properties*) which correspond to behaviour which we don't want the system to exhibit. These are complimentary activities in some ways, and run directly counter to each other in others.

We in the security community have tended to make a dichotomy between things that are the product of malice and things that are the product of bad luck. Roger Needham and Ross Anderson wrote a paper some time ago called "Programming Satan's Computer" [1] in which they almost argue that Satan is an adversary of a qualitatively different character to Murphy. A consequence of this view is that the techniques that we use to deal with a general kind of fault-tolerant threat are in some sense orthogonal to the techniques that we have to use to deal with a malicious opponent. So one question is, is this dichotomy still appropriate, or might we do better to treat Murphy and Satan as occupying extreme points of a spectrum, and think more about what is in the middle.[2]

In design exercises we are accustomed to designing a system by conceptually moving the system boundary around. If you're not sure how to design some part of the system then it's a good idea to try moving the system boundary across it and seeing what happens to your thinking about the rest of the system. Now that might perhaps tell us that trying to make a system secure by securing the system perimeter is not a good approach. Sometimes it may be more useful to consider the effects of moving the attacker across the system perimeter, and the same for the user or client, and for various bits of the infrastructure. I think the potential for interaction goes the other way as well. Roger Needham was fond of saying that if you had a completely secure system then at least turning cryptography on and off was a good way of checking whether you'd filled the configuration file in correctly.

---

[1] Computer Science Today, LNCS 1000, pp426–441.

[2] For example, see Geraint Price, Broadening the Scope of Fault Tolerance within Secure Services, LNCS 2133, pp155–169.

B. Christianson et al. (Eds.): Security Protocols 2005, LNCS 4631, pp. 1–2, 2007.
© Springer-Verlag Berlin Heidelberg 2007

We've already had a lot of experience in the security community with the idea that different participants in the system have different security policies and hence different threat models. A consequence is that when we're considering our interactions with someone else, we have to consider states of the system that are possible according to their threat model, but which according to our threat model are not merely contingently false but impossible *per se*[3]. Often one of the other participants in the system will insert a counter-measure to counteract a threat which they believe is real, and which we believe is imaginary, but actually we believe that the threat posed to us by their counter-measure is very real indeed. We spend a lot of time in practice trying to deal with the consequences of these counter-factual counter-measures, and there's a possibility that the design community might benefit from looking at systems in this kind of way. We've already had extreme programming, perhaps paranoid design is the next logical extension.

The ground rules are the usual ones. This is a workshop not a conference, and it's perfectly OK to talk about things that you haven't done yet. But of course it's also perfectly OK for people to interject from the floor about things they haven't done yet either. Try and look on this as leading a discussion rather than giving a presentation that you prepared before you came. Equally if you're interjecting try and make sure that you do let the person who's giving the talk say something important at some point, even if it's just at tea time. The computer is working perfectly so let's begin.

---

[3] LNCS 1796, pp63–64.

Experiences with Host-to-Host IPsec

Tuomas Aura, Michael Roe, and Anish Mohammed

Microsoft Research

Abstract. This paper recounts some lessons that we learned from the deployment of host-to-host IPsec in a large corporate network. Several security issues arise from mismatches between the different identifier spaces used by applications, by the IPsec security policy database, and by the security infrastructure (X.509 certificates or Kerberos). Mobile hosts encounter additional problems because private IP addresses are not globally unique, and because they rely on an untrusted DNS server at the visited network. We also discuss a feature interaction in an enhanced IPsec firewall mechanism. The potential solutions are to relax the transparency of IPsec protection, to put applications directly in charge of their security and, in the long term, to redesign the security protocols not to use IP addresses as host identifiers.

1 Introduction

IPsec is a network-layer security protocol for the Internet that is intended to provide authentication and encryption of IP packets in a way that is transparent to applications. IPsec can be used between two hosts, between two security gateways, or between a host and a security gateway. IPsec was primarily specified with the security gateways and virtual private networks (VPN) in mind, but the expectation was that it could also be used end-to-end between two hosts.

This paper explains some of the difficulties that arise when IPsec is used in a host-to-host setting. The paper is based on security analysis and experiments that were done during the deployment of host-to-host IPsec on a large production network (tens of thousands of Windows hosts). We believe that the problems discovered are not unique to one network or one vendor's implementation, and that they explain why there are few examples of successful host-to-host IPsec deployments in large or medium-size networks.

The problems identified in this paper arise mainly from mismatches between the identifier spaces used in applications, in the IP layer, and in the security infrastructure. For example, IPsec security policies are typically defined in terms of IP addresses but the addresses mean little to the application and they do not appear in authentication credentials. Another reason for the problems is the fundamental design principle in IPsec that it should be a transparent layer that has no interaction with applications, apart from the configuration of a static security policy at the time of setting up the applications. We show that, in order for IPsec to meet the real application security requirements, the transparency needs to be relaxed and applications need to become security aware.

B. Christianson et al. (Eds.): Security Protocols 2005, LNCS 4631, pp. 3–22, 2007.
© Springer-Verlag Berlin Heidelberg 2007

Most literature on security protocols concentrates on cryptographic algorithms and key-exchange protocols. We now know how to engineer a security protocol for authentication and encryption between abstract entities like Initiator and Respondent, or Alice and Bob. The latest IPsec specifications benefit from this work and represent the state of art in the field. The focus of this paper is on architectural issues, such as who defines the security policies and who has the authority over the various identifier spaces. We assume that the algorithms and protocols themselves are sound.

Arguments can be made that the vulnerabilities described in this paper are caused by flaws in the IPsec architecture. Equally well, it can be argued that we are using IPsec in the wrong way or that it has been implemented incorrectly. Either way, end-to-end encryption and authentication between hosts belonging to the same organization is clearly a reasonable security mechanism to ask for, and IPsec is a reasonable candidate to consider for the task. If IPsec in its currently implemented form fails, as we demonstrate it does, it then makes sense to ask what changes are needed to make the architecture meet our requirements.

The rest of the paper is structured as follows. We start with an overview of related work in section 2. Sections 3-4 provide an introduction to the IPsec architecture and to a well-known class of DNS-spoofing attacks. Section 5 shows how similar attacks are possible against host-to-host IPsec even if the name service is assumed to be secure. In section 6, we present a class of attacks that affects mobile hosts. Section 7 discusses an attack that was made possible by a non-standard extension to IPsec, and section 8 concludes the paper.

2   Related Work

IPsec is defined by the Internet Engineering Task Force (IETF). The earlier IPsec architecture specification [11] was based on early implementation experiences. The latest revised version [12] has a well-defined security model. There are also two versions of the Internet key exchange protocol, IKEv1 [10] and IKEv2 [7]. Where it matters, we use the latest specifications. All observations and experiments, however, were conducted with implementations that follow the older specifications.

The research community has paid a lot of attention to the cryptography and the key-exchange protocol in IPsec [3,8,13,19]. There is also some work on security-policy specification in large systems [9]. The architecture itself has received surprisingly little attention outside the IETF. The closest precedent to our work is by Ferguson and Schneier [8] who, in addition to evaluating the cryptography, make some radical recommendations for changes to the overall architecture, such as elimination of the transport mode. While the focus of this paper is on transport mode, all our observations apply equally well to tunnel mode when it is used host-to-host. Ferguson and Schneier also suggest that using IPsec for anything other than VPN will lead to problems but they do not elaborate on the topic. Meadows [16] pointed out that there might be problems with IKE if the authenticated identifiers are not based on IP addresses. A yet-unpublished article by Trostle and Grossman [23] also discusses identifier-space issues in IPsec that are similar to the ones we raise in section 5.

Recently, much attention has been paid to "weak" security mechanisms, such as cookie exchanges, which reduce the number of potential attackers or make the attacks more expensive [2,17,22]. While these solutions are suitable for many applications and, in particular, for denial-of-service (DoS) prevention, they do not provide the kind of strong encryption and authentication that are the goal of IPsec. Thus, we have to assume a Dolev-Yao-type attacker [5] and cannot argue that a vulnerability in IPsec does not matter because it is unlikely that the attacker will be in the right place at the right time to exploit it. We do, however, compare the consequences of having a secure (e.g., DNSSec [6]) and an insecure name service. The conclusions are valid regardless of how the name-service security is implemented.

One high-level explanation for some of the problems discussed in this paper is that IP addresses are both host identifiers and location addresses [4]. There have been several attempts to separate these two functions, including the host identity protocol (HIP) [18], and Cryptographically Generated Addresses (CGA) [1]. In HIP, routable IP addresses are used only for routing and hosts are identified by the hash of a public key. Cryptographically generated addresses (CGA) [1], on the other hand, are routable IPv6 addresses that have the hash of a public key embedded in the address bits. This makes them work better as host identifiers. Mismatches between the identifiers used to specify the security policy and the identifiers provided by the authentication protocol have been studied in other protocol layers, for example middleware [14]. While we believe that many of these approaches have merit, we have chosen to work with standard DNS names and IP addresses in this paper.

3   How IPsec Works

In this section, we give a simplified overview of the IPsec architecture with emphasis on the features that are needed in the rest of the paper. The architecture comprises protocols, security associations, and security policies.

IPsec, like most network security protocols, has a session protocol for the protection of data, and an authenticated key exchange protocol for establishing a shared session key. The session protocol is called the *Encapsulating Security Payload* (ESP). It takes care of the encryption and/or authentication of individual IP packets. There is another session protocol, the *Authentication Header* (AH), but its use is no longer recommended. The session keys are negotiated with the Internet Key Exchange (IKE), of which there are two versions (IKEv1 and IKEv2). The differences between the versions are largely unimportant to this paper.

The shared session state between two IPsec nodes is called a *security association* (SA). An SA determines the session protocol mode, the cryptographic algorithms, and the session keys used between the nodes. The SAs come in pairs, one for each direction. Security associations are typically created by IKE, but they can also be configured manually by the system administrator.

In addition to the protocols and associations, an important part of the IPsec architecture is the security policy. Each host has a *security policy database* (SPD) that determines an *action* for each packet: whether the packet should be protected, discarded, or allowed to bypass IPsec processing. The SPD maps the protected packets to the right SAs, and triggers IKE to create an SA pair if no suitable one exists. The policy applies to both outbound and inbound packets. For outbound packets, an SA is used to add the encryption and message authentication code as required by the policy. For inbound packets, the policy determines what kind of protection the packet must have. Inbound packets that do not have the right protection, i.e., ones that were not received via the right SA, are discarded by IPsec.

The SPD is an ordered list of rules, each one of which consists of *selectors* and an action. The packet headers are compared against the selectors and the first rule with matching selectors determines the action to be taken on the packet. The exact packet-matching algorithm has changed over versions of the IPsec specification and varies from implementation to implementation; we stick to what is common between many implementations. The selectors are typically ranges of packet-header values, e.g., source and destination IP addresses and port numbers. For example, the SPD of figure 1 mandates ESP protection for communication with peers in the subnet 1.2.*.* and a BYPASS policy for other peers. In theory, the selectors are not limited to IP and transport-layer header fields but can take into account other context, such as the hostname, process and user at the source or destination. In practice, such selectors are rarely implemented because they can cause layer violations and are, therefore, hard to implement. (We will return to names as selectors in section 6.4.)

In this paper, we are interested in the difference between two types of IPsec applications. The first application is a VPN, in which encrypted and authenticated tunnels connect geographically separate parts of a private network. Originally, IPsec tunnels over the Internet were used to replace leased telephone lines and the goal was to provide security equivalent to a leased line. The tunnel in that case is an IPsec SA between two security gateways. Increasingly, VPN technology is used to connect individual remote hosts to private networks. In that case, an IPsec SA between a remote host and a security gateway replaces a dialup connection. In both situations, the SA is set up in tunnel mode. When establishing a tunnel-mode SA, authentication in IKE is typically based on a pre-shared long-term key or X.509 certificates [24] issued by an organizational certification authority.

The second IPsec application is host-to-host communication. In that case, the IPsec SAs are established between end hosts and encryption and authentication are performed by the end hosts themselves. This kind of SA is usually set up in transport mode, although tunnel mode can also be used. The modes have subtle differences in packet headers and in policy lookup, but we need not consider them here. The host-to-host communication differs from VPNs in that one uniform policy cannot cover all traffic. Instead, hosts must support heterogeneous policies that allow them to talk simultaneously with peers that support IPsec and ones that do not. It may also be desirable to allow different authentication methods and certification authorities for different peers. The key exchange for transport-mode SAs is typically authenticated with certificates or Kerberos tickets [20], except for very small networks where pre-shared keys can be used. The lack of a global *public-key infrastructure* (PKI) for managing the certificates is often cited as the reason why host-to-host IPsec has not gained popularity in the Internet. However, we believe that there are other reasons (see section 5.1).

4 Classic DNS Vulnerability

This section explains how IPsec interacts with name resolution, and how an attacker can exploit the insecurity of a name service to circumvent IPsec. While we assume that the name service is DNS, the same conclusions apply to other name resolution mechanism like NetBIOS.

4.1 IPsec and Name Resolution

When IPsec is used for host-to-host protection of application data, the application usually starts with a DNS name of the peer host to which it wants to connect. For example, the application may have obtained the host name from user input. The following actions then typically take place:

1. The application asks the operating system (OS) to resolve the host name (e.g., "server-b.example.org") into an IP address. The OS consults the name service and obtains an IP address (e.g., "1.2.3.4"), which it returns to the application.
2. The application asks the OS to open a TCP connection to the IP address. The TCP protocol layer initiates a TCP handshake by trying to send a SYN packet to the given peer IP address.
3. Before the packet is sent to the network, its header fields are compared against the SPD. If a matching policy is found and it requires the packet to be protected, IPsec checks whether a suitable SA already exists. If one does not exist, IKE is invoked to establish a pair of SA's with the peer. The sending of the TCP SYN packet is postponed until the key exchange completes.
4. Finally, when the SA exists, the TCP SYN packet is sent encrypted and/or authenticated with the session key. The following data packets are similarly protected.

4.2 DNS Spoofing

In the well-known DNS spoofing attack [3], the attacker substitutes its own IP address (e.g., "3.4.5.6"), or someone else's address, for the DNS response. As

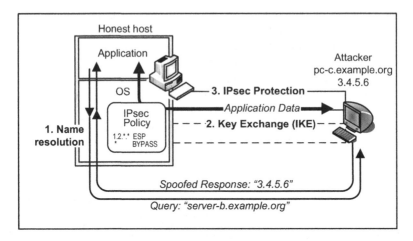

Fig. 1. DNS Spoofing Attack

a consequence, the application at the honest host connects to the wrong peer. This attack is shown in figure 1.

If the attacker is located at an IP address for which the honest host requires IPsec protection, then the attacker needs to authenticate itself to the honest host. This is usually called an *insider attack*. We will return to the insider attacks in section 5.1 where we show that they do not require DNS spoofing.

A more interesting DNS-spoofing scenario is one where the attacker is located at an IP address for which the honest host has a BYPASS policy (as in figure 1). In that case, the honest host will mistakenly skip authentication and send the packets unprotected. In practice, the honest host will always have a BYPASS policy for some peer addresses. First, there are hosts in almost every local network that do not support IPsec, such as network printers. The attacker may hijack the address of one such host. Second, most hosts will want to open unauthenticated connections to the public Internet. Thus, all IP addresses that are outside the honest host's own domain usually have a BYPASS policy.

Problem 1a: It is possible to bypass an IPsec policy with DNS spoofing.

Middle boxes, e.g., NATs, complicate the scenario but do not necessarily prevent the attacks. As long as the attacker manages to spoof the DNS response or is able to manipulate the DNS servers, the attack will succeed equally well from outside the NAT.

In the DNS-spoofing attack of figure 1, the wrong policy is applied to the packets because the attacker controls the binding of DNS names, which are the identifiers used by the application, to IP addresses, which are the identifiers used in the security policy. It is therefore tempting to blame the insecure name resolution mechanism for the attacks. This logically leads to the idea of introducing a secure name service. In the following section, however, we will argue that the current IPsec architecture makes the security of the name service irrelevant.

5   Identifier Mismatch

In this section, we assume that DNS spoofing is not possible. This allows us to focus on other design issues in IPsec. Indeed, we discover in section 5.1 that, regardless of whether the name service is secure or not, there still is a disconnection between host names and IP addresses in IPsec. In sections 5.2-5.5, we discuss potential solutions.

5.1   Attack Without DNS Spoofing

Recall that the security association between the honest host and its peer is created by the authenticated key exchange, IKE. A critical part of the key exchange is a step in which the peer host sends to the honest host a credential that proves its identity. The credential is usually an X.509 public-key certificate issued by a certification authority (CA) [24]. Equivalently, the credential could be a Kerberos ticket (in IKEv1 with GSS-API authentication [15,20]), in which case it is issued by a Kerberos KDC. We will use the word certificate below but the discussion applies to the other credential types as well.

The purpose of the certificate in IKE is to bind together the peer host's identity and its public signature verification key, which is then used for cryptographic authentication. The identifier in the certificate is typically a host name. While certificates can, in theory, contain IP addresses, they rarely do. Thus, while the SPD is typically specified in terms of IP addresses, the certificate that is used to authenticate the peer host only contains the peer's host name.

In figure 2, we trace the data flow when an application at an honest host tries to connect to a peer. The application starts with a host name ("server-b.example.org"). It uses the name service to resolve the host name into an IP address ("1.2.3.4"). This time, the answer is correct because we assume no DNS spoofing. The application then asks the OS to connect to the IP address, which triggers IKE. Within the IKE protocol, the honest host receives the peer's certificate. After the necessary cryptographic computations, it would be crucial for the honest host to compare the identifier in the certificate against the identifier that the application started with. But the only identifier in the certificate is a host name ("pc-c.example.org") and the only identifier known to the TCP/IP stack at this point is the peer IP address. Thus, the stack is unable to authenticate the peer, or to detect the use of a wrong certificate.

The next question is, of course, what do real IPsec implementations do when they encounter this impossible decision. One answer is that IPsec is not commonly deployed in host-to-host scenarios. It is used between VPN gateways that have static IP addresses and pre-shared keys, so that certificates are unnecessary. IPsec is also used in host-to-gateway VPNs, where the necessary checks can be made in a non-standard way by special VPN management software. (A mechanism for these checks is being standardized. See section 5.3.)

But there is an increasing demand to secure private networks from intruders with host-to-host IPsec. The only solution that we have seen in actual IPsec deployments is to skip the impossible check between the host name in the certificate and the IP address in the SPD and to continue as if everything were ok! (Appendix A contains instructions for a simple experiment to test this.)

The consequence of the failure to check the name in the certificate is to enable insider attacks. An attacker only needs to have a certificate issued by a CA that the honest host trusts. This means that, in an intranet, such as the large network we observed, any authorized host can impersonate all other authorized hosts. On the other hand, an intruder that plugs into the network or a host that is on a revocation or quarantine list cannot. Spoofed packets that manage to enter the intranet, e.g., via an unauthorized ingress route are also detected and discarded. In the network that we observed, these were the main security goals and spoofing attacks by authorized hosts were a secondary concern.

Another way to explain the situation is to say that host-to-host IPsec provides group authentication but not authentication of individual hosts. This is sometimes acceptable but not always. It is of paramount importance that those who rely on the authentication understand the limitations of the technology. Unfortunately, one is easily misled by IPsec literature on this point.

> **Problem 1b:** Host-to-host IPsec currently provides only group authentication. Hosts certified by the same CA can impersonate each other.

At present, host-to-host IPsec is not commonly used between Internet hosts that belong to different organizations. The reason for this is usually thought to be the lack of a global PKI. But even if a global PKI existed, host-to-host IPsec with certificate authentication on the Internet would be insecure because anyone with a certificate from the global PKI would be able to impersonate everyone else. The above facts are important to keep in mind because, with IKEv2, there will be the possibility of using TLS certificates for server authentication and passwords for client authentication (IKEv2 with EAP-PEAP authentication). While this could partially solve the PKI availability issue, it would not prevent the certified servers from mounting impersonation attacks against each other.

5.2   Secure Name Service

The honest host in figure 2 is faced with comparing a name ("PC-C") and an IP address ("1.2.3.4"). One's first thought, especially if one happens to be staring at that part of the code and not thinking of the high-level architecture, is to use secure DNS for this purpose. There are practical problems, however, in addition to the fact that secure DNS is not widely deployed.

If secure DNS is used to prevent the attacks, then we need both a secure forward lookup (find the address based on a name) and a secure reverse lookup (find the name based on an address). The forward lookup is required in the first phase where the application resolves the original name into an IP address. The reverse lookup is needed during the key exchange for comparing the IP address and the name in the certificate. Note that the OS was asked to connect to a specific IP address and, therefore, has to map from the address to the name and not the other way. Otherwise, the attacker could easily set its own DNS records to

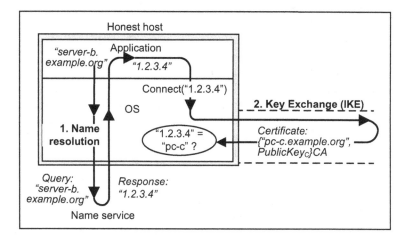

Fig. 2. Interaction of DNS and IKE

map its host name ("pc-c.example.org") to any address, including the authentic peer address ("1.2.3.4"). In other words, the secure forward lookup verifies that the owner of the name wants to associate it with a specific IP address, and the secure reverse lookup verifies that the owner of the IP address wants to associate it with the DNS name. For this reason, the reverse DNS records form a hierarchy that is isomorphic with the way IP addresses are allocated.

There are several practical issues with the secure reverse DNS lookup. Firstly, secure DNS is not any more widely available for reverse lookups than for forward lookups. Secondly, many hosts have dynamic addresses (DHCP or IPv6 autoconfiguration) and reverse DNS records are generally not updated for them. While reverse DNS is supposed to work for all Internet hosts, the response is often a generic name assigned by an ISP rather than the name actually used by the host. Thirdly, if an IP address has multiple names associated with it, the reverse lookup usually returns only one of them, and not necessarily the one used in the certificate. Hosts behind a NAT have the same problem because they share a single IP address, which means that there is no one unique owner for the address. Yet, they may still use IPsec with NAT traversal support. Fourthly, there are many ways in which the application may learn the IP address corresponding to the peer host name. IPsec does not require the use of one specific technology, such as DNS. In many cases, the IP address is obtained by an application-specific mechanism (e.g., in a SIP INVITE message) or from a proprietary name resolution mechanism (e.g., NetBIOS). It is therefore difficult to ensure comprehensive protection for name resolution.

These obstacles can sometimes be overcome within an intranet. For example, some DHCP servers automatically update the reverse DNS records when address allocation changes and IPsec can be used to protect the DNS queries and responses with an authoritative server. Nevertheless, it is clear that reverse DNS is not a generic solution to the identifier mismatch problem.

5.3   Peer Authorization Database

The latest version of the IPsec architecture specification [12] proposes the addition of a *peer authorization database* (PAD) to each IPsec host. The purpose of this database is to indicate the range of SPD identities (IP addresses) that each authenticated identity (name in the certificate) is authorized to use. The semantics of such a database is essentially the same as what we wanted to achieve with reverse DNS above: it determines which authenticated names may be associated with an IP address. The difference is that the PAD is implemented as a local database rather than as a lookup from a server.

For a VPN, the PAD solves the reverse mapping problem elegantly. For gateway-to-gateway VPN, it removes the need to distribute pre-shared keys. Instead, the gateways can be configured with a static table of peer gateway names and their IP addresses, and certificates can be used for authentication in IKE. In host-to-gateway VPN, the gateway typically allocates an intranet IP address for the remote host. IKEv2 even provides a standard mechanism to do so. In that case, the ownership of the IP address is immediately known to the gateway and the mapping can be added into the PAD. In both VPN scenarios, the PAD is a standard way to implement the checks that well-designed VPN software previously had to do in some ad-hoc manner. For host-to-host IPsec, however, the PAD is not so much a solution as a rephrasing of the problem. The question becomes how to implement the PAD, which is an equivalent task to that of implementing the secure reverse DNS.

5.4   Giving Up Statelessness

It is possible that all the attention given to secure DNS technology has lead us to look for the solution in the wrong place. The security property really required by the application is not a correspondence between a host name and an IP address. What the application cares about is that the host name in the certificate ("pc-c.example.org") is the same as the host name that it started with ("server-b.example.org"). If this can be ensured, the application does not care what the IP address is.

The problem is twofold. First, by the time the application calls *connect*, it simply passes to the OS an IP address without any indication of how the address was obtained. Second, the IPsec policy is stated in terms of IP addresses.

The first problem stems from the fact that the IP layer has been designed to be as stateless as possible. That is, the IP layer is not aware of higher-layer connections or sessions and does not maintain a state for them. This design principle has usually served protocol designers well. In this case, however, it would be beneficial for the OS to remember that it has previously performed the name resolution and to check that the name in the certificate is the one that it previously resolved to the same IP address. Care needs to be taken, however, when implementing this check. For example, it is not sufficient to look up the certified name in the local DNS cache. This is because the DNS cache stores the forward lookup result and, as we explained in section 5.2, a reverse lookup is needed.

In order to create a strong link between the resolved name that the application passed to the OS and the IP address that is compared against the name in the certificate, we can use the following trick: Instead of returning the IP address to the application, the name resolution returns a 32-bit or 128-bit handle, which is an index to a table that stores the actual IP address. When the application calls connect, the OS looks up the name and IP address from the table. During peer authentication, the name from the table is compared against the name in the certificate. This ensures that the peer is authenticated with the exact same name that the application started with. The idea comes from the HIP local-scope identifiers [18]. The disadvantage of this solution is that applications that do not treat IP addresses as opaque numbers will break. The same is true for applications that connect to an IP address obtained by some other means than a DNS lookup.

The second problem listed above is that the IPsec security policy is typically stated in terms of IP addresses. This means that authentication requirements can be different for different peer IP addresses. An attacker can exploit this by hijacking an address that corresponds to a BYPASS policy. As we explained in section 4.2, host-to-host IPsec policies always allow some peers, such as printers or non-intranet hosts, to bypass the protection. Thus, even if the authentication is always done with the right identifier, it does not prevent the attacker from turning authentication off, and IP spoofing allows them to do exactly that.

5.5 Giving Up Transparency

IPsec is designed to be transparent to the higher protocol layers. The security policy is specified by an administrator and enforced by the IP layer without any involvement by the applications. Yet, the purpose of IPsec is to protect application data. This conflict may be the best explanation for the identifier mismatch problem. The application cannot pass to the OS its security require-ments such as the CA and peer name to be used in the authentication. Neither can it check these parameters after the handshake. In many IPsec implementa-tions, an application can call *setsockopt* and *getsockopt* to switch on encryption or authentication and to query their state but it has no access to the certificate.

The solution we suggest is to compromise the transparency principle and to provide the application with the means to check what kind of protection is provided for its data. In the specific problem that we have discussed here, it is sufficient to provide an API for checking whether packets sent and received via a given socket are authenticated and/or encrypted, and to check the identifier that was authenticated in the key exchange. A more radical change to the IPsec architecture would be to replace the SPD with a per-socket policy. The system administrator may, however, still want to enforce some policies independent of the applications. This leads to problems of policy reconciliation, which is beyond the scope of this paper.

> **Solution 1:** Allow applications to specify the IPsec policy for their data and to check that the right kind of security is in place, including the authenticated peer identifier and the issuer of the peer credentials.

6   Attacks Against Mobile Hosts

Next, we will consider what effect host mobility, such as a laptop being moved to a different local network, has on IPsec. We first highlight, in section 6.1, reasons why DNS spoofing is much more serious a threat than is usually thought. In section 6.2, we show that confusion between different private address spaces can lead to attacks even without DNS spoofing.

6.1   Trusting Local Name Servers

It is quite clear from section 4.2 that a secure name service is required before IPsec can provide strong host-to-host security. Nevertheless, it is tempting to ignore the problems and to assume that DNS spoofing is sufficiently cumbersome to deter most attackers. For example, it is difficult for an attacker on the Internet to interfere with name resolution in the intranet. The goal of this section is to present a common scenario where the spoofing is trivial to implement. We assume, for a moment, that secure DNS is not in use.

When a mobile host, such as a laptop computer, connects to the Internet at a new access network, it usually configures its network connection based on information provided by a local DHCP server at that network. One of the configuration parameters provided by DHCP is the IP address of a local DNS server. Thus, a mobile host depends on the local DNS server to define the binding between host names and IP addresses. As a consequence, malicious administrators at the access network can provide false DNS responses and, therefore, circumvent the mobile's IPsec policy. Furthermore, all they need to do this is standard DNS server software.

Figure 3 shows an example of this attack. The mobile host unwisely trusts the DNS server at the access network to map a peer name ("server-b.example.org") into an IP address. By selecting an address for which the host has a BYPASS policy, the DNS server can both turn off IPsec protection and redirect the connection to the wrong destination. Since IPsec is usually bypassed for the public Internet, the attacker may be able to use its real IP address.

> **Problem 2:** The mobile host relies on a name server at an untrusted access network to define the mapping from names to IP addresses. Therefore, the access network can circumvent the mobile host's IPsec policy.

Another way to express the problem is to say that the physical location of the mobile host determines the authority in whose name space the DNS name resolution happens. However, the problem is not completely solved by the mobile connecting to an authoritative DNS server at its home network. This is because

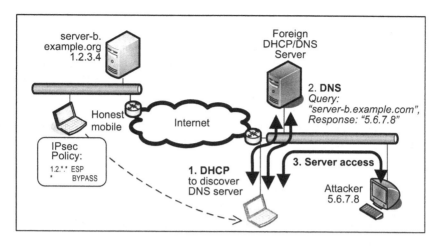

Fig. 3. Mobile host using a foreign DNS server

there are commonly available tools for intercepting the requests transparently and for redirecting them to a local server at the access network.

Secure DNS with signed resource records would prevent the attack as it is based on signature chains and provides the same level of security regardless of which DNS server a host uses. A less secure solution is to protect access to an authoritative, or just friendly, DNS server with a DNS transaction security mechanism or with IPsec.

> **Solution 2:** Never rely on insecure DNS at an untrusted access network. If secure DNS is not available, use IPsec to protect access to a more trustworthy name server.

The following section will, however, show that some attacks against the mobile host do not depend on DNS spoofing.

6.2 Ambiguity of Private Address Spaces

Some IP address ranges have been allocated for private use [21]. Anyone can use these addresses in their private network but packets with a private source or destination address must never be routed to the Internet. Examples of this kind of addresses are the ranges 10.*.*.* and 192.168.*.* in IPv4 and site-local addresses in IPv6. The most common use for private addresses is behind a NAT.

It is usually thought that private addresses provide a level of security because packets containing these addresses cannot cross network boundaries. If a host has only an address allocated from a private address space, then it will be impossible to route any packets from the Internet to the host, or from the host to the Internet, except when the communication is specifically enabled by a NAT. For this reason, it is common to place critical intranet resources, such as important file servers, into subnets with private addresses. It is also tempting to give this kind of protection to other hosts that should not be accessible from the Internet, e.g., printers.

The problem with the private addresses is that mobile hosts can move between two networks that both use the same private address range. The traditional wisdom that packets with private addresses cannot cross network boundaries is no longer true because the sender (or receiver) itself crosses the boundary.

For example, the mobile host in figure 4 uses an authoritative name server at its home network in order to avoid the attack of section 6.1. The name server maps a name ("printer-b.example.org") to a private address ("192.168.0.10"). But when the mobile host connects to this address, the packets are routed to an untrusted host at the access network. Even worse, the mobile host has a BYPASS policy for the address. Connecting to the wrong printer or server can cause the mobile host to reveal confidential information to the attacker. Sometimes, it can compromise the mobile host's integrity if the server, for example, distributes configuration information.

Problem 3: When a mobile host moves between physical networks, it can become confused about which private address space it is currently at. As a consequence, it may apply the wrong IPsec policy to packets destined to a private IP address.

This kind of situation can arise, for example, when most of the mobile host's communication, including DNS queries, is routed to its home network via a VPN connection but some addresses are excluded from the tunneling to allow the mobile to access resources (e.g., printers) local to the access network. Another situation that occurs commonly is one where the private address is statically configured (in a *hosts* file) or it is in the mobile's DNS cache at the time it attaches to the untrusted access network.

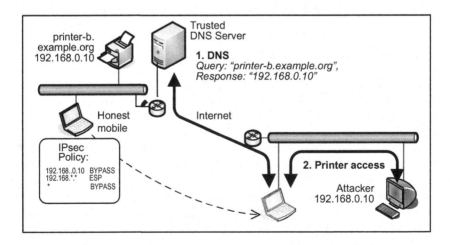

Fig. 4. Mobile host moving between private address spaces

The problem is similar to multihomed hosts and scoped IPv6 addresses. Multihomed hosts, however, have the benefit of being able to differentiate addresses by the interface on which they appear. Given that the scoping of IPv4 addresses has never been completely solved for multihomed hosts, we do not expect there to be any magic bullet for the mobile-host scenario either.

> **Solution 3:** When configuring the IPsec policy in a mobile host, one should not assume any degree of protection from physical or logical network boundaries. In particular, BYPASS policies for private and site-local addresses are dangerous.

6.3   Communication Failures in Private Address Spaces

There is another consequence of the confusion between private address spaces. If a host requires protection for a private peer address, communication with that address will fail unless the peer is able to authenticate itself. For example, the policy in figure 4 prevents the mobile host from communicating with any hosts in the access network that it is visiting (except with the attacker).

> **Problem 4:** A mobile host that requires protection for private or site-local peer addresses cannot communicate with hosts that use the same addresses in other administrative domains.

Stationary hosts do not experience the problem because they always reside in one administrative domain. Mobile hosts, on the other hand, move between networks. Configuring IPsec protection for a private address range in a mobile host effectively monopolizes that address range for use in only one domain.

We will not offer any immediate solution to this problem. In the light of the previous section, we feel that the communication failure is preferable to a security failure. It seems that private address spaces are fundamentally irreconcilable with an authentication mechanism that requires unique identifiers. System administrators have tried to solve the problem by guessing which sub-ranges of the private address space are not used by anyone else, a solution that is hardly sustainable if everyone adopts it.

6.4   Names in Security Policies

It is clear from the above that IP addresses are not the ideal identifiers for specifying a security policy for host-to-host communication, and we might want to replace them with host names or some other unique identifiers. This approach works in principle but is has a major limitation that we will explain below.

The IPsec specification allows policy selectors in the SPD to be specified in terms of host and user names but the semantics is not quite what one might, naively, expect it to be. The problem is that it is not possible to use the peer host name or user name as a selector in a BYPASS policy. While other types of selectors are matched directly against header fields of an inbound or outbound packet, the name selectors must be matched against the authenticated peer name from the peer's credential. Thus, any policy specified in terms of such selectors requires authentication of the peer. This means that name selectors can prevent insider attacks where there is confusion between two authenticated identities, but they cannot prevent the attacker from exploiting a BYPASS policy to get around IPsec. In this respect, the name selectors are similar to the peer authorization database. The following solution comes, therefore, with a major caveat:

> **Solution 4:** Redesign IPsec so that IP addresses are not used as selectors. However, this only helps if all peers are authenticated.

It is generally the case for all network security mechanism that, if some peers are allowed to bypass authentication, then the attacker can pretend to be one of them and, thus, bypass the security. The damage can be limited, as network administrators know, by making BYPASS policies as specific as possible, for example, by restricting them to specific port numbers.

Again, it appears that the ultimate solution is the one we already stated in section 5.5: putting the applications in charge of their own security. When authentication is provided by a transparent layer, the applications cannot know whether a specific packet has been authenticated or bypassed protection. On the other hand, if the applications are allowed to specify and enforce their own security policies, they can decide which data needs authentication and which does not.

7   IPsec as a Firewall

In this section, we will discuss an unexpected feature interaction in IPsec when it is used as a firewall. Although the attacks depend on a non-standard IPsec feature, they are interesting because they are an example of two security mechanisms, each of which is sensible and useful on its own, that together result in security failure.

The DISCARD policies in IPsec can be used to implement an elementary firewall policy. That is, IPsec can filter packets by any criteria that are expressible with the selectors in the SPD. Typically this means blocking port numbers or ranges of IP addresses. With standard IPsec, the firewall is necessarily stateless: each packet is processed individually and without regard to any packets sent or received previously. Nobody would expect to be able to implement complex application-layer policies with IPsec but it seems a pity that one cannot express the kind of simple stateful policies that even end users can configure in personal firewalls and home NATs. In particular, one would want to differentiate between packets that belong to a connection initiated by the local host and packets that arrive unsolicited.

Some IPsec implementations provide this kind of functionality, even though it is not a part of the standard IPsec architecture. One way to implement this is a policy that, upon sending an outbound packet to an IP address, creates a state ("soft SA") to allow further packets from that peer to bypass IPsec. This kind of policy is used, for example, to enable access to printers and embedded devices that do not support IPsec.

Another, seemingly unrelated, issue with the current IPsec specifications and implementations is that they lack full support for broadcast and multicast communication. There are two ways a system administrator can deal with the unsupported traffic: it can be discarded or allowed to bypass IPsec. In any system that depends on broadcast or multicast protocols for its operation, the choice is obviously to configure a BYPASS policy for these types of traffic. Encryption is usually unnecessary because these types of communication are accessible to large groups of hosts anyway. The lack of authentication is a bigger issue but it can be addressed with application-specific security mechanisms where necessary.

Unfortunately, the two features described above combine to create a vulnerability, as shown in figure 5. The honest host in the figure has been configured with a stateful policy because it needs to access printers that do not support IPsec and, in a large network, managing the BYPASS policies individually would be too tedious. In order to circumvent the stateful policy, the attacker needs to get the honest host to send an outbound unicast packet. If the honest host required authentication for all inbound communication, the attacker would not be able to manipulate it into sending such a packet. But when the policy at the honest host allows inbound broadcast and multicast packets to bypass IPsec, the attacker can use these to trigger the outbound packet. Indeed, there are several broadcast-based protocols that can be exploited for this. For example, the BOOTP, DHCP, and NetBIOS protocols send unicast responses to broadcast requests. In general, it is extremely difficult to determine at the IP layer which end host is the real initiator of the communication. Therefore, security policies that differentiate between the initiator and respondent tend to be fragile.

> **Problem 5a:** Stateful firewall extensions to IPsec can be exploited by triggering outbound packets with inbound traffic for which there is a BYPASS policy, such as broadcast and multicast packets.

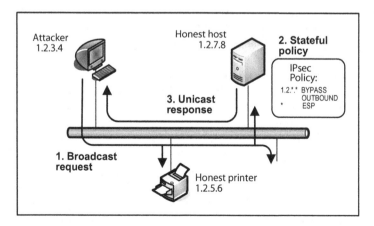

Fig. 5. Circumventing a stateful policy with broadcast

The difference between IPsec and dedicated firewall software is that the typical configuration for IPsec allows inbound packets to bypass protection if they belong to a traffic type for which there is no suitable protection mechanism. Otherwise, one would have to delay host-to-host IPsec deployment until the technology is in place to protect all possible types of communication. Firewalls, on the other hand, tend to discard packets by default. Thus, the above problem is, in part, explained by the different motivation for the administrator in configuring IPsec and firewall policies.

It seems that there will always be some IP packets for which no protection is available and which the honest host nevertheless wants to receive. For example, IPv6 is increasingly enabled on Internet hosts for experimentation, yet many IPv6 implementations still lack IPsec functionality or administrative support. This means that IPsec policies for IPv6 are often more relaxed than for IPv4. There is clearly a trade-off between security and availability of new services.

> **Problem 5b:** New protocols often lack full IPsec support. The attacker can often use them to circumvent IPsec protection of existing protocols.

> **Solution 5:** Care must be taken in reconciling strong security policies and availability of network communications during the deployment of new protocols.

8   Conclusion

This paper documents several vulnerabilities in host-to-host IPsec. There is no doubt that, over the years, administrators and developers have encountered all of these issues and either found solutions similar to the ones proposed here or moved to using other security protocols like TLS. Yet, it is a widely held belief that, if one implements and configures IPsec correctly, it can meet all of one's network security requirements. We aim to show that this is only possible with major changes to the philosophy that underlies IPsec. In particular, security should not be implemented as a transparent layer. Instead, applications should be allowed to manage their own security policies. Also, IP addresses are not meaningful identifiers for specifying security policies for application data.

We have observed all of the vulnerabilities described in this paper in actual IPsec implementations or configurations. One could claim that little is achieved by deploying host-to-host IPsec in its current form. There are, however, some mitigating factors. Firstly, some of the weaknesses result from compromises made for deployment reasons. For example, the need to have exemptions for multicast traffic and for non-IPsec-capable hosts may slowly disappear, perhaps with the transition to IPv6. Secondly, we found that attacks tested in laboratory conditions rarely work on production networks because modern applications and middleware (e.g., RPC mechanisms) implement their own security. Indeed, they have been designed with the assumption that the network layer is insecure. This leads us to the question whether there remains any role for host-to-host IPsec, but that discussion is beyond the scope this paper.

References

1. Aura, T.: Cryptographically generated addresses. In: Boyd, C., Mao, W. (eds.) ISC 2003. LNCS, vol. 2851, pp. 29–43. Springer, Heidelberg (2003)
2. Aura, T., Roe, M., Arkko, J.: Security of Internet location management. In: Proc. 18th Annual Computer Security Applications Conference, Las Vegas, IEEE Computer Society, Los Alamitos (2002)
3. Bellovin, S.M.: Problem areas for the IP security protocols. In: Proc. 6th Usenix Unix Security Symposium, pp. 205–214. USENIX Association, San Jose, CA USA (1996)
4. Carpenter, B., Crowcroft, J., Rekhter, Y.: IPv4 address behaviour today. RFC 2101, IETF Network Working Group (February 1997)
5. Dolev, D., Yao, A.: On the security of public-key protocols. Communications of the ACM 29(8), 198–208 (1983)
6. Eastlake, D.: Domain name system security extensions. RFC 2535, IETF Network Working Group (March 1999)
7. Kaufman, C. (ed.): Internet key exchange (IKEv2) protocol. Internet-Draft draft-ietf-ipsec-ikev2-17.txt, IETF IPsec Working Group, Work in progress (September 2004)
8. Ferguson, N., Schneier, B.: A cryptographic evaluation of IPsec. Technical report, Counterpane Labs (1999)
9. Guttman, J.D., Herzog, A.L., Thayer, F.J.: Authentication and confidentiality via IPsec. In: Cuppens, F., Deswarte, Y., Gollmann, D., Waidner, M. (eds.) ESORICS 2000. LNCS, vol. 1895, pp. 255–272. Springer, Heidelberg (2000)
10. Harkins, D., Carrel, D.: The Internet key exchange (IKE). RFC 2409, IETF Network Working Group (November 1998)
11. Kent, S., Atkinson, R.: Security architecture for the Internet Protocol. RFC 2401, IETF Network Working Group (November 1998)
12. Kent, S., Seo, K.: Security architecture for the Internet protocol. Internet-Draft draft-ietf-ipsec-rfc2401bis-03, IETF IPsec Working Group, Work in progress (September 2004)
13. Krawczyk, H.: SIGMA: The 'SIGn-and-MAc' approach to authenticated Diffie-Hellman and its use in the IKE-protocols. In: Boneh, D. (ed.) CRYPTO 2003. LNCS, vol. 2729, pp. 400–425. Springer, Heidelberg (2003)
14. Lang, U., Gollmann, D., Schreiner, R.: Verifiable identifiers in middleware security. In: Proc. 17th Annual Computer Security Applications Conference, New Orleans, LA USA, pp. 450–459. IEEE Computer Society, Los Alamitos (2001)
15. Linn, J.: Generic security service application program interface version 2, update 1. RFC 2743, IETF (January 2000)
16. Meadows, C.: Analysis of the Internet Key Exchange protocol using the NRL protocol analyzer. In: IEEE Symposium on Security and Privacy, IEEE Computer Society Press, Los Alamitos (1999)
17. Nikander, P.: Denial-of-service, address ownership, and early authentication in the IPv6 world. In: Christianson, B., Crispo, B., Malcolm, J.A., Roe, M. (eds.) Security Protocols. LNCS, vol. 2467, pp. 12–21. Springer, Heidelberg (2002)

18. Nikander, P., Ylitalo, J., Wall, J.: Integrating security, mobility, and multi-homing in a HIP way. In: NDSS 2003. Proc. Network and Distributed Systems Security Symposium, San Diego, CA USA, pp. 87–99 (February 2003)
19. Perlman, R., Kaufman, C.: Key exchange in IPSec: Analysis of IKE. IEEE Internet Computing 4(6), 50–56 (2000)
20. Piper, D., Swander, B.: A GSS-API authentication method for IKE. Internet-Draft draft-ietf-ipsec-isakmp-gss-auth-07, IETF, Expired (July 2001)
21. Rekhter, Y., Moskowitz, B., Karrenberg, D., De Groot, G J., Lear, E.: Address allocation for private internets. RFC 1918, IETF (February 1996)
22. Schuba, C.L., Krsul, I.V., Kuhn, M.G., Spaffold, E.H., Sundaram, A., Zamboni, D.: Analysis of a denial of service attack on TCP. In: Proc. 1997 IEEE Symposium on Security and Privacy, Oakland, CA USA, pp. 208–223. IEEE Computer Society Press, Los Alamitos (1997)
23. Trostle, J., Gossman, B.: Techniques for improving the security and manageability of IPsec policy. International Journal of Information Security 4(3), 209–226 (2005)
24. International Telecommunication Union. ITU-T recommendation X.509 (11/93) - The Directory: Authentication Framework (November 1993)

A   A Simple Experiment

The following simple experiment demonstrates that the OS is unable to check the correctness of the name in the certificate (as explained in section 5.1): First, set up the IPsec policy to use a transport mode SA and certificate authentication. Then, act yourself as the application of figure 2. In a shell window, use *nslookup* or a similar utility to resolve the peer host's IP address. Finally, invoke *telnet* to connect to the IP address. By the time you enter the *telnet* command, the only place where the host name is remembered is your head. Surely, the OS cannot have compared the host name in your mind with the one in the certificate.

Experiences with Host-to-Host IPsec
(Transcript of Discussion)

Tuomas Aura

Microsoft Research

I am going to talk about some problems with IPSec, especially about how IPSec policies are specified, and whether that matches the kind of security requirements we had in the beginning, and which were why we introduced IPSec. Maybe everyone is familiar with IPSec, but it might be useful to have the same kind of picture in mind, because you can look at these things from various points of view.

Most of the research in the past has been on things like, is this security protocol secure, is this authenticated key exchange protocol secure. In this talk I am just going to assume that you have some authenticated key exchange protocol and that it is secure. Also there's been lots of work on the cryptographic algorithms: is this encryption (or Mac) the most efficient and the most secure one known, or the best compromise between the two. And that's another thing that I'm not going to talk about, I shall just assume it happens. I'm more interested in the architectural type of thing, like the security policy and how it is specified.

IPSec is intended for end-to-end authentication and encryption in the Internet, but it's not quite clear what end-to-end means for IPSec because it's mostly used for gateway-to-gateway, or sometimes for host-to-gateway, and not really from host-to-host. In this talk I'm trying to look at what happens if it really is used end-to-end, host-to-host, without any security gateways. The goal of IPSec as stated is usually end-to-end security, but in fact the only application where it's really used in this way is for VPNs, and one might then ask, why is this, and can we actually use IPSec for securing all the communication on the Internet, or in your own home or corporate network.

We've done an experiment with this, not me personally, but I've seen a deployment of IPSec to a corporate network of tens of thousands of hosts. All traffic basically is protected with IPSec with a very small set of specific exceptions, and it's first of all difficult to configure it, to get it running, but as we then found out, it doesn't in fact do what you expected it to do, it doesn't provide you with the kind of security you wanted. One of the main design principles in IPSec is that it's a transparent layer, it hides the security mechanisms from you, and that's part of the problem, or at least causes difficulties.

The structure of IPSec is such that you have these protocols for key exchange, and you have then protocols for protection your session, and then in order to create session keys for the sessions, you run the key exchange authentication protocols, and you have a security policy that guides this process. So it tells whether certain IP packets should be protected in some way, that is, should you create a security association for it, and encrypt, and authenticate it, or

B. Christianson et al. (Eds.): Security Protocols 2005, LNCS 4631, pp. 23–30, 2007.

should you discard it, or (what's important in this talk) should you bypass it, should you let it go without protection. These policies are specified by the system administrator, and then IPSec tries to transparently implement them for *all* your applications.

The first and main problem that I'm going to present here is that IPSec is somehow tied in with the name resolution. So, here is a PC, and there's the applications, and the operating system, and the operating system has IPSec inside it (I'm trying to abstract as much as possible). And over there you have the peer computer that this PC wants to talk to. What happens when an application wants to talk to this peer computer, let's call it server B? First the application says, well, since I want to talk to server B, I must find its IP address, so it asks the operating system to resolve the name into an IP address, and the name service will get a query saying, where is server B, and it will return the address, it's at this address. The application gets the address and then it will ask the operating system to connect to that address. And there's an IPSec policy that says, well this kind of packet should be protected therefore I'm going to do a key exchange and then once I have the session keys, I'm going to protect the data with those session keys.

All that looks fine, but obviously I'm pointing out the name resolution there for a reason. IPSec, at least to some extent, depends on the name resolution being secure, so lets see what happens if the attacker can manipulate the DNS responses. Here is the honest PC trying to connect to a server but unfortunately an attacker is intercepting the traffic, and this is a well-known kind of problem. It's maybe not the obvious thing you would first think, but it's not new. Now the application asks for this name to be resolved and it gets the wrong IP address, because it's the attacker now feeding the response here. The application then asks the OS to connect to this IP address, and now you notice if you look at the details of the IPSec policy that for the true address of the server there is a policy of protecting the traffic, authenticating the server, but for this address the attacker gives, because that's the attacker's real address, it's just a node on the Internet, there is a BYPASS policy saying, no protection is required for all these other nodes, like websites, on the internet.

So in fact, there won't be any key exchange or IPSec protection taking place, all the traffic is sent plain text between here and there. The application did not get the protection that it was supposed to get based on the policy that the administrator had specified. So there's a problem in IPSec that your policy selection depends on the secure DNS, and by spoofing DNS responses an attacker can either force you to use a completely insecure connection, or just use different parameters for the authentication.

Now you might say, well we should not have such a default BYPASS policy there, but in reality while you want to authenticate the host in your own organisation, you certainly you don't want to use IPSec with everyone else on the Internet, so you usually have a default BYPASS policy at the end of your policy database. And the policies are resolved in this order, so you first look, do I match this policy, and then if you don't then you go to the last one. And you also usually have some special case, even if you say, this computer will not communicate with the Internet, it will only communicate with the hosts of our own organisation, you should use IPSec for everything, well too bad: your printer doesn't speak IPSec so you'll have a BYPASS policy for that, and all the attacker needs to do here is to take the IP address of the printer, and it can do the same attack. So we really do depend on secure DNS.

I guess that is quite well known, so the next thing I'm going to point out is that even if you assume that the DNS is secure, it still doesn't quite work. So let's now assume that we have some way of securing the DNS requests, or that for whatever reason, the attacker does not spoof this response: maybe there are security mechanisms, or maybe the attacker is just too lazy. Now everything works as it's supposed to, and the PC connects to the honest server. And we'll look at one detail of this authentication protocol, no matter what the authentication protocol, the server is going to send some kind of credential to this honest client to prove its identity. It could be an X.509 certificate issued by a CA that they both trust, or it could be a Kerberos ticket if you are using the GSS-API authentication as in Microsoft implementations on the Internet, and it could be something else if you are using IKE version 2, and EAP authentication in theory can use any kind of credentials in there. But anyway the credentials here will have something saying, some authority says that the cryptographic keys held by this server are somehow bound to this server name. I'll go through this process again:

The application starts with a server name, I want to connect to server-B, it does DNS name resolution here, or it could be any other kind of name resolution, it could be just locally configured hosts file, or anything. Secure name resolution gets the correct IP address response, and the OS passes it back to the application, the application now has the IP address for the host, and invokes the standard PCP connect API, and asks the OS to connect to this IP address. Now maybe security policy says, we'll have to authenticate the peer, and therefore the key exchange takes place, and here comes the certificate that says who the peer is. This should be the server name here in the certificate, it comes back and now, no matter which of the many key exchange and authentication protocols you use, the operating system during the authentication protocol must somehow now decide, is this name in the certificate the right name. Well how does it decide that? How does the client know whether this name is right? What the client should do is compare them: it was asked to connect to this IP address, and this is the name that is in fact in the certificate, so it needs to know whether these two things correspond. I wanted to connect to this kind of identifier, and I'm authenticating this kind of identifier, is there any way of comparing the two? Well the way IPSec is currently implemented there really isn't. Later we can discuss maybe the possible ways of making this the system, but currently there is no way this client can decide whether this is equal or not.

Pekka Nikander. Is that just a problem of this certificate value identifying the name of the server?

Reply. Oh you could certify the IP address directly, but that just doesn't happen anywhere, it's not what you want to do. Also client hosts have dynamic IP addresses so you couldn't possibly certify them, and also the client could be behind the NATS, and using NATS reversals, or sharing an IP address with someone else. So you couldn't really certify that IP address for this client, there are lots of reasons.

George Danezis. But I don't quite understand here, maybe I've missed something, what you're really wanting is that the person on the other side of the line is PCC, right, you don't care what their IP address is.

Reply. I think you're on the right track.

George Danezis. So what happens when you do authentication is that he is certified by a particular certificate which is saying that if the other person has carried through the certification protocol correctly, they are PCC, and I don't care what their address is. So at the end of the day if the protocol is correctly implemented then it is indeed PCC inside.

Reply. It's exactly as you say, at this point the operating system protocol here knows that the peer is PCC. But then the next thing is to ask, what do I do with this information? IPSec being a transparent layer that the applications don't know about, it cannot just tell the application, you've connected to PCC, so what does it do.

Matt Blaze. You haven't told us what the requirements are, so how can I tell if this is broken? [Laughter]

Reply. Well that's actually an easy way out. That's what you do when you're designing a key exchange protocol in isolation, you say, these are my requirements, and now I can maybe prove formally that my key exchange protocol meets these requirements. If this client here at the end of the key exchange protocol says, I authenticated PCC, that means at some point the PCC has said, I've authenticated, and yes, that property is in fact valid here, there's nothing wrong with the key exchange and authentication protocol. The real problem here is understanding what your requirements are, and also understanding whether the properties that your protocol provided were the ones that you actually wanted, and I think this step has been forgotten in IPSec. Really, what this process is about is understanding what your requirements are.

Matt Blaze. I don't even know where the requirements come from. Are they from the application, are they from the network, or from the administrator of some system, I'm not quite sure.

Reply. Yes, so it's quite silly in a way. The application certainly doesn't have any requirements in IPSec because it doesn't even know there is security, so it's the administrator who sets these requirements. But the way the administrator typically thinks is, I'd like to protect this application with that peer, and it starts with this IP, the name of the peer and the name of the application, and then it's a matter of, how do I implement it.

Pekka Nikander. So are there just different mappings between names, is it that simple? On the application level you're assuming that you are using DNS names also for security reasons, and then down here you're using IP addresses, and when you've got NATS there is no longer a 1:1 mapping between DNS names and IP addresses as there maybe used to be 15 years ago.

Reply. Yes, I think the real problem here is that we're using two different name spaces, and it really is like George said earlier, it just doesn't make sense to use IP address here. There are several ways of fixing this, one simple thing would be to change the API, to say well I'd to connect to server-B please, and then the stack here would know what the name was, and it could check it. Unfortunately changing the APIs, especially these kinds of APIs that have existed as long as the Internet, is not that simple, you can't just go and change all the legacy applications. One thing that we're actually going to do I'm sure is to make the application aware of security, but changing the APIs or making the application aware of the security, and allowing you to check whether the name was correct, that breaks backward compatibility, and it breaks the transparency.

Ben Laurie. Yes, but that didn't hurt the adoption of SSL, which is way more popular than IPSec.

Reply. Well SSL doesn't have this problem because everything is done on the application level there.

Ben Laurie. It doesn't change the fact that it's compatible, and it's very widely used.

Reply. Yes, I do believe that this problem will be solved by just changing the assumptions and breaking some of them, this is just the fact of how things work now.

Richard Clayton. In your first diagram, surely the issue was that the policy was written at the wrong level. If the policy said that server-B was to be protected then in order to apply that policy, you have to make the same DNS lookup as the application was made from, and then you'll not get any value out of the DNS spoofing.

You've done the binding to the IP address far too low, it's a binding problem rather than a problem per se. In this system I think you're wrong about the difficulty because in practice at the application level you don't use foreign DNS, and then the levels below do all the magic for you, that's perfectly possible, you wouldn't update lots and lots of programs when a system changes.

Reply. Well you would have to update programs wouldn't you.

Richard Clayton. Some programs maybe.

Reply. Well yes. But for legacy programs we can't really do much about it. There have been tricks proposed for this, one thing is for the operating system here to cache the DNS response, and then when it comes here it will check the cache, but that's a problem because you have other ways of resolving names than

DNS. So if you use any other proprietary protocol, if you get your IP address from the peer like in FTP or something like that, it doesn't work. That's a slight problem, in the sense that you can't make it mandatory as you should make a security protocol. If you allow exceptions then the attacker is going to take advantage of those exceptions.

Another approach to this is in the new IPSec architecture specifications, a so-called peer authorisation database: in addition to the security policy database, and security association database, you have this magic database that solves the problem. Basically there is some database here in which the operating system will look and find out whether this name is authorised to use that IP address or not. That works very well for VPNs, and when using gateway-to-gateway IPSec, because they can statically configure these databases, but if you are using it with a network with tens of thousands of hosts you can't possibly have this database anywhere realistic.

In theory, you could do a reverse DNS lookup. If you do a secure DNS lookup here, and then you do a secure reverse DNS lookup here, then you get the security, but the secure reverse DNS just doesn't exist. It exists, but in a less secure form than DNS.

Ben Laurie. I'm not sure that that's true.

Reply. As an academic problem we can say we have reduced the problem to a previously solved one, but as it's a real world engineering problem we say, well, that solution didn't quite work, we did something else.

Ben Laurie. Well, I could make it work securely.

Reply. Well if lots of people wanted reverse DNS to work securely then yes, it could be done. But at the moment secure reverse DNS doesn't work for various reasons, for example, you can't do the classless addresses because you need to have the 8 bit boundaries for resolving the reverse, and so on.

Ben Laurie. There's standard work that we've done with addresses to solve that.

Pekka Nikander. One practical reason why you can't really make a reverse DNS work in a public Internet is that many ISPs are just ignoring your queries, meaning that you just can't update your data reliably.

Reply. But it's obviously something that you want. If you just know one host-to-host security on your own network, you can't start by saying, OK, first thing I'll do is I'll wait for a secure reverse DNS to a peer. Anyway there's another picture of the same attack, and then we already discussed the various solutions.

Alf Zugenmaier. I think it is about the problem that you can't get transparent security. The application believes it could rely upon hiding that security, in fact it's totally transparent, the application doesn't know that it is there. But it should know that it's there, because it should have a certain policy set up with PCC, and one with server-B, but even knowing that you have just resolved that name, or you have just found out that these key addresses match doesn't really get you much further, because you could still have a mismatch between the policy that you wanted for a server and a client, it doesn't matter what you had before.

Reply. I'm not sure if that is always the case. There are some examples where it is more of a question of mobile hosts, and the problem that mobile hosts move from network to network. Resolving the host names relies on the foreign authorities in the place where it happens to be, and so it enters a different name space. When the laptop comes to this foreign network it first uses DHCP to discover the DNS server, it gets the DNS, from the DNS server it gets the IP address, and then it connects to this server. Well obviously the foreign DNS server is not really trustworthy so it could give you a wrong answer, and so it's just an easy way of implementing the DNS spoofing. It's trivial, you don't need to hack anything here, you just use a standard DNS server and configure it to give this answer.

Matt Blaze. Isn't this really a trust management problem, by encoding a name into an IPSec policy you're implicitly trusting the entire DNS system. That may or may not be what your intent was.

Reply. No, I think not. The problem we discussed earlier was that when you authenticate, you want to connect to a name, and you authenticate the name, and then you are done on the end-to-end authentication. But there's the other part that the IPSec policies specify in terms of IP addresses, and they probably shouldn't. But there's a major limitation to specifying the IPSec policies in terms of names, because that means you must authenticate everybody, you can't have a single BYPASS policy. You can't specify a BYPASS policy in terms of names, I don't want security for this name, because you don't know what the name is yet.

Mike Roe. Picking up on what Matt said, I think if you have an implementation in the operating system that goes from the names to the IP address, that way of implementing it does mean that you implicitly trust the whole DNS system. Now that's something you typically can't do because of some servers in the DNS.

Reply. To finish, I'll just show one more problem. This is at the IP address phase, so now we are specifying policies in IP addresses. IP addresses are usually thought to be global, unique identifiers for hosts, and we already know that they are not really because of NATs, and DHCPs, dynamic addressing, but in fact there's another thing that you have private address spaces. The addresses used here, in this local network, could be also used on this foreign network, and then you really get confused what you connect. I think the easier thing to understand is that this can lead to a failure of communications. If you have an IPSec policy that says, I must authenticate everything in this private address space, when you come to another local network where it uses the same address space, you simply cannot communicate.

For example, this printer uses an address for which you require authentication, and this address is in fact already used, for example in an intranet to protect the most secure parts of your intranet to use a private address space. So you make sure that no-one can route package to these hosts from the internet, or from them to outside, and then you have an IPSec policy for authenticating them. But that obviously means that if anyone, you go out anywhere to any other network and the same addresses are used there, you cannot communicate there. You can construct attacks from this as well if you want to, although again there may be an issue with definition; what was the requirement, is this an attack.

The problem would be smaller if you had more of these private address spaces, and if not everyone used this 254 address there.

Bruce Christianson. In the old days we used two address-matching gateways.

Reply. The point is that we know how to do authentication and key exchange securely, we know how to secure data after that, we even know in theory, not in practice, how to secure name resolution. What no-one seems to have thought much about was which identifier we wanted to authenticate, and therefore the host-to-host IPSec currently doesn't really work. If you're using it in your intranet it typically gives you group authentication: it means that any host who belongs to your organisation can pretend to be any other host, but that's the level of security you actually get. You can exclude outsiders, create a kind of virtual private network, but that's it.

Pekka Nikander. Basically you can't use IP addresses for security anymore unless you're in a very specific scenario where you actually can't spoof the IP addresses. So in general, if you have mobile you can have a large network, if you don't then you can't trust IP addresses for any security purpose.

Repairing the Bluetooth Pairing Protocol

Ford-Long Wong, Frank Stajano, and Jolyon Clulow

University of Cambridge
Computer Laboratory

Abstract. We implement and demonstrate a passive attack on the Bluetooth authentication protocol used to connect two devices to each other. Using a protocol analyzer and a brute-force attack on the PIN, we recover the link key shared by two devices. With this secret we can then decrypt any encrypted traffic between the devices as well as, potentially, impersonate the devices to each other. We then implement an alternative pairing protocol that is more robust against passive attacks and against active man-in-the-middle attacks. The price of the added security offered by the new protocol is its use of asymmetric cryptography, traditionally considered infeasible on handheld devices. We show that an implementation based on elliptic curves is well within the possibility of a modern handphone and has negligible effects on speed and user experience.

1 Introduction

Bluetooth is an open specification for seamless wireless short-range communications of data and voice between devices. It provides a way to connect and exchange information between wireless-enabled devices such as mobile phones, personal digital assistants (PDAs), laptops, desktops, printers, digital cameras and other peripherals. The specification was first developed by Ericsson, and later formalized by the Bluetooth Special Interest Group.

The Bluetooth authentication protocol is based on symmetric key cryptography and on a (typically numeric and short) password, called PIN, that the user enters into both devices. As first pointed out by Jakobsson and Wetzel [13], the protocol is vulnerable to a passive attack in which the eavesdropper brute-forces the PIN space and silently checks which PIN correctly reproduces the observed message trace.

We implemented this attack and successfully carried it out against several pairs of commercially available Bluetooth devices. Before proceeding any further, let us first review the original Bluetooth authentication and pairing protocol.

1.1 Bluetooth Authentication

Bluetooth natively provides authentication and encryption. Authentication is provided by a 128-bit link key, which is a shared secret known to a pair of Bluetooth devices which have previously formed a pair. The algorithms for authentication and for the generation of link and encryption keys are all based

B. Christianson et al. (Eds.): Security Protocols 2005, LNCS 4631, pp. 31–45, 2007.

on SAFER+ [22], here used basically as a hash. The cipher algorithm is E0—a stream cipher whose key can be up to 128 bits long.

The security architecture of Bluetooth defines three possible security modes for a device [5,4]. Mode 1 is non-secure, Mode 2 enforces security at the fine-grained service level and Mode 3 enforces security at the link level.

In the case of Modes 2 and 3, if pairing is turned on, when two Bluetooth devices meet for the first time, they pair using the following key:

$$K_{init} = E_{22}\{PIN, BD\_ADDR_A, RAND_B\}$$

where BD_ADDR_A is the device address of device A, $RAND_B$ is a random number contributed by device B and PIN is a shared password that the user must generate and then manually enter into both devices. (Clearly, BD_ADDR_A and $RAND_B$ will be available to an eavesdropper, while PIN won't.) Once two devices share a link key, the following protocol allows them to renew it and derive a new one, known as a combination key[1], which becomes the new link key used from that point onwards. The devices each produces a random number (LK_RAND_A or LK_RAND_B), masks it by XORing it with K_{init} and sends it to the other party. Both parties individually hash each of the two random numbers with the Bluetooth address of the device that generated it, using the algorithm E_{21}. The two hashes are then XORed to generate the combination key:

$$K_{AB} = E_{21}(LK\_RAND_A, BD\_ADDR_A)$$
$$\oplus E_{21}(LK\_RAND_B, BD\_ADDR_B).$$

The combination link keys calculated by each device after the key agreement should of course be the same if the procedure is successful. The old link key (either K_{init} or a previous K_{AB}) is then discarded.

Another, less secure kind of link key is the unit key K_{unit}, used by devices that don't have the memory to store a link key for each pairing. The restricted memory device will negotiate to use its unit key as the pairwise link key. It will then mask the unit key by XORing it to the K_{init} formed earlier and send it over to the other device.

For authentication, a challenge-response scheme is used. Device A sends B a challenge $RAND_A$, from which Device B must produce the authentication token $SRES$ and transmit it to A, based on the following:

$$\{SRES, ACO\} = E_1\{K, RAND_A, BD\_ADDR_B\}$$

The challenge-response is run bilaterally. If encryption is needed, the encryption key is derived from the link key.

---

[1] Both the initialization key K_{init} and the combination key are particular types of link key.

2   Breaking Bluetooth

2.1   Guessing the PIN

We used a Bluetooth protocol analyzer [24] to obtain a trace of Bluetooth transmission from the air and to decode the packets. We captured traces of transmissions from commercial Bluetooth devices such as handphones, PDAs, laptops, etc. The packets bearing the required pairing, key formation and authentication processes were analyzed.

We wrote a program that parsed the captured traces and extracted the relevant parameters as they appeared in the transmissions. The trace contains the device addresses, the random numbers exchanged, the challenge and response tokens and all other relevant parameters of one protocol run. Using these, we carried out a kind of dictionary attack (trying first the "easy" PINs such as those made of repeated or sequential digits) and then, where necessary, a full brute force search of the small PIN space[2]. For each PIN we first computed the K_{init}. Then, using the observed intermediate parameters, we computed the combination key and authentication token $SRES$. Both the key agreement using the combination key and the key transport using the unit key can be successfully attacked. If the trace showed that a unit key had been used instead, the number of intermediate parameters is even fewer. Guessing a PIN results in a $SRES$ value identical to the one observed in the trace. The reverse inference holds with high probability.

2.2   Quantitative Observations

The attack program was just a prototype and had not been optimised. Running it on a 1.2 GHz Pentium III laptop gave the following timing results (for randomly chosen PINs, of course—the ones subject to pseudo-dictionary attack could be cracked instantaneously). Note that cracking combination keys require more calls to E_{21} compared to cracking unit keys. Even with our non-optimised program, 4-digit PINs can be broken instantaneously, 6-digit PINs take less than a minute and 8-digit PINs can be cracked in less than an hour (Figure 1). This is due to the very small size of the PIN space.

We have found the unit key used in some models of Bluetooth-equipped PDAs. As will be clear to anyone who knows knows how how the unit key is used, as mentioned in [13] and elsewhere, once the unit key is discovered, the attacker can thereafter freely impersonate the device in its interactions with any other device. Fortunately, we found that at least the unit key was not set to the same string from device to device. The unit key is deprecated from version 1.2 onwards of the Bluetooth specification [6].

The only practical obstacle to widespread replication of the attack described here is that not every would-be eavesdropper will have easy access to a Bluetooth protocol analyzer ($\approx$ 3000 GBP). We expect however that enterprising

---

[2] The user interfaces of many Bluetooth devices further restrict the set of characters that may be used in the PIN. For handphones, this set is often just 0 to 9.

Type of key	No. of digits	Time taken
Unit key	4	0.15 s
	6	15 s
	8	25 mins
Combination key	4	0.27 s
	6	25 s
	8	42 mins

Fig. 1. Time to Crack PIN

hackers could in time figure out ways to use cheap standard Bluetooth modules to access the baseband layer directly, without requiring expensive debugging and diagnostic tools.

2.3   Improved Key Management — Frequent Change of Link Key

Although the protocol is broken by an attacker who eavesdrops on the key establishment phase, within its constraints of avoiding public key cryptography it is not an overly weak design. If the attacker misses the initial key establishment, this attack stops working. Moreover, as discussed in Part C, Section 3.4 of Version 1.1 [5] and Vol 2, Section 4.2.3 of Version 1.2 [6] of the specification, Bluetooth already supports renewal of the link key. An attacker who knows the previous link key and eavesdrops on the link key renewal exchange can trivially discover the new key, but if he misses that exchange then the two devices are safe from further eavesdropping, unless they recourse to bootstrapping a new link key from the weak PIN. This is a good security feature but unfortunately it is rarely exploited in current commercial Bluetooth devices. Change of link key is cheap for the user because it does not involve typing a PIN; yet most devices do not offer the option. We propose that devices provide users with the ability to initiate link key change whenever they wish and we further recommend that users exercise this option often. Frequent change of link key forces an attacker to be continually present when the two target devices are communicating. For resistance against an attacker who could be continually present when the link key is changed, then there is a compelling case to re-key via asymmetric techniques, which is not yet supported in the current specification. Frequent change of link key would also mitigate the risks of Barkan-Biham-Keller-style encryption key replay attacks raised by Ritvanen and Nyberg [27]. Fixes to the Bluetooth cipher algorithm and encryption key derivation are however, beyond the scope of this paper.

After we presented this paper at the workshop, another paper [29] appeared, which performed a similar attack to the one described in Sections 2.1 and 2.2. The computation speed of their attack seemed to be of the same order as ours. An interesting angle in that paper is that the authors attempt to force pairing and repeated pairing instead of passively waiting for one.

2.4   Further Comments

Our experiment confirms the expected result that short Bluetooth PINs can be cracked by brute force search with modest computational resources. It is not practical to seek protection in significantly longer PINs. As a rule of thumb, humans on average can reliably remember PINs up to only 7 digits in length, plus or minus 2 [23]. Software optimization and hardware implementations will bring further improvements in attack speed. Computing hardware continues to improve in performance, but the capacity of the human memory does not improve significantly over generations.

One may also observe, although this will have very little practical impact, that even a Bluetooth PIN of the maximal length (16 octets) allowed by the specification will not support the full diversity of 128 bits at the baseband. The PIN is represented at the user interface level by UTF-8 coding—a variable-length character encoding scheme which uses groups of bytes to represent Unicode. This means it is not possible to use the whole theoretical 128 bit PIN space even if the user interface could support it.

The short range of Bluetooth provides some protection against eavesdropping attacks, but an attacker can circumvent this with a high-gain antenna which extends the reach well beyond the Bluetooth nominal range.

A PIN-cracking attack of the kind described in this section could lead, among other threats, to an attacker recording the cleartext of the encrypted communications between your handphone and headset or between your PDA and the desktop machine with which it synchronizes. As a more elaborate follow-up, an active attacker might even be able to impersonate your desktop computer to your PDA and upload maliciously altered data into it, such as an address book with edited phone numbers.

3   Strengthening Bluetooth

After having ascertained the practical vulnerability of the Bluetooth pairing protocol, we did our best to repair it. Our first goal was to establish a strong, eavesdropper-resistant shared key between the two paired devices. We found no way of doing this within the thrifty constraints chosen by the Bluetooth designers, so we ended up having to resort to asymmetric cryptography, in particular to the Diffie-Hellman key agreement. We then sought to make this exchange resistant against active man-in-the-middle attacks. For this we turned to the vast literature on Encrypted Key Exchange [2] and derivatives.

Next, in order to mitigate the overall cost of the algorithm, we implemented the asymmetric cryptography operations using elliptic curves. Finally, to validate the feasibility of the approach, we implemented a single-machine simulation of the whole algorithm (with a single thread performing all the calculations that the two parties would in turn perform during a run of the protocol) and we ported it to a Bluetooth handphone. At the current stage of implementation we are not performing the protocol over radio, because the API of the phone does not allow us to modify the Bluetooth stack, but we are demonstrating that the processor in a modern handphone can perform the protocol with no appreciable penalty in terms of time or energy.

3.1 Password-Based Key Agreement

In the Bluetooth protocol, the eavesdropper may brute-force the PIN offline and learn the session key as we did. To improve on that, we use a variant of Encrypted Key Exchange (EKE). Regardless of the actual PIN, the eavesdropper cannot discover the session key, since it is established via Diffie-Hellman. The PIN instead is used to defeat active middleperson attacks and it cannot be brute-forced because the middleperson is detected at the first wrong guess.

EKE was introduced in 1992 by Bellovin and Meritt [2]. Thereafter, there have been a number of suggestions for password based authenticated key-exchange protocols. These include the schemes described in [11,12,32,7,15]. Some EKE variants add security features such as forward secrecy. Other different approaches include [10], which depend on parties knowing the others' public keys beforehand, [1], which uses collisionful hashes, and [28], which use 'confounders' but neither hashes nor symmetric cryptography.

We presented a protocol at the workshop, which was later discovered to be vulnerable to an active guessing attack when an attacker participates in a protocol run. Details of the protocol and the attack are given in Appendix A.

We thus revise our solution and provide one which is based on the AMP suite developed by Kwon [14,15,16], in particular AMP+. The password is entangled in such a way that an attacker who has no knowledge of the password is not able to mount such an active guessing attack, and also at the same time not able to compute the shared key formed between two genuine participating parties. The other advantages of this scheme include the following: its relative good efficiency, its simple and understandable structure, it can be easily generalised, ie. to elliptic curve (EC) groups, and a formal security proof is provided.

3.2 Proposed Protocol Implementation

Elliptic Curve Diffie-Hellman - Encrypted Key Exchange (AMP+).
The protocol may be sketched as follows. The participants share a weak password P. They hash the password with the parties' identifiers (ie. their device addresses) to produce the password hash s, which is then multiplied with G, the common base point of the elliptic curve, to produce V. Alice sends her ephemeral public key $G.r_A$ [3]. Both Bob and Alice hash their identifiers with Alice's public key to obtain e_1. Bob multiplies Alice's public key by e_1, adds it to V, and multiplies this with Bob's private key r_B. This result is Bob's password-entangled public key, Q_B. Bob sends Q_B to Alice. Both parties would hash both of their identifiers and both parties' public keys together to obtain e_2. Alice computes

---

[3] Analogous to the case of multiplicative groups in finite fields, where r_A and g^{r_A} would be the private and public keys respectively, likewise for the EC case, given r_A finding $G.r_A$ is easy, while given $G.r_A$ finding r_A is hard.

ω, using her secret key r_A, the password hash s, and the values of e_1 and e_2 computed earlier. After obtaining ω, and using Bob's password-entangled public key Q_B, Alice is able to calculate $(r_A + e_2).r_B.G$ and derive the shared key. Over at Bob's end, he knows r_B, and using Alice's public key Q_A and the value of e_2 he has computed, Bob would likewise be able to calculate $(r_A + e_2).r_B.G$ and derive the shared key. The resulting protocol is shown in Figure 2.

#	Alice	Bob
	$s = H_0(I_A, I_B, P)$	$s = H_0(I_A, I_B, P)$
	$V = G.s$	$V = G.s$
	Chooses random r_A	
	$Q_A = G.r_A$	
1	$\xrightarrow{\quad Q_A \quad}$	
	$e_1 = H_1(I_A, I_B, Q_A)$	$e_1 = H_1(I_A, I_B, Q_A)$
		Chooses random r_B
		$Q_B = (Q_A.e_1 + V).r_B$
2	$\xleftarrow{\quad Q_B \quad}$	
	$e_2 = H_2(I_A, I_B, Q_A, Q_B)$	$e_2 = H_2(I_A, I_B, Q_A, Q_B)$
	$\omega = (r_A e_1 + s)^{-1}(r_A + e_2)$	
	$K = H_3(h.Q_B.\omega)$	$K' = H_3(h.(Q_A + G.e_2).r_B)$
	$M_1 = H_4(I_A, I_B, Q_A, Q_B, K)$	
3	$\xrightarrow{\quad M_1 \quad}$	
		$M_1' = H_4(I_A, I_B, Q_A, Q_B, K')$
		Verifies $M_1 = M_1'$
		$M_2 = H_5(I_A, I_B, Q_A, Q_B, K')$
4	$\xleftarrow{\quad M_2 \quad}$	
	$M_2' = H_5(I_A, I_B, Q_A, Q_B, K)$	
	Verifies $M_2 = M_2'$	

Fig. 2. Password-based Key Agreement (based on AMP+)

The security of the AMP family as secure authenticated key exchange protocols has been asserted by a formal proof [14] (with the caveats of proofs in this field).

By inspecting the structure of the protocol, it can be seen that a passive eavesdropper would not able to compute the shared session key, unless he knows either r_A or r_B. This is the Diffie-Hellman number-theoretic problem considered hard. An active adversary, Eve, may attempt to carry out a protocol run (either full or partial) so as to obtain a trace to conduct a password guess (either online or offline). She does not have a high chance of success. If Eve attempts to masquerade as Alice, she has one chance at correctly guessing the password hash s, so as to calculate the correct K and subsequently send the correct M_1 to Bob. If she fails at one try, Bob will abort the protocol run without revealing more than one wrong guess. If Eve attempts to masquerade as Bob, and she contributes a password-entangled public key while not knowing the password hash s, even if she manages to collect an M_1 sent by Alice, Eve would need to solve the Diffie-Hellman problem to recover the corresponding r_B that would produce the same K solution which Alice has calculated.

Perfect forward secrecy in the protocol is provided through Diffie-Hellman, so an adversary is not able to calculate past session keys after knowing P or s. By the same token, there is also resistance to the Denning-Sacco or known-key attack, in which an adversary may attempt to attack the password after knowing a previous session key.

The protocol resists the two-for-one guessing attack [20] by an adversary which masquerades as Bob. The idea behind this attack is that an attacker can validate two password guesses on one connection attempt. Earlier versions of AMP and SRP [32] were vulnerable to this slight deficiency. The improved AMP version resists this by doing a EC multiply (or exponentiation in discrete logarithm notation) of Q_A by e_1 to obtain Q_B, which breaks the symmetry which would otherwise exist between Q_A and V. Many-to-many guessing attacks, first raised by Kwon [16], particularly affect three-pass protocols. We do not think that many-to-many guessing attacks are too risky for ad-hoc devices though, since it is not expected at present that the devices would participate in more than a single password-based key agreement run at any one time. We however choose to use a four-pass protocol, and not a three-pass one, even if the latter is more efficient, in case of future feature creep where ad-hoc devices become more powerful and get called upon to behave more like server-type machines supporting multiple connection instances.

Key Derivation. The co-factor h is used to provide resistance to attacks like small subgroup attacks.

$$K = H_3(h.(r_A + e_2).r_B.G)$$

Further, as recommended by IEEE 1363 Standard Specifications for Public Key Cryptography [25], a key derivation function is used because the output from an elliptic curve secret value derivation step may not always be appropriate to use directly as a session key, due to possible bias in some of its bits. A key derivation function based on some hash function will be able to utilize more effectively the entire entropy of the secret value. The hash also helps resist a known-key attack.

Key Confirmation. The key confirmation procedure is necessary to prove that the other party knew the password S and has established the same shared key K. It is bilateral. Including the identifiers of both parties adds explicitness and more defence-in-depth. The key confirmation functions H_4 and H_5 are hash functions. They may be differentiated by having different short strings pre-concatenated with their other hash inputs.

For subsequent mutual authentication between the pair of devices after they have established and confirmed the shared key, they may use the bilateral challenge-response steps similar to what is in Bluetooth's pre-existing specification. We use challenge-response with random nonces then instead of running the earlier key confirmation function again because freshness and resistance to replay attacks would then be necessary.

3.3   Hash Check Values

It has been suggested that checking a short code over a manual transfer channel [9] may be useful to help in key confirmation for wireless device imprinting. In our scheme, these mechanisms can be helpful, but are not essential, since there is already an existing manual data transfer mechanism, the out-of-band sharing of the password, which we assume is performed confidentially, and it is later entangled into the DH keys. The use of short hash check values would present to an adversary the opportunity to search the whole space of 2^r possibilities, where r is the bit length of the short hash, until he finds matching pre-images with which he would be able to carry out a certainly successful middleperson attack. Whereas entangling the password with public keys presents to the adversary a probability of a 1 in 2^t chance to guess correctly in one try the password, where t is the bit length of the password space, to be able to carry out a successful middleperson attack. The lengths of the password and the check value can reasonably be assumed to be of the same approximate order. Under the standard attacker model of a RF middleperson attacker, hash check values does not appear to be a better alternative.

In scenarios where it is not difficult to present a user-interface which can show check values of sufficient lengths, further using hash check values is recommended, and may even be substituted for the key confirmation step described earlier, to increase the difficulty further for the attacker, in the off-chance that he manages to make a correct guess of the password in one pass. The price is the increased burden for the user of a second "manual transfer" operation.

3.4   Implementation

We developed a demonstration program which implemented the entire key agreement protocol run described above. A 163-bit binary curve is used for the elliptic-curve cryptosystem. The hash function used is SHA-1[4]. Due to the difficulties of integrating this functionality described by the protocol into commercial Bluetooth devices, as changes are required at the baseband level of Bluetooth's protocol stack, we have not proceeded to implement this in a pair of Bluetooth demonstrator devices.

Laptop. The unoptimised simulation runs over a 1.2 GHz Pentium M laptop. Our program used routines from the MIRACL [19] library to do the elliptic curve operations. On average, it took 3 milliseconds to perform an elliptic curve multiply operation (the most expensive single operation). As an upper bound, we consider that each of the computations of Q_B and K' requires 2 EC multiplies. The other operations take negligible time with respect to the public-key operations. The entire protocol run is completed in the order of time taken for 6 EC multiplies, which is 18 milliseconds on our platform.

---

[4] This choice may be re-evaluated in the light of recent attacks [31], though the usages of the hash functions in the protocol do not appear to require random collision resistance [18].

Handphone. The software prototype was ported to a commercial handphone, a Nokia 6600 with a 104 MHz ARM processor and running the Symbian operating system. The timing results proved that this phone can run the protocol without any speed problems. An EC multiply of the said order took merely 80 milliseconds. Thus, ignoring communication delays, all the computations of the entire protocol run may be completed in around half a second. If V can be assumed to have been pre-computed, there is a saving of 80 milliseconds. Note that these public key operations, while intensive, are only required for key agreement, which is usually done once-off between a pair of devices. The rest of Bluetooth traffic encryption is carried out by symmetric means.

3.5   Further Work

Having established that asymmetric cryptography is affordable for a modern handphone, there is still the problem of simpler peripherals, such as Bluetooth headsets. It would be useful to develop an "asymmetric protocol", in which the more powerful device perform most of the computation. Another area that would need attention, assuming that the old protocol would be supported alongside the new for compatibility, is that of safeguards against the classic attack of persuading the devices to use the old less secure protocol even when they could both use the new one.

4   Conclusions

It was clear that the Bluetooth pairing protocol, based as it is on symmetric cryptography and on a low entropy PIN, would always be subject to a PIN-cracking attack. We implemented this known attack in order to verify the resources it required. Results indicate that 4-digit PINs (i.e. the ones in the format to which people are most used from their experience with bank cards, car radios and indeed handphones) can be cracked instantaneously. Longer PINs cannot be considered secure, since a non-optimised attack program cracks 8-digit ones in less than an hour. Even longer PINs, and especially PINs in which the characters were more varied than 0–9, would offer somewhat better protection; but we do not believe they are realistic. Within the limits of the existing protocol, frequent change of link key would make the life of the attacker harder. We propose that manufacturers promote the use of this facility.

We have attempted to strengthen the Bluetooth pairing protocol against the attack we could so easily mount. To do so, we have had to resort to asymmetric cryptography. In theory this could be considered as exceeding the design parameters, when taking into account the original design goals and constraints of Bluetooth. Having validated the protocol with a prototype implementation on actual handphone hardware, though, we now suggest that asymmetric cryptography should no longer be axiomatically considered taboo for Bluetooth-class devices. Yes, there will still be a legion of smaller Bluetooth-capable devices with much lesser computational capabilities and energy reserves than our handphone; but it is significant that running a public key protocol on today's mobile phone is much faster than running PGP version 1 or 2 was on a desktop computer of the day, which some of us considered perfectly acceptable.

For the new generation of powerful devices (phones, PDAs, laptops) that are the most likely custodians of digital data that is worth more protection, stronger authentication than that offered by the original Bluetooth protocol would be beneficial, and is now affordable.

Acknowledgements

We are grateful to the members of the Security group at Cambridge, particularly Ross Anderson and George Danezis, for useful comments about earlier versions of the protocol before we attended the workshop.

References

1. Anderson, R., Lomas, M.: Fortifying key negotiation schemes with poorly chosen passwords. Electronics Letters 30(13), 1040–1041 (1994)
2. Bellovin, S.M., Meritt, M.: Encrypted key exchange: Password-based protocols secure against dictionary attacks. In: Proceedings of the IEEE Symposium on Research in Security and Privacy, pp. 72–74. IEEE Computer Society Press, Los Alamitos (1992)
3. Bellovin, S.M., Meritt, M.: Augmented encrypted key exchange: a password-based protocol secure against dictionary attacks and password file compromise. In: Proceedings of the 1st ACM Conference on Computer and Communications Security, pp. 244–250. ACM Press, New York (1993)
4. Bluetooth SIG Security Experts Group. Bluetooth Security White Paper, 1.0 (April 2002)
5. Bluetooth Special Interest Group. Bluetooth specification volume 1 part b baseband specification. Specifications of the Bluetooth System, 1.1 (February 2001)
6. Bluetooth Special Interest Group. Bluetooth specification volume 2 part h security specification. Specification of the Bluetooth System, 1.2 (November 2003)
7. Boyko, V., Mackenzie, P., Patel, S.: Provably secure password authentication and key exchange using diffie-hellman. In: Preneel, B. (ed.) EUROCRYPT 2000. LNCS, vol. 1807, pp. 156–171. Springer, Heidelberg (2000)
8. Certicom Corp. SEC 2: Recommended Elliptic Curve Domain Parameters, 1.0 (September 2000)
9. Gehrmann, C., Nyberg, K.: Enhancements to bluetooth baseband security. In: Proceedings of Nordsec 2001 (November 2001)
10. Gong, L., Lomas, M., Needham, R., Saltzer, J.: Protecting poorly chosen secrets from guessing attacks. IEEE Journal on Selected Areas in Communications 11(5), 648–656 (1993)
11. Jablon, D.: Strong password-only authenticated key exchange. Computer Communication Review 26(5), 5–26 (1996)
12. Jablon, D.: Extended password key exchange protocols immune to dictionary attack. In: Proceedings of the Sixth Workshops on Enabling Technologies: Infrastructure for Collaborative Engineering, vol. 11, pp. 248–255 (June 1997)
13. Jakobsson, M., Wetzel, S.: Security weaknesses in bluetooth. In: Naccache, D. (ed.) CT-RSA 2001. LNCS, vol. 2020, Springer, Heidelberg (2001)

14. Kwon, T.: Authentication and key agreement via memorable password. Contribution to the IEEE P1363 study group for Future PKC Standards (2000)
15. Kwon, T.: Authentication and key agreement via memorable password. In: ISOC Network and Distributed System Security Symposium (February 2001)
16. Kwon, T.: Summary of amp (authentication and key agreement via memorable passwords) (August 2003)
17. Lenstra, A.K., Verheul, E.R.: Selecting cryptographic key sizes. Journal of Cryptology 14, 255–293 (2001)
18. Lenstra, A.K.: Further progress in hashing cryptanalysis (February 2005)
19. Shamus Software Ltd. Multiprecision Integer and Rational Arithmetic C/C++ Library
20. MacKenzie, P.: On the Security of the SPEKE Password-Authenticated Key Agreement Protocol (July 2001)
21. Mackenzie, P.: More efficient password-authenticated key exchange. In: RSA Conference, Cryptographer's Track, pp. 361–377 (2001)
22. Massey, J., Khachatrian, G., Kuregian, M.: Nomination of safer+ as candidate algorithm for the advanced encryption standard. In: Proceedings of the 1st AES Candidate Conference (1998)
23. Miller, G.A.: The magic number seven, plus or minus two: Some limits on our capacity for processing information. Psychological Review 63, 81–97 (1956)
24. Mobiwave. Bluetooth Protocol Analyzer BPA-D10
25. IEEE P, Standard Specifications For Public-Key Cryptography (1363)
26. Patel, S.: Number theoretic attacks on secure password schemes. In: Proceedings of IEEE Computer Society Symposium on Research in Security and Privacy, pp. 236–247. IEEE Computer Society Press, Los Alamitos (1997)
27. Ritvanen, K., Nyberg, K.: Upgrade of bluetooth encryption and key replay attack. In: 9th Nordic Workshop on Secure-IT Systems (November 2004)
28. Roe, M., Christianson, B., Wheeler, D.: Secure sessions from weak secrets. Technical report from University of Cambridge and University of Hertfordshire (1998)
29. Shaked, Y., Wool, A.: Cracking the bluetooth pin. In: 3rd USENIX/ACM Conf. Mobile Systems, Applications, and Services (MobiSys), pp. 39–50 (June 2005)
30. Stajano, F., Anderson, R.: The resurrecting duckling — security issues for ad-hoc wireless networks. In: Proceedings of the 7th International Workshop on Security Protocols (1999)
31. Wang, X., Yin, Y.L., Yu, H.: Finding collisions in the full sha-1. In: Shoup, V. (ed.) CRYPTO 2005. LNCS, vol. 3621, Springer, Heidelberg (2005)
32. Wu, T.: The secure remote password protocol. In: Proceedings of 1998 Internet Society Symposium on Network and Distributed System Security, pp. 97–111 (1998)

Appendices

A   Attack on Early Version of Protocol

The version of the protocol we presented at the workshop, later found to be insecure, is a variant of the EKE, using Diffie Hellman key exchange over an elliptic curve. We will describe the protocol in the more familiar notation of a multiplicative group over a finite field here. g is the generator of the group, and three hash functions H_0, H_1, and H_2 are used. The shared secret password is P, and its hash, $s = H_0(P)$. The co-factor, h is publicly known. At each instantiation of the protocol run, Alice and Bob choose random ephemeral private values r_A and r_B respectively. C_A and C_B are random challenge nonces. The protocol is shown in multiplicative group form in Figure 3.

#	Alice		Bob
	$Q_A = g^{s+r_B}$		$Q_B = g^{s+r_A}$
1		$\xrightarrow{\quad Q_A \quad}$	
2		$\xleftarrow{\quad Q_B \quad}$	
	$K = H_1((Q_B.g^{-s})^{r_A.h})$		$K' = H_1((Q_A.g^{-s})^{r_B.h})$
3		$\xleftarrow{\quad C_B \quad}$	
4		$\xrightarrow{H_2(I_A,I_B,K,C_B)}$	
			Verify hash
5		$\xrightarrow{\quad C_A \quad}$	
6		$\xleftarrow{H_2(I_B,I_A,K',C_A)}$	
	Verify hash		

Fig. 3. Early version of protocol

A.1   Active Guessing Attack

While this protocol is secure against a passive offline eavesdropping attack—the class of attack which we had implemented against the pairing protocol in the existing Bluetooth specification—one of us (Clulow) later found it to be vulnerable to an active guessing attack. An active guessing attack is one in which the attacker does not know the password, but participates in a protocol run with one of the legitimate parties, and uses the trace of the protocol run to calculate the password.

The vulnerability clearly exists in both the multiplicative group and EC group formulations of the protocol. We will describe it in the former formulation. Let P_i for $i = 1, \ldots, m$ be an enumeration of all possible passwords. We define $s_i = H_0(P_i)$. Eve pretends to be Bob, chooses random X, calculates $Q'_B = g^X$ and submits this value of Alice. Alice continues with the protocol calculating $K = (Q'_B.g^{-s})^{r_A.h}$, and the hash $H_2(I_A, I_B, K, C_B)$ which she sends to Eve. Eve then calculates all possible values of $K_i = (g^{r_A+s}.g^{-s_i})^{(X-s_i).h}$ for $i = 1, \ldots, m$. Eve is also able to calculate all possible values of $H_{2,i} = H_2(I_A, I_B, K_i, C_B)$. She compares the hash of each $H_{2,i}$ to the hash received from Alice. For the value of index i for which $P_i = P$, the hashes will be equal, allowing Eve to identify the original password P with high probability. The basic operations which Eve has to perform are merely exponentiations and hashings, which are computationally tractable. The complete attack is shown in Figure 4.

Depending on the computation power of Eve and the time-out period, she may be able to find the correct K' successfully, and be able to submit Message 6 in time to fool Alice within one protocol run. Alternatively, if Eve is unable

#	Alice	Eve
1	$\xrightarrow{g^{s+r_A}}$	
2	$\xleftarrow{g^X}$	
	$K = H_1((g^X.g^{-s})^{r_A})$	
3	$\xleftarrow{C_B}$	
4	$\xrightarrow{H_2(I_A,I_B,K,C_B)}$	
		Computes $K_i = (g^{r_A+s}.g^{-s_i})^{(X-s_i)}$ for $i = 1,\dots,m$ Find $K' = K_i$ such that $H_2(I_A,I_B,K_i,C_B) = H_2(I_A,I_B,K,C_B)$
5	$\xrightarrow{C_A}$	
6	$\xleftarrow{H_2(I_B,I_A,K',C_A)}$	
	Verify hash	

Fig. 4. Active guessing attack on protocol

to find K' before time-out, she at least has the trace of a failed protocol run to compute K' offline and find P, which she can then use in a subsequent attempt.

Finding an attack which expresses the attacker's view of the key as tractable exponentiation functions, where the inputs are a set of dictionary words, is not new. What may be considered more novel in this attack against this particular password-based protocol is that the search term s_i for dictionary attack is being applied twice in the expression, ie. $(g^{r_A+s}.g^{-s_i})^{(X-s_i)}$.

B   ECDLP-Based Solution

This appendix contains further details on our elliptic curve implementation of the protocol. A wireless ad-hoc scenario such as Bluetooth gains from having short keys without compromising on cryptographic strength. Storage requirements may be minimized. The computational load on the devices should be minimized, as should the number of messages passed. We can assume a balanced model. In a few applications such for the LAN gateway and the LAN client, the augmented model, similar to that described in [3],which confers resilience to key compromise impersonation, may be useful.

Instead of basing the key agreement on the Discrete Logarithm Problem in a multiplicative group of a prime field (whether it is a traditional discrete logarithm system or a subgroup discrete logarithm system), we may consider it advantageous to base it on the Elliptic Curve Discrete Logarithm Problem (ECDLP).

The algorithms for solving the Discrete Logarithm Problem are classified into index-calculus methods and collision search methods. The latter have exponential running time. Index-calculus methods run at subexponential time, but these require certain arithmetic properties to be present in a group to be successful. The absence of such properties has led to the lack of any known index-calculus attack on elliptic curve discrete logarithms. The best general-purpose algorithm to solve the ECDLP has exponential running time. The current lack of subexponential-time algorithms to solve the ECDLP, as well as the development of efficient implementations of elliptic curve arithmetic, are two main reasons why ECDLP has become attractive on which to base cryptosystems.

B.1 Elliptic Curve Discrete Logarithm

In our proposal, we use a simple construction based on elliptic curves over a binary field. Elliptic curve domain parameters over a binary field are a septuple:

$$T = (m, f(x), a, b, G, n, h)$$

The elliptic curve is specified over a field $GF(q)$ where q is $2m$ for some positive integer m. An irreducible binary polynomial $f(x)$ of degree m specifies the representation of $GF(q)$. Two elliptic curve coefficients a and b, which are elements of $GF(q)$, define an elliptic curve E.

$$E : y^2 + x.y = x^3 + a.x^2 + b$$

A positive prime integer n divides this number of points on E. And G is a base point (x_G, y_G) of order n on the curve. The parameter h is the co-factor. The choice of a binary field is made because this is easier to implement in hardware than the others. Elliptic curves over $GF(2m)$ generally consist of two types of parameters those associated with a Koblitz curve, and those chosen verifiably at random. Koblitz curves allow particularly efficient implementation, but their extra structure also aid attack to some degree. In our trade-off, we prefer randomly chosen parameters.

Based on the recommendations in [17], we may choose an elliptic key size which is equivalent to a symmetric key length of 86 bits (assuming no cryptanalytic progress), or equivalent to a symmetric key length of 79 bits (assuming cryptanalytic effectiveness doubles every 18 months). Such a length is suggested to be 163 bits. The reduction polynomial is:

$$f(x) = x^{163} + x^7 + x^6 + x^3 + 1$$

This is roughly equivalent to 1024 bit length of RSA and DH. Some suggested domain parameters are given in [8], and they are compliant or recommended under ANSI X9.62, ANSI X9.63, IEEE P1363, IPSec and NIST.

Repairing the Bluetooth Pairing Protocol
(Transcript of Discussion)

Frank Stajano

University of Cambridge
Computer Laboratory

The Bluetooth pairing protocol is the one that takes place when two Bluetooth devices get together and want to authenticate to each other. I shall start by giving a high level summary of our work.

Firstly, "Look Ma, we can crack Bluetooth!", we demonstrate a crack by a passive adversary. On its own this doesn't look very interesting academically because, from the protocol itself, it is clear that this could be done. So next we ask if this problem can be fixed. The answer is affirmative, and we show how, but this looks like cheating because we fixed it in a way that the original designers of the protocol thought was not allowed. However we then argue that this was a sensible thing to do, and that maybe it is appropriate to relax the constraints that they set on themselves in the first place.

(The speaker then describes how Bluetooth works and how they cracked it—see the paper.)

A basic way to protect the Bluetooth pairing protocol is to make greater use of the key renewal facility that is present in the specifications and allows you to regenerate a new combination key from time to time. Unfortunately, in practice most Bluetooth devices we have examined don't even offer the facility to initiate a regeneration of the combination key without going all the way to the beginning and typing in the PIN, which defeats the point. Key renewal, if used, would be an easy way to enhance the security. For example, every time you met the device again, you might renegotiate the combination key and then it would be quite unlikely that the snooper be listening every time you met that device. In practice, instead, I pair to my printer now, and I meet the printer the next day, and I meet the printer a week later, and so on, and I'm still using the same key without ever doing this renewal; in this case I will be subject to the attack I previously described if the attacker could listen to the first pairing.

What requirements did we consider in order to repair the protocol? Using a short PIN is not nice, from a security viewpoint, but it's a kind of necessary evil. When I was little I was often told that I should eat fish because it contains phosphorus which is good for the brain, promotes the growth of new neurons and so on. Now, no matter how much fish you eat, you still will not get a doubling of the number of neurons in your brain every 18 months as happens with the transistors in a processor under Moore's Law! So the number of digits we can reliably remember is still more or less the same as it was 20 years ago, or 200, or 2000, and there is no chance that we will be able to catch up with the enhanced brute-forcing capabilities of computers by lengthening the PIN. We are forced

B. Christianson et al. (Eds.): Security Protocols 2005, LNCS 4631, pp. 46–50, 2007.
© Springer-Verlag Berlin Heidelberg 2007

to rely on using short PINs if we are going to use PINs at all, because we cannot expect people to remember longer and longer PINs.

Now, before looking in detail at the repaired protocol, I will give an executive summary. The first thing we did was to establish a strong shared key despite having an eavesdropper, because that was the main problem of the previous protocol: an eavesdropper could find out the shared key between the devices. The second thing we did was to strengthen the exchange against an *active* middle person; this was not even discussed in the previous protocol because it wasn't even secure against a passive one. The objection of course is that from the very first point we are cheating because we are using asymmetric crypto. If asymmetric crypto had been allowed in the rules of the game, then the Bluetooth designers would have used it, and would have produced a better protocol in the first place.

Now on to the protocol. We are doing a Diffie Hellman exchange to establish a shared secret between Alice and Bob, and that would be sufficient in itself to fix the problem that we exploited in cracking the existing protocol. If we are only concerned about a passive attack, Diffie Hellman is sufficient to stop it, and we don't even need a PIN. Here we are still using a PIN, but now for a different purpose: we are using a PIN to prevent an active middle person attack. In summary we have Diffie Hellman, with an extra PIN along the lines of Encrypted Key Exchange[1] to defeat an active attacker, and also done over elliptic curves so that it will be less computationally expensive and will run on the cell phone.

Ben Laurie. If you use a four digit PIN, doesn't this still leave you open to an active brute-force attack? It could probably even be performed in real time.

Reply. If you are using the short PIN to derive a secret key, then an attacker can brute-force this PIN by trying all the possibilities, and basically the length of the PIN determines the amount of effort you have to do for brute-force. This is what we did in our own attack. If instead you are using this EKE-style construction to stop an active middle man, the PIN has a different function: it is there so that, if the attacker guessed the correct PIN, then he won't be detected, but if he guessed a wrong PIN then it will be obvious to the victim that he is there. If you have, for example, a thousand possible PINs, just three digit PINs, then the brute-force effort for cracking a PIN would be just trying a thousand times. But, used in EKE fashion, the significance of the thousand is different: it means the attacker has one chance in a thousand of not being spotted, and if he guesses the wrong pin he will be exposed.

Matt Blaze. So you're exposed, then what?

Reply. Then Bob says to himself "Hey, I'm not actually talking to Alice", so the authentication fails.

Matt Blaze. So what do you do then? Can you call the police?

Reply. Well, you just don't talk. Your device might play a siren to alert you, and you should react by saying "Wait a minute, who's around here? There must be an attacker!"

---

[1] See for example Christianson, Roe, and Wheeler, Secure Sessions for Weak Secrets, LNCS 3364, 190–212.

Matt Blaze. So, every time the victim is near the attacker, her siren will be going off? I'm asking a semi-serious question here, because a detection facility is only useful if there's a penalty for being detected. In a very hostile environment, where attacks are happening constantly, it becomes impossible to do anything about them. So is the detection actually an improvement?

Reply. At the lowest level there is a penalty, namely that the communication doesn't happen. While this is also a chance for denial of service, it is a penalty for the attacker in the sense that he cannot overhear or intercept the channel as he could if the middleperson attack went undetected. So the more malicious activities of the attacker are prevented.

Matt Blaze. But the victim has to try a thousand times before getting through.

Reply. If you are alerted to the fact that it's not working because an attack is in progress, then you can take countermeasures you wouldn't otherwise take, such as checking who is Blue-sniping you from the window.

Bruce Christianson. If you think of an analogy of trying to log-in, there are all sorts of things that an operating system can do when somebody repeatedly tries to log-in with the wrong password: you can suspend the account for a random period of time or you can have a two-level password where the system is suspended as the outer one is hacked and the inner one gets guessed wrong. It's the same problem. The thing you don't want is allowing an off-line attack.

Matt Blaze. Sure, absolutely, but I'm not convinced that, in a wireless environment, there's a significant difference between an on-line attack and an off-line attack for those purposes, because you have no way of identifying the attacker. For a remote log-in I might stop accepting connections from that IP address; but, in Bluetooth, what am I going to do? Stop accepting connections from the radio? I would love a protocol that allowed me to turn other people's phones off.

Reply. Back to the protocol and its implementation. The obvious objection was that using asymmetric cryptography is cheating, and the answer to that is to actually program the protocol for real and put it in a mobile phone. Ford got himself a mobile phone that he could program and wrote a simulation of the protocol to run on the phone. I mean a simulation because he couldn't make the phones talk a different Bluetooth version, but he could write some code that made all this computation run on a single phone pretending it was two phones and see how long it took. It was just a feasibility proof and a timing measurement, and the result was that doing one elliptic curve multiply took 80 milliseconds, and one full protocol run took less than a second. So the summary is that in a modern phone you can run this protocol with no trouble, and therefore it's not really cheating; rather, it's the original guidelines that were conservative. Although it's not realistic to assume that all Bluetooth devices will have a 100 MHz processor in them, it's still plausible to claim that the more powerful devices like your phone, your PDA or your laptop will have something like this or better. Fortunately there is a correlation between being a powerful device and holding many of your secrets, so there is a case to be made for saying that, although you might still have to use the old and less secure protocol when you are pairing small devices, when you are pairing powerful devices then it may be worth going for something more beefy and more computationally expensive.

Matt Blaze. So you need another protocol to prevent the attacker from persuading the victim to downgrade to an insecure mode?

Reply. Yes, that's the usual problem when allowing less secure alternatives, absolutely.

Let's now summarize the slides shown so far. We implemented and demonstrated the obvious Bluetooth crack, obvious in the sense that if you read the protocol it's clear that the passive eavesdropper could do that. It's conceptually trivial, but it's lethal: you are undetectable, you just gather traffic and do an off-line brute-force, and it doesn't take long. We fixed the protocol using, among other ingredients, asymmetric cryptography; we implemented the fix, and it doesn't take very long: the whole protocol runs in less time than it used to take to run PGP. When PGP 2 for DOS first appeared in the early 1990s, we had 33 MHz 386 computers and we were used to waiting several seconds for encrypting an email, never mind generating keys which took several *minutes*, and nobody really worried about it.

Ben Laurie. Nobody? Many people wouldn't use it at all, precisely because it was so time-consuming and inconvenient to operate.

Reply. Valid point. So let's rephrase: *those of us who were using it* didn't worry that it took several seconds to encrypt.

The moral of this story for me is that asymmetric crypto for Bluetooth should not be axiomatically taboo: there may be cases where it's starting to become justified. I was one of the people writing about the peanut processor and I said you cannot use asymmetric crypto for ubiquitous computing devices; but nowadays, while this is still true for the tiniest devices such as RFID, I'm starting to think that there are so many big processors being embedded into small objects that maybe for some of them we can relax our design constraints.

Mike Roe. So it's probably because you're using elliptic curves rather than RSA and that makes it just about fast enough?

Reply. Yes.

Bruce Christianson. Also you're not using any public key infrastructure at all?

Reply. Yes, that's right, that was one of our requirements.

Another thing I said but want to emphasise is that, for the case of the smaller devices that need to use the standard protocol, we recommend a much more frequent use of the existing facility to regenerate the combination key, which is totally wasted nowadays because it's something that would make the system more secure and yet is never used.

Kamil Kulesza. You mentioned very short PINs. Some research concerning the activation keys for nuclear devices found that the human being, under the stressful conditions of a crisis, can remember keys of up to 12–15 digits. Secondly

I think that, even if you need a longer PIN, you could have some sort of token that generated keys for you.

Reply. Yes, though somehow you would have to ensure that you have not lost the token and you are still in control of it. Maybe there's a kind of recursion here, where you have to activate the token by tapping in a PIN or something like that. At some point you will have to type in a PIN, and my argument was simply that the maximum length of a memorable PIN is limited: it cannot keep growing every time a new processor family comes out.

Yvo Desmedt. Talking of the fact that some people can remember one of these PINs, the problem is that there are people who have unbelievable memory. Someone could apparently memorize half the phonebook.

Reply. Indeed: when I was an undergraduate there were a number of us who took perverse pleasure in reciting hundreds of digits of π (which I have since forgotten). But it's one thing to perform this stunt and another to use it to secure your ubiquitous devices, particularly when you have tens or hundreds of them. It's not just your big-deal nuclear missile that needs a secret sequence, it's all these cheap and plentiful gadgets here and there and in every pocket, and you would have to share this human memory capacity among all of them. Besides, the fact that some people have a fantastic memory is hardly a problem: if anything, the problem is that all the others don't.

Mike Bond. Do you know of any research in the practical field of trying to make direct connectivity between devices easier? What I mean is you can take two devices and touch them together. Previously I guess we'd imagined a sort of small metal box which linked the devices. Is there not something which can be done, maybe using the casings, that uses some ingenious electronics so that you can literally touch devices more easily than without having to spare a particular contact pin or a particular connector?

Reply. As you know I have always been interested in this pairing business and in the original Resurrecting Duckling paper we advocated electrical contact as the safest solution. (This was then extended to say that you should do the initial key transfer over a more secure channel than the one over which you're doing the rest of the communication.) Whenever I talk to industry people about something like that, they always come up with objections: they say that having this metal contact is too expensive. You wonder how expensive it can be when we look at all the other stuff they put in, but still there is this argument, the manufacturing restrictions on providing extra electrical contacts. So wait until Ford's next talk[2] and he will describe interesting strategies for using alternative ways of transferring pairing information between devices.

---

[2] These proceedings.

Keep on Blockin' in the Free World: Personal Access Control for Low-Cost RFID Tags

Melanie R. Rieback, Bruno Crispo, and Andrew S. Tanenbaum

Computer Systems Group
Vrije Universiteit
Amsterdam, The Netherlands

Abstract. This paper introduces an off-tag RFID access control mechanism called "Selective RFID Jamming". Selective RFID Jamming protects low-cost RFID tags by enforcing access control on their behalf, in a similar manner to the RFID Blocker Tag. However, Selective RFID Jamming is novel because it uses an active mobile device to enforce centralized ACL-based access control policies. Selective RFID Jamming also solves a Differential Signal Analysis attack to which the RFID Blocker Tag is susceptible.

1   Introduction

Radio Frequency Identification (RFID) is coming, and it's bringing a streamlined revolution. Passive RFID tags are batteryless computer chips that are powered externally by their RFID readers. These "radio barcodes" can transmit information using radio waves, eliminating the need for a line of sight. RFID tags pose unique security and privacy challenges. Because of their severe processing, storage, and cost constraints, even standard security properties like access control are difficult to implement. Several access control solutions exist for high-end RFID tags, but these mechanisms increase the price of RFID tags beyond what some application scenarios (e.g. supply chain management) will allow. This leaves low-cost (<\$0.10) Electronic Product Code (EPC)-style tags without the ability to protect the privacy of their users.

In this paper, we suggest an access control mechanism for low-cost RFID tags called Selective RFID Jamming. Selective RFID Jamming extends protection to low-cost tags by enforcing access control on their behalf. Selective RFID Jamming achieves this by performing RF signal "jamming" (similar to the RFID Blocker Tag). However, Selective RFID Jamming has three unique characteristics: 1) It is implemented on active mobile device, 2) It utilizes ACL-based security policies, 3) It uses a Digital Signal Analysis (DSA) resistant jamming signal.

B. Christianson et al. (Eds.): Security Protocols 2005, LNCS 4631, pp. 51–59, 2007.

2   Radio Frequency Identification

Radio Frequency Identification (RFID) is the latest phase in the decades-old trend of the miniaturization of computers. RFID transponders are tiny resource-limited computers that do not have a battery that needs periodic replacement. RFID tags are inductively powered by their external reading devices, called RFID readers. Once the RFID tag is activated, the tag then decodes the incoming query and produces an appropriate response by modulating the request signal, using one or more subcarrier frequencies. RFID Tags can do a limited amount of processing, and have a small amount (<1024 bits) of storage.

RFID tags are useful for a huge variety of applications. Some of these applications include: supply chain management, automated payment, physical access control, counterfeit prevention, and smart homes and offices. RFID tags are also implanted in all kinds of personal and consumer goods. For example, RFID tags are used in passports, partially assembled cars, frozen dinners, ski-lift passes, clothing, and public transportation tickets. Implantable RFID tags for animals allow concerned owners to label their pets and livestock. Verichip Corp. has also created a slightly-adapted implantable RFID chip, the size of a grain of rice, for use in humans. Since its introduction, the Verichip was approved by the U.S. Food and Drug Administration, and this tiny chip is currently deployed in both commercial and medical systems.

2.1   RFID Threat Model

Like many other pervasive technologies, the success of RFID threatens to bring unwanted social consequences. RFID tags face unique security and privacy risks, not just because the transponders will be located everywhere, but because they are too computationally limited to support traditional security and privacy enhancing technologies. This lack of protection leads to some undesirable scenarios, like the unauthorized access of tag data, interception of tag-reader communications, and location tracking of people and objects.

A growing number of RFID security and privacy solutions have been proposed, but none have yet succeeded to ensure security and privacy in a wide range of RFID application scenarios. The least amount of progress has been made in protecting the application scenario that is the most common - supply chain management, using low-cost Electronic Product Code (EPC) tags. Low-cost RFID tags require new RFID security and privacy techniques. For the sake of clarity, we will now make a distinction between low-cost and high-cost RFID tags:

Low-cost RFID tags. Low-cost RFID Tags should cost between five and ten cents. They are usually used in supply-chain management, and they usually conform to the EPC standard. These RFID tags usually have a kill mechanism, but they are not powerful enough to support cryptography.

High-cost RFID tags. High-cost RFID Tags will cost more than ten cents. They are used in the numerous applications outside of supply-chain management,

Table 1. On-tag vs. Off-tag Security Mechanisms

On-Tag	Off-Tag
Kill commands	Faraday cages
Sleep/wake modes	Blocker tags
Pseudonyms	External re-encryption
Hash locks	
Cryptography/authentication	

and they can support many different standards. These RFID tags usually have one or more security mechanisms (kill/sleep/wake modes, cryptography).

3   Selective RFID Jamming

Selective RFID Jamming is a form of "off-tag" access control that produces a jamming signal when an access control check fails.

To understand how Selective RFID Jamming works, it is useful to understand the difference between on-tag and off-tag access control. Table 1 lists some on-tag and off-tag versions of access control mechanisms. As the name implies, on-tag access control mechanisms are located on the RFID tags themselves. On-tag access control is the most common type of RFID access control, with mechanisms including: tag deactivation, cryptography, and tag-reader authentication. In contrast, off-tag access control mechanisms put the access control mechanism on a device external to the RFID tag. Examples of this include the RSA Blocker tag and external re-encryption. Off-tag access control has the advantage that it can protect low-cost RFID tags (like EPC tags), because the access control doesn't require any extra complexity (hence, extra cost) on the RFID tag itself.

Here is how Selective RFID Jamming works:

1. An RFID reader sends a query to an RFID tag
2. The mobile device captures and decodes the query (in real-time), and determines whether the query is permitted
3. If the query is not allowed, the mobile device briefly sends a jamming signal that is just long enough to block the RFID tag response

The top-level concept is similar to the idea behind the RSA Blocker Tag[8]. However, Selective RFID Jamming has three unique characteristics: 1) It is implemented on active mobile device, 2) It utilizes ACL-based security policies, and 3) It uses a DSA-resistant jamming signal.

3.1   Active Mobile Devices

Selective RFID Jamming is always implemented in a battery-powered mobile device (e.g. PDA or mobile phone). This is important because Selective RFID Jamming needs to perform resource-intensive security protocols, such as signal

Table 2. Example Access Control List

Action	Source	Target	Command	Comment
block	*	MYTAGS	*	Suppress all queries targeting user's tags
allow	Home	MYTAGS	*	Home system can query user's tags
allow	Wal-Mart	MYTAGS	Read data block	Wal-Mart can read (not write) data from user's tags
allow	*	*	*	All queries to other RFID tags are OK

jamming and authentication. To implement such functionality on an RFID tag would cause severe restrictions in terms of power and storage. Using a device with an 'active' power-source avoids problems that 'passive' solutions like RFID tags face, such as the unreliable production of jamming signals based upon physical orientation. Adequate storage space is also important, because it limits the complexity of the access control policies that can be used. On-tag RFID access control mechanisms only have access to 1024 bits of storage at most. However, battery-powered mobile devices are full-blown computers, that have no comparable storage restrictions. This allows access control policies to contain enough entries that they can provide very granular access control.

3.2   Access Control Lists

Selective RFID Jamming uses Access Control Lists (ACLs) to represent security policies. It 'selectively filters' RFID tag responses, much in the same way that a firewall filters packets from a network. ACLs specify which RFID query responses are blocked or allowed, based upon the source (the reader issuing the query), the target (the RFID tags affected by the query), and the command (ex. read data/write data/inventory). Table 2 shows a sample ACL.

Selective RFID Jamming enforces access control for the localized RFID tags of a single user. This contrasts with the majority of RFID access control mechanisms, which protect individual RFID tags, wherever they may be. Since Selective RFID Jamming provides localized RFID access control, it could also be used protect fixed locations. (e.g. protecting a store from RFID-enabled corporate espionage).

RFID queries do not contain information about the issuing RFID readers, so the source of RFID requests are ascertained by means of an authentication protocol (using in- or out-of-band communications). "Friendly" RFID Readers may explicitly perform authentication ahead of time, swapping some information that can be used to create authenticated 'sessions'. These authenticated RFID Readers may have their own entries in the ACL, giving them special permissions to perform certain kinds of queries. "Unfriendly" RFID Readers (or RFID Readers that simply are not familiar with Selective RFID Jamming) will not perform any authentication protocol at all, and will simply issue their queries. The ACL should also specify a set of 'default' access control rules, that govern access for these unknown readers. Table 2 shows how authenticated RFID Readers from the user's home and the Wal-Mart, are given special dispensation to query the user's RFID tags. [1]

---

[1] Authentication requires shared keys, which require key setup between RFID Readers and the jamming device.

The jamming device extracts the targeted tags and the command type from the query signal, and match these values to the information stored in the access control lists. The jamming device may store lists of RFID tags, including 'tag ownership' lists, that specify tags owned or otherwise associated with the user. (Another one might list the former owners of RFID tags). Ranges of RFID identifiers might be represented similarly to ranges of IP addresses. For example, the mask "01.0000A89.00016F.0/60" specifies an 8-bit EPC Header, 28-bit EPC Manager, and 24-bit EPC Object Class, but not the 36-bit EPC Serial Number. Access is then restricted based upon the stored RFID tag information. Table 2 illustrates how access control is restricted for certain commands, for tags in a specific ownership list called MYTAGS.

Note that these access control checks must be performed in real-time. These real-time checks are possible because RFID Readers make a small pause between issuing queries and listening for RFID tag responses. (In the case of ISO 15693/18000, the pause is 300 microseconds long). In this time, a high-end microcontroller has enough available clock cycles to perform the required access control checks. Here is an example: the StrongARM SA-1100, running at 206 MHz has a performance of 235 MIPS. This means that it can perform over 70,000 operations in 300 microseconds. While this budget is not sufficient for performing public key cryptography, it does offers enough cycles for simple ACL checks, calculating checksums, or possibly even symmetric key decryption.

3.3   DSA-Resistant Jamming Signal

The Problem. RFID Blocker Tags[8], introduced by Juels, Rivest, and Szydlo, interfere with RFID Readers' tree-walk tag singulation algorithm by always replying with a '0|1' signal. This response causes a collision, which forces the RFID reader to traverse the entire ID space to discover the IDs of nearby RFID tags.

RFID Tags will usually not meet the singulation criteria, during the Blocker Tag induced full binary tree ID traversal. This means that the majority of the time during tag singulation, the Blocker Tag(s) are the only entities that are responding. Additionally, because the responses from RFID Blocker Tags are always the same, the analog signals received from the RFID Blocker will also be identical.

The Attack. In order to perform differential signal analysis, we need to modify an RFID Tag Reader to measure and record the additive waveform that results from the interference of all incoming RFID signals. If an RFID Reader records the analog signal received during tag singulation, the mode (or most commonly appearing) 'tag response' signal will be the combined waveform of the '0|1' responses, sent from the one or more Blocker Tags that are present. Because this signal never changes, it can be mathematically averaged out from the total recorded waveforms. The left-over signal will be the genuine RFID tag responses.

Illustrating the Attack. We will illustrate our attack through use of an example, shown in Figure 1 .

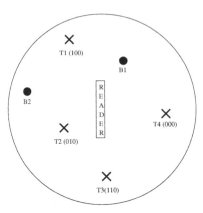

Fig. 1. Scenario: RFID Tags and Blockers

Let's hypothetically say that we use RFID tags with 3-bit ids (8 possible tags). We also assume that RFID tag IDs are unique – no two authentic RFID tags will use the same ID. We have an RFID reader in the center of a circular range, and four RFID tags (T1-T4), and two RFID blocker tags (B1-B2) are present.

It's easy to detect the presence of RFID blocker tags. If no (or few) tags seem to be missing during singulation, then it's likely that one or more RFID blocker tags are present. Additionally, if we attempt to perform singulation on each of the 'leaf nodes' (3-bit complete ID's), we will constantly get collisions, that will be composed of the combined signals shown in Table 3.

In each of these cases, we received collisions, so the reader will not be able to read the individual tag ID's. However the reader is able to detect total additive signal, produced by the multiple RFID tags.

Half of the measured analog waveforms received are equal to B1+B2. If we take the mode (most frequently occurring value) of all of the measured 3-bit ID signal strengths, we will get B1+B2. If we use 8-bit tag IDs instead of 3-bit tag ID's, the predominance of the mode throughout a range sweep will be even more obvious. Now all we have to do is subtract the signal (B1+B2) from each total signal received during the actual tree-walk singulation process, and we'll get the

Table 3. Analog waveforms received during an RFID tag sweep

Queried Tags	Combined Signal
Sub-tree starting with '000'	T4+B1+B2
Sub-tree starting with '001'	B1+B2
Sub-tree starting with '010'	T2+B1+B2
Sub-tree starting with '011'	B1+B2
Sub-tree starting with '100'	T1+B1+B2
Sub-tree starting with '101'	B1+B2
Sub-tree starting with '110'	T3+B1+B2
Sub-tree starting with '111'	B1+B2

Table 4. Subtracting blocker signals during RFID tag singulation

Singulated Node	Combined Signal	Subtracted Signal
Sub-tree starting with '0'	T2+T4+B1+B2	T2+T4
Sub-tree starting with '00'	T4+B1+B2	T4
Sub-tree starting with '000'	T4+B1+B2	T4
Sub-tree starting with '001'	B1+B2	No signal
Sub-tree starting with '01'	T2+B1+B2	T2
Sub-tree starting with '010'	T2+B1+B2	T2
Sub-tree starting with '011'	B1+B2	No signal
Sub-tree starting with '1'	T1+T3+B1+B2	T1+T3
Sub-tree starting with '10'	T1+B1+B2	T1
Sub-tree starting with '100'	T1+B1+B2	T1
Sub-tree starting with '101'	B1+B2	No signal
Sub-tree starting with '11'	T3+B1+B2	T3
Sub-tree starting with '110'	T3+B1+B2	T3
Sub-tree starting with '111'	B1+B2	No signal

following results, shown in Table 4. The RFID Reader can now easily determine which RFID tags are present.

Preventing Signal Analysis. Selective RFID Jamming produces a randomly modulated jamming signal, at a single frequency (ex. 13.56 MHz). The idea is that because the signal is randomly modulated, it cannot be easily averaged out. We use a single antenna to produce this jamming signal[2]. The only caveat to keep in mind is the following: if you collect enough samples of the same signal added with the random signal, you can often still average out the random signal. So careful attention must be paid to the design of the randomization function.

4   Discussion

Selective RFID Jamming provides centralized (multi-tag) access control, while most on-tag mechanisms provide decentralized (per tag) access control. This centralization has its advantages. Access control lists are easier to update, plus centralizing RFID access control has a cost advantage. A per-tag access control mechanism, like the RFID Blocker Tag, is used 1:1 in proportion with the RFID tags that are protected. Reproducing so many copies of the access control mechanism may be cost prohibitive in some applications. However, only one mobile device is necessary to protect hundreds of a user's low-cost tags using Selective RFID Jamming.

Selective RFID Jamming has an unresolved problem: Denial of Service attacks. If an attacker deliberately performs lots of unauthorized RFID queries, the jamming signal production will jam up the airwaves, causing interference with other nearby RFID systems. A secondary problem is that this repeated production of jamming signals will also drain the battery of the mobile device. Unfortunately, this is not an easy problem to solve.

---

[2] The Blocker Tag uses two antennas – one to produce the '0' response and one to produce the '1' response. However, this is not necessary to produce a '1|0' collision signal.

Selective RFID Jamming has a few other problems including: 1) The active mobile device is a single point of failure, 2) There might be legal problems, and 3) Selective RFID Jamming won't stop RFID readers using very directional antennas. We would like to further address these issues in future work.

5   Related Work

Off-tag RFID access control was pioneered by Juels, Rivest, and Szydlo with their RFID Blocker Tag. As described in Section 3.3, the RFID Blocker Tag interferes with RFID Reader singulation by "spoofing" the RFID Reader's tree-walk singulation protocol [8]. The Blocker Tag is different from Selective RFID Jamming because it is implemented on an RFID tag, it uses a static '0|1' jamming signal produced by two antennas, and it uses privacy-zones instead of access control lists. Several kinds of on-tag access control mechanisms also exist for RFID technology. Tag deactivation, otherwise known as "tag killing" was standardized by the EPCglobal consortium [1]. Juels also suggests the use of dynamic tag identifiers, called pseudonyms, that use a mechanism called "pseudonym throttling" to allow authenticated RFID readers to refresh the pseudonym list [7]. On-tag access control schemes work well for certain applications, but fail to protect low-cost EPC-style tags, which are too cheap to support these mechanisms. High-cost RFID tags may also support RFID tag-reader authentication schemes. Vajda and Buttyan offer lightweight authentication protocols [9], and Weis, et. al, proposed a randomized hash lock protocol for authentication [10]. Feldhofer, et. al, proposes an extension to the ISO 18000 protocol, that would enable the in-band transmission of authentication data [2]. Cryptographic primitives also exist that may work with high-cost RFID tags. Finkenzeller describes the use of stream ciphers [4], and Feldhofer, et. al, describes a low-cost AES implementation [3]. Gaubatz, et. al, describe a low cost NTRU implementation, designed for sensor networks, that brings public key cryptography closer to fitting the constraints of RFID [6]. Low-cost RFID tags can also be protected by social and legal factors. Simson Garfinkel proposes a legislative RFID "Bill of Rights", where he explicitly extends some ideas from the European Privacy Directive for use with RFID [5].

6   Conclusion

Selective RFID Jamming is an access control scheme that uses battery-powered devices to enforce ACL-based access control policies, with the aid of randomly modulated jamming signals. Selective RFID Jamming enforces access control on the behalf of low-cost RFID tags, which is useful for protecting cost-critical applications (e.g. supply chain management) that currently lack access control. It will combat RFID security and privacy threats, and can help fight the battle against the negative consequences that RFID technology will bring.

Future work will provide more detail about the earlier mentioned access control and authentication schemes. Additionally, we plan to implement this functionlity, to test the feasability of real-time RFID filtering.

- Introduce the RFID Guardian
  - (Battery-powered, mobile, 2-way RFID communications, personal RFID privacy management)
  - Implementable on already available devices (ex. RFID-enabled cellphones)
- Advantages
  - Active devices have fewer storage constraints
    * Enables very granular access control policies
  - Active devices have fewer power constraints
    * Reliable jamming signal production
  - Low-cost
    * Most RFID access control mechanisms are reproduced 1:1 with tags
    * Able to protect many tags with one device

References

1. EPCglobal. 13.56 mhz ism band class 1 radio frequency (rf) identification tag interface specification
2. Feldhofer, M.: An authentication protocol in a security layer for rfid smart tags. In: MELECON 2004. The 12th IEEE Mediterranean Electrotechnical Conference, vol. 2, pp. 759–762. IEEE Computer Society Press, Los Alamitos (2004)
3. Feldhofer, M., Dominikus, S., Wolkerstorfer, J.: Strong authentication for rfid systems using the aes algorithm. In: Joye, M., Quisquater, J.-J. (eds.) CHES 2004. LNCS, vol. 3156, pp. 357–370. Springer, Heidelberg (2004)
4. Finkenzeller, K.: RFID Handbook: Fundamentals and Applications in Contactless Smart Cards and Identification. John Wiley and Sons, Ltd., Chichester (2003)
5. Garfinkel, S.: An rfid bill of rights. Technology Review, p. 35 (October 2002)
6. Gaubatz, G., Kaps, J.-P., Ozturk, E., Sunar, B.: State of the art in public-key cryptography for wireless sensor networks. In: PerSec 2005. Proceedings of the Second IEEE International Workshop on Pervasive Computing and Communication Security, IEEE Computer Society Press, Los Alamitos (2005)
7. Juels, A.: Minimalist cryptography for low-cost rfid tags. In: Blundo, C., Cimato, S. (eds.) SCN 2004. LNCS, vol. 3352, Springer, Heidelberg (2005)
8. Juels, A., Rivest, R.L., Szydlo, M.: The blocker tag: Selective blocking of rfid tags for consumer privacy. In: Proceedings of the 10th ACM Conference on Computer and Communications Security, ACM Press, New York (2003)
9. Vajda, I., Buttyán, L.: Lightweight authentication protocols for low-cost rfid tags. In: Dey, A.K., Schmidt, A., McCarthy, J.F. (eds.) UbiComp 2003. LNCS, vol. 2864, Springer, Heidelberg (2003)
10. Weis, S., Sarma, S., Rivest, R., Engels, D.: Security and privacy aspects of low-cost radio frequency identification systems. In: Hutter, D., Müller, G., Stephan, W., Ullmann, M. (eds.) Security in Pervasive Computing. LNCS, vol. 2802, pp. 201–212. Springer, Heidelberg (2004)

Keep on Blockin' in the Free World

(Transcript of Discussion)

Melanie R. Rieback

Computer Systems Group
Vrije Universiteit
Amsterdam, The Netherlands

I am here today to talk about some of the security implications of Radio Frequency Identification. RFID tags are remotely-powered data carriers that resemble the theft control tags that you might find in a sweater when buying clothing from a store. Like theft-control tags, RFID tags are powered and accessed from a distance using radio waves, but RFID tags differ from theft-control tags in that they tend to have more storage space and processing power. RFID tags have security issues that have been exposed in the past few years. The heart of the problem is that RFID tags don't usually support cryptography, plus RFID application scenarios are usually not conducive to commonly performed security operations like key management; in fact, many security and privacy issues that generally exist in ubiquitous computing reappear in RFID applications specifically.

I will be discussing a new technique called Selective RFID Jamming that is an extension of a concept called RFID Blocking, that was originated by Ari Juels from RSA Security. However, Selective RFID Jamming has a number of features that makes it novel. So what is Selective RFID Jamming? It is a form of off-tag RFID access control. RFID tags can barely support on-tag security mechanisms, which is why it is desirable to take their security management and move it off the tags. Unlike RFID Blocker Tags, Selective RFID Jamming also utilizes a battery powered device. In other words, a person might carry around a small computer like a PDA or cell phone. This kind of active device has sufficient resources to harness traditional security tools like cryptography access control lists, it provides a means to introduce traditional security techniques to the realm of RFID. Another improvement is defense against a differential signal analysis attack that is faced by the RFID Blocker Tag. I'll explain that a bit later.

So first, we will delve into the differences between on-tag and off-tag access control. With on-tag access control, tags decide themselves which queries are authorized, and then respond accordingly (or don't respond). With off-tag access control, a third-party device mediates access between RFID readers and RFID tags; in a similar manner to the RFID Blocker Tag, mediators will determine which queries are authorized, it will jam unauthorized tag responses rendering them unreadable by the querying reader.

On-tag RFID solutions include a kill command, sleep/wake modes, hash locks, varying identifiers (called pseudonyms), and lightweight cryptography or authentication, using reduced AES and NTRU. Off-tag mechanisms include Faraday cages (a.k.a. tinfoil), blocker tags, and external re-encryption (where RFID

B. Christianson et al. (Eds.): Security Protocols 2005, LNCS 4631, pp. 60–68, 2007.
© Springer-Verlag Berlin Heidelberg 2007

readers periodically re-encrypt tag data). Each of these mechanisms have their pros and cons.

One advantage of off-tag mechanisms is that they can provide access control to low-cost RFID tags. Low-cost RFID tags, including EPC (Electronic Product Code) tags[1], should be cheap enough that you can embed them in everything. This allows tags to be found in a wide variety of real-world objects like consumer items, money, passports, drivers licences, and other identification cards. For low-cost items (e.g. a can of tuna fish), RFID tags should be sufficiently cheap that the incremental cost of the tag will not eliminate the profit margin on the tagged item. In other words, low cost is essential for making RFID-based computing possible, and the "ten cent tag" is a commonly cited goal.

High cost RFID tags may or may not offer privacy protection, at the discretion of the manufacturers. One example of high-cost RFID tags are subdermal RFID tags called Verichips[2]. Trend-conscious clubgoers in Barcelona and Rotterdam get these Verichips implanted into their arms, just below the shoulder. They use these chips to pay for their drinks, and access the VIP areas and hot tub; it is supposed to be quite the thing to do. But unfortunately, Applied Digital designed Verichips to rely upon obscurity for security and privacy protection, based upon their "proprietary readers". If an RFID tag manufacturer neglects to put security on their tags, the consumer needs other RFID security/privacy options. This underscores the utility of off-tag access control.

RFID blocker tags are the best-known example of off-tag access control. However, because they are implemented on an RFID tag, they are subject to all of the limitations of RFID tags, including power limitations, storage limitations, and reliability problems (an RFID tag incorrectly orientated with the reader will not even power-up let alone enforce access control. The blocker tag works by abusing the RFID reader's singulation protocol, that is invoked when there are multiple RFID tags in the interrogation field. Like several other kinds of broadcast media, some RFID tags use a "tree-walk" singulation algorithm to resolve tag collisions. Here is an example: RFID readers may query all tags that begin with a '1'. If the reader receives a collision, it then continues by querying all tags that begin with a '10'. If that collides, it queries again looking for tags beginning with '100'. The RFID reader continues in this fashion, increasing its mask length until it resolves the collision. Simply put, the RFID blocker tag interferes with this process by simulating collisions at every step of the way – it prevents readers from figuring out which tags are present by causing a full tag id namespace traversal.

Our technique of Selective RFID jamming was inspired by the RFID Blocker Tag, but it deviates from it in a number of ways. First of all, it uses a battery powered device, so it does not face the restrictions of a power-limited RFID tag. We are testing Selective RFID Jamming on a platform called the RFID Guardian, that we are currently developing together with the Delft University of Technology and Philips. The RFID Guardian is a battery powered portable

---

[1] See www.epcglobalinc.org
[2] See www.verichipcorp.com

device that leverages two-way in-band RFID communications. People have previously suggested managing RFID security with a Wi-Fi or Bluetooth PDA, which is a fine idea if you assume every cash register checkout will have Wi-Fi or Bluetooth communications available. However, this will often not be realistic, and so the RFID Guardian exclusively uses RFID protocols to conduct its security operations. More specifically, the RFID Guardian acts like both an RFID reader and an RFID tag emulator (using 13.56 MHz RFID, and ISO-15693 compliant).

For convenience purposes, we believe that the RFID Guardian can be best implemented in existing available personal devices, like PDAs and cell phones. Since Nokia has already put some RFID-enabled cell phones on the market, we do not believe that our vision is far-fetched.

Since it is battery-powered, the RFID Guardian can then perform any number of standard security protocols with RFID readers, (on the behalf of resource-limited RFID tags) which may include symmetric or public key security, and which could involve entire PKIs (if deemed necessary). In other words, the RFID Guardian provides traditional security tools for a non-traditional application scenario (RFID).

Because the RFID Guardian is battery-powered, it also has more than adequate memory for storing possibly complex access control policies. In contrast, RFID Blocker Tags might only have 1K bits of space for a security policy, which severely limits its possible complexity.

Thirdly, with RFID Blocker Tag approach you are likely to end up with not one but many security policies, because each tag has its own policy. It would be a big nightmare to keep these policies updated, and when tags have been deployed you will need updates to take care of the 50% of the tags that will be lost or destroyed. If you use a centralised device that manages the security of the tags within the radio range, you know at least that the security of the tags in near proximity (perhaps 1 meter) are going to be taken care of. Non-mobile RFID Guardians can also be placed in specific locations, to create zones of protection for RFID tags in specific areas (like at home).

Tuomas Aura. So you can have your mobile phone switch to shoplifting mode? [Laughter]

Reply. Indeed, but it's not the only (or necessarily the easiest) way to shoplift.

Another disadvantage of localizing RFID in individual RFID tags is that you are increasing the complexity and price of every single tag. This means if you have a thousand tags, you have a thousand implementations of the same access control mechanism. In contrast, with Selective RFID Jamming, you indeed have to purchase the device (which is a certain financial overhead), but then it can protect thousands of very low-cost RFID tags. So for applications where cost is a show-stopping factor, like supply chain management, centralizing the access control infrastructure is the best approach.

Matt Blaze. So the model is that, I have my phone and anything within RFID range of the phone is protected?

Reply. Yes.

Matt Blaze. So it's not tied to individual tags?

Reply. No.

Matt Blaze. So presumably the model is, I would be required to turn this device off as soon as I walk into a store, because as soon as I walk up to the cash register their systems are going to stop working.

Reply. Well not necessarily. This is the reason why our mechanism is called selective RFID jamming, and that's actually exactly what I'm about to discuss in my next slide.

Matt Blaze. So it is tied to an individual device?

Reply. Yes. So this is where we get into the whole access control part. Now this is going to look really familiar. You have block and pass access control lists, sources, and targets. Just like in a network packet filter. Here the target is a list called MYTAGS, which consists of a list of RFID tags that my RFID Guardian knows belongs to me. The purpose of this list is to make the distinction between jamming queries that are directed towards your tags, as opposed to queries directed towards tags that don't belong to you.

The targeted RFID tag IDs are extracted from the incoming RFID query, and this id value (which may or may not be in the MYTAGS list) is compared to the ACL to determine whether or not it is authorized; if not, the tag response is jammed on its way back to the RFID reader.

Determining the origin of the RFID query has to be handled a different way. The current RFID protocols do not offer room for a source address, and if there one were available, it would be just as easily-spoofed as IP addresses are. So the question is: how do you determine where an RFID query is coming from? The answer is that. Unfortunately, the RFID Guardian won't usually know where a query originates from, but in a small minority of the cases the RFID Guardian might encounter a "cooperative" RFID reader. For example, you might want your RFID tags to have more lenient permissions at home, since it is a trusted environment. In this case, you might install some special backend software on your RFID reader that cooperates with the RFID Guardian (the RFID reader hardware does NOT require modification for this). You could do this for the RFID reader at home, or at your mother-in-law's house. The local supermarket could also offer this as a service. However, keep in mind that while a select number of environments will have RFID readers that actively cooperate with the RFID Guardian, the grand majority of RFID readers will not be either helpful or even aware of what is going on. For RFID readers that are unknown, there should be some default settings in the access control policy.

Here's a basic example. If the RFID Guardian detects a query that targets your RFID tags, you may want to suppress the tag responses. However, if you happen to be at home, then you may allow the queries responses. If you are at Wal-Mart, you could possibly use either pre-exchanged keys or a PKI to authenticate the RFID readers. You can grant authorized read/write permissions if necessary. And for the rest, the RFID Guardian tries to disrupt the workings of the nearby systems as little as possible.

Ben Laurie. So what you're saying is if I want to read your tags I can stand near you in Wal-Mart with my RFID reader. I let you authenticate and then I read your tags.

Reply. That question actually leads us to the issue of authenticated sessions. Once a reader authenticates itself, it needs a way of determining which RFID queries originate from it (and hence are probably allowed). Source authentication is not currently part of RFID protocols, but we're currently taking a look at doing this one layer higher.

Frank Stajano. You mention MYTAGS a lot, but there is no inherent association between me writing this policy and the tags being mine.

Reply. Well the RFID Guardian manages the association between RFID tags and the owner of the RFID Guardian by performing periodic queries to find out what tags are nearby. The RFID Guardian can correlate the results of these queries over time to determine which tags are "affiliated" with you (either knowingly or unknowingly). In such a way, the RFID Guardian maintains a dynamic MYTAGS list. It needs to be this way anyways, because you will not necessarily know what tags you will own at the time that you're writing the policy.

Frank Stajano. So you're not even telling your guardians what your tags are?

Reply. There's several ways that you can establish the "ownership" of RFID tags. At home you might have an RFID system that can backup and synchronize ownership information with the RFID Guardian every night. You can also "acquire" new RFID tags from a store, for example when you are going through an RFID automated checkout. While the RFID reader performing the queries necessary for purchasing your items, the RFID Guardian can glean the purchased tag numbers directly from the queries. Friendly "Guardian-aware" RFID readers might even send explicit ownership information as part of the purchasing procedure. (After authentication, of course.)

However, for tags that are added covertly (e.g. an attacker drops an RFID tag in your handbag), then the only way that you can discover it is by correlating periodic RFID queries. This may happen when you get home at the end of the day, when you discover that you now have one RFID tag than that same morning (that wasn't explicitly added to the ownership list). The frequency of these periodic queries represents a trade-off between privacy, accuracy, and battery power.

Frank Stajano. You are talking here about how to automatically discover which tags are yours, but my point was a slightly different one which is that I as a malicious other person can pretend that, for example, your watch is one of my tags and I can tell my Guardian to jam it. In such a way, you can perform Denial of Service on other people's RFID tags. And surely the ID of the tag is not a secret so I don't have to be the owner of the product to jam a tag?

Tuomas Aura. No. There's nothing to prevent that. Obviously anyone can carry RFID tags, anyone else can jam them.

Mike Bond. It seems that in creating these RFID guardians, these high powered portable computing platforms that are capable of impersonating any tag, that we're putting a tool into the hands of people which is going to destroy the entire binding between a tag and an object, and suddenly I'll be able to walk around with a device and pretend I'm covered in tags if I want to, or I can jam tags wholesale, it just seems that if you look ten years down the line when everyone's got this capability in their mobile phones, and they can run little programs and do whatever they like, then, you know, what do tags mean anymore?

Reply. You've got a very good point.

Mike Bond. So, you know, the observation is that, I think RFID technology does not really scale up to a proper real world environment.

Reply. Yes, well once RFID is deployed on a wider scale I think it's going to have more problems than just rogue RFID Guardians. People who oppose RFID technology might remove or even switch the RFID tags on objects. This leads to a situation where RFID systems have to deal with false positives and false negatives, just like an intrusion detection system. This indeed cheapens the entire RFID infrastructure, if you cannot believe the information that you get from it.

Mike Bond. And you can do it all with your mobile phone, you don't need to actually hack out the tags from your clothes?

Reply. The RFID Guardian, like a lot of tools, has both good uses and bad uses. However, quite frankly if I don't build this kind of an RFID tag emulator, somebody else probably will.

Mike Bond. I think its a *good* tool. [Laughter]

Matt Blaze. It seems like the threat model here is kind of ill-defined because we don't really know how the tags are going to be used or how they can be misused. One of the problems getting the most attention is RFID tags that continue to exist well beyond their necessary lifetime. If they're intended for the supply chain to the consumer, once they reach the consumer, they should die at that point. But they don't, they're still around. They can be read, and an attacker can abuse that to figure out where a person has been walking around, and for all sorts of applications that they weren't originally intended for. That seems like a small subset of the overall problem space, and a solution to that problem seems relatively straightforward, relative to this general solution that you described. However, the RFID tags in my passport must continue to exist because I want to be able to go in and out of other countries without getting strip searched or whatever they do, when you don't have one. So if you take out the supply chain RFID tags that can just be destroyed before they get to the consumer, are you left with a problem that requires this kind of generality, and this kind of centralised device. How many of these other remaining RFID tags am I going to be walking around with?

Reply. Quite a few, perhaps. Let's say you buy a box of cream spinach and it has an RFID tag. In the glorious world of ubiquitous computing, a showcase example is the RFID-enabled microwave that reads the data off the box of spinach, to determine the cooking times. There are also similar projects with RFID-enabled washing machines that warn you when you put your red sweater in with your white socks, and it can automatically determine that your load of laundry requires a low temperature, no bleach. Automating the returning of products to a department store is another proposed use for non-deactivated RFID tags. People may want these tags for their value-added features, so it's not necessarily a matter as simple as killing all RFID tags at the checkout. That is why, in the long run, we need some kind of a solution that allows us to both protect our privacy, and preserve a bit of the functionality is promised by the visionaries behind RFID technology.

Matthew Johnson. Even if you've only got an RFID passport it is still useful to be able to jam it so you can verify it is a government passport if you've got a PKI infrastructure because then you can verify that its a government passport reader that is probing it, and you can block other requests.

Audience. So this is related to the problem of context with the RFID tags, so if I'm in Wal-Mart, I want Wal-Mart to be able to read Wal-Mart tags, not any of my tags. I don't want them doing marketing research as I walk through the checkout.

Reply. Exactly. You can sometimes configure your access control lists to filter blocks of RFID tags IDs, the same way you can filter blocks of IP addresses. For example, very much resemble the Class A, Class B, Class C, and Class D IP addresses. And if some blocks of EPC codes are associated with Gillette Razors or feminine garments, then I can block all of these things. Wal-Mart would also probably have its own manufacturer code, and the product might have a distributor code, item code, and unique item code. You can filter access to RFID tags, based upon any of these criteria.

Audience. But then you have the same problem you have with IPs which is the company gets taken over, and you didn't trust the new company who owns it, and so you start using other tag IDs so you've got exactly the same problem down the line.

Reply. This is why the management of the RFID tag access control lists could be a problem, just like management of network access control lists.

George Danezis. But if you assume that the RFID tags will be used for high level things like washing socks and cooking spinach, then you have a much better ability to actually identify which tags are yours, which tags should not be revealed, which tags are sensitive. If you assume that, you also can assume from a security point of view that you have much richer information to make decisions.

Reply. As in much of ubiquitous computing, the context of the RFID Guardian owner tends to be fuzzy and ill-defined. Can the fact that your RFID tag is spinach or a sock help you make access control right decisions and is there a methodical way to represent all of this, and to gain all this context information at the right time? Maybe. However, we would much prefer to keep our idea of context as simple as possible,. However, it's potentially open-ended what context you can store and respond to. It is an entire subfield in itself, actually. But you're right that context can be useful if you know how to harness it correctly.

Matt Johnson. But on the other hand, other readers should not be able to query that same context, like the manufacturer and the model of whatever it is you're wearing.

Reply. Context in this case should help determine the amount of access that will be granted to that reader. If singulation starts occuring in the proximity of sensitive articles, than the RFID Guardian might start jamming singulation at that moment. All of this can be represented as a policy.

Audience. But that means that you'll jam anybody else around you if you have some kind of clothing?

Reply. One of the big unresolved issues here is the denial of service, because our system has the potential to harm its environment, by interfering with other RFID systems. This may even cause legal problems. But our hope is that, if you make the jamming procedure selective enough, we'll be able to prevent interfering with the RFID systems around us.

Another disadvantage of the RFID Guardian is that it is a single point of failure. If somebody steals your Guardian, you've got a problem. We think it's a good idea to use PIN codes to lock the user interface, so we can provide at least some kind of a barrier against attackers extracting the information from stolen RFID Guardians. However, once the device is physically in the attacker's hands, well you have problems anyways. Another precaution is to store as little data in your RFID Guardian as possible. For example, your RFID Guardian might only want to keep the key information for tags that were present when you left the house that morning. This minimizes the consequences of losing your Guardian.

Another problem is RFID readers with massively directional antennas. In other words, an RFID reader with a big Yagi antenna will perform its query silently to the RFID Guardian. Unfortunately, the RFID Guardian can't enforce what it can't hear. Quite frankly, I'm not sure what we can do to solve this. At least it's a comfort that the attacker is going to look pretty silly walking around with that big antenna.

Frank Stajano. What do you mean you can't even hear a query?

Reply. Since the radio waves are directional, the RFID tag would be able to hear it, but the RFID Guardian (in a different location) wouldn't be able to hear the query. And if the RFID Guardian cannot hear the original RFID query because it's so directional, it has no way of determining if it is unauthorized, and stopping it. However, for this attack to work, the attacker needs to know the exact location of the RFID tag that it is querying.

Mike Bond. If you were able to put tags to sleep, then maybe the solution is when the tags come into the range of the RFID Guardian, they can fall asleep and then the device just pretends to be the tag until they are released again.

Reply. Yes, definitely. What I've discussed today (the Selective Jamming) is only one fraction of the total functionality that you can actually implement on an RFID guardian. In July, I will be presenting a paper at the ACISP Conference[3], that also discusses topics like context-based tag activation and deactivation. This may even be preferable to doing Selective Jamming, assuming that sleep/wake functions are available on your RFID tags, because of Selective Jamming's possible legal issues. So you're right.

---

[3] Melanie Rieback, Bruno Crispo, and Andrew Tanenbaum. RFId Guardian: A Battery-Powered Mobile Device for RFID Privacy Management. (Australasian Conference on Information Security and Privacy - ACISP, July 2005).

PIN (and Chip) or Signature:
Beating the Cheating?

Dan Cvrcek, Jan Krhovjak, and Vashek Matyas

Masaryk University in Brno, Faculty of Informatics
cvrcek@math.muni.cz,{xkrhovj,matyas}@fi.muni.cz

Abstract. Our paper first reviews some of the most critical issues related to the introduction of Chip & PIN card payment authorisation, and
then outlines one part of our experiment[1] that we decided to undertake to
validate some of our views and ideas. Our experiment examines, in two
phases, whether introduction of this authorisation method is advantageous for an opportunistic thief and whether the customer truly benefits
from the Chip & PIN technology with respect to this opportunistic thief.

1 Introduction

Many discussions of the ongoing introduction of the Chip & PIN "technology" for
purchase authorisation – and hopefully also authorised cardholder authentication
– end up with a declaration that the new means obviously are – or are not –
easier to circumvent for an opportunistic thief. We see this opportunistic thief as
an individual or a small group of loosely organised individuals that do not have
any special hardware for card analysis, cloning, etc. And it is the opportunistic
thief we focus on in our experiment proposed farther below.

Card PINs are typically restricted to the length of four digits (only rarely one
can see systems allowing for use of up to six digits, e.g. in Switzerland) and even
then is their entropy rather questionable [1]. A reasonable assumption is that
such short strings typed onto a "3-by-3" PIN keyboard are easy to spy on.

1.1 Problems with PINs

We are currently of the view that while Chip & PIN authorisation will likely
increase the cost of card counterfeiting as well as complicate (at least at the first
sight) abuse of stolen cards, it may have an adverse effect on Chip & PIN card
users in the time prior to card loss detection and reporting. We see two potential
problems here.

The first problem with PIN authorisation lies in repudiation – while the customer can fight reasonably well against a loss with a track in the form of a poorly
faked signature, it will be quite hard to fight the loss after one's correct PIN has
been entered. There will be no track in the purchase/authorisation documents,

---

[1] This experiment was partly supported by the FIDIS (Future of Identity in the Information Society) Network of Excellence.

B. Christianson et al. (Eds.): Security Protocols 2005, LNCS 4631, pp. 69–75, 2007.

and relevant camera recordings might be hard to get from the merchant – either due to their short retention time, or perhaps when considering where lies the interest of the merchant in an investigation of a disputed purchase. A closely related issue here is the use of cards stolen from mail, where the thief will quite likely also get the PIN – this can be partly addressed by the card activation procedure.

And a second drawback follows – current systems do not deploy different security mechanisms (or at least settings) for differing threat environments – different PINs for low- and high-level transactions. And so if the opportunistic thief can spy on your PIN while you do your bookstore or restaurant transaction, he can use that PIN with your card for a merry shopping spree at a jeweler.

While signatures in general have more entropy than PINs, their long-term problem has been that merchants often did not bother checking them (for a number of reasons) as many investigators have verified in reality [2]. Some of the indirectly related (yet that we do not want to treat in detail in this experiment and related discussions unless really useful or necessary) issues are:

- we have to allow for a co-existence of both Chip & PIN and signature authorisations and so we get drawbacks of both combined;
- the technology change introduces the opportunity for some participants to shift the parameters of risk exposure;
- what information can be read from the card chip at any merchant's reader and how can this information be used for other fraud, e.g. in countries or shops not involved in the Chip & PIN exercise?

The technological change from strip and signature to Chip & PIN surprisingly lowers the difficulty of some of low-tech attacks on cards. The main reason lies in the change in handling the cards. It is easier to spy on PINs than before (since they have to be used more frequently, and often in overcrowded shops where spying on one's PIN is much easier than at ATM machines). It will also be easier to create a satisfactory surface of the cards – the necessity of a PIN-card being inserted in the reader during the entire transaction also reduces the opportunity for the merchant to check some card details such as the physical security when compared with the signature purchase authorisation. The one (and only?) thing that will improve is the difficulty to obtain the machine-readable information from the card.

Let us assume that the opportunistic thief (working on his/her own or in a small loosely organised group) without a dedicated hardware will stick to the use of genuine (pickpocketed) cards, and let us examine whether the new or old authorisation approach is more favourable to this thief. We refer the reader to [3] for a detailed discussion of most problems with the Chip & PIN card payment authorisation.

2   The Experiment – PIN v Signature

We are verifying whether it is easier to get a correct PIN than to forge a signature. And so we decided to undertake an experiment where in realistic conditions the following would be examined:

1. Can the PIN entry spying be easier than the signature falsification?
2. Under what conditions does the above hold true or false?
3. What are other alternatives for purchase authorisation using chip-equipped payment cards?

Results from this experiment can help us and indeed the broader community (since Chip & PIN is in fact one of the largest computer deployment exercises with security as a major factor) answer the question related to this year's Workshop – is such a system your friend and should you like it?

We decided to abstract from the possibility of merchants colluding with the attackers, e.g. through the use of cameras, and so we have to stress that the experiment results are based on the assumption of honestly behaving merchant. (We disregard the possibility that the merchant is able to easily eavesdrop PINs, e.g. by installing CCTV or modified PIN-pads. Yet we understand that this type of attack has a very high potential.)

This experiment is being undertaken in at least two phases throughout the year 2005:

1. *Trial phase* – at this stage we examined the success rates of PIN observation and signature falsification in near-realistic conditions as described in this paper. Results from this phase are provided in this paper.
2. *Mature test* – we will undertake this phase of our experiment in realistic conditions this Autumn, with settings modified according to both our experience from the trial phase and also feedback from the discussion of the trial phase results.

3   Trial Phase

This phase was undertaken in two rounds, the first round focusing on the success rates of observing a customer entering the PIN and the second round (more-or-less a verification round at this phase) on the success rates of falsifying someone else's signature (without the shop assistant's detection). Students and staff of our university took part in this phase, and the payment operations happened in the university bookstore.

The first round was undertaken with 32 "customers", 4 observers (of which typically only 3 were active at any given time), 3 (plus one of the observers) bystanders that did not cooperate with the observers and were not observing the customer, and obviously the shop assistants (2 – the bookstore owner and another person from a jewelry store to verify the signatures since the bookstore we used does not accept card payments), and three experiment supervisors. We also made sure in both rounds (using the shop plus two other separated rooms) that customers after their participation in a given round of the experiment did not exchange information with customers who were yet to take part in the given round of the experiment.

3.1   Cover Story

A good cover story is critical for customers' as well as merchants' behaviour to be unbiased (or, better said, as little biased as possible) when they participate in the payment operations. We therefore decided to inform both the merchants and the customers at the start that this experiment is conducted to survey pros and cons of two different methods of payment authorisation (PIN-based authorisation is used only in a minority of card payments in the Czech Republic, so it is known as an authorisation method overshadowed by signatures). We stressed that we would focus on measuring the time that all related operations take and on the issue of user comfort and acceptance, together with the facts that we use two different types of PIN-pads (and customers would be split into two groups). We also emphasized the request that both the customers and the merchant followed all security and logistic provisions they are supposed to follow in reality. The customers were requested to fill opinion survey questions at the start of the experiment to assure them in this belief.

Last but not least, the cover story was presented by a person who was not known to the "customers" and who posed herself as a researcher from the School of Social Studies, with members of our research group posing as technology consultants in this experiment.

At the end of the experiment, obviously, the participants were informed about the real purpose of the experiment.

3.2   Round One

In this round we took all thirty-two customers into one room and gave each of them a purchase card with a PIN that we randomly generated. Then we split them into two groups (one for each of the PIN-pads used) of 17 and 15 participants where each group used a different PIN-pad – one with a massive security/privacy shielding, and one without any shielding. Then we sent the customers one by one into the bookstore. Each of them had to pick one item at random and to approach the counter (or the queue at the counter). We started timing the operation once the customer handed the selected item to the merchant, let the card operation with PIN entry (correct at the first attempt) be performed and set the delay for purchase authorisation and receipt printing at a constant time of ten seconds. We read the time at the moment when the merchant handed the item and a receipt to the customer.

Once the customer left the bookstore we recorded the guesses of the PIN from our observers, and called the following customer.

3.3   Round Two

In this round we took all thirty participants from the first round and split them into two groups of fifteen and seventeen members. The first group was issued cards with own signatures on the back, the second was given cards with signatures of someone else. Participants from the second group were given time of twenty, and at a special request thirty, minutes to practice the given signature.

The merchants were informed that there would be some customers falsifying someone else's signatures, without any indication of the rate of these customers.

The customers attended the bookstore again one at a time and their purchase time was measured as in the first round. The merchants, however, had to decide about the signature validity right at the time of the purchase (and were allowed to request the signature to be repeated if in doubt).

4   Results from the Trial Phase

4.1   Opinion Survey

While we asked the participants to fill the opinion survey forms at the start of the trial phase of our experiment in order to strengthen their belief that this experiment was about the user friendliness of customer authorisation technologies, results of this survey are worth mentioning before we discuss the ultimate experiment results.

There were 25 participants (out of the total 32) who used magnetic strip cards for payments and about half ever used a Chip & PIN payment cards. The overall level of satisfaction with magnetic strip card payments was substantially worse than that with Chip & PIN card payments (3.4 mark against 2.5 on a five-point scale where 1 is the best and 5 is the worst mark).

Given the options of 10, 20, 30, 40 and 50 seconds as the maximum acceptable time for the entire payment operation the participants agreed on 21 seconds on average. And finally, the participants have experienced (on average) in 89% of their transcations no problem with the card payment, in about 7.5% experienced a minor nuisance, in 2% a major problem, and in less than 2% were unable to pay with their card.

4.2   PIN-Pad with Privacy/Security Shielding

For the seventeen "customers" who performed their experiment card payments using PINs there were six (35.3%) cases where the observers would succeed in guessing the PIN. And in five of those six hits the thieves would guess the PIN right at the first attempt, where for three PINs two observers got the PIN right and for two PINs one observer learned the PIN. In the sixth case the observers were able to build the PIN based on their shared knowledge.

Viewing the recordings from another point of view, the observers correctly guessed 75 digits (48%) in 39 tips of the four-digit PINs (i.e., for 156 digits altogether).

4.3   No Privacy/Security Shielding PIN-Pad

Results for this PIN-pad were shockingly different – for the participants "lost" their PINs to the observers in twelve out of fifteen, i.e. 80%, cases! And ten PINs out of this unlucky dozen would be guessed correctly right at the first attempt, with two PINs being seen by all four[2] observers, one PIN was seen by three observers, four by two, and finally three just by one observer. The remaining two correct guesses were built from the shared knowledge.

Using the alternative view, from the 46 tips of 4-digit PINs (i.e., 184 digits) provided by the observers there were 129 digits guessed correctly (70.1%).

4.4   Round Two – Signatures

For the seventeen cheating "customers" the merchants have correctly identified twelve of them as fraudsters, i.e. five of them bypassed the merchant control. Eight out of the identified dozen there were pointed out as fraudsters right after their first attempt, and four after their second signature. In the group of twenty (five fraudsters and fifteen signing their own signatures) successful "customers" there were only four participants who had to sign twice to convince the merchants. It is worth noting that both the participants and the supervisors for this experiment were of the view that the merchant check was quite thorough – we are of the view that this was caused mainly by the fact that the signature verifier works in a luxury jewelry store where the checks are on a higher level than in a supermarket or bookstore.

5   Conclusions

Considering that both signature forgers and PIN-entry observers were new to their tasks, the results of 29.4% signature forgeries going undetected and 35.3% or even 80% PINs being observed are rather unpleasant for most card users. With no paper trail allowing for later verification in case of disputed transactions, the figures for the Chip & PIN card are not exactly encouraging. Also, the comparison of the last two above mentioned figures definitely supports the view that privacy/security shielding for PIN-pads makes a lot of sense.

While we want to undertake the second phase of our experiment before we start with a detailed discussion of the results, the first phase indicates that we are perhaps going for a replacement of a weak biometric by even weaker secret information as the means for customer authorisation of their(?) payments. However, we see the biggest problem not in going for a weaker authorisation method – we see the related problem of repudiability for PIN-based authorisation as the issue customers should worry about.

Results from the second phase of our experiment, together with a detailed discussion of results from both phases will be provided in a follow-up to this paper than can be requested from the authors (contact the last author regarding this experiment).

---

[2] While the instructions said that always one of the four observers should abstain from watching the "customer" and engage in some interaction with the bystanders, in four cases all four observers reported some results with the fourth observer noting that "he couldn't have helped it" seeing the ease of PIN entry observation even at a distance, while talking to the bystanders.

Acknowledgements

Thanks are due to the FIDIS NoE for supporting our experiment, to Monet+ for providing the PIN-pads, to Pavel Marecek for the cooperation in and with his bookstore, to Dalibor Hanak for his cooperation in verifying the customer signatures, and last but not least to more than three dozen students who assisted us in this experiment. We also wish to thank Petr Hanacek, Marek Kumpost and Petr Svenda for stimulating discussions about the experiment plan.

References

[1] Kuhn, M.: Probability Theory for Pickpockets – ec-PIN Guessing. COAST Laboratory, Purdue University, USA, http://www.cl.cam.ac.uk/ mgk25/ec-pin-prob.pdf

[2] Hargrave, J.: Credit Card Prank. http://www.zug.com/pranks/credit/

[3] Anderson, R., Bond, M., Murdoch, S.: Chip and Spin. Paper available at http://www.cl.cam.ac.uk/~mkb23/spin/spin.pdf webpage "Chip and SPIN!" at http://www.chipandspin.co.uk/

PIN (and Chip) or Signature:
Beating the Cheating?
(Transcript of Discussion)

Vashek Matyas

Masaryk University in Brno, Faculty of Informatics

This work has been done with over 40 participants in a simple experiment we decided to undertake in Brno this year. With the introduction of Chip-and-PIN payment authorisation we very often hear that that shoulder-surfing is easier than forging the signature, and different groups of people argue against or for this statement. We were not sure whether the authorisation of the transaction from the point of view of the customer, the signature or entering the PIN, really makes a difference for an opportunistic thief who can observe your transaction in the shop, then steal your card and try to forge the operation on your behalf afterwards. And so we decided to undertake an experiment that would answer this question to us. And here we didn't care about any other threats, we considered the opportunistic thief, and a simple transaction in the shop with the point of sale terminal.

We hired 32 students and we undertook the first phase of our experiment at the University bookstore. We gave the customers, our students, who were about to forge the signatures, about thirty minutes to practise the forging. I would like to note that there are certain groups of students who have previous practice in forging the signatures, namely signatures of their parents. There are also groups of students who don't have much practice in this area. In any case the signatures that they forged had been created by the supervisors of the experiment just 20 minutes before the experiment started, and the students had no other influence than just the choice from about 20 signatures. The observers that we had then in the shop to observe the transactions with the PIN had about two hours to practise the shoulder-surfing, so again, we didn't give them much time to practise the art. And we would sincerely hope that none of these two groups were real professionals in their specific areas.

We want to undertake the second phase of our experiment in realistic conditions somewhere in the City centre of the Brno, and we want your feedback on what have we done wrong, and what to do next.

So for the first phase we had all the 32 people, one by one, going through the bookstore, first purchasing their item with the card and then they went into another room, and we didn't allow any communication between these two rooms. We wanted the subjects to behave as if it were normal shopping so we gave them a cover story, presented kindly by someone who didn't have much technical background, we told them this is an experiment given by the Institute of Social Studies together with Faculty of Business Administration, and that we from the Faculty of Informatics, assist there only to make sure that the

B. Christianson et al. (Eds.): Security Protocols 2005, LNCS 4631, pp. 76–81, 2007.
© Springer-Verlag Berlin Heidelberg 2007

conditions are realistic from the technology point of view. They were told that we cared about things like user interfaces, whether they liked working with this method or that method, that we cared about the behaviour being realistic as if it were their own cards, and we were measuring the time during the experiment doing things like that to make them believe that this is not about security, this is about interface behaviour at the till, and so on. We also gave them a form to fill in that basically beefed up the cover story, they were asked what cards they are using, how they feel about using them, and so on, and the merchants were giving the same cover story.

As a side effect of the cover story we got the questionnaire, it might illustrate a bit what the conditions and what the subjects were like. Most of them used magnetic strip cards, half of them used Chip cards, they actually, prior to the experiment, would prefer the methods with Chip and PIN, or they didn't have any big problems with the use of the cards previously.

So for the first round we used two devices, one with quite massive privacy-shielding, the other one without any shielding at all, each for about half the subjects. The observers who were present in the room reported their guesses to me after the customer left the room. They were either giving tips in the form of four-digit strings, which was most typical, and they could give weights to the digits, either if they were sure that the digit reappeared in the PIN, or if they were sure about the digit and its position, so we took the weights for individual digits of the PIN as well. Other types of guesses were like the last column, or the first row of the PIN-pad. As I said before, the cover story required that we measured the time. We disregarded the issue of the security threat from the merchant in the experiment.

In the second round again we split the customers into two groups, the first half was given an empty strip to sign with their own signature, the other half chose the signature that they had to forge out of the group of 20 signatures we made available, and they had 20 to 30 minutes spare time to get ready to forge an acceptable signature. Since the bookstore as such doesn't accept cards yet we used an assistant who has got a jewellery shop in the city centre and who accepts cards for years, who was checking the signatures. A remark both from myself as the experiment supervisor, and also from the subjects, is that the checking of the jeweller is considered different than checking in general stores, and that this guy has been quite thorough.

In the first round, where we used the PIN-pad with the most security shielding, the observers succeeded in guesses of six out of the 17 PINs being used, this is built on the shared knowledge considering all the tips, all the weights, and everything that the observers put together. In five cases out of the six they would be able to guess the PIN at the very first try. Other interesting stats out of the tips that the observers provided, 48% digits have been guessed correctly.

With the PIN-pad without any shielding around, observers in ten out of the twelve correct guesses would guess the PIN at the very first try, in the other two they would need two or three tries to get the right PIN. And of the tips provided by the observers, over 70% of the digits have been guessed correctly.

With the signatures, we had 17 customers who forged the signatures of others, the merchant detected 12 out of them, that means only five of them passed. Out of those 12 detected, eight were detected immediately after their first signatures, four of them after, or in one case, during the second signature when the guy just gave up, he wasn't able to face the questioning merchant. Out of the 20 successful customers, those 15 who signed their own signatures, and those five that forged well enough, 16 of them passed immediately after the first signature, four of them have been asked to sign twice.

Mike Roe. The customer who gave up after the second signature, was that one actually trying to forge the signature?

Reply. Yes. Our guy from the jewellery shop knew that there will be guys who will forge the signatures, we tried to create realistic conditions, and since he knew that he was a bit rough then when he was asking them sign for the second time, he wouldn't treat the customers in the same way, that's why the guy gave up.

Mike Roe. The first issue is that if he really checked that hard then probably even some people who aren't forging a signature can't just get their own signature right even if they want, you query them and they go away and don't succeed.

Reply. I have to admit that once this also happened to me, I had to sign in a supermarket about five or six times to get the goods.

Matt Blaze. Were there any incentives in this game that you set up? For example, in real life if somebody tries to forge a signature and are unsuccessful eventually the police get called, similarly if you are a merchant and you say, that's not your signature when it is, you lose your business, so there's an incentive system to be right in the real world. Were there bonus incentives?

Reply. No, not in this phase of the experiment, the only incentive here for the students was they were promised interesting results of an interesting experiment, and we gave them some moderate financial compensation for the two hours of assistance.

Mike Roe. It's quite common if you pay participants to pay them slightly more if they get it right.

Reply. Yes, we could have done that but I presume we still have to verify the results through a realistic experiment. The observers were mainly grad students, they had enough incentive with the fun during the experiment.

We found, by the way, a great way that we hadn't thought of before: if you take a mobile phone with you and you are loud enough, and you speak about something completely irrelevant, how you are, should your dog go to the vet, or something like that, and you stand in the queue behind the guy who is entering the PIN, the guy couldn't care less. If you pretend to read a book the guy next to you enters the PIN, then he re-checks that you are looking in the book, and then you have the PIN or its part. Our guy with the phone was able to get almost behind the shoulder of the guy who was entering the PIN, just by speaking on the phone about what kind of beer he wants in the evening, the other guy couldn't care less. Keep talking about something irrelevant and you can work with your eyes very well.

Bruce Christianson. Texting on a phone would be quite a good one as well because you can take moving pictures now?

Reply. Yes, we deliberately avoided things like use of cameras, we took just human observers for this.

Frank Stajano. With texting you can also make a record of the PIN instead of having to memorise it?

Reply. Yes, that was also tricky, that while the customer really got out of the bookstore and I went to record the guesses, sometimes the observers said they had a hard time to recall what their guesses were.

We saw that using the security shielding makes sense on the PIN-pads. However, we've seen examples of students having real problems to enter the PIN, and I would say that it sometimes goes into the other extreme, that once you have really bad security shielding you will force the guy to enter the PIN with the finger really pointing out what keys you are pressing. An interesting observation was that the last digit guess was always the most successful one, it was almost 90% guessed correctly.

Our observation from this phase of the experiment would be that from the point of the threat of the opportunistic thief, there is not any improvement from the introduction of PIN authorisation by the customer. On the contrary, and there are few ways possible to improve it in the short-term. There is a paper by Ross Anderson, Mike Bond and Steven Murdoch[1], they point out very well that the ATMs where we have been used to enter PINs and the tills where we are supposed to enter the PINs today are very different environments.

Matt Blaze. Presumably there is some baseline data in that the card issuers, the financial companies, know what their fraud rate is. It would be interesting to find out how your data matches the real world fraud rates.

Reply. From my personal point of view it's like the ongoing argument for years that there has been first some reduction of fraud in France, but that has been countered by the fraud increase of cards being used abroad in the neighbouring countries like UK, Spain, or Germany. I used to have some figures while working for a bank, but these figures are treated as semi-confidential, the bankers are not supposed to release them, what gets released are processed sums that say very little.

Matt Blaze. But presumably there is some risk that my PIN will be compromised, that is in some way proportional to the number of transactions that I

---

[1] R. Anderson, M. Bond, S. Murdoch. Chip and Spin. Paper available at http://www.cl.cam.ac.uk/~mkb23/spin/spin.pdf, webpage Chip and SPIN! at http://www.chipandspin.co.uk/.

perform, so you can calculate a per transaction risk, of compromise of the PINs, if you knew what those numbers were.

Reply. And if we had these numbers separately, we could do that for the cards that are authorised by the signature and by the PIN.

Matt Blaze. Right, exactly, and presumably those numbers are hard to get, but somebody could calculate them, and it would be very interesting to see how your experiments match those numbers.

Richard Clayton. The figures you get from existing real world fraud would mislead you, because the standard method of doing the fraud is you take your stolen card into a shop where you have a friend behind the counter, and somebody who's getting a rake-off, they then don't look for a particularly good validation of the signature. They approve something on the basis this is plausible and that the owner might have written that signature if they're having an off day, you can't actually demonstrate that in fact they could see very well that it was a fraudulent card and just let it go.

Reply. I was told by this friend of mine who helped us with the experiment, the jewellery owner, about the procedures used by the banks to verify what signatures are OK, and what not. The bank official comes to check in the shop if the signature, or rather the transaction, is claimed as fraudulent by the owner of the card. Very often they have cases where it's clear that the signature is completely different, then it's the problem of the merchant and eventually of the shop assistant. But they have sometimes these fuzzy cases where the signature doesn't look entirely the same, but it's like if I use my card that I signed five years back, in different conditions. I was told that it's the arbitrary decision of the bank officer to say, yes, this is still acceptable, we won't blame you for this, or no, this is not acceptable. And we are not aware of any real court cases where it is up to the court to decide whether, in that fuzzy case, the bank official is right, or whether the merchant is right.

Kamil Kulesza. If you have a friend behind the counter of the shop then you can practice the signature more than once, till it's more or less accepted.

Reply. In that case, yes, but as Richard said, the statistics won't be of much relevance.

Mike Bond. In the experiment, were the customers typing in their real PINs, or a PIN they'd made up for the purpose of the experiment?

Reply. PINs that we made up for them. We generated PINs, and we gave them innocent looking cards.

Mike Bond. If you were to repeat the experiment it strikes me that maybe you should use PINs which they might plausibly have.

Reply. No, in the real conditions this is hard. That's why I want a sponsor to take up the cost of replacement of the card, because I want the customers to use their real card, the cards to be recalled right after the experiment, destroyed, and they will ask their bank for a new one.

Mike Bond. Then you get PINs which the customers have practised, because I know that I find it very difficult to securely enter a PIN the first time I use it.

Frank Stajano. There's a difficulty here. Maybe PINs are slightly less risky than passwords, but if you get a password that people have chosen themselves as opposed to things that they've been assigned to by the bank, then you have an insight into what they choose, you have a sort of preferential avenue for guessing what their next set of passwords is going to be.

Reply. That's true here, but it won't apply in our case because in the Czech Republic with the vast majority of the banks you can't change your PIN. Well it does matter for the reason that Mike said, that you practise with it and so on, but for this purpose it doesn't.

Richard Clayton. I think that the sort of place where you do your second phase experiment is going to make a real difference because, rightly or wrongly, I assess my risk of entering a PIN. In Tesco's in broad daylight, complete strangers standing in the queue behind me are very unlikely to know who I am, very unlikely to be able to rob me on the way to the car park, so my risk if I expose my PIN to them is very low. Whereas the risk that I run by entering a PIN in a clear banner on a box in a relatively large street in Cambridge at 2 in the morning might be very different if someone was standing behind me.

Yvo Desmedt. Everybody is focusing on PINs, but the problem is that you can still do certain transactions without PINs, for example, when we go on the Internet. So when you are shopping at your favourite shop, one issue is do you trust the person there, the cashier, who may actually not be interested in the PIN but actually be trying to read the card number. It seems there is quite a problem there. The PIN is only one issue.

Richard Clayton. Yes, there's lots of problems with using cards in general.

Insecure Real-World Authentication Protocols (or Why Phishing Is So Profitable)

Richard Clayton

University of Cambridge, Computer Laboratory, William Gates Building,
15 JJ Thomson Avenue, Cambridge CB3 0FD, United Kingdom
richard.clayton@cl.cam.ac.uk

Abstract. The users of online banking systems are currently at risk from "phishing" scams. Confidence tricksters persuade them to visit fraudulent websites and use their authentication credentials to steal from the victims' accounts. We analyse the authentication protocols used for online banking, find that they are entirely inadequate, and consider how to improve systems design so as to discourage attacks.

1 Introduction

"Phishing" is the use of email messages to entice customers of legitimate companies into the sharing of passwords or other credentials such as credit card numbers or PINs. The third party who has successfully conned the customer into revealing their details is then able to masquerade as the customer in order to steal money or services.

The earliest recorded use of the word "phishing" is in a Jan 2 1996 Usenet article by drspamcake@aol.com [2] and relates to the theft of America Online (AOL) passwords. However, the actual attacks are far older and, for example, the sending of instant messages, apparently from AOL staff, that asked for a password was so widespread that by 1995 the AOL software package contained a specific "report password solicitation" button [5]. A 1990 paper on a closely related attack, obtaining passwords from public terminals by altering the firmware [4], uses the spelling "fishing".

In recent years, the term phishing has come to be specifically associated with the operation of fake websites that purport to be a bank or an online system such as eBay (www.ebay.com) or PayPal (www.paypal.com). The customer is sent an email that claims to be from the bank and is invited to click on a link within it. This takes them to the fraudster's site where a superficially plausible web page is used to capture the customer's access credentials. The fraudster then uses these credentials to impersonate the customer.

Phishing emails and the associated websites are now almost indistinguishable from legitimate activity (not least because marketing departments continue to value the use of clickable links in their emails). MailFrontier have run a couple of online quizzes [6] and found that about 30% of respondents make at least one mistake in categorising ten emails into legitimate or con-trick. So

B. Christianson et al. (Eds.): Security Protocols 2005, LNCS 4631, pp. 82–88, 2005.
© Springer-Verlag Berlin Heidelberg 2007

we should look to the authentication protocols and the overall system design to prevent phishing, rather than to user education or a change to the email standards.

In this paper we consider the inadequacy of current authentication protocols in section 2. Since no easy solution is apparent we consider how websites are authenticated in section 3. A real fix still being absent, in section 4 we consider how client certificates can also fail to deliver. We conclude that existing security primitives and security protocols fail to provide the tools needed to secure real-world online applications, though all is not lost because high-level system design changes may be sufficient to make online banking "secure enough".

2   Authentication Protocols

The standard protocol used for an online banking session with a bank B is for the Alice the user A, to supply a login name and a shared secret (password) S:

$$A \longrightarrow B : A, S$$

If the phisher, P, persuades Alice to visit his website then clearly he can masquerade as Alice:

$$A \longrightarrow P : A, S$$
$$P \longrightarrow B : A, S$$

In fact, because there is no freshness in this protocol, P can do this at any future time until Alice changes her password (or the Bank freezes the account).

This can be tackled by using a one-time password S_n which can never be reused. Example implementations would be a pad of single-use random numbers shared between Alice and the Bank, or a hardware token device such as RSA's SecurID [7]. This does not prevent the man-in-the-middle attack:

$$A \longrightarrow P : A, S_n$$
$$P \longrightarrow B : A, S_n$$

but P can only use the one-time password on the one occasion. The usage must also be done quickly. In the SecurID case, the password is inherently time-limited; but in both cases Alice is very likely to try and contact the bank again and as soon as she reaches the correct destination she will probably discover any attempted fraud before any money has been transferred.

The phisher can discourage Alice from making a new connection by acting as a man-in-the-middle for the entirety of her session. Most simply this would mean relaying all messages back and forth between Alice and the Bank except for a final "logoff"; thereafter P can perform extra transactions to his own benefit.

The bank can prevent extra transactions that are unknown to Alice (and force the phisher into providing a live service) by insisting on a fresh password for every transaction, such as paying a bill, that occurs within the banking session. Essentially Alice is signing each transaction T_n by the password S_n.

Unfortunately, since there is no binding between T_n and S_n this still does not prevent the man-in-the-middle attack where P replaces T_n ("pay the gas bill") by a wicked ("send all A's money to P") transaction W_n.

$$A \longrightarrow P : T_n, S_n$$
$$P \longrightarrow B : W_n, S_n$$

Of course, if this was a purely cmputer protocol in the Needham-Shroeder tradition then one would be looking to establish a binding between the signature and that which was signed, viz we'd design messages such as:

$$A \longrightarrow B : \{A, B, \text{nonce}, T_n\}_{K_A^{-1}}$$

where the messages are cryptographically signed with Alice's private key K_A^{-1}. Since Alice will be unable to perform cryptography in her head, we've moved into a more complex area than we've considered so far. We'll return to cryptography below, but first we'll consider another notion: the use of secure channels.

2.1 Secure Channels

If a secure channel from the Bank to Alice is available then this can be used to prop up an otherwise insecure protocol. By a secure channel we mean for example delivering a "text message" to Alice's mobile phone, or sending an email to a previously agreed address. Although P has managed to persuade Alice to visit the wrong website, P is not omnipotent enough to interfere with the rest of Alice's activities.

Of course it would be best if all transactions were carried out over secure channels ! – but email and text messages are not as convenient as using a website, because they are slower and far less interactive.

As an example of "propping up", perhaps at the end of the session the Bank could send Alice an email containing a summary of transactions. Alice would then compare this with her records and any wicked transactions could be undone. Bank transfers currently take several days, so Alice can be given the time to do her checking before an irreversible event occurs. In protocol terms, using the symbolism $\overset{secure}{\longrightarrow}$ to mean a message from the Bank over the secure channel we would have:

$$A \longrightarrow B : A, S_0$$
$$A \longrightarrow B : T_1, S_1$$
$$\cdots \qquad \cdots$$
$$A \longrightarrow B : T_n, S_n$$
$$B \overset{secure}{\longrightarrow} A : A, T_1, \ldots, T_n$$

In practice this scheme would fail if P was able to borrow one of Alice's transaction keys to validate a change to her email address (viz to alter the secure channel) and then supply a forged email contained a spurious set of transactions. Similarly, the Bank is very likely to report upon transactions in human friendly terms such as "Payment to 'Gas Company' (a/c 01–02–03 1234567), £100" and so there is a risk that P can change the account number associated with the Gas Company and Alice will fail to see the fraud.

This suggests that there is a need for multiple levels of authentication; run-of-the-mill validation of transactions, and higher levels for operations such as changes to payees, inspection and alteration of out-of-band contact details. Further thought will show that the lower level of authorisation need not be onerous since it just prevents denial-of-service attacks (why would P go to considerable trouble to cause Alice to make specious payments to the Gas Company, who can be trusted to refund the excess?). However, the authenticators S_n will have significant value when a sensitive operation is occurring. The highest level of authentication (perhaps using old-fashioned pen and ink?) is needed for changes to the secure channel itself, which can be made even more robust by insisting that it is impossible to inspect the current setting.

However, the effect of all of this analysis and invention is merely to change the nature of phishing from "visit my website and type in an authenticator" to "visit my website and perform sensitive operations" which, since there are many plausible reasons for having to do sensitive operations, is unlikely to slow down the confidence tricksters significantly.

It is clear that we need proper cryptographic signing of Alice's messages, but this requires special software to achieve. Some cryptographic software ships as standard within web browsers. Maybe we can prevent phishing by having Alice realise that she has reached the wrong website?

3   The Standard Website Security Model

Secure Sockets Layer (SSL) was invented by Netscape Development Corporation in 1995 and version 3.0 [3] has become widely deployed. A closely related protocol called TLS (Transport Layer Security) was standardised by the IETF in 1999 [1]. By convention, websites using these protocols have URLs that commence `https` rather than `http`.

SSL/TLS is intended to provide a private connection, which cannot be eavesdropped, between two entities using symmetric encryption with a specially negotiated session key. The connection is reliable in that a message integrity check is used to ensure that messages have not been altered in transit. The entities can establish each other's identity by inspecting cryptographically signed packets. Certificates issued by a mutually trusted third party can be exchanged to demonstrate the authenticity of those signatures.

In practice, web sites have a certificate signed by a CA (Certificate Authority) such as Verisign. The consumer's browser is pre-loaded with the root certificate for the CA and can verify that the certificate presented by a website is owned by that website. Unfortunately, customers seldom understand what has been verified by an `https` connection and believe that very different guarantees are in place.

If a fraudster obtains a certificate for `www.fakebank.com` then the certificate issued by Versign would correctly show that the site being connected to was indeed the promised `www.fakebank.com` and not an imposter. However, the consumer will believe that Verisign is promising that the site is wholesome and indeed that it is somehow related to the `www.truebank.com` that the customer thought they were visiting. This is entirely clear in protocol notation:

$$P \longrightarrow A : \{\, \texttt{site-P} \,\}_{K_{CA}^{-1}}$$

where A reads `site-P` as `site-B` and also believes the CA guarantees P's probity.

In the real world, if a fraudster obtains a certificate, sets up their site to resemble a major bank and then sends out a phishing email to attract the gullible then the emphasis placed on the value of using `https` is likely to make this a more successful con than if `http` had been used. The only reason this is not more common is the high cost of certificates and a slight risk that the CA might become aware of the fraudster's identity.

4   Client Certificates

As noted above, SSL is capable of securing both ends of a conversation. For this to occur the customer must install a "client certificate". The bank (who will not confuse `site-A` and `site-P`) can verify that there is no man-in-the-middle. In essence, the two parties A and B swap certificates signed by the CA, then use the Diffie-Hellman protocol to agree a communication key K_{Comm} and sign messages attesting to its value:

$$A \longrightarrow B : \{\, \texttt{site-A}, K_A \}_{K_{CA}}, \{K_{Comm}\}_{K_A^{-1}}$$
$$B \longrightarrow A : \{\, \texttt{site-B}, K_B \}_{K_{CA}}, \{K_{Comm}\}_{K_B^{-1}}$$

P is unable to forge either of these two messages and cannot interpose himself between A and B without causing the communication keys on the two links to differ – because those keys are constructed from secrets supplied by both ends of each link and A and B will not choose the same values.

The problem with client certificates is that it is expensive to operate the necessary certificate issuing system and it will prevent customers from using random machines (at the office, or on holiday) to do their banking. Therefore the use of client certificates has been restricted to high value systems such as share trading where the inconvenience of only being able to use a machine with the certificate installed is not significant.

However, if a certificated connection was only needed for the special transactions we identified earlier then this might be an acceptable solution. One could visit a beachfront cybercafé to pay the gas bill, but could only set up a new payment destination from the living room at home.

It is also possible to use the secure channel mentioned above to replace the client certificate. The Bank can be verified by making an `https` connection, albeit with the risks already mentioned. The user must then compare the value of K_{Comm} on their machine with the value sent over the secure channel.

$$B \stackrel{secure}{\longrightarrow} A : K_{Comm}$$

Although in theory this works well, the main difficulty is that it hard to display the value of K_{Comm} within today's browsers and downloading a program to display it provides another opportunity for the phishers to con the users. Even if the value was displayed correctly, a phisher acting as a man-in-the-middle might be able to overlay that part of the screen with a misleading value[1], much as phishing sites today overlay "lock symbols" and URLs with their own graphics.

Of course, if phishers change their *modus operandi* into asking Alice to mail in her certificates ("we've discovered a security fault and need to replace them") then user certificates will become a significant liability because they do not usually require any password or other authorisation to be activated.

5 Conclusions

The types of authentication currently employed by online banking systems are, when analysed as security protocols, entirely ineffective. Some simple changes can make the phisher's task significantly harder – requiring them to run realtime man-in-the-middle attacks and forcing them to persuade customers to perform unnecessary sensitive operations. Although being in "the middle" and dynamically altering the traffic is conceptually simple, there are a number of things that banks could do to ensure that it is far from straightforward – and hence it might become difficult for the phisher to automate.

Cryptography fixes the problem at the protocol level, but in the real world there are significant limitations in how it can be effectively deployed.

However, from the banks' point of view, it may not be necessary to provide a perfect solution. If they can make phishing for bank details harder than capturing merchant accounts on Amazon or Tesco then the attackers will change their targets. As when two hunters are being chased by a bear, it is not necessary to outrun the bear, but merely to go faster than the other fellow.

References

1. Dierks, T., Allen, C.: The TLS Protocol, Version 1.0, IETF, RFC2246 (January 1999)
2. DrSpamcake: Get on aol from off aol. alt.online-service.america-online (January 2, 1996)
   http://groups.google.com/groups?selm=4calah$eoh@newsbf02.news.aol.com
3. Freier, A.O., Karlton, P., Kocher, P.C.: The SSL Protocol Version 3.0. IETF Internet Draft (November 18, 1996) draft-freier-ssl-version3-02.txt
4. Harriman, D.D.: Password Fishing on Public Terminals. In: Computer Fraud and Security Bulletin, pp. 12–14. Elsevier Science Publishers, New York (1990)

---

[1] P knows the value of K_{Comm} that will be sent via the secure channel, because P is using that key for their own connection to B.

5. Lee, L.: AOL scam warning. bit.listserv.christia (September 29, 1995) `http://groups.google.com/groups?selm=950929165422_112740484@mail02.mail.aol.com`
6. MailFrontier Inc: MailFrontier to Unveil Phishing IQ Test II at Inbox East. Press Release (November 11, 2004) `http://www.mailfrontier.com/press/press_phishtest2.html`
7. RSA Security Inc: RSA SecurID Authentication. `http://www.rsasecurity.com`

Insecure Real-World Authentication Protocols
(or Why Phishing Is So Profitable)
(Transcript of Discussion)

Richard Clayton

University of Cambridge, Computer Laboratory

I want to talk about the real world, where authentication protocols are extremely insecure, and I'm going to try and explain to you why phishing is so profitable.

Why does phishing work? Basically because con artists are really good at persuading people to do really dumb things – and we just have to face up to this. What's changed recently is that in order to run a con you no longer need a printing press in the cellar to produce all the props. Anybody can produce web pages which look just as good as the professional stuff. But the really deep problem is that the underlying protocols are rubbish and that's what my paper is about.

This is the real-world authentication protocol that we are used to, Alice comes along and says to the bank, hello, my name is Alice and this is my secret which we share. If the con artist, the phisher person, can persuade Alice to talk to them instead of to the bank, then Alice will hand over the secret to the phishing person, and the phisher will then go along to the bank and say, I am Alice, which is of course a lie, but here is the secret, at which point the bank will accept their word for it.

We can fix some of the problems with this. We can fix the freshness, we can arrange for Alice to sign on using a secure ID, or taking the next one-time password out of the little booklet which the bank has sent them, which is what they do in Germany, or you can have a token which is sent over your mobile phone in an SMS message, or all sorts of other two-factor things. This works really great, but you can still run a man-in-the-middle attack on this, although you have to do it real time. Mike you sit in the middle, Alice says to you, I am Alice and here is my special one-time password, and you immediately pass it on to the bank saying exactly the same thing, and the bank accepts it.

In the phishing example, Alice is talking to the phishing person who talks to the bank, and will happily do the first couple of transactions, and then when Alice has gone on the phishing person will extend the session and arrange that now all of the rest of the money in Alice's account will be transferred to a bank account in Nigeria, or Russia, or Penge, or somewhere like that.

Alf Zugenmaier: Even when you have a man-in-the-middle, can't you fix the session extension problem by using one-time PINs for every instruction?

Reply: Yes you can defeat session extension, where the phishers issue more commands when you've finished your banking, if every time you do a transaction the bank asks for a fresh one-time password. So what the phishing person does is that instead of passing your real transaction to the bank they replace it by

B. Christianson et al. (Eds.): Security Protocols 2005, LNCS 4631, pp. 89–96, 2007.
© Springer-Verlag Berlin Heidelberg 2007

another transaction that benefits them. It's more complex to do, but it's still a viable attack.

Tuomas Aura: But this means that you actually have to run an on-line man-in-the-middle attack, where normally the phishing site just collects the credentials, and then the phisher would log on later in his pare time and transfer the money?

Reply: You have only changed the technology – and put the bad people who clone websites out of business. The new bad people just pass packets backwards and forwards. This is much easier because you don't get all the difficulty of trying to scrape websites and fix up the HTML so it will work on your box. It's sometimes suggested that we should all use random colours on websites, so that I think that the Barclays website is red, and you think the Barclays website is green. This stops the cloning attacks, because the phishing website will be the wrong colour. But if you run a real-time man-in-the-middle attack there's no need to know about colours, you just pass the packets backwards and forwards.

What people have come up with is some ideas of using secure channels to improve matters. I've already talked about the idea to deliver one-time tokens over your mobile phone, this doesn't actually help you, but maybe we can do some other things with secure channels. And by secure in the context of a phishing attack I mean out of band. The main difficulty is that secure channels are slow and less convenient because otherwise we'd always use them, in which case we wouldn't have a problem.

One of the things we might be able to do with a secure channel is at the end to send people a summary of everything that happened so that if any of the transactions have been replaced then an out of band message turns up and says, these are the transactions you've just been doing, so that you can check them, and I've put in these little padlocks into the arrows to indicate this is a secure message. This has some merit.

James Malcolm: Your secure channels are really just bank statements aren't they?

Reply: Yes, although the secure messages turn up a bit faster than paper bank statements. You should also note that it will be a brilliant solution from the banks' point of view because now if Alice doesn't complain immediately then it will be Alice's fault, and the banks will have dumped all the risk onto their customers.

Mark Lomas: I had a phone call from my bank asking me if I had bought a 3-piece suite in Dublin the previous week because they'd worked out statistically it was unlikely for me to have done what I did. That's actually a useful system, the bank statement only comes once a month, but here the bank has actually gone out of its way to talk to me.

Yvo Desmedt: But a phisher probably knows about this. How were you sure it was the bank who rang you up?

Mark Lomas: They knew my telephone number and what to ask about.

Yvo Desmedt: That doesn't really define their identity.

Mark Lomas: Somebody else can ask me whether I bought a 3-piece suite and if I say "no" I'm not giving away very much information. Whatever question they're likely to ask, I'm likely to say "no".

Mike Bond: Maybe one of the problems with this is that you get the constant invasion of privacy from banks ringing people up to double-check whatever it is they've been doing. I've seen a wide variation in capability of these statistical systems which either ring people up three or four times about the same transaction and drive them absolutely nuts, or don't ring up at all even when very bizarre things happen.

Reply: Although the credit card companies have been ringing people up to verify transactions for many years, they've got a bit more proactive about this recently. This reflects the amount of fraud they're getting, and how well they're managing to control it.

Alf Zugenmaier: We already have the problem with on-line banking, that you sign up to agree that whatever the bank thinks happened did happen.

Reply: My simple answer is that if you're a monopoly, there's a limit to what you can do to dump risk onto people if it's not perceived to be fair. Eventually the politicians, the regulators, will step in and say, "you may not dump risk that way". The point of this summary of events being part of the protocol is that it looks fair to dump the risk in that manner, and therefore it's much harder for a regulator to say, "you can't do that".

But the difficulty with this scheme is that if all of the tokens are essentially the same, just one-time passwords, then instead of the phisher using them for transactions, they can use some of the tokens to change the contact details. Now the phishing person can generate the email containing an appropriate looking summary, and meanwhile they can do as many other transactions as they can get passwords for. Remember my first starting point, conmen are really good, so if you go to your bank website and a message says, "I'm terribly sorry we're having a computer error today, can you enter another password please", or "extra security this week", you'll probably keep on typing in extra passwords happily, and providing as many as may be needed.

Matt Blaze: So are the banks being dumb in training their users to cooperate with what is asked of them?

Reply: I think the answer is that we still have the wrong question, and we're trying to fix the wrong thing.

What about client certificates? Client certificates fix man-in-the-middle. The difficulty is that they have a number of other side effects as well. First of all they kill off account aggregation, those sites where you can manage all of your bank accounts from one central place.

Ben Laurie: If they issue client certificates which they all agree on, then they can still do aggregation.

Reply: The banks want to kill off aggregation. Not because they consider it insecure, because they don't necessarily trust these third parties, but because one of the points of having a banking site is to be able to show adverts for your products. And the point of an aggregation site is to be able to put up other adverts, and get rid of all the adverts from the bank.

Ben Laurie: Sure, but it's not the client certificates that are killing off aggregation.

Mike Roe: You can still have aggregation by having the customer give their keys to the aggregation site, if the customers agree to the risk.

Reply: Client certificates also stop you doing your banking from cybercafés unless you take your client certificates with you. Also, remember these are con-men. What happens if the phishing people write you an email saying, "here's your new client certificates, and please could you mail back your previous ones so that we can destroy them securely?" [Laughter] What if the next virus goes looking for client certificates and mails them in? What exactly is the binding between Alice and the client certificates? Have we not in fact, by shipping lots of client certificates, made the whole situation rather worse?

Tuomas Aura: Suppose I keep the certificates on a chip card. That stops them being mailed in.

Reply: If you bind Alice to the chip card and arrange that every cybercafé has a reader, yes, you can build systems like that.

Tuomas Aura: People who do banking in the cybercafé deserve what they get anyway. [Laughter]

Reply: We can also fix things with crypto. What we should be sending around of course is not all this nonsense saying, "I am A and here's the secret". We should be sending messages with As and Bs, and nonces and signatures. But Alice has to trust the program doing the crypto, so what if the conman sends her an email saying that there is a new improved version, and she should download it from `bankname.newsoftware.com`. Many people think you can fix phishing by fixing the DNS, and stopping people registering wicked things like bankname with two Ms, but for this attack `bankname.com` will be totally unaware, because it's all delegated within the DNS. The first they will know is customers complaining about the new software not working.

Matt Blaze: I just updated my DNS to serve `barclays.crypto.com`!

Bruce Christianson: So if you want your old software back you can fetch it from Matt.

Matt Blaze: It's going to be operated with every care. I'm promising the security of all of your bits.

Reply: Another way of looking at this is that crypto isn't the solution because all we've really done is we've punted. How does the crypto program authenticate Alice? You have just moved the problem, and the crypto program now has to authenticate Alice rather than the bank having to authenticate Alice.

People are very keen on running some extra software along with your browser in a pop-up to warn you about certificate validation and all the real-time checks that nobody can ever be bothered to do. The difficulty is that the browser is extremely insecure. The phishers already overwrite the padlocks, they overwrite the URL being visited, and it's really hard to rely on anything on the screen being at all valid. Frankly it's not credible to say to customers that before doing some banking you need to turn off Java, and you need to turn off JavaScript, and you need to turn off Flash, and you need to turn off ActiveX.

Frank Stajano: Most of the banking websites won't even work if you do that.

Reply: Exactly.

Mike Roe: I disable all that stuff for all sites *apart* from my bank. So if I see a flash animation, or whatever, it's not from a phishing site. And if my bank is trying to defraud me, they can do it more directly.

Reply: The question we're beginning to ask is, is the problem actually authentication at all? Bruce Schneier is saying it as well, this is a quote from the last Cryptogram, "if we're ever going to manage the risks and effects of electronic impersonation, we need to concentrate on preventing and detecting the fraudulent transactions"[1]. The implication is not to be wasting effort on better authenticating the person doing them.

Tuomas Aura: Does that mean the kind of statistical approach we were talking about?

Reply: This is exactly the sort of thing which the credit card companies having been doing for years, which with suitable tuning doesn't impact a lot of people. People will get occasional unnecessary phone calls, if they have a weird lifestyle, but this seems to work, and it is keeping the level of fraud under control. The initial people who targeted Barclays in this country had a certain amount of success. They didn't steal very much money, they stole £9.99 from each account, but marked it "monthly transfer". They were clearly in it for the long haul. Now as it happens, Barclays was fairly quick off the ball and was able to match the things together from their own internal record and find all the places where this was occurring, or so everybody believes. One of the things Schneier is suggesting is that the real fix is to make the financial institutions responsible for every fraudulent transaction and not let them wriggle out in any way. Not that this is a solution, but it is a way of generating a solution.

Tuomas Aura: Just like making software companies liable is a way of getting rid of bugs?

Reply: That's probably a way of getting rid of the software. [Laughter]

So, what will work? There are lots of small improvements which are possible. In particular, moving to one-time passwords will mean that phishers have to run a real-time man-in-the-middle. If you have client certificates, you've at least changed the attack surface to something rather different from today. Browsers could do a lot more real-time checks on websites and DNS. If you were the first person to visit you might be in trouble but maybe after a few hours somebody will have spotted the problem, and you can leverage that community knowledge. Websites could look harder at the incoming IP address. This is not a complete fix, but if I'm coming from a cybercafé in Latvia then it can take a different view of transactions than if I appear to be sitting at home in Cambridge, and the IP address will at least tell you that to an approximation. If nothing else you push up the cost to the phishing people; to attack me they have to put their

---

[1] B. Schneier, Crypto-Gram Newsletter, 15 April 2005.

intermediate website somewhere near Cambridge rather than somewhere near Latvia. Banks could have multiple levels of authentication. At the moment one size fits all, whereas we'd do a lot better if paying your gas bill didn't require very much authentication at all, but changing the destination of your gas company's account required more, setting up a new payee whilst sitting in a cybercafé in Latvia maybe needs a lot of authentication, etc. I would suggest that we need to encourage the banks to introduce them all at once, so suddenly the security landscape changes from looking like a series of small hills to a sort of Kilamanjaro effect. The other thing I'd like to stress is that the banks don't actually have to fix everything, all they have to do is to make it harder to attack the banks than to attack Amazon, or Tesco, or whatever, rather like the two hunters pursued by the bear, the trick is not to outrun the bear, but to outrun the other hunter.

Tuomas Aura: Just one more to add to your list – which is already being used – you delay your transactions over a certain amount so they will only take place in three days time.

Reply: In the UK all transactions are in three days time.

Tuomas Aura: But some kind of extra delay would give you some time to find out that something is wrong.

Reply: There is a difference between a payment going to the gas company, a respected UK company who, if there is something going wrong, will give it back. A payment to an overseas bank is different because there'll be significant difficulties in getting the payment to come back again.

Pekka Nikander: One problem that you didn't address that I would like to highlight is that many of the technologies that we're using are not only relying on the user or the password, but also how the user knows to whom the browser is talking. Also we are heavily reliant on the DNS. One of the more fundamental problems is that we don't have any secure name space. From a broader point of view, it really looks like we need something like IPsec as well.

Matt Blaze: There's an underlying issue that we as crypto people understand, which nobody else gets (although there's things we don't get that everyone else does in complement) and that is this wonderful invention in the crypto and protocols world that the ability to verify something does not entail the ability to forge it yourself. So you can prove who you are in some cryptographic sense, and you can give the verifier the ability to verify without giving him the ability to forge your identity. There's no analogue to that in the real world, and of course most people don't have the computational set-up to be able to exploit it, so this is a non-intuitive notion. The thing *we* don't get is that this isn't very useful because it's a non-intuitive notion. So a lot of what you're describing as the countermeasures to phishing attacks are very straightforwardly (and I think your paper recognises this) solved by the deployment of very straightforward protocols, that people don't intuitively trust.

Reply: But the protocols merely move the trust about, by shifting where the issue of authentication takes place. They don't actually fix the problem, they just move it so that you can trust this piece of wire from the bank to Alice's machine, and there's still a bit of an air gap between.

Matt Blaze: To understand what the trust is requires having intuitions that not many people have.

Reply: One of my recent insights is that the session extension attack is not necessarily as easy as it looks, because what you're trying to do is to pick things out of the packets flowing backwards and forwards. The chrome, the browser graphical components, is hard enough to distinguish properly, but you also have to pick out the material to be forged, and that can be made pretty difficult. There's some work I've recently become aware of from Georgia Tech[2], where they are generating pictures that contain coded objects, in this example dice, which the user will then recognise as being their coded objects, Also the transaction which you're currently trying to verify is sitting in here as a visual object as well, with reflections of it in shiny mirrors and so on. The notion is that the man-in-the-middle may find it extremely difficult in a short period of time to identify which bits of this they should change, and reconstruct a picture with their forged information placed into it.

Yvo Desmedt: This is going back to Turing tests. It seems that we want things that are easy to generate, but can be different each time, and then hard to extract.

Reply: Yes, these are visual CAPTCHAs, it's a hard problem for a computer and the idea is that even if you have a human sitting there helping the computer, with current tools it may be very difficult for the human even to tell the computer what needs to be changed in the picture to persuade Alice that there is no man-in-the-middle. There are inelegant things about this solution, but maybe this is the way forward. Force phishers to be man-in-the-middle and then make it really hard to alter the traffic.

Pekka Nikander: I have a slightly more daring question. Why we are trying to authenticate the users that much? It seems to me more or less obvious that everybody basically is carrying a trusted device. Of course there are problems of what happens if you lose a trusted device, but I don't see how we can continue for much longer without that kind of help. Most of us are already carrying our cell phone and we rely on that quite a lot.

Yvo Desmedt: The operating system is the problem. Really it's no longer a cell phone from ten years ago, it's now a Windows machine, or...

Reply: With all the security enhancement that implies.

Bruce Christianson: But the hope is you can push the trust requirement. Instead of having to trust something remote, you just have to trust something local.

Virgil Gligor: Treating it much as a black box?

Matt Blaze: Or understanding it?

Bruce Christianson: Having a PhD in Computer Science.

Frank Stajano: I think that this Georgia Tech approach is flawed, and for a general reason which applies to most of what you have described. It may not

---

[2] J. King and A. dos Santos, A User-Friendly Approach to Human Authentication of Messages. In A. S. Patrick and M. Yung (ed.): Financial Cryptography and Data Security: 9th International Conference, FC 2005, Roseau, The Commonwealth Of Dominica, Feb 28 – Mar 3, 2005. LNCS 3750, Springer, pp. 225–239.

be easy to replace one message with another message, with everything matching in the reflections in the mirrors and so on. But only a forensic scientist could know this, whereas the person who is doing the check doesn't look at all the requirements. They just check, "are the dice there, and what does the information say?" The reason why phishers are successful is because they understand the psychology of this, and in the example you so brilliantly had, they look at `www.barclays.software.com` and they don't realise that `software` overrides `barclays`. They just check, is it Barclays? If it has the logo of flying fish, or whatever Barclays logo is, then it must be Barclays. So I think although the scheme is trying to make everything verifiable in a way that a forensic scientist would not be able to spot the difference, it's quite sufficient to make it plausible enough that the average person says, that's alright, I'll go there.

Mike Roe: It's a bit like the problem you have with forged banknotes.

Tuomas Aura: If a banknote or a credit card has a hologram on it then whoever is looking at it is happy it has a hologram. How many will remember what that hologram should look like?

Mark Lomas: When the first euro notes came out, the forgers didn't try to copy them; they just invented new denominations.

Mike Bond: Maybe we should put our research into trying to turn the handle on the sausage machine backwards so that when things start to go wrong we can just wind back time. Try instead to solve the problem that you can't get the money back once it's gone to Columbia. Maybe that's where the research should be heading?

Authorisation Subterfuge by Delegation in Decentralised Networks

Simon Foley and Hongbin Zhou

Department of Computer Science,
University College, Cork, Ireland
{s.foley,zhou}@cs.ucc.ie

1 Introduction

Trust Management [1,4,10] is an approach to constructing and interpreting the trust relationships among public-keys that are used to mediate security-critical actions. Cryptographic credentials are used to specify delegation of authorisation among public keys. Existing trust management schemes are operational in nature, defining security in terms of specific controls such as delegation chains, threshold schemes, and so forth.

However, Trust Management approaches tend not to consider whether a particular authorisation policy is well designed in the sense that a principle cannot somehow bypass the intent of a complex series of authorisation delegations via some unexpected circuitous route. In an open system no individual has a complete picture of all the resources and services that are available. Unlike the administrator who 'sees everything' in a traditional closed system, the principals of an open system are often ordinary users and are open to confusion and subterfuge when interacting with resources and services. These users may inadvertently delegate un-intended authorisation to recipients.

In this paper we introduce the problem of *authorisation subterfuge*, whereby, in a poorly designed system, delegation chains that are used by principals to prove authorisation may not actually reflect the original intention of all of the participants in the chain.

2 Authorisation Subterfuge

2.1 Delegation of Authorisation

A simple model is used to represent delegation of authorisation between public keys. A signed credential, represented as $\{\!|\,K_B, p\,|\!\}_{K_A}$, indicates that K_A delegates to K_B, the authorisation permission p. Permissions are structured in terms of lattice $(PERM, \leq, \sqcap)$, whereby given $p \leq q$ means that permission q provides no less authorisation than p. A simple example is the powerset lattice of $\{\mathsf{read}, \mathsf{write}\}$, with ordering defined by subset, and greatest lower bound defined by intersection.

B. Christianson et al. (Eds.): Security Protocols 2005, LNCS 4631, pp. 97–102, 2007.

Given a credential $\{\!| \, K_B, q \, |\!\}_{K_A}$ and $p \leq q$ then there is an implicit delegation of p to K_B by K_A, written as $(\!| \, \hat{K}_B, p \, |\!)_{K_A}$. Two reduction rules follow.

$$\frac{\{\!| \, K_B, p \, |\!\}_{K_A}}{(\!| \, K_B, p \, |\!)_{K_A}} \qquad \frac{(\!| \, K_B, p \, |\!)_{K_A}; p' \leq p}{(\!| \, K_B, p' \, |\!)_{K_A}}$$

If delegation is regarded as transitive, and if K_A delegates p to K_B, and K_B delegates p to K_C, then it follows that K_A implicitly delegates p to K_C.

$$\frac{(\!| \, K_C, p \, |\!)_{K_B}; (\!| \, K_B, p' \, |\!)_{K_A}}{(\!| \, K_C, p \sqcap p' \, |\!)_{K_A}}$$

This corresponds to SPKI certificate reduction [4] (greatest lower bound is equivalent to SPKI tuple intersection). It is not unlike a partial evaluation over a collection of KeyNote credentials, resulting in another credential. At this point, we do not consider permissions that cannot be further delegated.

2.2   Incompetence in Delegation

Bob (represented as public key K_B) holds credential $C_1 = \{\!| \, K_B, \mathsf{buy100} \, |\!\}_{K_A}$ reflecting an authorisation to make purchases for his organisation (K_A) up to a limit of €100. Bob delegates this authority to another staff member Clare by signing $\{\!| \, K_C, \top \, |\!\}_{K_B}$, where $\top$ represents the highest value in the permission ordering and K_C is a public key owned by Clare. Bob believes that this is a reasonable strategy as,on the basis of his view of the world, certificate reduction gives $(\!| \, K_C, \mathsf{buy100} \, |\!)_{K_A}$ (and no more).

In this case, Bob's delegation strategy is *incompetent* as in an open system it fails the principle of least privilege. Bob does not consider the possibility of the existence of other certificates, for example, $\{\!| \, K_B, \mathsf{buy1000} \, |\!\}_{K_A}$ (where $\mathsf{buy100} \leq \mathsf{buy1000}$), indirectly authorising Clare for purchases up to €1,000 (and possibly unknown to Bob). Thus, when writing delegation certificates one must be careful to exactly specify the desired permission and no more. Bob should have signed $C_2 = \{\!| \, K_C, \mathsf{buy100} \, |\!\}_{K_B}$. An implication of this is that a systematic naming scheme for permissions becomes critical in ensuring the principle of least privilege. For example, Keynote suggests a global registration scheme (for example, IANA/ICANN) to ensure uniqueness of permission attributes.

2.3   Confusion in Delegation

Continuing the example above, suppose that Bob also works for an organisation with public key K_Z and is unaware of the existence of the certificate $C_3 = \{\!| \, K_B, \mathsf{buy100} \, |\!\}_{K_Z}$. Bob signs certificate $C_2 = \{\!| \, K_C, \mathsf{buy100} \, |\!\}_{K_B}$, as recommended, believing that the resulting certificate chain (with $K_A \rightarrow K_B \rightarrow K_C$) provides the appropriate $\mathsf{buy100}$ authorisation for Clare (as an employee of K_A).

Unknown to Bob, Clare could use certificate C_3 to provide an alternative chain $K_Z \to K_B \to K_C$ as proof of authorisation for buy100.

This confusion may introduce problems if the certificate chains that are used to prove authorisation are also used to determine who should be billed for the transaction. Bob believes the chain $K_A \to K_B \to K_C$ provides the appropriate accountability for Clare's authorisation; his view of the world has not considered the existence of C_3. In this case we think of Bob as more *confused* in his delegation actions rather than incompetent; the permission naming scheme influences his local beliefs and it was the inadequacy of this scheme that led to the confusion. Perhaps Bob has too many certificates to manage and in the confusion looses track of which permissions should be associated with which keys.

Such inadequacies can lead to vulnerabilities when certificate chains are used to provide evidence of accountability for an authorisation. For example,

- K_Z, collaborating with K_C conceals $\{\!| K_B, \text{buy100} |\!\}_{K_Z}$ from K_B so that Clare can order from an unintended supplier (authorised via K_Z).
- K_Z conceals $\{\!| K_B, \text{buy100} |\!\}_{K_Z}$ from K_B and K_C and then, unknown to Clare, cut-and-pastes certificate chain $[C_1; C_2]$ from Clare to $[C_3; C_2]$.
- K_Z, collaborating with K_A conceals $\{\!| K_B, \text{buy100} |\!\}_{K_Z}$ to facilitate plausible deniability (for K_A) on the validity of an order. A third party cannot confirm the intent of the original delegation, viz, whether it should be billed to K_A or K_Z.

Certificate chains have been used in the literature to support degrees of accountability of authorisation, for example, [3,8,2]. The micro-billing scheme [3] uses KeyNote to help determine whether a micro-check (a KeyNote credential, signed by a customer) should be trusted and accepted as payment by a merchant. In [8], delegation credentials are used to manage the transfer of micro-payment contracts between public keys; delegation chains provide evidence of contract transfer and ensure accountability for double-spending. These systems are vulnerable to authorisation subterfuge (leading to a breakdown in accountability) if care is not taken to properly identify the 'permissions' indicating the payment authorisations when multiple banks and/or provisioning agents are possible.

2.4   Dishonesty in Delegation

Bob has a legitimate expectation that so long as he delegates competently then he should not be liable for any confusion that is a result of poor permission design. Bob can use this view to act dishonestly. In signing a certificate he can always deny knowledge of the existence of other certificates and the inadequacy of permission naming in order to avoid accountability. While Bob secretly owns company K_Z, he claims that he cannot be held accountable for the 'confusion' when Clare (an employee of K_A) uses the delegation chain $K_Z \to K_B \to K_C$ to place her order.

3   What's in a Name?

A number of ad-hoc strategies can be used to avoid the problems of incompetence, confusion and dishonesty. One strategy would be to ensure that Bob had different roles (public keys) corresponding to the different organisations (K_A and K_Z) that he works for. This assumes competence on Bob's part to ensure he is in the right role when delegating authorisation.

Another strategy would be to ensure that each permission is sufficiently detailed to avoid ambiguity. For example, including a company name as part of the permission $\{\!| K_B, \texttt{<OrgA:buy100>} |\!\}_{K_A}$ may help avoid the vulnerabilities in the particular example above. However, at what point can a principal be sure that a reference to a permission is sufficiently complete? Achieving this requires an ability to be able to fix a permission within a global context, that is, to have some form of global identifier and/or reference for the permission.

In addition to global uniqueness, it is preferable that permission identifiers also be *non-transient*. Including just a globally unique organisation name within a permission may not be sufficient. Organisation names and their ownership can change. For example, the domain name registration mishap concerning `panix.com` [11] may result in subterfuge when delegating permission `<panix.com:buy100>`.

In Trust Management frameworks such as KeyNote and SPKI/SDSI, public keys provide globally unique identifiers that are tied to the owner of the key. These can also be used to avoid permission ambiguity within delegation chains. For example, given $\{\!| K_B, \texttt{<}K_A\texttt{:buy100>} |\!\}_{K_A}$ there can be no possibility of subterfuge when Bob delegates authority to Clare with $\{\!| K_C, \texttt{<}K_A\texttt{:buy100>} |\!\}_{K_B}$. In this case the certificate makes the intention of the delegation very clear and provides accountability in the delegation chain for the authorisation held by Clare.

Needless to say that this strategy does assume a high degree of competence on Bob's part to be able to properly distinguish between permissions `<`K_A`:buy100>` and `<`K_Z`:buy100>`, where, for example, each public key could be 342 characters long (using a common ASCII encoding for a 2048 bit RSA key). One might be tempted to use SDSI-like local names to make this task more manageable for Bob. However, in order to prevent subterfuge, permissions require a name that is unique across all name spaces where it will be used, not just the local name space of Bob. In Bob's local name space the permission `<(Bob's Alice):buy100>` may refer to a different Alice to the Alice that Clare knows.

Another possible source of suitable identifiers is a global X500-style naming service (if it could be built) that would tie global identities to real world entities, which would in turn be used within permissions. However, X500-style approaches suffer from a variety of practical problems [5] when used to keep track of the identities of principals. In the context of subterfuge, a principal might easily be confused between the (non-unique) common name and the global distinguished name contained within a permission that used such identifiers.

One practical difficulty when relying on public keys as global identifiers is that their use is often *transitory*. A public key serves as an identifier (for its owner) for as long as the key is regarded as valid. If the (private) key is compromised, or if the owner decides to re-key then authorisation certificates will have to be re-issued by all participants on delegation chains involving the permission. If K_A re-keys to K'_A, and issues a new certificate $\{\!|\ K_B, <K'_A:\text{buy100}>\ |\!\}_{K'_A}$ then Bob (and everyone else) will have to issue new certificates $\{\!|\ K_B, <K'_A:\text{buy100}>\ |\!\}_{K_A}$, and so forth. This is contrary to the trust management strategy [10] whereby role memberships can be maintained independent of the permissions that are delegated to them. This contrasts with the use of X500-like global names. In this case, we assume that the name is non-transitory while the key is transitory. A re-keying results in the issuing of a new identity certificate. The owner uses their new key to re-issue existing authorisation certificates, whose permissions refer to the name of the principal rather than the public key. Other authorisation certificates signed by other principals remain valid as their permissions are based on non-transitory global names rather than transitory keys.

4   Conclusion

In this paper we described how poorly characterised permissions within cryptographic credentials can lead to authorisation subterfuge during delegation operations. This subterfuge results in a vulnerability concerning the accountability of the authorisation provided by a delegation chain: does the delegation operations in the chain reflect the true intent of the participants?

The challenge here is to ensure that permissions can be referred to in a manner that properly reflects their context. Since permissions are intended to be shared across local name spaces then their references must be global in nature. In the paper we discuss some ad-hoc strategies to ensure globalisation of permissions. In particular, we consider the use of global name services and public keys as the sources of global identifiers. In general we are interested in systematic ways of determining whether a particular delegation scheme using particular permissions is sufficiently robust to be able to withstand attempts at subterfuge. For the example above, Bob would like to know whether is is safe for him to delegate permission <panix.com:buy100> to Clare.

Trust Management, like many other protection techniques, provide operations that are used to control access. As with any protection mechanism the challenge is to make sure that the mechanisms are configured in such a way that they ensure some useful and consistent notion of security. We would like some assurance that a principal cannot bypass security via some unexpected but authorised route. It is argued in [6] that verifying whether a particular configuration of access controls is effective can be achieved by analysing its consistency, that is, whether it is possible for a malicious principle to interfere with the the normal operation of the system. This type of analysis [7,9] is not unlike the analysis carried out on authentication protocols. In the case of mechanisms based on trust management it is a question of determining consistency between potential delegation chains. Developing a suitable verification framework for the consistency of delegation chains is a topic of ongoing research [12].

Acknowledgements

This work is supported by the UCC Centre for Unified Computing under the Science Foundation Ireland WebCom-G project and by Enterprise Ireland Basic Research Grant Scheme (SC/2003/007).

References

1. Blaze, M., et al.: The keynote trust-management system version 2. Internet Request For Comments 2704 (September 1999)
2. Blaze, M., Ioannidis, J., Ionnidis, S., Keromytis, A., Nikander, P., Prevelakis, V.: Tapi: Transactions for accessing public infrastructure (submitted for publication, 2002)
3. Blaze, M., Ioannidis, J., Keromytis, A.D.: Offline micropayments without trusted hardware. In: Financial Cryptography, Grand Cayman (February 2001)
4. Ellison, C., et al.: SPKI certificate theory. Internet Request for Comments: 2693 (September 1999)
5. Ellison, C.M.: The nature of a usable PKI. Computer Networks 31, 823–830 (1999)
6. Foley, S.N.: Evaluating system integrity. In: Proceedings of the ACM New Security Paradigms Workshop, ACM Press, New York (1998)
7. Foley, S.N.: A non-functional approach to system integrity. Journal on Selected Areas in Communications 21(1) (January 2003)
8. Foley, S.N.: Using trust management to support transferable hash-based micropayments. In: Proceedings of the 7th International Financial Cryptography Conference, Gosier, Guadeloupe, FWI (January 2003)
9. Foley, S.N.: Believing in the integrity of a system. In: IJCAR Workshop on Automated Reasoning for Security Protocol Analysis, ENCS. Springer, Heidelberg (2004)
10. Rivest, R., Lampson, B.: SDSI - a simple distributed security infrastructure. In: DIMACS Workshop on Trust Management in Networks (1996)
11. Zeller, T.: New York Times (January 18, 2005)
12. Zhou, H., Foley, S.N.: A logic for analysing authorisation subterfuge in delegation chains. In: Submitted for publication (2005)

Authorisation Subterfuge by Delegation in Decentralised Networks
(Transcript of Discussion)

Simon Foley

Department of Computer Science,
University College, Cork, Ireland

This talk is about work by myself and Hongbin Zhou, who's a PhD student in Cork (except he's here today). One of the problems that we're interested in is just simple authorisation, whether or not somebody is allowed to perform some action, get access to some resource. In the good old days we had the traditional view of system administrators who had control over everything, and they had, or at least liked to think that they had, a very clear picture of what the resources were for, and who should have access to the resources, and so on. As a consequence they tend to exercise very tight control, they don't like giving away authorisation to resources, and it's usually a battle for somebody to get additional access to any resource. Administrators in these closed systems exercise their principle of "no privilege", nobody's allowed to do anything. As a consequence, the opportunity to subvert an administrator is very small, so you really have to work hard to get anywhere within one of these closed systems.

Well, this kind of system isn't very practical, it's very hard to use, everything has to go through these administrators who just don't want to help us, because they just don't understand us. So we moved to a more decentralised model, or an open systems view, where the resource owners and creators are the people who can decide who can have authorisation to use those resources. The argument being that these are the people who are familiar with the resources and therefore they're best placed to hand out authorisation, and they would typically rely on their working practice to decide whether or not they should give authorisation: a manager decides, I give my clerks authorisation. What we have then is a principle of "flexible privilege", people tend to get the privilege that they need, sometimes more, sometimes less, but it's a bit more flexible than the first case.

However, the question that I'm asking is, what's the opportunity to subvert user intentions in this situation. You've got the scenario where you have this despotic god-like administrator who sees everything, and knows everything, and exercises tight control; versus, what is in effect a free-for-all, with all of the individuals making their own decisions, and thinking they know what they're doing. So what's the possibility, or what are the chances, of being able to subvert these people.

And the motivation for this work then is, supposing you have users who have these certificates which give them authorisations to do things,these bags of potentially very large numbers of certificates, which maybe they're carrying around with them, or maybe they have them stored on web servers somewhere,

B. Christianson et al. (Eds.): Security Protocols 2005, LNCS 4631, pp. 103–111, 2007.

the question is, when a user decides to give some authorisation away to another user, is it possible to subvert their intention. Has the delegation scheme been sufficiently well-designed that it's not possible to create any surprises, or basically to create subterfuge. That's what the talk's about.

So we're going to look at this idea of authorisation subterfuge. Some basics first just so we're all on the same wavelength when it comes to the notation: we assume we've a lattice of permissions with the usual orderings, public keys go round writing certificates, so here we are, KB is authorised to do p by KA, and we can build up our certificate chains by just writing lots of certificates. And then we have the notion of certificate production, I would assume that everyone can delegate to everybody else potentially, we're not going to worry about the delegation bit, so here KA delegates to KB the permission p, and KB delegates to KC the permission p prime, and in effect KA is delegating to KC the intersection of those two permissions p and p' on the lattice.

If we just take a very simple example, we have our principal Alice who is trusted by some service to make purchases up to a limit of £100 each, and it turns out that Bob and Clare work for Alice, and Alice has decided that she's going to delegate her authority to Bob to use the service to buy things, and Bob chooses to also delegate authorisation to Clare. Now as far as Bob's view of the world is concerned he has the authority buy100 delegated top to Clare so therefore by reduction Clare also has authorisation to buy100. There's nothing particularly startling here, and the idea is that my certificate chain here provides evidence that Clare has been authorised by Bob, who's authorised by Alice, who's the person the service trusts to make these kinds of purchases, so there's nothing very hard here, and ultimately Alice is going to be accountable for purchases because she decided to pass that authority on to Bob who passed it on to Clare.

But the problem here was in the way that Bob wrote the certificate, he just wrote a certificate delegating all his authority to Clare, but maybe he didn't realise that there was also another certificate that Alice had issued, which had delegated the authority buy1000 to Bob. Now the reduction means that Clare is also authorised to buy items up to a value of 1000. So from Bob's perspective, he thought his view of the world was just, well I'm authorised to buy anything up to £100, yes, and I'm happily passing that onto Clare, but really I was very incompetent when I wrote this credential, I shouldn't have written the credential like that because it turned out there was this other credential and Clare ended up being able to do something I didn't want to pass on to her. So if Bob was to behave in a more competent way, what he should have done was issued an exact credential saying, Clare you're authorised to buy up to 100. But of course we could extend that argument and say, well, Alice should also have been a lot more competent in the first place, she should have said, I'm not just giving Bob authorisation to buy anything up to a 100, it's only to buy things up to a 100 for department X.

So really to avoid this kind of incompetence, or what is effectively subterfuge as we'll see, we need to be putting an awful lot more information into our permissions, into the authorisations that we're giving to people. The question that we have to ask ourselves is, well, when is the information that we put inside the permissions sufficient. Clearly putting just buy100, or buy1000, wasn't enough, we should put in more information.

Ross Anderson: Simon isn't it the case the electronic signature of the protocol needs people to be in top delegations as a default?

Reply: I'm not familiar with the electronic signature regulations.

Ross Anderson: If you have a qualifying electronic signature creation device then you are bound for any signature that it produces, regardless. So the regulations are pushing people in the direction of general delegation rather than...

Reply: ... being very specific. True, true, yes. But really when people delegate they need to be a lot more precise. They can't just say, oh everything I've got you can do, because otherwise, where does it stop.

Mike Roe: Which is why there is a tremendous amount of regulation concerning how you can do it, if you wish to do such permission delegation.

Bruce Christianson: But it's a useful thing for people who are mentally incompetent, they need a general Power of Attorney to delegate everything to somebody more competent. [Laughter] It seems we have to mark these certificates.

Tuomas Aura: It just needs people to delegate exactly what was in the first certificate, for example, by putting a hat on that certificate.

Reply: You're on the right track, as you'll see when we go on a bit further.

Frank Stajano: I guess at the higher level the fact that you are delegating everything to a subordinate gives you a chance to put the blame on the subordinate. If you delegate very precisely then you share the blame if they do something wrong.

Reply: Yes, exactly. This is something we're going to be coming to in later slides, the idea really is that you want to design a delegation scheme which avoids all of these scenarios. I want a scheme where people can't duck out of their responsibility, and where people can't introduce subterfuge. So it's all about saying, how much information do we have to put into the permissions, so that we can get a handle on what exactly is being delegated and by who, and for what, so that we have some chain of accountability.

So let's suppose this more competent Bob says, I'm going to delegate this £100 purchasing to Clare, and I'm following the rules now, being a lot more careful. However it turns out that Bob also works for Zac and overlooked the existence of this other credential that was around the place, which was Zac authorising Bob also for the same named permission. Now remember that Bob has this big bag of credentials, he probably doesn't read half the information in them, or may not even be aware of all of the credentials that are out there.

Ben Laurie: This doesn't sound very realistic to me, because surely the buy100 is going to be spend 100 of Alice's money really. So the final 100 in the second case will be spend 100 the next time?

Reply: Exactly, however, where does it stop. How much information do you have to put into the permissions, when does it stop.

Ben Laurie: Ah, I don't know, because I'm not designing the system.

Reply: OK, so Clare provides proof of authorisation, and now we have this problem if the chain is being used for accountability purposes. Bob had done this delegation delegating 100 to Clare and not realising that there was this other potential chain linking it back to Zac, and as a consequence could introduce these problems that the bill ends up going to Zac, whereas in Bob's mind everything that Clare buys should be going back to Alice. And yet everyone's right, you can just add in more information to permissions, but that's not ...

Frank Stajano: How does Clare even know about the existence of that other credential? When she provides her proof of authorisation, how does she know anything other than the chain she knows?

Reply: Well maybe she went to a website and she found these extra credentials, maybe she's been working in collaboration with Zac.

Mike Roe: You have to assume they're publicly available, or else you get another lot of problems.

Reply: Yes. Remember the certificate chain is used to provide evidence, of who should be held accountable for the delegation and the authorisation, at least that's the interpretation I usually attach to a certificate chain. Alice employs Bob, Bob also works for Zac, and Clare works for Bob. So Zac and Clare collaborated, and they concealed this credential – the fact that Zac had delegated authority to Bob so that Clare can order from an unintended supplier authorised by Zac. Another scenario is perhaps Zac conceals the existence of this credential from everybody, and then does what is in effect a cut and paste attack on the certificate chain that Clare presents as her authority. Clare's presenting authority saying, OK, I'm allowed to buy things up to £100 and the buck stops at Alice, as she sends the chain back it gets intercepted by Zac and he puts this in instead. Clare doesn't know this has happened, Bob doesn't know it's happened, but this is the evidence for the authorization.

Frank Stajano: Are the certificates presented to some kind of arbitrator?

Reply: There's some service saying, I trust Alice for purchases, I trust Zac for purchases, or maybe they're two different companies. At the end of the day in my mind the certificate, the chain is providing evidence of delegation, where the person got the authorisation from, Clare got it from Bob, Bob got it from Zac.

Frank Stajano: Why is there a problem, because eventually Zac would be billed.

Reply: Yes but the point is, that it is not what Bob intended when he delegated this permission buy100 to Clare.

Ben Laurie: Both of them are going to issue a purchase order thinking that it will be paid by Alice.

Frank Stajano: But Bob has not lost any of the money from Alice if the money can only come from Zac.

Reply: But the issue is accountability. The authorisation for Clare to buy this never came from Zac, and it wasn't supposed to come from Zac in the first place, Zac will turn around and say, hey, I never said that people like Clare should be making these kinds of purchases.

Tuomas Aura: But if Zac allowed the delegation then Zac actually said that anyone who has a valid claim can do it. What you lose here is that there's no record of which authorisation was used in the transaction.

Reply: Yes. I don't disagree with any of these remarks. Every time I throw something up people are saying, oh, but you can do this, or this, and it works fine, and you won't have that problem, or, it's not a problem because that's the way you've written these certificates, and I say, yes, that's fine. But if you look at it from the point of view of Bob, Bob is using this delegation scheme but there's subterfuge going on, he doesn't realise that these things are possible. So Bob would like to say how should I do my delegation to try and protect myself from these kinds of subterfuges that can happen.

Tuomas Aura: What I'm trying to understand, is Bob being cheated out of anything?

Reply: That doesn't matter. At the end of the day the chain is providing evidence of accountability as to how the authorisation is obtained. Now as to how it's subsequently interpreted and who gets hurt with it...

Tuomas Aura: Aha! The protocol you're presenting does not provide any evidence of which authorisation chain was actually used, it could have been some other chain that's not showing on this slide.

Reply: Yes, exactly.

Ben Laurie: And for every attack where Alice frames Zac there's a dual attack where Zac claims falsely to have been framed by Alice.

Reply: So maybe Zac and Alice collaborate, they conceal the existence of the credential where Zac is giving authorisation to Bob, and then that gives them this plausible deniability. It's not giving you any accountability, but Bob thought it was, when he wrote that authorisation he thought he was authorising Clare for the transaction, and that effectively the buck, which came from Alice in the first place, stopped at him.

Frank Stajano: When you say concealed, concealed from whom?

Reply: From Bob.

Pekka Nikander: So, in a way, if you make me your proxy, in the legal sense, then I should know about that, and if I don't know about that then you can later claim that I have done something bad just because you made me a proxy. And maybe I haven't done something bad.

Reply: Yes, something like that. If we move on hopefully it will start making more sense. So we can have another form of subterfuge by dishonesty, where in this case Bob is actually Zac as well, it's the same person. Bob having delegated authority to Clare, Clare went off, bought something with it, presented what she thought was the right chain, and Bob then presents another chain saying, hang on a second, this isn't proper accountability because it's possible for there to be another chain which could account for that purchase. So here we could have subterfuge by dishonesty.

What we're interested in is how do we avoid this kind of subterfuge when designing the delegation scheme, when we start passing permissions around the place how do we articulate permissions in such a way that we won't be subject to these flavours of subterfuge attacks.

Tuomas Aura: Well you don't need to change the permissions, you can also change the transaction protocol.

Reply: I suppose so. We thought of it from the point of view of permissions, but maybe that's. . .

George Danezis: What Tuomas said is a good point, I have been sitting here wondering why you're presenting a broken protocol. Why not bind this action to the chain in a secure way, with the authorisation you could include the hash of the authorisation chain.

Reply: OK, so you're saying that if you add in additional details into the protocol, like for example, taking a hash off the chain that was presented, that then becomes part of the transaction. Yes, that's another solution.

What I'm trying to point out here is that these kinds of subterfuge attacks can exist where you consider broken protocols. I haven't claimed that any of these worked in the first place, they are all broken, right, and all I'm trying to draw out here is an understanding of what is it that we're expecting from this certificate chain. Really what we're thinking of is that the delegation chain is giving us some form of accountability, or evidence of how the authorisations were passed from person to person. And the subterfuge happens when we can't precisely account for how a particular authorisation gets held: Clare gets some authorisation but, gee, it could have come from Zac, or it could have come from Alice, because there wasn't enough information in the permission. And so we want to design our scheme so that we can avoid the subterfuge, so that on the basis of the certificates I'm aware of, and given that I might be held accountable for anything that I'm going to sign, any credential that I'm going to issue, then is it safe for me to delegate some authorisation to some other person on that basis. In other words, where does the buck stop if there's going to be trouble.

And so when we then take these broken scenarios that we were looking at and try and fix them in practice one strategy is that we could just say, well clearly when somebody works for different companies they should have different public keys for their different roles, and Alice should delegate the appropriate authority to Bob in his role as working for her company, and Zac should do the same to a different role or public key. So here we make the delegation more explicit. And so you see KA to KB working for a different public key altogether, a different role, and that way we avoid the subterfuge. But of course that's assuming that our principles are going to be competent in distinguishing between all of the different roles that they can hold, and how do we know whether we've introduced enough roles? It's an ad hoc situation, oh this is best practice, we go off, we come up with a bunch of keys for different people's roles, and everything seems to work fine.

Another scenario would be to put more precision into the permission names. We saw at the beginning that just having a simple buy100 isn't enough, so what we should do is put in the name of the department that the person's allowed to buy for. But then is the name sufficiently precise? When do we know we have enough information in the name, in effect what we're saying is that the permissions, or the authorisations, that we write should be global in some sense. Where do we get this information from? In trust management schemes like KeyNote, they do things like going to Iana, or Ican, for effectively global names which would correspond to parts of permissions, so that you can uniquely identify your applications that the permission was concerned about. Or maybe you go down the route of having some global name server, or an X500 name, and so on. There's lots of different ways you could try to make your permissions more global. We're still not really sure how in practice.

Ben Laurie: You need to hash your public key.

Reply: Another scenario is we use public keys as global identifiers, and so we encode a key into the permission name like this. But the problem then is that the humans are looking at these permissions and they're saying, woe, there's all these hex values in front of the buy100, what does it all mean, and they'd probably do what Ross is suggesting and say, oh just delegate all authority because it doesn't make any sense to me. And going down the route of something like local names isn't going to work either because local names are local to local name spaces, while permissions need to be global across all named places.

Another problem is that we have transient permissions. Remember these are authorisations to use resources, should they be transient or non-transient, do they change with time. So things like public keys change with time, so if you have a public key encoded in a permission as representing a unique global name for that particular, or accessing a particular resource, what happens when that public key has to be revoked and replaced with another one, all of those certificates involved in that permission are going to have to be reissued, which flies in the face of what some of the trust management system schemes would have you do. Of course you could have global names like domain names but look at say panix.com, who'd have thought that a domain name would be transient, but panix.com wasn't transient at all, it's something that changed, it was the same name but all of a sudden there was a different company behind it. And of course there's this overhead of having to reissue certificates that contain transient permissions.

If you look at non-transient permissions, these are permanent global permissions that stick around forever, but of course don't forget the certificate that the permission is in can have a time limit. To my understanding, X.500 is a non-transient way of naming things, we could have some kind of global name directory services, and presumably these would be non-transient as well. One question given that transience is something that's inevitable, should certificates be transient and contain non-transient permissions, or should we also allow transient permissions, permissions that can change. I don't know.

What we began thinking about was this scenario where people do these delegations, passing permissions around the place, and we're worried about this notion of subterfuge, ensuring accountability along the delegation chain. And we're effectively asking this question, is it possible for some malicious user to interfere with the certificate chain with a view to influencing authorisation accountability, and that started sounding very like what we do when we check an authentication protocol. It's like a sort of freshness attack, if we think of a protocol step, it's an encrypted message exchanged between principals while the certificate is more or less the same kind of thing, it's a signed message exchanged between principals, an authentication protocol is a sequence of protocol steps, a certificate chain is a sequence of certificates, freshness in a protocol attempts to fix a message to a rung of a protocol, while what we're trying to do with accountability is try and make the permission delegation accountable within some particular chain.

So a superficial view of subterfuge is a freshness attack, but the idea is to take the existing protocol analysis techniques and to adapt them to be able to analyse delegation schemes for subterfuge, if you're willing to believe that subterfuge is some kind freshness attack. Hongbin has been working on this, and has more or less completed a logic called subterfuge logic which can be used to analyse subterfuge in delegation schemes.

To conclude, we started off with the premise that a certificate chain gives us delegation accountability. We saw that if we're not careful about how we design chains we can end up with the potential for authorisation subterfuge. Now normally in the real world there would be some ad hoc techniques, or strategies: we'd put public keys in the permissions, we use global names, or X.500 names, we add all this stuff into the permissions in a sort of best practice way, that gives us confidence that there won't be any subterfuge. But really what we should be doing is trying to analyse our delegation scheme, the way we're putting the permissions together, and the way they get delegated, using some kind of logic so that we that we get some kind of assurance that subterfuge isn't possible. In effect, where does the buck stop when we do a delegation chain.

Mark Lomas: Is there anything to say for using dual control schemes, I delegate the red key to X, provided X did not have the blue key to do it.

Reply: Hongbin has an authorisation logic which builds on top of the subterfuge logic, and the authorisation logic is a more powerful version of delegation logic, or RT logic, it's like delegation logic but with ability to deal with subterfuge. So the kinds of things that you can say, things like separation of duty rules, could be said within this more extended logic. Is that fair?

Frank Stajano: Please correct me if I have a wrong model, my view of this delegation certificate chain is that, in the context of the buy100 example, they are only usable once. So if I give someone the delegation to buy100, they can buy100, and then they have used it up and then they can come back to me for another one if they need to buy100 again. Is this true or false?

Reply: False.

Frank Stajano: So how can you stop the abuse if someone has buy100 and they buy100 a million times in an hour?

Reply: You're allowed to make individual purchases, up to a limit of 100, so the 100 is like a cheque card, it's just saying on any individual transaction you have the authorisation to buy up to 100, but of course you can make multiple transactions. I'm not trying to prevent Clare from going out and spending a million, all it's doing is putting a control on the size of things that she can buy.

Frank Stajano: The reason why I was asking this is because if it were a once only thing, then that would be a fairly strict resource allocation control which we would seem in my eyes to nullify the problem of the subterfuge, because you would know if it has come that way.

Reply: Yes, indeed, what you're doing is like saying, if I can put freshness into my credential, the subterfuge goes away. And doesn't that sound familiar, like the kind of things we do with authentication protocols, we try to make sure messages are fresh, or at least fresh to the run of the protocol.

Ben Laurie: Your objections to putting public keys on this is that local names don't work. I don't buy that because I only use local names for the permissions that I've actually been given. I only need to know my local name of the guy who gave the permission to me.

Reply: But if you have a permission, and you've got a local name for that permission, you're then going to give it to somebody else. How, in your local namespace, to translate to another local name in somebody else's namespace.

Ben Laurie: It doesn't matter. What I've got is a number, and I map it to a name that's meaningful to me, and they get the same number and they map it to a different name.

Reply: OK, so you're saying that the number, would be like a public key for that local name, assuming that the public key is unique, so yes, OK. If you want to use the public keys underneath the local names, which is what we were saying, you can use public keys within the permission. But the disadvantage of that is that they're transient, what happens if you need to re-key, you must throw all your permissions out and start again from scratch.

Multi-channel Protocols

Ford-Long Wong and Frank Stajano

University of Cambridge

Abstract. We examine several ad-hoc pairing protocols that strengthen their radio exchanges with additional transmissions over another channel, for example a screen showing graphically encoded information to a camera. Additional channels may have limited capacity and may still be subject to eavesdropping, but they may offer specific advantages over radio such as data origin authenticity. A single protocol may profitably use more than one channel, each with its own specific security properties, for different messages in its trace. Making this option explicit allows for further advances in protocol design.

We also present an intriguing asymmetric protocol that achieves results comparable to mutual authentication even though the verification happens only in one direction.

1 Introduction

The problem of authentication between two devices that meet for the first time has been extensively studied and is particularly significant in ubiquitous computing. In this paper we revisit the problem subject to the following constraints. We first assume that the devices cannot rely on a certification authority, on a Kerberos-style authentication server or on any other kind of third-party introducer. We then assume that their main communication channel is radio, meaning that they can never be sure whether they are talking to the expected device or to any other compatible device within range. We also consider that attackers may eavesdrop on the radio channel (obvious) and even insert or modify messages (non-trivial but still possible[1]). Under these constraints, reliable authentication is hard if not impossible.

We make the situation more manageable by assuming the presence of an extra channel between the devices: if, for example, one device has a screen and the other a camera, a suitable graphical encoding can be used to transfer bits from the first to the second over a visual channel. This possibility has obvious practical relevance given the growing popularity of camera phones in recent years. A slight variation on this theme is for the second device to have a keypad, and for the human operator to enter into the second device a sequence of characters displayed on the screen of the first. There is a great variety of options for extra

---

[1] The simplest case in which this might happen is one in which devices A and B are out of range of each other but both in range of the attacker-in-the-middle M. A more elaborate setting is described by Kügler [7] in the context of Bluetooth: M establishes connections with both A and B but on different hopping sequences.

B. Christianson et al. (Eds.): Security Protocols 2005, LNCS 4631, pp. 112–127, 2007.

channels including direct electrical contact, infrared, typing the same PIN into both devices, modulated audio beeps, voice and so on. Several of these, and among them the visual channel available to camera phones, enjoy the useful property of "data origin authenticity" that the radio channel does not possess: the user of the receiving device knows for sure that the received data was sent by the intended source device.

1.1   Contributions

We offer two main contributions in this paper.

The use of more than one channel, each with different security properties, in the context of a single security protocol, is not in itself new: in the context of ad-hoc authentication and pairing the Resurrecting Duckling model by Stajano and Anderson [11] specified that, in contrast with any other messages later exchanged between Mother and Duckling over the wireless channel, imprinting had to be carried out using direct electrical contact. The problem of pairing, and the idea of supplementing a radio interaction with communication over another medium, was revisited by several researchers. Among the most significant recent contributions we recognize at least Gehrmann and Nyberg [3], who use the "manual transfer" channel of typing a code on a keypad; Hoepman [6], who discusses various types of "authentic" and "private" channels; and McCune et al. [8], who apply a visual channel based on cameras and 2D barcodes to the protocols originally proposed by Balfanz et al. [1]. Outside the context of authentication, Stajano and Anderson built the Cocaine Auction Protocol [10] on the primitive of "anonymous broadcast" and then explored channels that would provide it, either natively or through the intermediation of a sub-protocol.

However, with hindsight, there are much older examples of multi-channel protocols: one is the geek practice of printing the hash of one's PGP key on one's business card (which offers higher integrity than the web page with the full key); another, as old as cryptography itself, is the fundamental idea of transmitting the symmetric key using a more secure channel than the one used for the ciphertext. Multi-channel protocols have therefore implicitly existed for millennia. We argue, however, that recognizing them as such is a significant change of perspective.

One of the original contributions of this paper is to explicitly introduce multi-channel protocol modelling as a new powerful design and analysis tool. The other is a surprising multi-channel pairing protocol for the asymmetric situation in which only one of the two devices can acquire a code from the other over the extra channel.

1.2   Structure of This Paper

We review and compare a number of pairing protocols that make use of multiple channels, discussing advantages and limitations of the channels used. Our original contributions mentioned above are in sections 8 and 7 respectively.

Section 2   We start with a trivial example of multi-channel protocol by showing that a Diffie-Hellman exchange over radio requires an extra channel to resist middleperson attacks.

Section 3 The limited capacity of the extra channel (how long a PIN will your users be willing to type?) opens the door to a brute-force attack by a middleperson.

Section 4 Cameras and screens in mobile phones provide a channel that, while still of limited capacity, can carry a long enough code to defeat the attack of the previous section. A protocol that uses this technique is SiB.

Section 5 With the proliferation of CCTV, many of the proposed extra channels can no longer be considered as guaranteeing confidentiality. Following this insight, we revisit a protocol built to resist the attack of section 3, MANA III, and show that it becomes vulnerable if the attacker can eavesdrop on the extra channel.

Section 6 We discuss a variant of the previous protocol, broadly equivalent to φKE, that uses short codes on the extra channel but remains secure against middleperson even in the presence of an eavesdropper on the extra channel.

Section 7 We present a new pairing protocol for the asymmetric case of a uni-directional visual channel. It appears incomplete at first sight, which is what makes it interesting.

Section 8 Finally, against the backdrop of the protocol design and analysis of the previous sections, we discuss the general applicability of multi-channel protocol modelling and some of the research challenges of this new field.

2   Diffie-Hellman Key Establishment over Radio

An established session key may be used to authenticate subsequent requests and an encryption key may be derived from it to protect communication confidentiality. During the key establishment process we want to ensure that the key is being established with the intended correspondent. As we said, we assume we cannot rely on a third-party introducer; we therefore exclude the use of static asymmetric-key or symmetric-key certificates.

In the Resurrecting Duckling model [11], trust is bootstrapped from a secret transferred via a secure channel between the two parties. The recommended secure channel is physical contact: it gives a strong guarantee that the shared key has been established between the two chosen devices and no others, with high confidentiality and integrity. It makes cryptography redundant for key establishment. Wired contacts on personal devices, however, are surprisingly expensive in the eyes of manufacturing engineers once we take into account not just the cost of the connectors but the additional board area and the geometrical and ergonomic constraints on industrial design.

It should be clear, however, that carrying out a Diffie-Hellman exchange over RF gives no guarantees about the party with which one is establishing a key. The process is therefore vulnerable to a middleperson attack. Even if each of the two parties successfully challenges the other to prove ownership of the established

#	Alice	Bob
	Basic DH	
1	Chooses random a	Chooses random b
2	$- g^a \rightarrow$	
3	$\leftarrow g^b -$	
4	$K = (g^a)^b$	$K' = (g^b)^a$
	B challenges A	
5		Chooses random C_b
6	$\leftarrow C_b -$	
7	$M_1' = H(K, C_b)$	$M_1 = H(K', C_b)$
8	$- M_1' \rightarrow$	
9		Verify $M_1' = M_1$
	A challenges B	
10	Chooses random C_a	
11	$- C_a \rightarrow$	
12	$M_2 = H(K, C_a)$	$M_2' = H(K', C_a)$
13	$\leftarrow M_2' -$	
14	Verify $M_2' = M_2$	

Protocol Trace 1. Diffie-Hellman with key confirmation

key, as in steps 5–9 and 10–14 of Protocol Trace 1, the confirmation phase can never prove that the key was established with the desired party.

The obvious remedy is to have steps 8 and 13 take place over an extra channel, such as manual transfer [3] or visual transfer [8], that guarantees data origin authenticity. Manual transfer may be implemented by displaying on the first device a string that encodes the MAC and by having the user type this string into the other device. This channel has limited capacity because it is unpleasantly laborious for human users to transfer long strings manually without making mistakes. One may then have to transmit a truncated MAC. This leads to an attack.

3   Attack Against Short Codes on the Extra Channel

As pointed out by Gehrmann et al. [4, section 2.3], if the manually transferred authentication code is too short then a middleperson attack is still possible.

The attack is shown in Protocol Trace 2. The column 'Ch' describes whether the step consists of a transfer over the radio (RF) channel or over the manual (M) channel. In the context of this protocol trace, when we say RF we mean a channel subject to eavesdropping and substitution attacks and with no data origin authenticity, but no practical limits on capacity. When we say M we mean a channel offering data origin authenticity but with very limited capacity, of the order of 10–20 bits per message.

As the MACs must be short in order to be transmitted over the M channel, it is computationally feasible for middleperson Carol to search for second

#	Ch	Alice	Carol	Bob
1		Chooses random a		
2	RF	$- g^a \rightarrow$		
3			Chooses random a'	
4	RF		$- g^{a'} \rightarrow$	
5				Chooses random b
6	RF		$\leftarrow g^b -$	
7			$K_{bc} = (g^b)^{a'}$	$K_{bc} = (g^{a'})^b$
8				Chooses random C_b
9	RF		$\leftarrow C_b -$	
10			$M_1 = H(K_{bc}, C_b)$	$M_1 = H(K_{bc}, C_b)$
11			Chooses random b'	
12	RF		$\leftarrow g^{b'} -$	
13		$K_{ac} = (g^a)^{b'}$	$K_{ac} = (g^{b'})^a$	
14			Finds C_b' s.t. $H(K_{ac}, C_b') = M_1$	
15	RF		$\leftarrow C_b' -$	
16		$M_1' = H(K_{ac}, C_b')$		
17	M	$- M_1' \rightarrow$	$\rightarrow$	$\rightarrow$
18				Verify $M_1' = M_1$
19		Chooses random C_a		
20	RF	$- C_a \rightarrow$		
21		$M_2 = H(K_{ac}, C_a)$	$M_2 = H(K_{ac}, C_a)$	
22			Finds C_a' s.t. $H(K_{bc}, C_a') = M_2$	
23	RF		$- C_a' \rightarrow$	
24				$M_2' = H(K_{bc}, C_a')$
25	M	$\leftarrow$	$\leftarrow$	$\leftarrow M_2' -$
26		Verify $M_2' = M_2$		

Protocol Trace 2. Middleperson Attack on Short MACs

pre-images. After intercepting Alice's key contribution (step 2), Carol pretends to Bob that she is Alice and establishes a key with him (steps 3–7).

At this point Bob wishes to challenge his RF correspondent, whom he hopes to be Alice; the verification code will be received over the extra channel (step 17) and will therefore undeniably come from Alice. What does Carol do to fool Bob?

After receiving Bob's challenge C_b in step 9 and computing the keyed hash value M_1 in step 10 from the session key shared with Bob, Carol forms a session key with Alice (steps 11–13) and performs a brute force search (step 14) to find a challenge C_b' such that the keyed hash value M_1' derived from it equals M_1. She sends the forged challenge C_b' to Alice (step 15). Alice computes M_1' (step 16) and shows this result over the manual transfer channel (step 17) to Bob, who verifies it (step 18) against his computed result M_1 and finds that it matches. Bob has been fooled.

Carol then performs the same forgery in the symmetrical situation of Alice challenging Bob (steps 19–26), fooling Alice as well.

The effort required by Carol to attack each challenge-response is of the order of 2^r trials, where r is the bit length of each short MAC. Assuming an adversary with powerful computing resources who is able to perform 1 billion trials a second, and a device time-out of 10 seconds, Gehrmann et al. [4] calculate that a 48-bit code is needed to defeat this attack. But manually transferring 48 bits (which correspond to 12 hexadecimal digits) is tedious and prone to error. One alternative is to use an extra channel of greater capacity.

4   SiB and the Camera-Phone Visual Channel

It is possible to acquire the code from the screen with a camera instead of typing it on the keypad. The number of bits that can be reliably transferred is slightly greater and usability improves significantly [12].

At the time of writing, the camera phones commercially available in Europe have reached resolutions of $1280 \times 1024 = 1.3$ megapixels (3.2 megapixels in Asia). In reality, the limiting factor for data transmission is not so much the camera resolution but the screen resolution, which is the lower of the two. Screen resolutions have reached 66 kilopixels, though 36 kilopixels are still more common. Based on these figures, with a suitable 2D encoding the screen-to-camera channel can reliably provide about 40 to 100 bits per message. This is still not enough for a full hash but it is sufficient for a longer code that would solve the problem described in the previous section.

We built a prototype on a Nokia Series 60 handphone, using 2-track SpotCodes [5] that provided 46 bits. We used Diffie-Hellman over elliptic curve groups. The protocol we developed, which we shall discuss in section 6, was later discovered to be basically equivalent to Hoepman's φKE [6]. In our implementation, one run of the protocol took several seconds. A good fraction of this time was taken by aligning the camera phone with the other phone displaying the code. Current phones are usable but not optimal for this task: there are problems of focusing distance, resolution and illumination.

The idea of transferring short cryptographic codes visually between camera phones was originally proposed by McCune et al. [8]. Their SiB protocol, based on earlier work by Balfanz et al. [1], closes the vulnerability pointed out in section 3 by transferring a longer code over the extra channel. The protocol would still fail if the attacker could find a preimage but, because the camera phone channel used by the authors allows 68 bits per transfer (well over twice the capacity of a manually typed PIN), the brute force search is no longer feasible in real time. In other words, SiB requires at least a "medium length" code, not a "short" code[2].

---

[2] Our very informal semantics for "short", "medium" and "long" codes in this context are as follows. "Short" is a code that can be brute-forced in a few seconds, during a run of the protocol, for example 10 bits. "Medium" is a code that can be brute-forced in an hour, a day or a month but not in real time during a protocol run, for example 50 bits. "Long" is a full length code that, assuming the hash function is not otherwise broken, cannot be brute-forced in hundreds of years, for example 250 bits. If we were being more formal about these terms then we would say something

5   MANA III and Eavesdropping on the Extra Channel

There is however another threat. In protocols that implicitly or explicitly use an additional channel, as happens in many EKE variants in which a strong session key is formed from a weak PIN, there is often the assumption that the additional channel is somehow "local" and safe from eavesdropping.

We argue that, for the manual (screen and keypad or keypad and keypad) and for the visual (screen and camera) channel, this assumption is no longer realistic with the current proliferation of CCTV cameras, both indoors and outdoors. In many cases such cameras even operate covertly, hidden behind opaque domes that allow them to pan and zoom without the victims knowing where the cameras are pointing.

In this section we discuss the consequences of this change in the attacker model.

The MANA III scheme by Gehrmann et al. [4], developed as a variant of Larsson's SHAKE[3], is shown in Protocol Trace 3. It aims to establish that both parties have correctly received each other's public key. It complements the radio transmissions with an exchange of short codes using manual transfer. As the authors themselves say, "Informally, the security of the scheme relies on the fact that R remains secret to the attacker (it is never sent over the air)...". In the presence of a passive attacker in the optical domain, which we believe can no longer be dismissed, this protocol can be cracked.

I_A and I_B are identifiers of Alice and Bob respectively and are publicly known. D is a data string formed from the concatenation of Alice's and Bob's public keys g^a and g^b. K_1 and K_2 are long keys. M_1 and M_2 are long MAC values formed using the function m. R is a short randomly selected string shared between Alice and Bob over the manual channel. Alice will only send K_1 after she has received M_2, and Bob will only send K_2 after he has received M_1.

Crucially, after the verification (step 14), each device must signal whether the verification succeeded (steps 15 and 16), over a channel (e.g. red/green LED) guaranteeing integrity and data origin authenticity. Although the M channel could be reused here, we indicate this channel as L (LED), rather than M, to point out that its requirements are less demanding than those of the channel used in step 6. In particular, its required capacity is only one bit per message. Note the additional subtlety that the LED is signalling to the *operator* of the device(s), not to the other device directly.

As noted in the original paper, if Bob were not told that Alice's verification failed, middleperson Carol could send Alice a random M_2 in step 10, grab K_1 from Alice in step 11, ignore the rest of the protocol run with Alice, find R by brute force and successfully impersonate Alice to Bob, who would not notice the forgery.

---

about the distinction between finding collisions and finding second preimages; but we aren't, so we don't.

[3] This work is cited in the bibliography of the Gehrmann paper but we have not been able to obtain a copy of the Larsson paper or even to confirm the correctness of the citation.

#	Ch	Alice	Bob
1		Chooses random a	Chooses random b
2	RF	$- g^a \rightarrow$	
3	RF	$\leftarrow g^b -$	
4		$D = g^a \mid g^b$	$D = g^a \mid g^b$
5		Chooses random R	
6	V	$- R \rightarrow$	
7		Chooses random K_1	Chooses random K_2
8		$M_1 = m_{K_1}(I_A \mid D \mid R)$	$M_2 = m_{K_2}(I_B \mid D \mid R)$
9	RF	$- M_1 \rightarrow$	
10	RF	$\leftarrow M_2 -$	
11	RF	$- K_1 \rightarrow$	
12	RF	$\leftarrow K_2 -$	
13		$M_2' = m_{K_2}(I_B \mid D \mid R)$	$M_1' = m_{K_1}(I_A \mid D \mid R)$
14		Verifies $M_2 = M_2'$	Verifies $M_1 = M_1'$
15	L	$-$ outcome $\rightarrow$	
16	L	$\leftarrow$ outcome $-$	

Protocol Trace 3. MANA III

The reason why the attack of section 3 no longer works is essentially because the short code exchanged over the extra channel is not the MAC but the challenge: the MAC, now transmitted over radio, is full length and not subject to second preimage attacks. The protocol's security, however, relies on the challenge R being kept secret from the middleperson attacker.

If this assumption is violated, the attack is as follows. Assume that middleperson Carol is able to observe the string R being keyed into the devices. She may then send modified public keys to both Alice and Bob, such that Alice's and Bob's copies of D are different from each other's, but match the two copies held by Carol. Thereafter, Carol can individually choose different K's and generate the M's so as to authenticate successfully with both Alice and Bob. Note that this attack is independent of the length of the MACs.

6 Short Codes and Eavesdropper Resistance

Sections 3 and 4 have shown protocols that can be cracked if the attacker can brute-force in real time the short code sent over the extra channel; they therefore require at least a "medium length" code. Section 5 has shown a protocol that resists brute force even with a short code, but which is vulnerable if the attacker can eavesdrop on the extra channel. Is it possible to come up with a protocol that transmits only short codes (rather than "medium" ones) on the extra channel but, despite that, is not broken by eavesdropping?

We developed such a protocol as a variant of MANA III and presented it at the workshop, although we later discovered that it was essentially equivalent to Hoepman's earlier φKE [6]. In both cases, the extra channel (whether

#	Ch	Alice	Bob
1		Chooses random a	Chooses random b
2	RF	$- g^a \rightarrow$	
3	RF	$\leftarrow g^b -$	
4		Chooses random R_a	Chooses random R_b
5		Chooses random K_a	Chooses random K_b
6		$H_1 = H(I_A \mid g^a \mid g^b \mid R_a \mid K_a)$	$H_2 = H(I_B \mid g^b \mid g^a \mid R_b \mid K_b)$
7	RF	$- H_1 \rightarrow$	
8	RF	$\leftarrow H_2 -$	
9	V	$- R_a \rightarrow$	
10	V	$\leftarrow R_b -$	
11	RF	$- K_a \rightarrow$	
12	RF	$\leftarrow K_b -$	
13		$H_2' = H(I_B \mid g^b \mid g^a \mid R_b \mid K_b)$	$H_1' = H(I_A \mid g^a \mid g^b \mid R_a \mid K_a)$
14		Verifies $H_2 = H_2'$	Verifies $H_1 = H_1'$
15	L	$-$ outcome $\rightarrow$	
16	L	$\leftarrow$ outcome $-$	

Protocol Trace 4. Our MANA III variant

screen-to-camera or screen-to-keypad) is exploited for its integrity and data origin authenticity rather than for its confidentiality.

For our proposed protocol, given in Protocol Trace 4, the core objective remains the same—to assure that a session key is being established with the correct party. The pre-conditions are an RF channel having low confidentiality and low integrity, and a bandwidth-limited optical channel having low confidentiality but high integrity and high data origin authenticity.

R_a and R_b are short random nonces. K_a and K_b are long nonces. H_1, H_1', H_2 and H_2' are long hashes.

Each party generates an ephemeral Diffie-Hellman private value, computes the corresponding public key and sends it to the other party. Alice chooses a short random R_a (step 4), a long random K_a (step 5), and hashes the concatenation of these with her identifier I_A and the public keys, into a long hash H_1 (step 6). Bob does likewise and produces a long hash H_2. Next, Alice and Bob both send over the RF channel their computed hashes to each other, which represent their commitments (steps 7 and 8). Bob must indicate that he has received a hash, and only then, and not before, Alice may release R_a over the visual channel and K_a over the radio channel. Similarly, Alice must indicate that she has a received a hash and only then, and not before, is Bob allowed to release R_b and K_b. After all the R and K have been received, both sides proceed to compute the hashes and verify that they match the copies they had received earlier in steps 7 and 8.

The length of the long hashes determines the size of the complexity theoretic problem a potential middleperson attacker would face for finding their second pre-images. The length of the visually exchanged R values determines the probability or "luck" the attacker would have in choosing coincidentally the same R

values for the commitments as Alice and Bob might later choose. (We'll get back to this at the end of this section.)

The protocol is symmetric: steps 7, 9 and 11 prove to Bob that he is communicating with Alice; conversely, steps 8, 10 and 12 prove to Alice that she is talking to Bob. If one set of steps is absent, the authentication is only unilateral. We explore this case in section 7.

Compared to MANA III, this protocol relies on the strong data origin authenticity property of the extra channel rather than on its confidentiality: when an R value is exchanged, we have high confidence that it originated from the observed party. The difference is that, here, both parties must issue their commitments H before the release of any of the R and K values. Therefore an attacker Carol who manages to observe the R values will be too late to compromise the key agreement, because she must have already committed to a fake H for which she will not be able to generate a matching K.

One may wonder why we need the K values, if the unforgeable R values are there. This is because, if there were no K_a, middleperson Carol could otherwise intercept Alice's H_1 in step 7 and try all possible values for R_a until she found the one that produced the correct hash. At that point Carol would be able to substitute her own key $g^{\tilde{a}}$, compute the hash $H(I_A \mid g^{\tilde{a}} \mid g^b \mid R_a)$ and send it to Bob. Since the R_a is the genuine one that Alice will later disclose, Bob will find that the H'_1 he computes in step 13 will match this one he received from Carol in step 7 (all the inputs are the same). So the K values are there to prevent Carol from brute-forcing the R values out of the H values.

If step 14 completes with successful mutual verification of the hashes, both parties will have high confidence that the party from whom each has visually obtained the R value is the same party from whom each has received a public key. As in the original MANA III protocol, both devices must finally indicate (steps 15 and 16) whether the verification succeeded or not: each device should only consider the protocol run successful after receiving proof that the *other* device also succeeded during step 14.

As hinted at above, the middleperson attacker Carol has basically two options. In the first option, she guesses an R value, inserts a modified public key and a hash computed from a random K value, and then hopes that the spoofed party will coincidentally choose the same R value. The probability of this attack succeeding is 2^{-r} where r is the bit length of the R value. Carol has less than 1% chance of success for an R as short as 7 bits. In the second attack option, Carol inserts a modified public key and a random hash. After the R value is disclosed by the spoofed party, the attacker embarks on a search for a K value which can yield the hash she has already committed to. The complexity of such a search is of the order of 2^h where h is the bit length of the hash. Since we said H was "long", this is by definition infeasible.

Thus the protocol is strong even under the model of a powerful attacker who is able to eavesdrop on the extra channel and rewrite messages on the RF channel, and in a situation in which the extra channel can only carry a "short" (not even "medium") payload.

7   Asymmetric Pairing

Now imagine the case in which the devices are not peers and the visual channel can only be established in one direction. For example, one device is a large stand-alone screen with some local processing power; it sits in a shop window and displays a pre-programmed sequence of text and graphics. The other device is a PDA that, every week or two, uploads a new sequence into the screen over radio.

The screen needs to be imprinted to the PDA of the shopkeeper so as to prevent anyone else from uploading messages to the screen. We assume that the PDA has a camera but the screen doesn't; and that, owing to industrial design constraints, it is not possible to use a wired connection between the two. Our goal is to devise a sufficiently secure method to perform the Resurrecting Duckling's imprinting operation in the absence of a wired contact.

Taking Alice as the mother duck PDA and Bob as the duckling screen, we cannot perform all the exchanges in Protocol Trace 4 because the visual channel only works from B to A; the message in step 9 cannot be sent and this cancels out the whole subprotocol in which A acts as prover and B as verifier (steps 7, 9, 11, 16 and Bob's half of steps 13 and 14).

The bits we can still do are in Protocol Trace 5. After successful completion, Alice the PDA is assured that she has established a key with Bob the screen, but Bob receives no proof that he is being imprinted to the correct PDA. This seems incomplete, which is what makes this protocol interesting.

What we wish to avoid is for Bob to be persuaded to imprint itself to another device Carol. How can this be stopped if Bob knows nothing about the device with which it is pairing? In the Resurrecting Duckling policy, introduced in [11] and formalized in [9, section 4.2.5], Bob the duckling imprints itself to the first mother duck he sees, whoever she is. What we want here is to prevent Carol from

#	Ch	Alice (mother duck)		Bob (duckling)
0	PW			Start imprinting
1		Chooses random a		Chooses random b
2	RF		$- g^a \rightarrow$	
3	RF		$\leftarrow g^b -$	
4				Chooses random R_b
5				Chooses random K_b
6				$H_2 = H(I_B \mid g^b \mid g^a \mid R_b \mid K_b)$
7	RF		$\leftarrow H_2 -$	
8	PB		$- \text{ack} \rightarrow$	
9	V		$\leftarrow R_b -$	
10	RF		$\leftarrow K_b -$	
11		$H_2' = H(I_B \mid g^b \mid g^a \mid R_b \mid K_b)$		
12		Verifies $H_2 = H_2'$		
13	PB		$- \text{outcome} \rightarrow$	

Protocol Trace 5. Asymmetric pairing

appearing in front of Bob for imprinting before he has a chance to see Alice. A crucial element of the solution is the presence of a human operator who wishes to imprint Bob to Alice.

Although manufacturers would love to get away with a Bob that had no other inputs than a wireless interface, we believe we also need at least the following:

1. a way to ask Bob to start imprinting;
2. a way to tell Bob whether to proceed or not, before committing to a proposed imprinting.

These two input mechanisms must be available only to a human operator Hermione having physical control of device Bob. The intention is to construct a protocol that cannot be subverted by hidden middleperson device Carol so long as human operator Hermione has physical control of duckling device Bob during the imprinting phase. Once imprinting is over, duckling device Bob may be left unattended: the Duckling policy will ensure that it can't be taken over by Carol or anyone else unless the mother duck device Alice first voluntarily relinquishes control.

Mechanism 1 could be implemented as nothing more than the act of switching on device Bob when he is still in his imprintable state. This is indicated (very poorly) as step 0 in the trace, with PW indicating the "power" channel. Mechanism 2, on the other hand, could be implemented as two mutually exclusive pushbuttons (yes/no, ok/cancel, proceed/abort...), indicated as channel PB in step 13.

The exchange presented in Protocol Trace 5, obtained from Protocol Trace 4 by removing the steps in which Alice authenticates to Bob[4], proves to Alice that she and Bob are using the same two public keys g^a and g^b. Once human operator Hermione is satisfied that device Alice completed her verification succesfully in step 12, Hermione presses the "yes" pushbutton (step 13) on duckling device Bob, thereby ordering Bob to compute and commit to the imprinting key g^{ab}. If Hermione observes that Alice's verification failed, she presses pushbutton "no" (or lets Bob abandon the protocol by timeout[5]) and Bob forgets the previous exchange and remains imprintable.

An unattended attacking device Carol, with ability to eavesdrop on the V channel and with ability to rewrite messages on the RF channel, cannot imprint Bob to herself unless she can also *press* the "yes" pushbutton used in step 12 to commit the imprinting. Even if Carol had a mechanical finger that allowed her to press Bob's button, it is expected that Hermione would notice this and disallow it—that's the point of Hermione "having physical control" of Bob.

---

[4] Note that we had to introduce a "content-free" step 8 to maintain synchronization. Bob should only display R_b after being sure that Alice received a hash. In Protocol Trace 4, this was achieved implicitly by Alice having to send something useful in step 9. Here, even though she has nothing useful to send at that stage, she must still signal to Bob, over the unforgeable extra channel, that she received the hash and that he can proceed.

[5] This could also be exploited as a way to allow just one pushbutton rather than two.

This protocol is interesting because it seems incomplete. Alice never proves herself to Bob. Bob doesn't actually know with whom he paired. Something appears to be missing. And yet, it works: Bob can only pair with the correct Alice (even if he can't recognize her) because Hermione won't let him proceed otherwise.

In the protocol of section 6, we achieved mutual authentication with a bidirectional "short" extra channel. In this protocol we show that we can achieve the same result even with a unidirectional "short" extra channel channel coupled with an even shorter "one bit only" extra channel in the opposite direction. In a sense, Bob is delegating his trust to Alice and Hermione.

Note that this core idea (tricky delegation-based mutual authentication despite asymmetric extra channel) could have been demostrated with a much simpler protocol if the unidirectional extra channel had been allowed to be "long" rather than "short"; but this is true of most of the other protocols we discussed, which would have all basically reduced to a Diffie-Hellman augmented with unforgeable transmission of the hashes of the keys.

8   Multi-channel Protocols: Towards More Expressive Protocol Modelling

We have looked at a variety of modern protocols that make use of multiple channels. As we noted in section 1.1, multi-channel protocols have been implicitly used for thousands of years but it is time to recognize that thinking explicitly in terms of multiple channels is a powerful technique for protocol design and analysis. We shall now highlight our future work plans for expressive modelling of multi-channel protocols.

To reason accurately about multi-channel protocols we need first of all a good **notation**. The protocol traces in this paper have used line-by-line listings with an explicit indication of the channel used in each step; while we believe this to be an improvement over previous practice, this notation is still not satisfactory and does not capture all the relevant details.

For example, messages 17 and 25 in Protocol Trace 2 are transmitted over the manual channel M and therefore, unlike the others, cannot be rewritten by Carol. We have shown them as "going through" Carol but this is not entirely accurate. This notation does not clearly distinguish whether Carol may or may not observe them—indeed, in section 3, where that protocol trace appears, we still assume she can't, while in section 5 we assume she can.

Stajano and Anderson [10] discussed channels whose transmission primitive was point-to-point send, point-to-domain broadcast or point-to-domain anonymous broadcast and then proposed a notation to make such distinctions explicit. Unfortunately it is not sufficiently general for analyzing all possible multi-channel protocols.

The intermediation and consent of a locally present human, featured in the last step of Protocol Traces 3, 4 and 5, should also be captured more explicitly by the notation. It might perhaps be abstracted away through a more rigorous definition of the associated one-bit channel, but the special role of Hermione in the asymmetric protocol of section 7 must also be taken into account.

The interaction with the human operator should also be described more clearly in step 0 of Protocol Trace 5: it is human Hermione who forces device Bob to start the imprinting, but this is not clear from the protocol trace which only describes the interactions between devices Alice and Bob.

There should also be a more explicit mention of temporal dependencies. In Protocol Trace 4, for example, there are pairs of messages that might be swapped without affecting the protocol (for example 2 and 3); but there are other cases in which return messages are implicitly used as ACKs, for example when Alice's reception of Bob's message 8 is significant not just for its contents but also because it signals that Bob received Alice's message 7, meaning that Alice may now release R_a over the visual channel. See what happens in Protocol Trace 5 when we remove the interleaved messages: it is necessary to reintroduce an "empty" message precisely because we need an ACK before proceeding (cfr. footnote 4). A notation that specified which dependencies really matter, perhaps inspired by PERT charts, might be more expressive and would highlight alternative linearizations, possibly leading to more efficient (e.g. shorter, when two adjacent messages may be collapsed into one) message sequences.

The notation should also feature a legend detailing the properties required of the various channels used. In this paper we have discussed primarily confidentiality, integrity, user-friendliness, origin authenticity and carrying capacity. There are of course other properties, including at least anonymity, covertness, range, cost (equipment costs and running costs) and latency. For some of these properties a boolean qualifier makes no sense; for most of the remaining ones it is at best an oversimplification. And then are the trade-offs: for a channel of limited carrying capacity per message, one could increase that capacity by sending several messages in a row, probably at the expense of latency, usability and running costs. It will be hard to settle on the correct level of abstraction— not so generic that is becomes content-free but not so detailed that it becomes unusable.

Following on from this, while in this paper we have used ad-hoc descriptions in the main text, it would be useful to have a uniform and coherent **taxonomy** of channel properties and of channels so as to be able to compare the channel requirements of any two protocols. Listing such requirements explicitly will clarify whether a given protocol may be run over any other channels than the ones originally intended—perhaps new ones that had not even been invented when the protocol was designed. More importantly, it will make the protocol authors more aware of the details of their design, which in itself may help avoid some errors. The expressiveness and clarity of the notation used to express an idea is an important factor in avoiding implementation errors, as is well known from programming languages.

Note also that, once its properties have been stated, a complex channel may be implemented on top of a more primitive channel that had different properties: see the discussion of anonymous broadcast in the cited Cocaine Auction paper but also all the composite channels offered by the likes of IPSEC and SSL on top of a basic packet network.

Finally, the last and perhaps the most important tool we need is a **logic** for multi-channel protocols in the spirit of BAN [2]: a framework of simple rules (sending a message on a certain channel leads to certain consequences, properties and beliefs for the various parties involved) that either allows a protocol designer to prove that a protocol achieves its goal or, if it can't, gives clues as to why it probably doesn't.

9   Conclusions

With this paper we explicitly open up the field of multi-channel protocols. Until now, protocols were described primarily in terms of sender, recipient, payload and sequencing order. Instead, it may be advantageous to send different messages of the protocol over different channels and take into account the different properties of the various channels.

We have presented a surprising asymmetric pairing protocol: by carefully exploiting the properties of its channels, it provides mutual authentication even if the proof only happens in one direction.

Finally, we have charted in detail the plans for some future work that will enable effective modelling of multi-channel protocols. We believe that multi-channel protocols will become a fertile new field for security protocols research.

Acknowledgements

Thanks to Alf Zugenmaier for pointing us to Hoepman's work.

References

1. Balfanz, D., Smetters, D.K., Stewart, P., Wong, H.C.: Talking to strangers: authentication in ad-hoc wireless networks. In: Network and Distributed System Security Symposium (February 2002)
2. Burrows, M., Abadi, M., Needham, R.: A Logic of Authentication. Tech. Rep. 39, DEC SRC (February 1989)
3. Gehrmann, C., Nyberg, K.: Enhancements to Bluetooth Baseband Security. In: Proc. Nordsec 2001 (November 2001)
4. Gehrmann, C., Mitchell, C.J., Nyberg, K.: Manual authentication for wireless devices. Cryptobytes 7(1), 29–37 (2004)
5. HighEnergyMagic. "SpotCode" (2004), http://www.highenergymagic.com/
6. Hoepman, J.-H.: The Ephemeral Pairing Problem. In: Juels, A. (ed.) FC 2004. LNCS, vol. 3110, pp. 212–226. Springer, Heidelberg (2004)
7. Kügler, D.: Man in the Middle Attacks on Bluetooth. In: Wright, R.N. (ed.) FC 2003. LNCS, vol. 2742, pp. 149–161. Springer, Heidelberg (2003)
8. McCune, J.M., Perrig, A., Reiter, M.K.: Seeing is Believing: Using CameraPhones for Human-Verifiable Authentication. Tech. Rep. CMU-CS-04-174, Carnegie Mellon University (2004)

9. Stajano, F.: Security for Ubiquitous Computing. John Wiley and Sons, Chichester (2002)
10. Stajano, F., Anderson, R.: The Cocaine Auction Protocol — On The Power Of Anonymous Broadcast. In: Pfitzmann, A. (ed.) IH 1999. LNCS, vol. 1768, Springer, Heidelberg (2000)
11. Stajano, F., Anderson, R.: The Resurrecting Duckling — Security issues for Ad-Hoc Wireless Networks. In: Malcolm, J.A., Christianson, B., Crispo, B., Roe, M. (eds.) Security Protocols. LNCS, vol. 1796, Springer, Heidelberg (2000)
12. Toye, E., Madhavapeddy, A., Sharp, R., Scott, D., Blackwell, A.: Using camera-phones to interact with context-aware mobile services. Tech. Rep. UCAM-CL-TR-609, University of Cambridge Computer Laboratory (December 2004)

Multi-channel Protocols

(Transcript of Discussion)

Ford-Long Wong

University of Cambridge

Ben Laurie: So these protocols only work if you actually try and connect devices to each other?

Reply: Because of this type of auxiliary channel, yes, they would need to be next to each other.

Bruce Christianson: If you want to be sure that the two things that you're holding are connected to each other and not to some third party, yes?

Reply: Yes. In the past, someone who can eavesdrop on this auxiliary channel will be able to break your system, so what we're saying here is that with our protocol, they can eavesdrop all they like, but by the time they eavesdrop it's too late. They have to break the hard problem, to calculate the right keys.

Bruce Christianson: Can you remind us why it's not enough for Alice and Bob to just exchange g^a and g^b over the radio channels, and *then* send each other some bits of g^{ab} over the auxiliary channels. Why is that not enough?

Reply: Because an attacker would compute, by brute-force, the possible bits of g^a and g^b which would output the same hash as the particular g^{ab}.

Bruce Christianson: Yes, you'd need 20 bits of that. So the attacker pre-computes a whole range of exponentials?

Reply: Yes. It's necessary only up to the length of the hash, and we know that the auxiliary channel is of a low bandwidth. Let's say the truncated hash of the shared key is only 20 bits, then the difficulty of my attack is just finding a $g^{a'}$ and a $g^{b'}$ such that $g^{ab'}$ and $g^{a'b}$ both hash to the same 20 bits, and since it's only 20 bits, it can pre-computed rather quickly.

Ben Laurie: But how many bits can you transmit over a visual channel?

Reply: You might be able to transfer by hand 8 digits without error. Looking at some camera-equipped devices, people have developed 2D codes - various coding constructs, having different bit lengths. You can even pack up to 83 bits in one type of 2D code tag. You may not always have a camera-equipped device, with a screen and a camera handy, but when you do, you can capture these codes, sufficiently long, and without error. Also, the length of the code in bits is actually just some rule of thumb, ultimately the actual length is influenced by the camera's focal length, the camera resolution, the screen size, screen resolution, and various other factors. Basically these devices are not really designed to be operating at centimetre ranges, and the optimal focusing distance may be one metre or so. So it is pushing the existing technology a bit, and we've learnt quite a lot by looking into this, but we still do manage to capture the 2D codes with the handphone cameras.

B. Christianson et al. (Eds.): Security Protocols 2005, LNCS 4631, pp. 128–132, 2007.
© Springer-Verlag Berlin Heidelberg 2007

Mike Bond: If you want to use phone cameras, how are they related to the spatial resolutions? Is there any reason that you can't add time series of different images in the spatial encoding scheme in order to get a 4-bit scheme?

Reply: Yes, you can do that to increase the entropy.

Mike Bond: Let me guess how it may apply here: rather than try to transmit the MACs between the two phones, or transmit to the verifier, if you're on a set of 1000 items, that's about ten minutes of information, then you have a series of five icons, you put the two screens next to each other and then watch it just verify the visual packets.

Mike Roe: A few years ago, you had each of them play some random generated tune based on a key generator, and if they're playing the same tune you can recognize it.

Pekka Nikander: Well, actually you also have a microphone so you can have one other device sending Morse code to the other.

Reply: So the suggestion is, to address the need for longer length, bigger bandwidth on a visual channel, would that be what you're saying?

Mike Bond: Yes, I mean you might not need to in this case but in the general case if you wanted to transfer more bits over a visual channel, and is that a possibility?

Reply: Yes, exactly, this protocol is in response to, what we consider to be, a realistic requirement that the code needs to be short for the auxiliary channel. But really, the other characteristics of this visual channel are high integrity or more precisely, high data origin authenticity - properties which you don't have for the RF channel, and which we attempt to explicitly take advantage of in our protocol. Coming to your suggestion, say you try and send visually from a big dictionary of images, where each image has been indexed by some number or string. Such that a particular image maps to some value. The question would be: what really is your entropy? It might actually be small after all.

Mike Bond: I think about 30 bits.

Reply: Yes, even up to 50 bits may be fine, and can be reliably sent visually.

Mike Bond: Because it's very quick for a human to identify even quite accurately whether or not two images are completely identical, and the icons here, let's say are 7000, can be chosen, so they don't have to spot the different properties, they could all be quite different things, you know 100 can be apples, 100 could be kitchen utensils, and just think of 100 different things. I'm not sure about the storage part to fit it all, to fit a decent set of these, for example, if you get ten bits and a set like that you require just enough time to register.

Reply: Speaking of the bits, do you mean that the number of distinct objects span the full 50 bits of entropy, or do you mean that each image is composed of 50 bits? If the latter, an attack is simple. Suppose there are only 2^{10} images though each image is encoded by 50 bits, then the entropy is only ten bits. This is as susceptible as the original protocol is to a brute-force attack on the short hashes. If there are instead 50 bits worth of plausible hashes, that means you actually have the full entropy, the full cardinality, the attacker has to cycle through 50 bits and, that's still tough by today's computational power, as 50 bits is over a quadrillion possibilities. Now you can time-out the devices in ten seconds, so if you do not receive the right hash in a timely fashion, the attacker has not been able to compute a quadrillion possibilities (or on average half of that) by then, just shut him out.

Jun Li: Why would you call this 'multi-channel'? From my understanding, it's just two channels. One is the radio channel between the two devices and the other an observation over a visual channel.

Reply: We are trying to say that these protocols are based on different channels with really different characteristics, different bandwidth: one's got high integrity, one's got low integrity; one is like susceptible to passive attack, one is susceptible to active man-in-the-middle attack; and there may be other classes that we haven't covered, so this is our first step. We use multi-channel to refer to two or more channels. This one is essentially a bi-channel protocol, but it is possible to conceive of other channels and their different properties.

Jun Li: How is such authentication strong? Do you want to authenticate the people who are using the phones? Because it's quite different, a really different context if you need strong authentication.

Reply: We are authenticating devices. Often, I may think that my device is talking to a particular device. For example, if I see this hash on that device, does it really mean that my device has formed a secure pairing with that device? We can't be sure, as it could be some man-in-the-middle attacker has formed a shared key with me whose hash also computes to this.

Jun Li: Do you authenticate the person who is using this device?

Reply: Our protocol objective is to do device-to-device key agreement and authentication, with human in the loop.

Bruce Christianson: The first step is to make sure that your wireless keyboard really is talking to your wireless computer screen.

Reply: Yes, so that's where this visual channel comes in, when you can bring it up close enough.

Frank Stajano: As co-author of this I wanted to continue answering the question about the multi-channel protocol. We feel that in this study we have come across protocols that were using different channels for sending different messages in the sequence. We have done that ourselves before in the Resurrecting Duckling[1] when, with Ross, we advocated that the first channel for establishing the key should be a different channel, a more secure channel, rather than the one that you use to address the protocol. Now with Ford, we think that this should be something that is modelled explicitly because some of the properties of the channels are very different, and make a significant difference.

For example, with the radio channel, you really don't know who you're getting the message from, whereas with the video channel at least you're very sure as the user of the thing that it came from that particular cell phone: you may have someone overlooking you, but it's almost impossible to do a man-in-the-middle where someone fakes which device is sending you this message, you would

---

[1] F. Stajano and R. Anderson, The Resurrecting Duckling: Security Issues for Ad-Hoc Wireless Networks, LNCS 1796, 172–182.

immediately notice that there is a man-in-the-middle, whereas it's not so obvious in other channels, in a packet network, or in a radio, or something like that.

So at a higher level than any of the individual protocols that have been exposed in this talk, our message with this research is that there's mileage in considering multi-channel protocols, as multi-channel things to be studied as such. For message number two, I need a channel that guarantees data origin, but I don't actually care so much about confidentiality, for message three, then I want one where I am sure that if I'm talking to it, then nobody else is going to overhear you, or something like that. So if you look at the paper there is a notation which we are still basically inventing where we have a numbering of lines and then next to it, there are some bits that are sent over video, and then in an appendix to the protocol you should say the RF channel is the one that needs to have those characteristics, the video one has to have these other characteristics. So other than thinking of the individual protocols we discussed already, and about protocols we break, also think about this paradigm of multi-channels as a way that can make the study of protocols wider, opening new horizons.

Mike Bond: The other important feature is being explicit about who has to check what at each step. Usually we assume protocol participants are out of sight of each other and communicating over some long range network. This is the opposite problem. The potential for protocols like this is very much greater I think, than just the protocols that are in Ford's paper: the whole issue of what is captured in a model, such as this is substituting the electrical channel.

Reply: Yes.

Frank Stajano: You could say, I advocate an electrical contact here because of these properties, and not an electrical contact there, because of the other properties required there.

Mike Bond: One of the things that's quite interesting is that idea of a human who is capable of comparing things, at a reasonably high bandwidth. Would that be a bizarre new channel that has not yet been considered and modelled? It seems two devices could use it.

Frank Stajano: Yes, the human comes in some other channels we were discussing such as, for example, someone looking at the hash on one device and hiding it from the view of another person, and that's a channel with other properties: it is not guaranteed, it may transpose digits, it has a limited capacity because they are not going to bother attacking anything that's longer than five or eight characters, it has a strong data origin authenticity, and so on. So channels should not be limited to just radio and video, they're just illustrative.

Reply: Yes, just to follow on what Mike said about making part of the protocol explicit, Alice has got to be certain that she's received the H_2 commitment from Bob before she releases her R_a, because her receipt of H_2 would indicate that Bob has safely received the H_1 commitment from her, which is an essential preparatory step for Bob to be able to verify Alice in later steps. Similarly, Bob has to be certain he has received R_a from Alice, before he releases R_b. From this point onwards they can go on to exchanging K_a and K_b. They can then be sure that the attacker truly faces the difficulty of trying to derive K_a or K_b

from committed information. None of the protocol messages are concurrent, I hadn't specially emphasized that before, but that's how they ought to be run. In London, they already use CCTV for number-plate tracking for congestion charges. Immigration and Customs at airports are using high-resolution visual recognition systems to try to pick out terrorist suspects, so perhaps it may not be such a long shot for a hostile adversary to use CCTV to peek at your hashes or other codes on your personal devices, use that intelligence to transmit messages on the radio medium, thereby conducting man-in-the-middle attack.

Combining Crypto with Biometrics:
A New Human-Security Interface
(Transcript of Discussion)

Feng Hao

Computer Laboratory, University of Cambridge

I present my research on combining cryptography and iris biometrics. This is work with Ross Anderson and John Daugman. It is a short talk so I will leave out the technical detail.

The motivation of the research is to incorporate advanced biometric authentication features into cryptography. We find that cryptography lacks the involvement of a human factor. In authentication, you would use a password or a token, but there is no real human factor involved. We studied the iris biometric because it is one of the most reliable biometrics discovered so far. There are however certain issues with the iris biometric. First, it is fuzzy. Second, its storage is quite controversial for privacy reasons. And third, it cannot be kept secret by its very nature. These limitations apply to biometrics in general.

In Unix, you don't store the password in plain text. Instead, you apply a one-way hash function. But you cannot do the same with iris codes because they are fuzzy. If you hash an iris code, it would destroy all the information content. So in our research, we devised a method to map the 2048-bit fuzzy iris code into an exact 140-bit string. This mapping is repeatable with a 99.5% success rate.

Our technique is based on error correction codes. First I will explain the error characteristics in the iris codes. There are two types of errors. First there are random errors – errors dispersed randomly across an iris code. Second there are burst errors – caused by undetected eyelashes and specular reflections. We devised an error correction scheme to deal with these two types of error. At the top level, we wanted to design an error correction scheme in such a way that it will have the error correction capability at a cutting point to correct errors just enough for authentic users, and not more than that.

We segment the iris code into 32 blocks with 64 bits in each block, and we apply a Hadamard code to correct up to 25% of the bits in each block. This is roughly the cutting point to discriminate between the same eye and a different eye. However, certain errors are clustered in some blocks to give us error blocks. Hence, we have a second layer of error correction using a Reed-Solomon code which corrects these burst errors.

Here is a basic scheme. It is a two-factor scheme. Key reproduction is based on two factors: iris and token. The token is something that we can keep secret, but the iris is not. On the left-hand side of this diagram is the registration part which is also the encoding part. We generate a 140-bit random string, and encode it to 2048 bits. Then we XOR this with an iris code, which is also 2048 bits. The

B. Christianson et al. (Eds.): Security Protocols 2005, LNCS 4631, pp. 133–138, 2007.
© Springer-Verlag Berlin Heidelberg 2007

result is called the locked code. We store it on a token together with a hash of
the key so that we can verify later whether it was generated correctly.

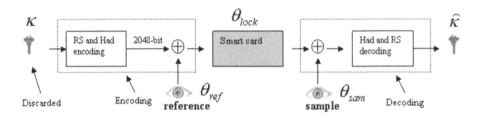

On the right hand side of the diagram is the key generation part, that is the
decoding part. We have an authentic iris code which is not identical but close
to the reference one. By going through the decoding procedure, we are able to
recover this 140-bit key exactly. Here we let e denote the Hamming difference
between the two iris codes. If the iris code is authentic, then e has a relatively
small Hamming weight. On the other hand, if the sample is not authentic, the
Hamming weight will be relatively big. We designed a coding scheme to handle
the errors with e up to 27%. Below this threshold we are able to correct the
effect of the noise, and recover the exact string. We can check against the hash
value which is stored on the token.

What is the performance of this scheme? Here, we must decide the number
of error blocks we want to correct using the Reed-Solomon code. We choose a
Hadamard matrix size of 64-bit, so we have 64 bits in one block and 32 blocks in
total. RS is the number of error blocks we can correct. We find a suitable choice
is RS = 6. At this point we can get a key length of 140-bit, and the false rejection
rate is pretty low, only 0.5%. This performance is much better than other key
generation implementations based on biometrics, like, voice, handwritten signature, fingerprint, and face. The common false rejection rate is 20%. Our 0.5% is
much smaller.

Here is the histogram of the database we use. At this stage we haven't included the mask information into our coding scheme because of some technical
difficulties. We will do that in our future research. The diagram on the right-
hand side is a histogram without using the mask information. As you can see,
there is some overlap here and that's why we cannot get zero error rates. Ideally
if we can include the mask information, we can surely reduce the error rates even
further.

What is the security of this scheme? The initial motivation of our work is
that if you have, for example, a biometric ID system, then you will have to
store the iris code for each person in a central database. That will cause a lot of
privacy concerns. Our thinking is to just store a random sting, and the person
is identified by regenerating that random string. The privacy concerns for this
approach are much less.

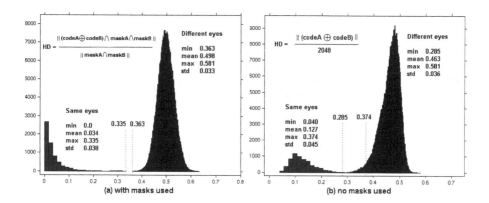

There are some other applications of our technique. For example, you may want to use the generated key as a cryptographic key. In that case it'd be better to add another factor, a password. We can use a password to permute the Hadamard matrices, so that if an attacker wants to derive this key then he has to compromise all three factors.

Each of the three factors has intrinsic limitations. For example, a password can be stolen, or guessed. As for the token, it can be stolen or reverse-engineered. But it is possible that a password and a token can be kept secret by a careful person. For the biometric, a biometric copy can be stolen. An attacker may be able to obtain your fingerprint. In the case where the attacker has the token only, he may present his own iris and try his luck to see whether he can get through the system. But the probability of that is very small. But the problem is that the iris biometric cannot be kept secret by its nature.

In our 3-factor scheme, if the attacker wants to compromise the key, he has to compromise all three factors.

Mark Lomas: Can I suggest that the problem is not that the biometric can't be kept a secret. The problem is the need for a secure channel from whatever makes the measurements to whatever does the composition which you have just explained. So I think your approach is a sensible one if I can incorporate the crypto part into the camera that does the scan, but not if I'm presented with, say, a smartcard that does the processing and an untrusted camera. Secrecy is not actually the issue.

Frank Stajano: Well it is in a sense. John Daugman has this famous story of the Afghan girl on the cover of National Geographic[1]: you can recover her iris data from just a photograph of her, so in some sense even if the camera does the crypto you can still fool it by presenting a picture of an iris.

Mark Lomas: But if you recall some of John's earlier papers he explains how you work out whether this is a live iris as opposed to just a photograph.

Bruce Christianson: I think Mark's original point is right, the trick is to ensure that the channel between the person and the crypto really does have all

---

[1] See http://www.cl.cam.ac.uk/~jgd1000/afghan.html

the properties that we want it to have, and this includes checking that you've got a live person, not a head attached to a pump in a hatbox.

Frank Stajano: That's a longer channel, to the iris not just to the camera.

Reply: It's actually not that easy to steal an iris image. You need a special camera. A digital camera doesn't work. It's a near infra-red camera and the image is captured within one meter.

Matt Blaze: So one way to do that is by setting up a biometric scanner that the person is required to use?

Reply: Yes, that is correct.

Mike Roe: In previous talks we've discussed the proliferation of CCTV cameras in the UK, there's even some have been developed which use infrared to see in the dark. As you walk down the street there's already all the technology needed to get you iris image looking at you.

Ross Anderson: But I think the point of this is different. In the real world everything can be faked, forged, guessed, etc. Sure you can end up with a database of the iris of most people in the UK by setting up some strategic cameras, but you won't know their names unless we've also got scanners which read the ID cards in their wallets. You know most of their passwords, because an on-line dictionary is just one mouse-click away, and you can steal large quantities of tokens by subverting some person at the post office. Now all of these have a probability attached. If you take the NSA mathematicians view that if it's not perfect it's no good, and you consider that you will only ever thing about security mechanisms if you're absolutely guaranteed by a complexity theoretic proof that you've 128-bit minimum security, then I suppose this work has no place whatsoever in that lecture course. But that doesn't imply that it has no place here.

Matt Blaze: Ross, I'm sorry, I think you've been replaced with somebody who looks like Ross Anderson. [Laughter] I'll used my biometric scanner just to be sure, but the old Ross never would have agreed to use it, and I know that if you agree to use it, then you are in fact an impostor.

I think the underlying problem is not that it's cryptographically imperfect, or that there's some attack in which we convert every molecule on earth into a super computer, and run it for ten thousand years and break it. The fundamental problem is that it doesn't solve is, I subvert one person using this biometric authentication system, either by collecting their database, or replacing the software that does the collection with something that sends the data to me as well, and then I can use that information to subvert your biometric authentication of these users everywhere else they go.

Ross Anderson: If all I were doing is deriving a single key from somebody's biometric, which is what most schemes do, then that's a fair statement, but in this scheme here we have a different key for every application.

Matt Blaze: But if we can get your biometrics by stealth, if I'm not misunderstanding, this scheme only works if everyone is using it, but if somebody, somewhere, is using a dummy scheme then I can recreate the biometrics for the purpose of fooling you.

Ross Anderson: True. In that case you would fall back on the password. I suppose a security evaluation of a scheme like this is to ask, how good is the best that we can do given the apparent limitations of the underlying technology.

Matt Blaze: The technology is very limited.

Ross Anderson: And if it gets the most bangs that it is possible to get out of that technology then it's a good scheme. But how do we go about systematizing that kind of evaluation?

Alf Zugenmaier: How stable is the biometric in time? Are there problems like, a woman becomes pregnant, the iris totally changes, and will not be recognised again, so the key is wrong for good.

Reply: No, the iris is fixed for a lifetime.

Hoon Lim: Even after a night at the Eagle?

Reply: Yes. Although I also saw reports that some patients had a cataract operation and that changed the iris structure. But I think the main point in our scheme is that the key is random, and completely independent from biometrics. That is quite important because biometrics, by nature, cannot be kept secret. What happens when the biometric copy is stolen? It has no impact on the key because the key is completely independent from biometrics.

Yvo Desmedt: There are people who make artificial irises. All you need is a personal computer and a printer, and an infrared camera, and access to some published papers.

Mike Bond: One of the interesting challenges here is normally in the active counterfeiting scenario: you have anti-counterfeiting measures which mean that you need a really expensive press to print bank notes. Whereas we've got this one unique source of decent irises, ourselves. Now it seems a lot of the anti-counterfeiting protection in irises is currently in the measuring of the irises, whereas once you've got the data from it with your infra-red camera, which costs £1000 today but tomorrow costs £10, that's it. So how do we exploit things that aren't in the measuring phase in verification?

Ross Anderson: There's now a proposal that US Immigration and Naturalisation Service think about egress controls, so that when you leave America on a plane, some pleasant young man or young lady will come up to you, look at your boarding card, scan one of your fingerprints, and if it matches against the fingerprints that you gave when you entered the country then you'll be allowed to leave. So if the future contains a world in which this kind of biometric scanning is done, (which may be evil, but if it's going to happen anyway) then many of the liveness problems can be overcome at a critical level. For example, you can design next generation mobile phone cameras to scan somebody's iris.

Virgil Gligor: I think that all that happens is the border with Mexico will become very popular.

Frank Stajano: Another problem is to keep people out, not not allow them to leave.

Mike Roe: There's scope for some protocol attacks here. You've only got one pair of irises, you don't get a separate iris for each security application. So firstly we've got to secure against the possibility that there is some other protocol using this mechanism that will cause the iris code of everybody in the world to become public. Secondly, you have to design the protocol so you don't break any other protocol that relies upon the mechanism. I think you've got the pieces here to do it, but it's not straightforward.

Ross Anderson: And that's why you have to have statistically independent keys, because you just have to assume that you're using your iris to do many different things.

Bruce Christianson: This is a nice mechanism, particularly the mangling of the iris data with the key and the potential integration of that with access class. But it's going to take a long time to work out some of the other implications, and it certainly brings a whole new meaning to the phrase "cardholder not present" [laughter].

User-Friendly Grid Security Architecture and Protocols

Liqun Chen[1], Hoon Wei Lim[2], and Wenbo Mao[1]

[1] Hewlett-Packard Laboratories
Filton Road, Stoke Gifford, Bristol BS34 8QZ, UK
{liqun.chen,wenbo.mao}@hp.com
[2] Information Security Group,
Royal Holloway, University of London
Egham, Surrey TW20 0EX, UK
h.lim@rhul.ac.uk

Abstract. We examine security protocols for the Grid Security Infrastructure (GSI) version 2 and identify a weakness of poor scalability as a result of GSI's authentication framework requiring heavy interactions between a user-side client machine and resource suppliers. We improve the GSI architecture and protocols by proposing an alternative authentication framework for GSI, which uses dynamic public/private key pairs to avoid frequent communications to a significant extent. The improvement to the GSI security protocols is enabled by a novel application of an emerging cryptographic technique from bilinear pairings.

Keywords: Security Protocols, Grid Security, Grid Security Infrastructure, Public-key Authentication Framework, Dynamic Public Keys.

1 Introduction

1.1 Motivation

A computational grid [8,10] is a distributed computing system comprising a large number of computational resources which form a virtual organisation (VO) that services a group of users with resource demanding jobs. In general, within a grid environment, a user (more precisely, a user's proxy, UP, which is a user's client acting on behalf of the user) must conduct potentially a large number of instances of mutual authentication with these resource contributing sites (each site is managed by a resource proxy RP) in order to gain secure access to them.

The Grid Security Infrastructure (GSI) version 2 [9] enables a secure way of resource allocation with a set of three security protocols. These protocols are run between UP and RP to achieve mutual authentication between these two entities. Entity authentication in these protocols are achieved by straightforward applications of the standard SSL Authentication Protocol (SAP). Here, UP and RP are assumed to have possessions of standard X.509 [12] public-key cryptographic credentials called *proxy certificates*.

B. Christianson et al. (Eds.): Security Protocols 2005, LNCS 4631, pp. 139–156, 2007.

In GSI, UP is in general a user-end average computer platform; however it is also in a computationally heavily loaded point both in computation and in communication. The authors of GSI conceded that the security architecture in GSI has a poor scalability [9] which limits the number of resource allocation sessions that a UP can make which in turn limits the degree of high-performance grid computing services available to a user. We believe that this scalability limitation is due to the fact that the GSI is based on a straightforward application of the conventional X.509 certificate-based PKI authentication framework, which is inherently highly interactive.

There are two important features which are necessary for a grid security solution and which GSI has solved nicely by applying the standard X.509 PKI:

- User single-sign-on: The user U should be able to authenticate itself once by using one cryptographic credential and then can enjoy grid services which may be provided by many resource contribution sites.
- Unattended user authentication: The user proxy UP can conduct authentication sessions on behalf of U even when U is not present; this is very important since the duration of a grid can be sufficiently long and new resource allocation request may be needed after U has left, so the protocols have to be run by UP in an unattended manner.

In this work, we attempt to improve the performance and scalability of GSI and our improvement must not lead to any reduction to the quality of these two features.

1.2   Our Contribution

We apply a novel application of the bilinear pairing technique to achieve a dynamic public key management scheme in which a static public-key certificate (e.g., in the X.509 style) can be used to compute ephemeral public keys using predetermined formulae and the certificate owner can also compute the matching ephemeral private keys. These ephemeral keys have the following important property: any of the ephemeral private keys cannot be used for deriving either the static private key behind the static certificate or any of the past-used or future-to-evolve ephemeral private keys. Thus a computer lacking a strong means for protecting long term cryptographic keys, e.g., a usual client platform which is vulnerable to malicious-code attacks, a laptop computer or a hand-held device which are vulnerable to loss or theft, can be programmed to use frequently evolving ephemeral private keys. Assuming a user's long-term private key is stored in a secure computing platform such as smart card, protection for his short-lived private key can therefore be lightweight, such as keeping the key in the file space under the usual file access control protection. Compromise of such a short-lived key can have a limited danger. Because the matching evolving public keys are publicly computable using the static key certificate, the use of ephemeral public keys will not incur a high cost for key management. This technique has a potential to expedite a wide deployment of the X.509-like public-key authentication framework in the vast client environment.

The remainder of this paper is organised as follows. In Section 2 we review related work. In Section 3 we make a quick technical review on bilinear pairings and the security services that they provide. Section 4 describes our key dynamation concepts. In Section 5 we present our improvement to GSI security protocols. Finally we conclude in Section 6.

2   Related Work

Many researchers have tried to solve the same problem that we are interested in this paper in different ways. For instance, Tzeng and Tzeng [19] proposed a key-evolving public-key encryption scheme which aims at limiting the exposure of ciphertexts encrypted under a user's private key within a certain period of time. They make use of Shamir's (t, n)-secret sharing idea to create one public key corresponding to t valid private keys. However, the scheme requires the user to interact with a trusted authority to update his private key. Dodis et al. introduced the notion of key-insulated security in [7] which essentially has the same objective. Despite the fact that their scheme is non-interactive with the TA, it requires two-stage update before a private key can be updated. First, a user must interact with a physically secure device which stores the master secret key to generate a partial secret key. This partial secret key is then provided to a second key-update algorithm which takes as input some other parameters such as time period and current private key to produce a new private key.

Both schemes proposed in [7,19] assume that the public key is fixed. This may seem a desirable feature for many applications as all the users do not need to update the public keys of other users in their directories. However, our method shows that a dynamic public key is equally useful whereby it can be used as an input for generating a fresh shared session key with another communicating party. More interestingly, in our approach, the length of public/private keys are independent to the number of private keys.

In another related aspect, the concept of *identity-based cryptography* (IBC) was proposed by Shamir in 1984 [18]. The idea of an identity-based system is that a public key can be derived from an arbitrary string, and the corresponding private key is created by a secure bonding of the public key and a system master key. This means that if a user has a string corresponding to its identity, this string can be used to derive the user's public key. In [18] Shamir proposed an identity-based signature scheme, but for many years identity-based encryption had remained an open problem. The problem was solved nearly two decades later [3,5,16,17]. In [5] Cocks proposed a solution based on quadratic residuosity. In [16,17], Sakai, Ohgishi and Kasahara proposed an identity-based key setting on elliptic curves, which was then used to build an identity-based encryption scheme using bilinear pairings. In [3] Boneh and Franklin defined a well-formulated security model for identity-based encryption, and gave an IBE scheme using bilinear pairings as well. The Boneh and Franklin scheme has drawn much attention mostly because of its provable security in the security model. In [15], Sakai and Kasahara proposed another IBE scheme using bilinear pairings on elliptic curves based on a different identity-based key setting.

Unlike IBC schemes using a *trusted authority* (called key generation center in literature) that generates private keys for its users using some master key, in our scheme, a user plays the role of their own key generation center. The user generates dynamic public/private key pairs by using his own static public/private key pairs.

3   Background of Bilinear Pairings

Using the notation of Boneh and Franklin [3], $\mathbb{G}_1$ denotes an additive group of a large prime order q and $\mathbb{G}_2$, a multiplicative group of the same order. $\hat{e}_q$ denotes a bilinear, non-degenerate and efficiently computable map from $\mathbb{G}_1 \times \mathbb{G}_1$ to $\mathbb{G}_2$. Typically, $\mathbb{G}_1$ can be realised by a q-torsion subgroup of points on a supersingular elliptic curve defined over a finite field K, $\mathbb{G}_2$, the order-q subgroup of a suitable finite field extension of K, and the map $\hat{e}_q$, derived from either the Weil or Tate pairing on the elliptic curve. By $\hat{e}_q$ being bilinear we mean that for $P, Q, R \in \mathbb{G}_1$, the following equations hold

$$\hat{e}_q(P + Q, R) = \hat{e}_q(P, R) \cdot \hat{e}_q(Q, R) \quad \text{and} \quad \hat{e}_q(P, Q + R) = \hat{e}_q(P, Q) \cdot \hat{e}_q(P, R).$$

By $\hat{e}_q$ being non-degenerate we mean that for any non-unity element $P \in \mathbb{G}_1$ (i.e., P is not a point at infinity), we have $\hat{e}_q(P, P) \neq 1_{\mathbb{G}_2}$. By $\hat{e}_q$ being efficiently computable we mean the computation of $\hat{e}_q(P, Q)$ can be done in time polynomial in $\log q$. We denote $k = \log q$ and call it the security parameter of the problem. We notice that the efficiency of computing the pairing parameterised in k is compatible to that of a public-key encryption operation in a widely applied public-key cryptosystem, such as the RSA [14], parameterised in k. We refer to [1,3,11] for more comprehensive descriptions of how these groups, pairings and other parameters should be selected in practice for striking a good balance between efficiency and security.

Now we state a few facts about the difficult and easy problems which base the security and the working principle of our technique.

3.1   The Difficulty of Elliptic-Curve Discrete Logarithm Problem

For any $a \in \mathbb{Z}_q^*$ and $P \in \mathbb{G}_1$, we write aP for P being added to itself a times, which is also called scalar multiplication of P by an integer a. The scalar multiplication is efficient. However, the reverse problem of finding the integer a from a given pair (P, aP) is intractable, i.e., cannot be done in time in polynomial in

k, deterministically or probabilistically. This is the well-known assumption on the hardness of the elliptic-curve discrete logarithm problem.

3.2 The Difficulty of Elliptic-Curve Computational Diffie-Hellman Problem

In addition to the difficulty of the elliptic-curve discrete logarithm problem we will also need the following hardness assumption. Given a tuple $(P, xP, P') \in \mathbb{G}_1$ with unknown $x \in \mathbb{Z}_q^*$ and the discrete logarithm relationship between P and P', compute xP'. This problem is also intractable in k. This is the well-known assumption on the hardness of the elliptic-curve computational Diffie-Hellman problem [6].

3.3 The Difficulty of the Bilinear Diffie-Hellman Problem for $(\mathbb{G}_1, \mathbb{G}_2, \hat{e}_q)$

We will need one more hardness assumption. Let $\mathbb{G}_1$, $\mathbb{G}_2$ and $\hat{e}_q$ be as above. The Bilinear Diffie-Hellman problem for $(\mathbb{G}_1, \mathbb{G}_2, \hat{e}_q)$ is as follows. Given a tuple $(P, xP, yP, zP) \in \mathbb{G}_1$ with unknown $x, y, z \in \mathbb{Z}_q^*$, compute $\hat{e}_q(P, P)^{xyz} \in \mathbb{G}_2$. This problem is also intractable in k. This hardness assumption is called the Bilinear Diffie-Hellman assumption [3].

3.4 The Efficiency of Decisional Diffie-Hellman Problem in $\mathbb{G}_1$

In the general case of a group G (e.g., let G be defined in the general setting of an elliptic curve), given a tuple $(P, xP, yP, zP) \in G$, answering the following question is a hard problem:

Is the tuple (P, xP, yP, zP) a Diffie-Hellman instance?
The answer is YES if and only if $z = xy$ (mod the order of G).

We do not know any algorithm which can answer this question in polynomial time in k. This is the well-known hardness assumption called the decisional Diffie-Hellman assumption.

However, in the group $\mathbb{G}_1$ in which we have defined an efficient and non-degenerate bilinear pairing, we can provide an efficient answer to this question. Given a tuple $(P, xP, yP, zP) \in \mathbb{G}_1$, we can answer YES if and only if

$$\hat{e}_q(P, zP) = \hat{e}_q(xP, yP).$$

Indeed, by bilinearity and non-degeneracy, this equation holds if and only if $xy = z$, i.e.,

$$\hat{e}_q(P, zP) = \hat{e}_q(P, P)^z = \hat{e}_q(P, P)^{xy} = \hat{e}_q(xP, yP).$$

Clearly, this question can be efficiently answered since the evaluation of the bilinear pairing is efficient.

Being able to efficiently answer the decisional Diffie-Hellman question is the very reason why we can let the user use dynamic public/private key pairs and thereby avoid large number of communications in the grid security protocols.

4   Key Dynamation

In this section we provide some technical background of the grid security applications that will be specified in Section 5.

In order to expose the central idea of our key dynamation scheme clearly we will confine ourselves to a special and simple case of key dynamation as a publicly evaluable function of a time period. In this special case, a user's dynamic public key can be a function of (i) the user's static key certificate, and (ii) a time period value. In this case, a user's dynamic public key can be easily computed by any principal who has the user's static certificate without the need of any interaction with the user. It is easily imagined that the user's dynamic public key can also be a function of additional public information; for example, a user's dynamic public key can be computed as a public function which also takes as input the identity of a principal who is delegated by the user.

4.1   Static Certificate and Key Pairs

Let Alice pick a random point $P \in \mathbb{G}_1$ and random integer $a \in \mathbb{Z}_q^*$. The integer a is Alice's static private key. She generates her static public key as (P, aP). Let this static public key material be certified by a key certification authority CA in the X.509 PKI setting. The certification result is a static public-key certificate which can be denoted by

$$Cert_A = \text{Sign}_{CA}(\text{Alice}, P, aP),$$

i.e., CA creates $Cert_A$ by digitally signing Alice's identity together with her static public key material.

4.2   Dynamic Key Pairs as a Function of a Time Period

Let f be a publicly evaluable function which maps from a bit string of arbitrary length into $\mathbb{G}_1$. The function f must satisfy the collision resistance property, that is, it is intractable for one to find two different bit strings $s_1 \neq s_2$ such that $f(s_1) = f(s_2)$. We know that there exist cryptographic hash functions which satisfy this property.

Let the system agree on the following key evolution scheme:

$$Q(X, UTP) = f(Cert_X, UTP).$$

Here, "UTP" (which stands for "Unique-Time-Period") is a bit string which is application dependent. For example, it is "Date" represented in the 24-hour system defined under a universal clock setting such as the Greenwich Mean Time.

In the date "Date", Alice's dynamic public key is the elliptic-curve point $Q(A, Date)$ in $\mathbb{G}_1$. Notice that anyone having $Cert_A$ can compute $Q(A, Date)$.

Let the system agree on the following dynamic private setup algorithm:

$$T(SK_X, Q(X, UTP)).$$

For example, given Alice's static private key $SK_A = a \in \mathbb{Z}_q^*$, Alice's matching dynamic private key is $T(SK_X, Q(X, UTP)) = aQ(A, Date)$, which is another point in $\mathbb{G}_1$. We assume that the latter computation is conducted in a secure computing environment, such as a smart card possessed by Alice.

One can verify the relation between the static asymmetric key pair and the dynamic asymmetric key pair by checking if the following equation holds,

$$\hat{e}_q(P, aQ(A, Date)) = \hat{e}_q(aP, Q(A, Date)).$$

Let Alice stores the dynamic private key $aQ(A, Date)$ in a relatively less secure computing environment, e.g., in the file space of a low-end computing device. The low-end computing device can use this dynamic private key as a cryptographic credential on behalf of Alice. In this manner, the system needn't require Alice to conduct cryptographic computations in the secure computing environment. This is important in applications in which Alice may be unavailable most of the time (a typical situation in the grid services).

A brief analysis of difficulty of finding such private keys is given in Appendix A.

4.3   An Aggregate Signature Scheme

A grid environment requires the use of a signature chain which could bind a large number of signatures from different resources. For the purpose of reducing complexity of the signature chain, we introduce a new aggregate signature scheme. The concept of aggregate signatures was first proposed by Boneh et al. in [2]. The proposed scheme is a special aggregate signature mechanism, where the first signer uses a master private signing key and the i-th signer uses the received $(i-1)$-th aggregated signature as the private signing key. Anyone can verify the aggregate signature by only using the matching master public key.

The following is an example with three signers, as the same case in the proposed grid solution that will be described in next section. Let Alice be the first signer and hold a master private signing key $s \in \mathbb{Z}_q^*$, and a master public verification key $(P, sP) \in \mathbb{G}_1$. Let Bob and Colin be the second and third signers respectively. They perform as follows:

1. Alice signs the first message m_1 under s to obtain

$$Sig_A(m_1) = sH_1(m_1),$$

   where H_1 is a suitable hash function that maps a string to a point in $\mathbb{G}_1$. Alice sends m_1 and $Sig_A(m_1)$ to Bob in a secret and authenticated way.
2. Bob signs the second message m_2 by performing the following steps:
   (a) Pick a uniformly random number $r \in \mathbb{Z}_q^*$;
   (b) Compute $X = rP$;
   (c) Compute $h_1 = H_2(X, m_2)$, where H_2 is a suitable hash-function;
   (d) Compute $Z = rsP + h_1sH_1(m_1)$;
   (e) Send m_1, m_2, X and Z to Colin in a secret and authenticated way.

3. Colin signs the third message m_3 by performing the following steps:
   (a) Pick a uniformly random number $r' \in \mathbb{Z}_q^*$;
   (b) Compute $X' = r'P$;
   (c) Compute $h'_1 = H_2(X', m_3)$;
   (d) Compute $Z' = r'sP + h'_1 Z$;
   (e) Send m_1, m_2, m_3, X, X' and Z' to a verifier.
4. The verifier checks validation of the aggregate signature by performing the following steps:
   (a) Compute $Y = H_1(m_1)$;
   (b) Compute $h_1 = H_2(X, m_2)$;
   (c) Compute $h'_1 = H_2(X', m_3)$;
   (d) Check if $\hat{e}_q(Z', P) = \hat{e}_q(X' + h'_1 X + h_1 h'_1 Y, sP)$; accept the signature as valid if and only if the equation holds.

Optionally, in order to indicate the identities of signers, m_1 can contain Bob's identity, m_2 can contain Colin's identity and so on. This aggregate signature scheme is efficient in computation because the verification only requires two pairings, which is independent on the number of the signers and signatures involved.

5 Improvement to Grid Security Infrastructure

5.1 The Security Architecture for GSI

We now overview the security architecture for grid [9].

As shown in Figure 1, there are three different principals in GSI: a user U, a user proxy UP and a resource proxy RP. In a general grid application there can be many RPs and Figure 1 only depicts two of them as "Site 1" and "Site 2".

These principals have the following relations. In order to use the grid resources, U first communicates with UP by running "Protocol 1" so that UP will be able to act on behalf of U for a specified period of time. Then UP will allocate resource for U by running "Protocol 2" with RP in a remote site (e.g., "Site 1"). If more resource is needed, resource allocation can be done likewise between UP and RP in other remote sites (e.g., "Site 2").

GSI specifies the following security requirements.

- *Single sign-on:* U should be able to authenticate itself once by using one cryptographic credential and then can enjoy grid services which may be provided by many resource contribution sites. UP can conduct authentication sessions on behalf of U even when U is not present; this is very important since the duration of a grid can be sufficiently long and new resource allocation request may be needed after U has left and so the protocols have to be run by UP in an unattended manner.
- *Protection of credentials:* User credentials (passwords, private keys, etc) must be securely protected.

- *Interoperability with local security solutions:* While security solutions may provide interdomain access mechanisms, access to local resources will typically be determined by a local security policy that is enforced by a local security mechanism. It is impractical to modify every local resource to accommodate interdomain access; instead, one or more entities in a domain (e.g., interdomain security servers) must act as agents of remote clients/users for local resources.

- *Uniform credentials/certification infrastructure:* Interdomain access requires, at a minimum, a common way of expressing the identity of a security principal such as an actual user or a resource. Hence, it is imperative to employ a standard (such as X.509v3) for encoding credentials for security principals.

- *Support for secure group communications:* A computation can comprise a number of processes that will need to coordinate their activities as a group. The composition of a process group can and will change during the lifetime of a computation. Hence, support is needed for secure (in this context, authenticated) communication for dynamic groups.

- *Support for multiple implementations:* The security policy should not dictate a specific implementation technology. Rather, it should be possible to implement the security policy with a range of security technologies, based on both public and shared key cryptography.

In the remaining of this section, we will modify the three aforementioned GSI protocols using dynamic public/private key pairs.

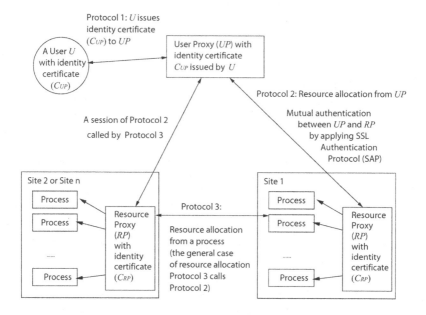

Fig. 1. Grid Security Infrastructure

5.2   The Improvement

We now improve the GSI security protocols.

In our notation, each entity $X \in \{U, RP\}$ has a static credential denoted by C_X, which could include a static public key, $PK_X = (P, s_X P) \in \mathbb{G}_1$, the corresponding static private key, $SK_X = s_X \in \mathbb{Z}_q^*$, and a static public key certificate (such as X.509v3).

Protocol for User Proxy Credential Creation. "Improved Protocol 1" is run between a user U and its proxy UP. The output is that UP obtains a short-term cryptographic credential so that the latter can allocate resources for U. We notice that UP in our architecture needn't be local to U. It can reside on a high-performance platform such as MyProxy Server[1] which serves as a grid portal that allows the user to access grid resources from anywhere.

The following protocol does not show how U authenticates UP. We assume that U is able to do so if it is requested.

Improved Protocol 1: Creation of User Proxy Credential

Assumption. *A user U has access to a user proxy UP; UP has access to an authenticated static public key PK_U of U.*

U and UP interact as follows:

1. *U performs the following steps:*
   - *Compute a dynamic public key $PK_{UP} = Q(U, Date)$, where Q denotes a dynamic public key setup algorithm.*
   - *Compute the corresponding dynamic private key $SK_{UP} = T(SK_U, PK_{UP})$, where T denotes a dynamic private key setup algorithm.*
   - *Set $C_{UP} = (U, Date)$. This is called UP's dynamic public key credential.*
   - *U sends to UP C_{UP} and SK_{UP}.*
2. *UP checks if C_{UP} and SK_{UP} are created correctly. If the check does not pass then UP rejects C_{UP}; otherwise UP's dynamic private key for U is SK_{UP} and the respective matching dynamic public key is C_{UP}.*

The dynamic key setup algorithms, Q and T, and how to check the correctness of the resulted keys have been described in Section 4.2.

The dynamic private key SK_{UP} with UP can be treated with lightweight protection. Notice that in the event of this dynamic private key being compromised, it cannot be used to derive U's static private key s_U, or dynamic private keys for other dates. The hardness of trying to derive these keys from a compromised SK_{UP} is discussed in Appendix A.

---

[1] MyProxy is a high-end secure Web services-based system which stores the users' long-term credentials so that the users can access grid resource from anywhere by logging into the MyProxy Server and have their proxy credentials securely generated by the server [13].

"Improved Protocol 1" is functionally the same as "Protocol 1" in the GSI, except that in the latter case, C_{UP} output from "Protocol 1" is in the conventional public key certificate in the certification infrastructure X.509. The improvement is in the following sense:

- C_{UP} output from "Improved Protocol 1" is a function of Date and U's static key certificate, which can be computed from U's static key certificate (and used) by a remote party without the need of an additional communication;
- C_{UP} output from "Protocol 1" of GSI is random, and has to be communicated to a certificate verifier (which in this case is the user himself), even if a remote party already knows U's certificate.

The advantage of being able to save communication before using C_{UP} by a remote party can be important. This will become clearer in the following proposed protocols.

Protocol for Resource Allocation by UP. "Improved Protocol 2" is run between UP, who holds a dynamic secret key SK_{UP}, and a resource proxy RP. The purpose of this protocol is for UP to allocate resource through RP. Recall that UP acts on behalf of U.

Improved Protocol 2: Resource Allocation.

Assumption. *UP has PK_{RP} which is an authenticated copy of the static public key of a resource proxy RP. RP has access to an authenticated copy of the static public key PK_U of U. UP has the dynamic private key SK_{UP}. H_1 and H_2 are two suitable hash functions. $\mathcal{E}$ is a suitable symmetric key encryption algorithm.*
UP and RP interact as follows:

1. *Let a message r be a resource allocation request specification. UP signs r under its dynamic private key SK_{UP} to obtain $Sig_{UP}(r)$. This can be done by using the IBS mechanism described in Appendix C. UP then sends r and $Sig_{UP}(r)$ to RP in a secret and authenticated way such as encrypting them under PK_{RP} using the IBE mechanism described in Appendix B.*
2. *Upon receipt of r and $Sig_{UP}(r)$, RP checks validation of the signature. If it is valid, RP checks whether U is authorised by local policy to make the allocation request. If the request can be honoured, RP creates a resource-credential tuple m, containing the user's name U.*
3. *RP securely passes the resource-credential tuple to UP. It can be done by using the IBE mechanism.*
4. *UP examines the resource-credential tuple, and, if it wishes to approve it, signs the tuple to produce a process credential, C_{RP}, for the requesting resource. UP securely passes C_{RP} to RP. Again, the signing and secure passing process can be done by using the IBS and IBE mechanisms, respectively.*
5. *RP allocates the resource and passes the new process(es) C_{RP}, where C_{RP} is a signature $Sig_{UP}(m)$. As all of the other credentials, C_{RP} should be kept secret in RP.*

"Improved Protocol 2" is also functionally similar to "Protocol 2" in GSI. In the latter case, RP in Step 2 will verify UP's signature using a random certificate of UP, and then further verify the authenticity of the random certificate. Now in Step 2 of "Improved Protocol 2", the verification of the signature uses UP's dynamic public key certificate $(U, Date)$ which is computed from U's static certificate rather than received from UP. This seems to be a small improvement. However, it can be significant in the general case of resource allocation from a process. Let us further discuss this in "Improved Protocol 3".

Improved Protocol 3: Resource Allocation from A Process.

Assumption RP_1 in "Site 1" and RP_2 in "Site 2" have access to an authenticated copy of a static public key PK_U of U. RP_1 has a process credential $C_{RP_1} = Sig_{UP}(m)$ created in "Improved Protocol 2". UP has the dynamic private key SK_{UP}. They all have access to an authenticated copy of the other's static public key. H_1 and H_2 are two suitable hash functions. $\mathcal{E}$ is a suitable symmetric key encryption algorithm.

1. Let m' be allocation request parameters including the names U, RP_1 and RP_2. RP_1 first signs m' under an aggregate private signing key $Sig_{UP}(m)$ to obtain $Sig_{RP_1}(Sig_{UP}(m), m')$ by using the aggregate signature mechanism described in Section 4.3. RP_1 sends the allocation request parameters and the signature to RP_2 in a secret and authenticated way, such as encrypting them under the RP_2's static public key.
2. Upon receipt of m' and $Sig_{RP_1}(Sig_{UP}(m), m')$, RP_2 checks validation of the aggregate signature. If it is valid, RP_2 checks whether U is authorised by local policy to make the allocation request. If the request can be honoured, RP_2 creates a resource-credential tuple m'', containing the user's name U.
3. The following steps are the same as in Protocol 2. RP_2 securely passes the resource-credential tuple to UP.
4. UP examines the resource-credential tuple, and, if it wishes to approve it, signs the tuple to produce a process credential, C_{RP_2}, for the requesting resource. UP securely passes C_{RP_2} to RP_2. This can be done by using the IBE and IBS mechanisms.
5. RP_2 allocates the resource and passes the new process(es) C_{RP_2}, where C_{RP_2} is a signature $Sig_{UP}(m'')$. As with all other credentials, C_{RP_2} should be kept secret in RP_2.

Protocol for Resource Allocation by a Process. In the general case of resource allocation in the grid, it is a process in a resource site that is the initiator for a resource allocation request. This is because in the general case a process which has been allocated to a user may need more resource dynamically. In GSI, this is done by "Protocol 3" in which a process in "Site 1" (see Figure 1) finds more resource in "Site 2" and then calls "Protocol 2" which is run between UP and RP in "Site 2". Through this way of resource allocation, UP must be the initiator in "Protocol 2". Thus, UP is in a centre position and has to initiate cryptographic operations in order to run Protocol 2 with a new RP in additional sites. Figure 1 only depicts "Site 2", however the general case can be "Site n". We consider this a major weakness: UP can be vulnerable to a denial-of-service attack.

"Improved Protocol 3" changes the way of operation by UP, it is now in the position of a responder. When new resource in "Site 2" (or "Site n") is needed, RP in that site can be an initiator and it processes cryptographic operations which will then be sent to UP. Notice that by using our dynamic public key cryptographic technique, RP can compute the public key of UP for the day from U's static certificate without the need of interacting with UP. This is not possible in the GSI using the conventional X.509 proxy certificate since a proxy certificate is random and RP must first communicate with UP to obtain it.

Note that the public key of UP involved in "Improved Protocol 3" might not be the same as UP involved in "Improved Protocol 2". This is because the lifetime of the public key might not last longer than the time needed to complete the job carried out by P. Without loss of generality we denote $(U, Date_1)$ as the public key of UP involved in "Improved Protocol 2" and $(U, Date_2)$ as the public key of UP involved in "Improved Protocol 3".

In "Improved Protocol 3", UP can be in the position of a responder because its dynamic public key can be computed by any party which has the static certificate of the user U for whom UP is the proxy. In a grid application, UP may be at a client platform of U or may be at a server platform which serves many end users; in the former case the client is usually a low-end platform, and in the latter case, the server is in a highly demanded position. Both cases put UP in a performance bottleneck position within a grid environment. In the GSI, the use of a conventional public key certificate by UP means that UP must always first transmits its proxy certificate to RP before running "Protocol 3". Thus in the GSI, UP seems to be placed in the centre of heavy communications and computations.

We should recap that a grid application may have a lengthy duration (consider a long period of cooperative work among a group of scientists). Thus, in a dynamic VO, a newly recruited RP in "Protocol 3" or "Improved Protocol 3" in general does not have a long term relationship with the members in the VO. In our improved case, a newly recruited RP can compute dynamic public key identifier $(U, Date_2)$ to create an "authenticated" public key for the UP from a given static certificate of U.

Our improvement in "Protocol 3" particularly suits the case that UP is on a server which serves many end users. In this case, a user U can sign-on to the server and request for a dynamic private key. All the subsequent authentication which involves the user can be carried out by UP on the server. Being in a more lightweight responder position, such UP is less vulnerable to denial-of-service attacks. In such an architecture, the server can be a "resource broker" which serves as a portal for the user to enter a grid VO.

6 Conclusions

We have proposed improvements to the security architecture and protocols in GSI version 2. The technical enabler of our improvements is a non-interactive authentication notion from a newly identified cryptographic application of bilinear pairing technique. In our proposed modification to the GSI architecture, remote resource providers can compute a user's dynamic public key without interactions with the user's proxy platform, and can thereby play the initiator's role in mutual entity authentication. The user's proxy platform in the modified architecture can have the following features:

- It can be provided dynamic private keys of a user without endangering any long-term security of the user.
- The non-interactive way of entity authentication means that the user proxy can operate in a responder's role, and with lightweight cryptographic performance.
- It can either be a low-end client platform, or be placed in a central server position to act as a resource broker. In the latter case, grid services can become widely available to users who do not have high-performance platforms. This is exactly what grid computing means as a future computing model.

The GSI version 2 seems to have poor performance and low scalability. This is mainly because the user's proxy platform is heavily involved in performing mutual entity authentication with other resources. Our modified architecture and protocols improve this situation.

References

1. Barreto, P.S.L.M., Kim, H.Y., Lynn, B., Scott, M.: Efficient algorithms for pairing-based cryptosystems. In: Yung, M. (ed.) CRYPTO 2002. LNCS, vol. 2442, pp. 354–368. Springer, Heidelberg (2002)
2. Boneh, D., Gentry, C., Lynn, B., Shacham, H.: Aggregate and verifiably encrypted signatures frombilinear maps. In: Biham, E. (ed.) EUROCRPYT 2003. LNCS, vol. 2656, p. 416. Springer, Heidelberg (2003)
3. Boneh, D., Franklin, M.: Identity based encryption from the Weil pairing. In: Kilian, J. (ed.) CRYPTO 2001. LNCS, vol. 2139, pp. 213–229. Springer, Heidelberg (2001)
4. Cha, J.C., Cheon, J.H.: An identity-based signature from gap Diffie-Hellman groups. In: Desmedt, Y.G. (ed.) PKC 2003. LNCS, vol. 2567, pp. 18–30. Springer, Heidelberg (2002)
5. Cocks, C.: An Identity-Based Encryption Scheme Based on Quadratic Residues. In: Honary, B. (ed.) Cryptography and Coding. LNCS, vol. 2260, pp. 360–363. Springer, Heidelberg (2001)
6. Diffie, W., Hellman, M.E.: New directions in cryptography. IEEE Trans. Info. Theory IT-22(6), 644–654 (1976)
7. Dodis, Y., Katz, J., Xu, S., Yung, M.: Key-Insulated Public Key Cryptosystems. In: Knudsen, L.R. (ed.) EUROCRYPT 2002. LNCS, vol. 2332, pp. 65–82. Springer, Heidelberg (2002)

8. Foster, I., Kesselman, C.: The Grid: Blueprint for a New Computing Infrastructure. In: Computational Grids. ch. 2, pp. 15–51. Morgan Kaufmann, San Francisco (1999)
9. Foster, I., Kesselman, C., Tsudik, G., Tuecke, S.: A security architecture for Computational Grids. In: Proceedings of the 5th ACM Conference on Computer and Communications Security, pp. 83–92 (1998)
10. Foster, I., Kesselman, C., Tuecke, S.: The anatomy of the Grid: Enabling scalable virtual organizations. International Journal of High Performance Computing Applications 15(3), 200–222 (2001)
11. Galbraith, S.D., Harrison, K., Soldera, D.: Implementing the Tate pairing. In: Fieker, C., Kohel, D.R. (eds.) Algorithmic Number Theory. LNCS, vol. 2369, pp. 324–337. Springer, Heidelberg (2002)
12. ITU-T. Rec. X.509 (revised) the Directory — Authentication Framework, International Telecommunication Union, Geneva, Switzerland (equivalent to ISO/IEC 9594-8:1995.) (1993)
13. Novotny, J., Tuecke, S., Welch, V.: An online credential repository for the Grid: MyProxy. In: Proceedings of the 10th IEEE International Symposium on High Performance Distributed Computing (HPDC-10 2001), pp. 104–111. IEEE Computer Society, Los Alamitos (2001)
14. Rivest, R.L., Shamir, A., Adleman, L.: A method for obtaining digital signatures and public-key cryptosystems. Communications of the ACM 21(2), 120–126 (1978)
15. Sakai, R., Kasahara, M.: ID based Cryptosystems with Pairing on Elliptic Curve. Cryptology ePrint Archive, Report (2003)/054
16. Sakai, R., Ohgishi, K., Kasahara, M.: Cryptosystems Based on Pairing. In: The 2000 Symposium on Cryptography and Information Security, Okinawa, Japan (January 2000)
17. Sakai, R., Ohgishi, K., Kasahara, M.: Cryptosystems Based on Pairing over Elliptic Curve. In: The 2001 Symposium on Cryptography and Information Security, Oiso, Japan (January 2001) (In Japanese)
18. Shamir, A.: Identity-Based Cryptosystems and Signature Schemes. In: Blakely, G.R., Chaum, D. (eds.) CRYPTO 1984. LNCS, vol. 196, pp. 47–53. Springer, Heidelberg (1985)
19. Tzeng, W., Tzeng, Z.: Robust Key-Evolving Public Key Encryption Schemes. In: Deng, R.H., Qing, S., Bao, F., Zhou, J. (eds.) ICICS 2002. LNCS, vol. 2513, pp. 61–72. Springer, Heidelberg (2002)

A   The Difficulty of Finding Private Keys

In this appendix, we examine whether the disclosed key material of Alice can lead to disclosure of any form of Alice's private keys. We consider three different cases of private key disclosure from the known information.

i) Alice's static private key a from the static public key or from additionally disclosed dynamic private keys;

ii) Computing any dynamic private key from the static public key;

iii) Computing any future dynamic private key from the static public key and a disclosed past or the current dynamic private key.

The problem in case (i) is clearly the elliptic-curve discrete logarithm problem. In fact, because P is a generator of $\mathbb{G}_1$, we can view $Q(A, Date)$ being generated by P (i.e., $Q(A, Date) = zP$ for some unknown $z \in \mathbb{Z}_q*$) and hence $aQ(A, Date)$ is also generated by part of the static public key aP. An attacker can generate as many points as possible $aP' = b(aP) = a(bP)$ by applying the scalar multiplication. These actions won't reduce the difficulty of the discrete logarithm problem.

The problem in case (ii) is to use the known information

$$(P, aP, Q(A, Date))$$

to compute a dynamic private key $aQ(A, Date)$. Observe that this is the computational Diffie-Hellman problem and hence is intractable.

The problem in case (iii) can be presented as follows without loss of generality: using the known information

$$(P, aP, Q(A, Date_1), aQ(A, Date_1), \cdots, Q(A, Date_i), aQ(A, Date_i), Q(A, Date'))$$

to compute the dynamic private key $aQ(A, Date')$ where $Date'$ is different from $Date_1$, $Date_2$, ..., $Date_i$. Notice that because collision resistance property of the function f, the point $Q(A, Date')$ can be considered to be independent from the points $Q(A, Date_1)$, $aQ(A, Date_1)$, $\cdots$, $Q(A, Date_i)$, $aQ(A, Date_i)$. Therefore, the only input values which are relevant to the problem are still $(P, aP, Q(A, Date'))$, and hence the problem in this case remains being the computational Diffie-Hellman problem.

B Application I of Key Dynamation: Encryption

Let Bob have in possession of Alice's static certificate $Cert_A$. To send a confidential message m to Alice which can be decrypted by Alice's client machine on the date $Date$, Bob performs the following encryption operations

1. Pick a random number $r \in \mathbb{Z}_q^*$ and compute

$$rP, \quad k = H(\hat{e}_q(rQ(A, Date), aP))$$

   where P and aP are points taken from $Cert_A$, $Q(A, Date)$ is Alice's dynamic public key on the date $Date$, and H is a suitable hash-function.
2. Send to Alice the ciphertext pair

$$(rP, \mathcal{E}(k, m))$$

   where $\mathcal{E}$ is any secure block cipher algorithm.

To decrypt this message, Alice's client machine computes

$$k = H(\hat{e}_q(rP, aQ(A, Date))).$$

Notice that this value is the same as the key used by Bob, since

$$\hat{e}_q(aQ(A, Date), rP) = \hat{e}_q(Q(A, Date), P)^{ra} = \hat{e}_q(rQ(A, Date), aP).$$

Hence, having the dynamic private key $aQ(A, Date)$, Alice's client machine can indeed use the correct key to decrypt the ciphertext $\mathcal{E}(k, m)$ and obtain the confidential message m.

Notice that the decryption can be done by the client using an ephemeral private key even when Alice is not present with the client. This is the central point of our key dynamation technique.

We assume that the encryption algorithm doesn't have weakness and that the best attack to obtain any knowledge about m from the ciphertext $\mathcal{E}(k, m)$ is to find the encryption key k. Then for an opponent who has the public information $(P, aP, Q(A, Date), rP)$, the task of finding $k = \hat{e}_q(rQ(A, Date), aP)$ is that of breaking the bilinear Diffie-Hellman problem. This is indeed the case if we consider $Q(A, Date) = zP$ for some unknown $z \in \mathbb{Z}_q^*$.

This encryption scheme is that of Sakai et al [17] and that of Boneh and Franklin [3]. We will refer to the scheme as IBE henceforth, since it is commonly called identity-based encryption.

C   Application II of Key Dynamation: Signatures

Let Alice's client machine have the dynamic private key $aQ(A, Date)$. Let H be a cryptographic hash function mapping from $\{0, 1\}^*$ to $\mathbb{Z}_q$. To sign a message m, the client performs the following steps

1. Pick a uniformly random number $r \in \mathbb{Z}_q^*$;
2. Compute $U = rQ(A, Date)$;
3. Compute $h = H(U, m)$;
4. Compute $V = (r + h)aQ(A, Date)$;
5. Output (U, V) as the signature.

Let Bob have $Cert_A$. To verify the signature (U, V) on the message m, Bob performs the following steps

1. Compute Alice's dynamic public key $Q(A, Date)$;
2. Compute $h = H(U, m)$;
3. Check if $\hat{e}_q(P, V) = \hat{e}_q(aP, U + hQ(A, Date))$; he accepts the signature as valid if and only if the equation holds.

We notice that due to the bilinearity of the pairing, Bob's evaluation of the pairing equation shows him that the point V satisfies

$$V = a(U + hQ(A, Date))$$

where the unknown integer a is the same as that in aP which is part of Alice's static public key material. The signature verification an easy decisional Diffie-Hellman question in $\mathbb{G}_1$, namely, answering the following question

Is $(P, aP, U + hQ(A, Date), V)$ a Diffie-Hellman instance in $\mathbb{G}_1$?

Since this question is easy in $\mathbb{G}_1$, Bob can make the correct decision efficiently. However, to create the valid signature, the only known algorithm is that Alice or the client authorised by her use the dynamic private key $aQ(A, Date)$. From this argument, only Alice or the client authorised by Alice could have created the signature.

This signature scheme is that of Cha and Cheon [4]. We will refer to the scheme as IBS henceforth, since it is commonly called identity-based signatures.

User-Friendly Grid Security Architecture and Protocols
(Transcript of Discussion)

Hoon Wei Lim

Information Security Group,
Royal Holloway, University of London

My talk which includes some background information about grid computing, grid security, security infrastructure, and also some of the limitations, our proposal on some security protocols, what are the improvements, and a summary.

A computational grid allows a user to submit a very computational intensive job from different kind of platforms to some remote resources, so that these remote resources can execute the job on behalf of the user, and return the relevant result back to the user. The nature of the job is normally very complex and complicated such as those for advanced science and engineering applications which normally require a long time to complete.

Currently the Globus Toolkit is the most widely used open-source toolkit for building a grid system, and its security component is called the GSI, which provides some standard security services, and also some grid specific security services such as single sign-on and delegation. The GSI is based on PKI, but with some additional properties because it uses two types of certificates: standard X.509 certificates and proxy certificates which are short-term certificates that will usually last for less than 24 hours.

One of the limitations of the GSI is its scalability. Potentially within a single job submission the user has to interact with more than one resource, and that means he has to perform mutual authentication many times via the standard SSL or TLS protocol. For a lower than average user platform, this may seem to be a bit expensive in terms of computational power and bandwidth requirement. In our paper, we propose a different kind of key management technique from the conventional PKI approach by using some properties from bilinear pairing. It allows a user to compute a short-term public key, called a dynamic public key, on-the-fly, by using some static information which is publicly available. Any users who have a copy of my certificate can compute a new fresh short-term public key on-the-fly without actually interacting with me. You will see how this can be applied in a grid environment in a short while.

Here's a list of grid security requirements. I'm not going to go through each of these but I just want to mention single sign-on can be very important within a grid environment because, as I mentioned earlier, within a single job submission session potentially the user has to perform mutual authentication with more than one server, so it would be very useful if the user can logon once, and all the subsequent authentication can be performed by the user's machine automatically without any physical intervention from the user. As with any

B. Christianson et al. (Eds.): Security Protocols 2005, LNCS 4631, pp. 157–161, 2007.
© Springer-Verlag Berlin Heidelberg 2007

other distributed systems, protection of credentials is very important, especially a long-term private key, therefore within a grid environment normally a short-term public/private key pair are used for job submission.

This is an overview of the GSI. We have a user, the user proxy, which is some sort of session manager which acts on behalf of the user to interact with all these resources, and within each resource there exists a resource proxy which is created for a single user, so each user will have a different resource proxy. And if the job submitted by the user can be divided into many sub-tasks which can be run in parallel, then many processes can be created to handle all these sub-tasks.

Today we're going to look at a few protocols which run on this architecture. The first one is about issuance of proxy credential to the user proxy from the user. This is pretty straightforward, it's just a generation of a short-term public/private key pair. The second protocol that we'll look at is about resource allocation from the user proxy to a remote resource. Protocol 3 is about resource allocation from the process rather than from the user proxy, and this protocol is a bit complicated because it requires a call to Protocol 2 which is between the user proxy and the resource proxy.

In Protocol 1, the user gains access to his computer and creates a short-term public/private key pair, and then the user will sign the short-term public key using his long-term private key. The proxy credential will contain the user's ID, validity period, and so on. In Protocol 2, first of all, the user proxy and the resource proxy will perform mutual authentication via the standard TLS handshake protocol. After that the user proxy sends a signed request which contains some job information to the resource proxy. The resource proxy will verify the signatures and perform some checks, if it's OK it will then create a resource credential which contains the user ID, and send it back to the user proxy. The user proxy will check the resource credential, and then sign the resource credential using his short-term private key, and then send it back to the resource proxy. So this is called the process credential, which will be held by the process within the resource. By doing that the resource proxy allocates the resource to the user.

Now this is a protocol which will be called by a process within the resource to another remote resource. Say, for example, we have two sites, Site 1 and Site 2. If a process in Site 1, widentifies that the job requires some additional remote resources to finish the job, it will first contact the user proxy, and then the user proxy will again perform mutual authentication with Site 1, so in Protocol 2 that we looked at earlier, the user proxy has already performed mutual authentication once, now he has to perform it again. The process will send a signed request to the user proxy, if the user proxy is happy with the request, he will call Protocol 2 which will be run between the user proxy and Site 2. So again, another mutual authentication.

These are some limitations of the GSI. Key generation may be a problem for some low-end platforms. RSA key generation is widely known to be very computationally expensive, therefore this may not be a good thing for low-end user platforms since every time when the user submits a job he has to generate some short-term public/private key pairs. Also the short-term public key has to be certified with a proxy certificate, and then be forwarded to the remote resource before it can be used, and it is very user-oriented because every time the Site to which the user has submitted the job identifies some additional resources, this new Site has to go back to the user and perform mutual authentication, and so on as in Protocols 2 and 3, before the new resource can be allocated.

We propose two techniques which seem to be useful for grid environments. The first one is using dynamic public keys. A dynamic public key, or short-term public key, is actually a function of a user's identity and a date. Anyone can compute a new fresh short-term public key by using some fixed information from the certificate.

The second is an aggregate signature scheme. This scheme allows different users to sign different messages, and these signatures can then be aggregated and form an aggregate signature which can be verified by any verifying party, by using only two pairing computations, regardless of the length of the signature chain. This can be quite useful within a grid environment.

Here's our proposed proxy creation protocol, it's almost the same as the one that I talked about earlier, except that the short-term public key can be created by anyone using the user's static certificate, because this is publicly available, and also the date is assumed to be known by every entity.

This is our proposed Protocol 2. It's pretty much the same as the previously described Protocol 2, except that after the user proxy has sent a signed request to the resource proxy, the resource proxy can verify the signature using a dynamic public key, which the resource proxy can create on-the-fly by using the user's static certificate. So this can save some computational power, and also some bandwidth resource from the user's site.

This is Protocol 3. Again for this example, we have two Sites. If a process in Site 1 identifies some additional resources, then rather than going back to the user, the resource proxy in Site 1 can now actually contact Site 2 straightaway by using the aggregate signature scheme that we propose. Resource proxy in Site 1 will send a signed request to resource proxy in Site 2, so RP2 will verify the signature, check if everything is OK, and create a new resource credential, and only then he'll send it back to the user proxy. Please note that there isn't any mutual authentication involved between the user proxy, Site 1 and Site 2 at this point. What the user proxy needs to do is just to verify this resource credential, and if he's happy, he can create a process credential, and send it back to the new Site directly.

So as you can see, rather than be user-oriented, most of the mutual authentication can be performed at the server site. This can cut down quite a bit the computational power required at the user site and also, because the user proxy has become more lightweight now, we can actually allocate the user proxy on a very high performance server that can act as a resource broker which can serve many user proxies.

Summary. We have proposed a different kind of key management technique from the conventional PKI approach. Our approach seems to be more lightweight than the conventional approach. In the conventional approach, every time the user wants to submit a job he has to create a new public key, certify the public key, and send it to the user proxy. Every time when the user requires additional resources the user has to perform mutual authentication with the new additional remote resources. So we think that our approach can improve the performance of the grid system because of the lightweight key management approach.

James Malcolm. The original GSI supports delegation, whereby one resource server can delegate work to another resource server. However, this requires the second resource server to go back to the user to get authentication. Why didn't the original delegation protocol support a longer chain of delegation?

Reply. Well GSI version 2 uses a delegation protocol, but just between the user proxy and the resource sites. Maybe I should show you this slide again. The user proxy indeed delegates his credentials to the resource so that the resource can act on behalf of the user to communicate with other resources, but then has to go back to the user again to perform mutual authentication. So the delegation is just between the user proxy and Site 1, it's not a long delegation. This is, I think, the architecture for the older version of the GSI which is still in use in some grid projects. The new version has fixed this problem, but it still has the issue of using long chains of delegations between many sites. Our proposed aggregate signature scheme can be used in that case as well for the efficient signature verification.

Bruce Christianson. Is it easy to correlate a dynamic key or a public key with the public key that it evolved from, if you haven't been given the correlation itself?

Reply. Do you mean a short-term public key, a new public key?

Bruce Christianson. Yes.

Reply. The user has to send a copy of his static certificate to other sites before these sites can compute the short-term public key, based on some parameters on the certificate.

Bruce Christianson. Oh sure, but a third party may not know the long-term public key from which the short-term public key was generated. Can a third party correlate the short-term public key within the environment in which it's arrived without knowing that static certificate?

Reply. The answer is no. The short-term public key is useless unless the third party has information about the parameters contained in the certificate. Any party can verify the short-term public key created by anyone, but only based on some parameters from the certificate.

Simon Foley. What's your opinion of the ways that the grid gets used in practice? What impression do you get about this tortuous process of certificate generation and issuance, and then in turn this tortuous process of getting authorisation to use various machines on the grid itself. It's not a very easy system to administer.

Reply. Yes, that's the problem! That's what currently happens. Every time, before the user submits a job the user has to create a proxy certificate, and then the user has to forward both certificates, the long-term and the short-term, to a remote resource via the SSL handshake.

Simon Foley. But how do the actual long-term certificates themselves get processed by the CAs. My experience is that it's tortuous to actually try and get a CA to certify your public key.

Reply. Yes, I agree with you.

Simon Foley. So are you familiar with any work that's trying to make it a bit easier to administer the certification process?

Reply. Not really! For people from the grid community, they think that PKI is a stable and widely used technology, so they just make use of existing technologies. Yes, I agree that it's really a pain that grid systems require extensive use of certificates. That's why we've come up with this proposal, trying to cut down the use of certificates.

Countering Automated Exploits with System Security CAPTCHAS

Dinan Gunawardena[1], Jacob Scott[2], Alf Zugenmaier[3,*], and Austin Donnelly[1]

[1] Microsoft Research Cambridge, UK
{dinang,austind}@microsoft.com
[2] UC Berkley, CA, USA
jhs@ocf.berkley.edu
[3] DoCoMo Euro-Labs, Munich, Germany
zugenmaier@docomolab-euro.com

Abstract. Many users routinely log in to their system with system administrator privileges. This is especially true of home users. The advantage of this setup is that these users can do everything necessary to fulfil their tasks with the computer. The disadvantage is that every program running in the users context can make arbitrary modifications to the system. Malicious programs and scripts often take advantage of this and silently change important parameters. We propose to verify that these changes were initiated by a human by a ceremony making use of a CAPTCHA (Completely Automated Public Turing Test to Tell Computers and Humans Apart). We compare this approach with other methods of achieving the same goal, i.e. passwords, secure path and access control based on zone of origin of the code.

1 Introduction

Most users need to fulfil at least two roles when dealing with their computer. In one role they do their day to day activities with the system. In the other they perform systems administration. Most users are usually logged in with the maximum privileges that they ever need, which often are local system administrator privileges. It has often been proposed to give users minimum privilege, however in many cases that is not feasible as users will on occasion have to change crucial system parameters. Spyware, scripts, and viruses are usually crafted in such a manner that they initially are executed in the users context. They then change system parameters that allow them to do their evil deed, such as spy on the users network activity, change the dial-up phonebook entry to a premium rate number, or ensure that they are executed every time the computer is booted up. We try to find a user friendly way in which the user can be asked for permission to change important parameters. This should happen in a way that cannot be subverted programmatically. Ellison [1] is the first to describe ceremonies as an extension of network security protocols. Ceremonies try to include the actual

---

* This work was done while the authors were at Microsoft Research Cambridge.

B. Christianson et al. (Eds.): Security Protocols 2005, LNCS 4631, pp. 162–169, 2007.

humans sitting in front of the computer as an important active entity that is vital to achieving security properties. We propose a ceremony ensuring a human authorises changes to protect important configuration parameters of a computer system from inadvertent change through the user or a program running in the users context. The concept is based on the system issuing a challenge to the user that can only be solved by a human. This challenge acts as a warning that something crucial is being altered and also as a barrier for automatic exploits. This article is structured as follows: First we describe the concept of system security CAPTCHAS, the ceremony that proves that a human was involved in the protocol and not just a program that has taken over input and output. We then present a preliminary evaluation of the idea, based on a small prototype. Potential alternatives are discussed in Section 4. The paper finishes with conclusions.

2   System Security CAPTCHAs (SSCs)

In a Turing test a person tries to determine whether the entity responding to his or her inputs is a human or a computer [2]. Completely automated public Turing tests (CAPTCHAS) [3,4] are in some respect a reverse Turing test – a computer is trying to determine that an entity responding to its inputs is a human. When combined with access control, they represent a way of ensuring that a human was involved in the decision to access a specific resource. The response to a CAPTCHA cannot be scripted. Web based email providers already successfully employ this technique to mitigate creation of a large number of email addresses that could be used to send unsolicited bulk email. Usually CAPTCHAS are based on a hard AI problem, such as recognition of severely distorted characters or audio streams.

These CAPTCHAS can now be used in a discretionary override of access control. The concept of discretionary override of access control [5] is based on the observation that currently deployed access control policies only have the option to allow or disallow an action. Sometimes an action should be disallowed at most times, but there should be a way to override this decision. System parameters (e.g. the Windows registry) are subject to access control, such as NTSEC. With System Security CAPTCHAs (SSC), the security policy can specify not only allow or deny, it could also require a user to correctly solve an SSC. The configuration change is either allowed or disallowed subject to the validation of the SSC. The system has to store some additional context or message to present to the user related to the parameter that some application has attempted to change (e.g. if this were an attempt to disable the firewall, an appropriate message to present to the user could be retrieved from a system string table).

To decide which parameters could be protected protect using SSC we did a cursory analysis of malware, and some brainstorming. The complete obviously depends on the system to be protected.

Some examples of parameters and API calls thet lend themselves to be protected with SSCs:

- Enabling or disabling the SSC configuration
- Automatic startup extensibility points [6]
- Firewall reconfiguration
- Virus protection configuration
- System software installation
- API to change security permissions
- API to access non-sandboxed resources
- Attempt to change telephone number for the system telephone dialler application (i.e. block rogue diallers)
- Maximum number of incomplete TCP connections allowed (Windows XPSP2 scanning worm propagation mitigation technique) configuration changes.
- Attempt to change registry settings regarding the network stack layers which is a favourite place to install Spyware
- Attempt to change the Start-up sequence (Autostart folder etc.)
- Enabling the exporting of a file system e.g. sharing C\$ on the network should test whether a human is really attempting to perform the action.
- Verifying system activation and similar system licensing related API calls.

Because changes to the parameters often come in bulk, it makes sense to wrap the changes into a transaction that either commits all changes made by one process or discards all changes. The following list gives some examples of parameters and API calls that are unpracitcal to protect with SSCs.

- Every disk access
- Installation of signed/trusted software

2.1 A Credit Based Extension for Reducing CAPTCHA Usability Overhead

To reduce the overhead of asking the user for a CAPTCHA for every single security critical interaction, a scheme is possible whereby each security critical parameter has a virtual cost associated with its alteration (with that cost being proportional to the severity of the security impact of the parameter being changed). Users start with a credit threshold above which they must answer a CAPTCHA. If the CAPTCHA challenge is failed, the configuration changes are undone (back to the state at the last successful challenge or some well defined snapshot from a system point). The scheme is as follows:

1. System starts up, all security critical parameters have been audited and assigned a credit cost P_i for their reconfiguration by the user. Any parameter without an associated credit cost may be (optionally) given a nominal cost P_{default} as set by system policy. The system associates a SSC subsystem callback with each of the security critical parameters identified in the audit, the system startup parameter values are snapshot and stored in secure storage by the SSC subsystem.

2. When the user logs on, her SSC parameter modification cost U_p is set to 0. The SSC system retrieves the users associated SSC credit threshold U_t and stores it (with U_p) in secure storage. In addition, the SSC subsystem stores an empty list L_p in the secure storage (this will be used to store parameter change tuples).

3. When a user modifies system parameters that the SSC is monitoring, P_i is added to U_p.

    (a) If $U_p < U_t$, the parameter changed is added to a list of parameter tuples changed by the user (L_p), along with the old value of the parameter i.e. ¡parameter identifier, old parameter value¿.

    (b) If $U_p \geq U_t$, the user is issued with a SSC challenge.

        i. If the challenge is passed, U_p is set to zero and the parameter change is allowed and the list of parameters changed is set to the empty list.

        ii. If the challenge fails, U_p is set to zero, all the parameters in Lp are reverted to the old parameter value and Lp is set to the empty list. The snapshot value for the last 'good' configuration parameter is updated to reflect the current parameter value.

2.2   Optional Extensions of the Credit Based Scheme

The following extensions are independent of each other. 1. Time period linked credit: The credit may be allowed to build up using some standard leaky bucket based scheme so that the value U_t is automatically and dynamically calculated based on the token bucket parameters associated with the U_t update as set by system policy. Obviously there is the danger of a script delaying its actions sufficiently that U_t is always 0. 2. Automatic and distributed calculation of P_i and U_t: To avoid a full audit of security parameters, $P_{default}$ can be set to some unit value. Every time a parameter is updated, Pi can be incremented by $P_{default}$. If any P_i exceeds some threshold P_g set by group policy, the parameter identifier can be forwarded by the SSC subsystem to a group administrator, following a local SSC challenge. The administrator may then decide whether this parameter is security critical or not and push down a fixed P_i to all users in the administrative group, by group policy. The same mechanism can be used to set U_t dynamically in this case, P_i values may be dynamically calculated or fixed. If U_p exceeds some threshold U_g set by group policy, the parameter value list L_p can be forwarded by the SSC subsystem to a group administrator following a local SSC challenge. The administrator may then decide whether the L_p chain is too long or too short for the level of security required and push down a fixed U_t to all users in the administrative group by group policy.

Either of the above schemes could be used whilst a system is under test (prior to deployment) to calculate reasonable static values for per configuration parameter credit costs or thresholds.

2.3   Possible Drawbacks of the Credit Based Scheme

If unit cost is known to attacker, changes can be aimed to stay below threshold. Accurately determining the criticality value of a system parameter is difficult. In addition, criticality of parameters may not be additive. Many of these problems are mitigated if commit happens on exit of program and SSC will be raised in all cases if $U_t > 0$.

2.4   Non Security Centric Applications for SSC

Some ideas for applications that go beyond the protection of API calls or the Trusted Computing Base (non-User/Kernel e.g. Master Boot Record, BIOS, firmware, microcode etc.) that have already been suggested include:

Human in the loop check for *safety* critical systems. There are numerous computer systems / processes that are critical to safety e.g. nuclear power plant monitoring, railway/flight traffic control systems, security monitoring of premises where it is important to ensure that the system is being actively monitored by a human. In these scenarios, if a malicious script or automated process were to be able to subvert the 'human in the loop' test then there might be dire consequences for safety. It is possible to use a SSC to verify the continued presence of a human being to avoid the threat. This somewhat akin to a 'dead man's hand' switch concept.

Service still in use (by a human) for billing purposes. With the migration to software as a service, one possible billing model is usage (time) based billing. Current billing models for software are usually based on upfront license fees and the use of some explicit of implicit license server. This model is suboptimal when the user can rent the use of an application for shorter periods on an ad-hoc basis. One problem with distributed application renting is it is hard to distinguish user inactivity from user session completed but not logged out correctly. This has a ramification for billing and charging. I.e. the billing system will bill the user from the last time the user interacted with the system plus some inactivity time-out (in the case where the user did not correctly terminate the session e.g. by logging out). One could suggest a simple 'this application has been idle for some time, would you like to keep this application open YES/NO' type query. This could be subverted by malicious automated software on the users system (the incentive for the malicious software is to keep a usage based billing channel open to unduly load/deny service at the server or to increase the revenue for a disreputable service provider). It is possible to use a SSC instead of this simple 'YES/NO' dialog to avert this problem. Consequently, there might be fewer billing queries from the user.

3   Evaluation

This evaluation is based on a small prototype that protects a chosen registry key using a SSC.

Security. Even though the program being run in the users context has full permission of the user, it cannot make full use of them. In our example human intervention is necessary to alter the protected registry key. This prevents automatic exploits from changing that registry key.

Possible attacks. For a program it may be possible to copy the SSC into different context, i.e. into a window claiming to change a different parameter than what is actually changed. But then, as soon as the SSC window pops up user should become suspicious anyways. In addition, responding to an SSC requires more effort than just clicking OK on a popup dialog box. In addition, just clicking o.K. could be scripted by a program taking over the user input. The malicious program could try to proxy the SSC to some real person over the Internet if necessary, this may be mitigated by not permitting network I/O while a SSC is being presented. This also requires the SSC to time out after a short period, so that network I/O can resume. An alternative approach so that unwitting users are not tricked into solving CAPTCHAs would be to bind the content of the CAPTCHA somehow to the request that triggered it.

Furthermore, a program that can access the security function directly (e.g. has kernel access) can circumvent the protection.

Usability. We have not done a proper usability study, yet. The usability will very likely depend on how often the SSCs get triggered. If it happens rarely (less than once a day), we expect the SSCs to be a real help. This depends very much on careful selection on the parameters to be protected. Software installation may require the installation of a large number of services and/or configuration changes to the system. If a CAPTCHA were requested for each of these changes, the user would quickly disable the SSC protection owing to intrusiveness and lack of usability.

Choice of CAPTCHA content. Whilst the exact content of the CAPTCHA presented to the user is outside the scope of this document, the recommendation is the CAPTCHA present a challenge that is contextually relevant to the security configuration change or user operation requested. The rationale behind this is to bind (mentally) the SSC solved with the action the user wants and expects to execute. In the absence of such a binding, the user may not consider the importance of solving the SSC. User complacency in this regard will reduce the value of the SSC subsystem mechanism as a whole.

4   Comparison with Other Approaches

Passwords. The alternative of having users remember a password for logging in with minimal privilege and using that for day to day business and an alternative password to that gives them system level privilege may be the right thing to do from the security standpoint, but has the drawback of too much cognitive burden. In addition, once the password is compromised, it can be used for all kinds of automated exploits.

User switching. Consciously switching users from normal to superuser requires foresight on part of the user. Often the user does not know in advance that the program he or she is about to execute requires system level privileges. This is often found out by the user at a later stage, the user then has to rerun the program to get it to execute in the correct context.

Trusted path. Proving that human intervention is involved in a specific process could also be done by using trusted path for input and output (e.g. CTRL-ALT-DEL). All programs possibly interacting with the user interface would have to be disabled for that period of time. Therefore, using a SSC has the advantage of being less intrusive. It also has the additional feature of requiring more human interaction than just clicking OK in a window, possibly leading to greater reflection of the person doing the SSC about what he/she is authorizing.

SSCs can also be used to lower the bar on trusted path. If the trusted path only provides secure output (i.e. it can be made sure that no other application can overlap or grab the content of the SSC window), but not secure input, the randomization of the required input ensures that the user input is useless for all other applications that may divert the input.[1]

Code origin. This is the approach taken by e.g. Internet Explorer that authorises code depending on where code that is to be executed comes from (e.g. which security zone). The drawback with this solution is that it is too easy to convince the computer that the code comes from a trusted zone (e.g. cross site scripting attacks or saving the code first on local disk).

5   Conclusion

The proposed ceremonies involving system security CAPTCHAS seems to be less secure than passwords, user switching, and secure path, but more useable. Code origin seems more usable but has been shown to be brittle. The SSC ceremonies try to explore further the possibilities of making automatic exploits more difficult while keeping the user in control. It tries to give the user a second chance with the first immutable law of computer security "once the bad guy has convinced the user to run his code, game over" [7].

References

1. Ellison, C.: UPnP Security Ceremonies Design Document (October 2003), www.upnp.org/download/standardizeddcps/UPnPSecurityCeremonies_1_0secure.pdf
2. Turing, A.M.: Computing machinery and intelligence. Mind 59(236), 433–460 (1950)
3. Ahn, L., von Blum, M., Hopper, N.J., Langford, J.: CAPTCHA: Telling humans and computers apart. In: Biham, E. (ed.) Advances in Cryptology – EUROCRPYT 2003. LNCS, vol. 2656, pp. 294–311. Springer, Heidelberg (2003)

---

[1] With secure output the challenge does not even have to be a hard problem, randomization is sufficient.

4. Ahn, L., von Blum, M., Hopper, N.J., Langford, J.: The CAPTCHA Web page; `http://www.captcha.net`
5. Rissanen, E., Firozabadi, B.S., Sergot, M.: Towards A Mechanism for Discretionary Overriding of Access Control. In: World Computer Congress (2004)
6. Wang, Y.-M., Roussev, R., Verbowski, C., Johnson, A., Wu, M.-W., Huang, Y., Kuo, S.-Y.: Gatekeeper: Monitoring Auto-Start Extensibility Points (ASEPs) for Spyware Management. In: Proc. Usenix LISA (November 2004)
7. Microsoft Corporation. 10 Immutable Laws of Security. Technet, `www.microsoft.com/technet/archive/community/columns/security/essays/10imlaws.mspx`

Countering Automated Exploits with System Security CAPTCHAS

(Transcript of Discussion)

Alf Zugenmaier

DoCoMo Euro-Labs, Munich, Germany

This talk is about putting the human in the loop, or rather making sure that there is a human in the loop. Sometimes we have this feeling that, while we're still responsible for what the computer does, we don't have control over what it does, and it would be nice to make sure that at least some human has seen what goes on. So this is about countering automated exploits with system security CAPTCHAs, I know it is a bad idea to have an acronym in the title but I was at Microsoft Research when we did this work. CAPTCHA for those of you who don't know, it is a Completely Automated Public Turing Test to Tell Computers and Humans Apart.

Agenda: first I will make the problem statement clear, then I'll present some existing approaches, or at least the ones that I found, and you can tell me about more possible approaches, then I'll explain what we did using CAPTCHAs for system security, then I'll come up with some issues which I am sure, at least the people who are awake will spot, the ones who are asleep probably have spotted them already, then finally conclusions. If I have time for that.

Problem statement: the way that computers work in most home environments, and actually also in quite a few office environments, is that users have admin rights, they don't maintain these roles separately, they just login, because some program requires them to run as admin they just always run as admin. Otherwise you know, we want to install something new it tells you, you don't have sufficient privilege, so eventually you give up and say, alright, I'll just always run as admin. So this principle of minimum privilege, that we have been preaching for I don't know how many years is violated, and so you run into this problem that scripted exploits can do anything they want to, they can install rogue dialogues, they can install [diversion here all laughing].

OK, you get these windows which tell you, click here to view that file, you click there and it starts installing applications. It may also be erasing a hard disk, because what's in the text and the window doesn't really have to do anything with the program code that's executed. These scripted exploits also may simulate user input, just take over control of your mouse and click on OK for you, even though you didn't really want to do that, or it just cleverly changes the focus of your window manager, just before you hit return it changes this thing to the "click here to delete all files".

B. Christianson et al. (Eds.): Security Protocols 2005, LNCS 4631, pp. 170–179, 2007.
© Springer-Verlag Berlin Heidelberg 2007

This is a bit of a problem, so we looked around, what are the approaches to solve this? Unix has explicit user switching, so if you run as user, you don't have all these admin rights, if you want to do anything like that you would say SU, and then VI /ETC/password, or whatever the editor of choice would be nowadays, and that's explicit user switching, you do that before you actually run the command that requires you to run as admin. That means you have to know in advance which of these programs require you to run as admin.

Ben Laurie: That's when you haven't setuid, right?

Reply: Yes, once you have setuid even a rogue program can start the setuid program. Basically anyone can start it. You have given away all rights for the setuid program.

Ben Laurie: But isn't to set UID better than just doing SU because if somebody does SU root...

Reply: Well at least you have the advantage of having a entered a password in case of SU root. If you use setuid then anyone can just start the program and it runs.

Simon Foley: If it really worries you that you have to know in advance then you can write a two line script, instead of the one line script you need with SU.

Reply: Yes, OK. That goes here. Then rather like that, there's the kind of password protection which the Mac has, which tells you, you have to enter your root password now, because you want to run this program requiring root rights. I keep having to enter this root password. So, up pops this window, enter root password now, and again, enter root password now. You do that about five times a day. You somehow lose track of why did the system now ask for this root password. It could be a website popping up this window saying: enter root password now, I am the kind of person who would say: why *now*, is that some kind of attack?

Pekka Nikander: Actually, with the Mac you can see the program which is asking you for the password, but you have to explicitly state you want person to see the program name. It tells you the name but it doesn't understand what the program is doing, and I actually don't sometimes understand what the program is about, but you can see it if you want to, and then you can go to the install scripts if you want to but that requires initiative from the user.

Reply: And this kind of solution still requires you to enter the root password. Once it is sent off over the Internet because some application has conned you into entering it, well, that's your root password gone. Virgil would probably say we need trusted path, trusted path is great. On Microsoft machines there is a trusted path. If you give the three finger salute, you get trusted path.

Simon Foley: That's not trusted path.

Reply: It will give you trusted path.

Simon Foley: Not if you can just overwrite the software. The really good password sniffer programs would also overwrite the interrupt vectors so it appears as if you got trusted path when in fact you didn't.

Frank Stajano: You have no guarantee that you were running Windows in the first place.

Simon Foley: So a true trusted path is what used to be like a break key, which would give you hardware connection into your kernel software.

Mike Roe: Yes, but the reason for this design was, how do you know the program is supposed to be able to intercept that keyboard input?

Tuomas Aura: It seems there are several levels where maybe you trust the operating system to partly protect against root applications, and maybe you trust the hardware to protect against the operating system.

Mike Roe: The hardware wouldn't necessarily work either because it's partly the way you've written the interrupt data.

Reply: So yes, I think that about covers what I had planned to say about trusted path. Assuming then that there are no bugs – trusted path is code that has looked very similar for a number of years now and that's because people don't really want to touch a piece of code that works well. Now if you should do more and more additional functionality with trusted path, and then add more stuff to it, eventually you will have a complete operating system being incorporated into "access to trusted path". Suddenly you have exactly the same problem with access to trusted path as with operating systems in general.

Another approach would be to have code signing, so only use code that has been signed by some authority, and of course that some authority knows where the code comes from, now this all funnels down to the user's machine, you can decide that this code is actually good to be run, sounds a bit like Active X, and I think there were enough demonstrations that this sometimes work, and sometimes doesn't.

Another approach would be a gatekeeper, this is something that was also done at Microsoft Research in Redmond, they were proposing to monitor all these automatic start-up extension points like the autostart folder, and so on. At about 150 start-up points that they had identified for Windows, they can hook things that are loaded automatically, and all these points are monitored, and after they have been changed there comes up a pop-up saying, this auto start-up point has been edited, and it looks like you have installed Gator, or, it looks like you have installed Spyware, and then you can say, oh I don't want to have this in start, and revert all these auto start-ups sensibly, and this is actually the closest approach to what we are doing.

Frank Stajano: Does this thing exist?

Reply: Yes, at least the paper was published in 2004[1]. I don't know whether they have made the software available for download, so you have to check the Internet.

---

[1] Reference [6] in the position paper.

Ben Laurie: Well would you count things like Immunix as being gatekeeper like, or are they different? Immunix certainly lets you run stuff in a mode where it asks you questions, and then from there on you can configure it.

Reply: No, I think gatekeeper is different from that approach. Any more additional approaches that you would see there? OK.

Our approach was to say, well we have overrideable access control, so we run whatever gets run in this mode where it basically runs as if it were a user, but if it wants to change something that you need admin rights for then you ask the user, is that OK, and then you can agree on where you may override it. What we see here as a problem is to prove that the user is actually involved in this taking of an overriding decision: if it's only a pop-up window then how do we make sure that it's not a scripted thing that will click OK for you, so we have to find a way of countering scripting, and this is where the CAPTCHAs comes in.

So the Completely Automated Public Turing test to tell Computers and Humans Apart proves that a human is involved, and it does that by taking a hard computer science problem (hard as in the algorithms that we have really are not really as good as a human yet, like OCR or Speech Recognition), and then it would tell you, look at this thing here, please enter the characters that you see, so B6GH.

Ben Laurie: Can I ask you about your threat model, is your computer running hostile code at this point?

Reply: At maximum in user mode. So the attacker's code doesn't go down to the kernel, you need some kind of trusted platform.

Ben Laurie: So the attacker can't mess around with your CAPTCHA software.

Simon Foley: Have you a trusted path to the software offering you this test?

Reply: That's one of the open issues, man-in-the-middle attacks could overlay the CAPTCHA by another window which grabs the input and uses it somewhere else.

Simon Foley: That's the key point, you're assuming that the human being is really talking to your CAPTCHA, just as the CAPTCHA's trying to figure out if it's talking to a human.

Reply: Yes. You need to make sure that this bit [the graphic containing the CAPTCHA] is not just lifted off somewhere. And of course the other thing is if you have a network in-between, and someone then just got the screen shot and sends it over the network to someone hacking in.

Mike Roe: This is the same problem as popping up a window to ask you for your password, and which is software edited: pop up a window to ask you to solve CAPTCHAs at random times, the malicious software will also do this in order mainly to attack somebody else's system. The pop-ups are asking: "can you read this for me because of <some random reason>."

Reply: Yes, that is true. I believe that the quality of compromise is different from the root password compromise, because solving a CAPTCHA has a one-time effect. The root password you re-use. But the attack exists is exactly as you say.

Frank Stajano: Well wait a minute, in this case you're only proving that there is a human, not the human who knows the root password. So shouldn't you mix it with some kind of authorisation, otherwise anybody would recognise the things just because he is human, not because he's supposed to be root and allowed to authorise. What do you do about that?

Reply: Well for this you would have to combine both.

Frank Stajano: So you do that and ask for the root password next?

Reply: You could if both are required. If you just want to counter automatic exploits, just things that spread virally, our solution works because you at least have a human that has to do something. So the difference is being attacked by a real human and not just by an automatic script.

Ross Anderson: It's also important than when a human gives instructions the machine should absorb the consequences. An NS terminal server will use anti spyware, but when it starts up and asks permission from me to change my home page, I refuse permission. It does it anyway, and that sends it to an Internet Explorer advisory page which says inappropriately strong security settings, I then go back and change my home page to back where it was, and it pops up more crud saying MAC was disabled and so on. There has to be, I think, a rather holistic approach to the problem of putting the user in command of the system.

George Danezis: If there is a trusted path from the computer to the human and the malicious potential program only runs in user mode and has to ask the operating system for permission, via the trusted path you then get a pop up saying, are you human, are you entitled to this application. Somehow you have to make sure that this comes from the trusted computing base, and that it doesn't come from the application, but if you have a trusted path then you don't actually need a CAPTCHA per se.

Reply: There's also another aspect to solving a CAPTCHA because it takes you more time than clicking OK/Cancel. You have an additional feature in our CAPTCHA solution which is, if you get to see this then you may actually read the text on top because of the time it takes to solve this puzzle. It is easier to hit cancel than to solve this puzzle. I know that I very often click OK before I have finished reading what the text of the pop-up says. It's kind of a reflex, you are now connecting to a secure web page blablabla, I think, OK, I've read this before – click. But then it may be something different. So the CAPTCHA solution has more of a warning function than just a pop-up OK/Cancel.

Simon Foley: So for a particular application you might say, well the trusted path is sufficiently resilient to the kinds of mistakes that users make, and the purpose of the CAPTCHA is to make the human resilient to the mistakes that they make.

Reply: Yes, it is a bit like if you sign things, if you start a new job you sign a lot. I think I signed at least 20 or 30 papers. Eventually you get into this habit. Signatures just come out of your hand. You can't really remember whether you've just signed, that in case of fire you will evacuate, or whatever. Sometimes they tell you, initial here, initial here, initial here, which makes sure that you get pointed at the important bits. This CAPTCHA solution may be similar. You get pointed at: this pop-up now is important. It will take you time to solve the puzzle, If you are not sure what the program does, and you don't really care, then you should hit cancel.

But we have not done user tests in that way yet, no.

Simon Foley: A psychological study from years ago was done while and people were registering for the conference. Half way through the registration process the person behind the desk bends down to pick something up, and comes back up again, and carries on the registration process. Afterwards the people were asked, did you notice anything peculiar when you registered? Only 20% of the people noticed that in actual fact half way through the registration the person looking after the registration changed, so when they bent down somebody completely different came back up again. Most people didn't know that they were now dealing with a completely different person.

Reply: So you're saying that this may only have 20% of users? Well that is a result, then I would say, great, we have 20% of users, we may have made life really terrible for the other 80% because they say, I really prefer to just click OK every time I get asked something.

Mike Roe: It's quite hard to speculate correctly whether this would work or not but you could do some user testing experiments to see what people do.

Frank Stajano: If you just have an API that says, this is how you issue an important value box, then the program will just say, OK, my name is important, and the user will be bombarded with tons of these, just like you have with your trusted password, and then why is it any better.

Ben Laurie: There needs to be a limit on the number of questions asked.

Richard Clayton: A key problem in CAPTCHAs is that there is no binding between the problem that you are solving and the question that you are being asked. That is why an automated attacker can just send them off, and get people on other systems to solve the CAPTCHA, which people are allegedly having to do, and then the answer will be fed back.

You are also making a very deep assumption which is completely wrong which is, when you ask a human, shall I do this wicked thing, that the human is actually in a position to say, no, I think that would be very unwise. A good example of this is if you have recently visited a dodgy porn site then perhaps if you're asked a question in the next ten minutes it might be a good idea to say no, right, but if you're just sitting there the following morning and it pops up and the name has something to do with some printer or something, you're sitting there thinking, well yes, I might want to print to that, yes of course I'll answer this question yes.

That's basically the key problem, something like Windows has I'm told 450,000 files in the standard install, there is absolutely no way that anybody, even in the development teams, has any idea what some running DLL which wants to have access to the Internet, who wants you to solve the CAPTCHA in order to be able to do something exciting, whether or not you should answer yes or no.

Reply: The Microsoft way of doing this is the following: of course it's signed by Microsoft, therefore you know that it's good.

Richard Clayton: Well we went through a whole lot of that stuff yesterday[2], it's signed by Microsoft.Barclays.crypto.org, so of course it's good, it's signed by a bank. Humans are not in a position to answer these questions, I really don't think so.

Bruce Christianson: Can I ask about the assumptions for the trusted path. There's a trusted path from the secure bit of the operating system to the user, what's it's range?

Reply: The way that the assumption here works is saying: we need to have a user involvement. We currently would accept all these attacks that scrape the screen, send it off somewhere else, and someone else does the CAPTCHA for you. At least there are no automated attacks coming in.

Bruce Christianson: But the assumption is that you've got a channel which preserves secrecy as well as integrity as far as the user?

Reply: Well currently we don't even say that, so our security is much weaker than what you were hoping.

Bruce Christianson: If the assumptions are weaker, that's great, I'm just not sure how you know which human you're talking to.

Reply: You don't.

Bruce Christianson: Oh right, OK.

Reply: You really have less security than you would want in the ideal world.

Bruce Christianson: If it doesn't matter then it's less of a problem, I'm just worried about denial of service.

Mike Roe: Yes, it would be better if you had confidentiality to the user so that you can image some train buffer that the user can see on the screen that the program is able to read.

Reply: Yes, that would be good to have, but I don't think we currently do. With the way modern graphics card work they are almost like computers with lots of code on them.

Ben Laurie: It wouldn't make it any stronger unless the user knew that he was using it, right, you'd have to say, this part of the screen can only ever be used like this, or you have to draw it specially or something, so people know what it looks like.

---

[2] Richard Clayton, these proceedings.

Mike Roe: Well no, I was imagining when you get a pop up from this part of the operating system it comes in front of everything else, nothing else running knows that pop-up's there, and it's got both messages, it says what the effect of answering this CAPTCHA is going to be, and what you have to sign in, nothing else, nobody else will get told of that at that stage.

Frank Stajano: Yes, but suppose you had an application that has a window that just looks the same.

Reply: But the thing here is that the information an attacker can learn from grabbing the input is not so valuable because it's not reusable.

Simon Foley: But when people used to worry about things like trusted path, they looked at designing multi-level security, and all sorts of issues as to how you place windows on a multi-level worktop, you can't have a secret window, for example, sitting on top of one that is not secret, and the whole purpose there was to stop these kinds of attack.

Ben Laurie: But that's a different thing because there you want the user to know when they're in which level, in this you don't even want the user to know they're in the current operating system, so I could open a window and pose a CAPTCHA.

Reply: Yes, but that doesn't matter because you have solved the CAPTCHA but you can't do anything else with this solution. The only solutions that really matter are the ones that are from the correct window.

Frank Stajano: Yes, you are educating the user to just type CAPTCHAs whether they are from the operating system or not.

Ross Anderson: Can't you bind the CAPTCHA to the question that the person's trying to solve, as Richard suggested.

Reply: Well you could try to present some text here that would do that.

Ross Anderson: I've seen this done before, it's a natural way to bind the CAPTCHA to the problem that somebody thinks he's trying to solve, and what's more, if you have got some trusted, or semi-trusted application, you can share some information with it which in some way is embedded in the text of the CAPTCHA, so you can play around at the fringes and send via a trusted path, provided you don't see the CAPTCHA that's in the black box.

Simon Foley: So then it's more than just proving that a human was involved, it's proof of the human understanding the question.

Ross Anderson: The human understands the question, and he agrees to the proposition that the question came from some piece of software that he interacted with.

Reply: I think we have a problem though. Like Richard says, the person who wants to see that picture doesn't care whether the CAPTCHA he solves actually says, yes I want to delete all files.

Bruce Christianson: But this is the point, if you had some way of ensuring that the genuine CAPTCHAs went to the part of the screen that only they can go to. OK you've got to make sure there isn't a camera on the screen, and that sort of thing, but at least you've got some hope.

Mike Roe: Digital rights management is really a way of getting paper on the screen, that can possibly be screen-scraped by some other program, and sent to everybody else on the Internet, and you have exactly the same problem.

Reply: Maybe the visual CAPTCHAs are going in the wrong direction, we could do audio CAPTCHAs. They talk letters and numbers, so at hotmail where I scraped this one from [points to CAPTCHA on slide] they also have a link which says: if you can't read this click here. There is an audio file which is then played. I was incapable of understanding it. So by these standards, I'm not a human, I'm a computer. These things are apparently clearly understandable to an American.

Frank Stajano: What everybody seems to agree is that you need some amount of trusted path in order to even ask a question. Why don't you use an untrusted path just to ensure that the thing is typed by someone instead of a script?

Reply: Yes, we could do that, but the advantage of the CAPTCHAs is also that you get more user attention to the problem to be solved than just click OK.

Ben Laurie: You can click the OK button and run away.

Reply: Yes, I've seen that before, it does make you read that window again when it jumps to the side when you click OK.

Bruce Christianson: Actually that's a good point, if you can be sure the nonsense being typed into a keyboard is actually from a human you wouldn't care too much about where the question came from.

Simon Foley: This probably is worth looking at. We did some work for an airline logistics terminal; if you have each airline on a different terminal, and your coordination centre has retype stuff from one machine to another machine, because there's no uniform standard, so they came up with a screen-scraper and then a software keyboard, so basically you now have a machine-run keyboard which goes out through a piece of a hardware plugged into the back of the other machine. So as far as the machines were concerned the software was a human.

Reply: But that's something most users would notice when someone starts installing special hardware to them.

Simon Foley: If you're a user of this, after a while you forget about the fact that what you're typing in on one keyboard, you're not quite sure which machine it's going to, not just that, the machines themselves are receiving keyboard input, but it's actually coming from a program.

Reply: But that is something that happens, I have two computers sitting on my desk and I don't know how many times I've thought, oh, thank goodness, I'm not logged in as root on this machine, rm -rf, oh no, wrong keyboard, where did that go, oh, login window, that's good.

Mike Roe: With digital rights management the user had the incentive to buy some special pack that let them copy. Here the trusted party is acting for the user, so the user doesn't have an incentive to go and install hardware to subvert it.

Reply: So we had a discussion about denial of service, and which parameters can be protected, and of course you should only protect parameters that you rarely run into problems with, while if you have things like disc read rights, then eventually it becomes impractical. If you say virus protection on/off is something that you really want to protect then that is very practical.

Other uses could be in safety critical systems, when you want a dead man's handle that makes sure that you still have an operator sitting there, and not some script: meanwhile the train runs on. Or you could test whether the system is still in use by a human for billing purposes, if there is software running on your computer that keeps your DSL line alive and keeps sending out messages, every once in a while it would say, you know, you seem to be really heavily using this line, and are you still there, and do you want to be using this line, so in that way it would be protecting the user. The other way round would be if maybe some operator wants to make sure that you only, as a user, use your connection, and you don't just put up a server behind that cheap residential connection, so you could say, well, at least every once in a while you need to solve this.

Open issues: one of the things that came up was, how do you convey the effect of a system parameter change? You get this pop-up saying, printer.dll wants to access the network. In the gatekeeper approach they have this known star database, which is known good, known bad, and they take hashes of our applications and so on, and you look up in that database and it tells you, this program is known to be good, or unknown, or it is known to be bad. Of course the person who owns that database has a lot of power by saying, I think software by Apple is not good, it's known to be bad, or, software by Microsoft is known to be bad, so there's quite a bit of power in this known star database. And what is the overhead of an intrusive network to the user, how many of these things are you really willing to solve.

I conclude: our proposed solution is a user friendly (very big question mark) way of overriding access control. It has some finality and cautionary function. If you compare with signatures. signatures have finality and cautionary function, they have identification, and repudiation properties. The System Security CAPTCHA has this finality and cautionary function. Only changes up to the point of entering the CAPTCHA are accepted The cautionary function is also more present than within a popup because popups are easy to click away and System Security CAPTCHAs is a bit more difficult. Also, it is an indemnification for the system to perform potentially unwanted actions. The system manufactures can claim they have done all to warn you: If you didn't want to have this piece of software installed in the autostart folder, you should not have solved that CAPTCHA. I'll stop here and let the next person start with 20 minutes delay when they have solved the CAPTCHA. Thank you.

The System Likes You?

(Transcript of Discussion)

Mark Lomas

Arabella (Arab Bank Group)

The theme of the workshop is that the system likes you and wants to be your friend, so rather than look directly at security issues, I'm going to consider whether my system is actually friendly, and see if there are any observations that may be helpful to us in improving the security.

I start off by looking at some of my experience with trying to use DNS from a bog standard PC. Now you might say that DNS is rather an easy target to attack from a security perspective, but what I'm going to address here isn't really the security aspect of it, it's just the way that this system seems to behave.

How does a certain well-known system from Redmond operate if for some reason your DNS service is unreliable – it's not that anyone has actually broken it, but there may be, say, an unreliable network connection, or the system is behaving very slowly. From my experience, my mail service breaks, my news service breaks, and my web browser breaks. And you might think that's actually a little extreme, because my mail server seldom changes its IP address; my news server seldom changes its IP address; and although I might go to a number of websites, by and large I'm most likely to go to Google, and although its IP address may change because of round robin addressing, if I were to use the same address chances are I will get to the Google server. So why should DNS cause me these problems?

One of the reasons is that this system, unless somebody can tell me how to do it, doesn't seem to cache the name to address mappings.

Richard Claydon: It does a bit.

Reply: Well it does for a very short period of time, it seems to drop an address within about a minute of it being used.

Mike Roe: What you need is stashing rather than caching. Caching is where you keep a copy for performance, so you don't bother checking if the master is available, whereas stashing is where you try and get hold of the master if you can, and only if you can't do you then revert to this previous copy which might not be up to date, but it's all you've got so you're going to use it anyway.

Reply: Yes, I'd be perfectly happy to do that, and if you can tell me how to do that I will. But for now let's get back to security. People often say that the reason DNS is insecure is that we don't want to take the resources to sign all of the messages, and run a proper authentication protocol. But note that if I solve the problem of unreliability then I can reduce the number of messages that

B. Christianson et al. (Eds.): Security Protocols 2005, LNCS 4631, pp. 180–186, 2007.

I actually need to do the signature verification on. So trying to fix apparently separate problems at the same time can actually be less costly.

Another question, why when my DNS service does come back does Internet Explorer not notice? You often find, if the DNS service fails and then comes back, that you still cannot get at the web page you wanted. If you shut down Internet Explorer and start it up again, suddenly it finds the server's there, and I've no idea why.

Mike Roe: I could guess that it might have cached the non-reachability of your target (laughter) so it's a self-fulfilling prophesy.

Reply: Next reasonably common experience. At home I've got an ADSL router that has both Ethernet and WiFi network connections on it. I like it, it works well, it's convenient to use, but it has a few annoying little niggles. One is that the default setting is that absolutely anyone can connect to it. Now in the case of the Ethernet that doesn't really bother me because the device is inside my house and the only people who could plug into it are people who are already in the house. But it does bother me that neighbours have access via the Wireless LAN network, and they can either route onto any of the systems that I've got connected to that router, or they can use my ADSL connection to go out onto the Internet.

How do we fix this? Going back to what I said earlier, we start by examining whether our system is trying to be friendly with me. On my particular router, firstly I have to choose some authentication key and put it into the router. There's a dire warning in the manual, make sure you do it at the router first because otherwise you'll break your network connection and not be able to talk to the router at all.

Tuomas Aura: One of my routers had a tendency to crash, and revert to the default settings. [Laughter]

Reply: You then have to find a carefully hidden configuration utility on the machine that you're going to communicate from, enable encryption, and then type in this long shared key, and then you reconnect. The default is that you type in this long hex stream, although I think most users wouldn't have a clue what hex is, but they also give you a nice convenient non-default mode where you can switch it to ASCII, in which case your key length has then been greatly reduced.

Ben Laurie: It's exactly the same length, because it's the same key.

Reply: Well you're right of course, but if you type in a similar number of hex characters you will end up with a rather shorter key than you thought you had.

So I have been through all this with my router, and eventually got a secure connection. But then I thought, before coming to this workshop I'll set the auto-detect mode on the network connection: you can have your WiFi connection in what they call infrastructure or ad hoc mode, and there's also an auto-detect option that allows you to recognise both. The net result if you do actually pick that setting is that you break the security configuration that you've just set up, and again, I have no idea why.

Pekka Nikander: Some systems like MacOS X actually remember a number of keys, and they automatically open up the network, even if you haven't been there for a long time.

Reply: Yes OK, that would be nice.

Ben Laurie: There's different places that you can set the key. Just when you're creating a wireless network doesn't mean you have to put a key on it then.

Reply: OK, but my observation is, I've got a degree in computer science, my PhD dissertation is in network security, and I have difficulty connecting commodity network equipment, so what hope has an ordinary user?

I've got a few suggestions, one is I'd like the people who are designing these to read some of Frank Stajano's papers on ubiquitous computing, to show how you might make these devices talk to each other without having to cause the user to type in long keys.

And I would like the protocol between the router and the network card designed in such a way that, instead of bothering me with all these keys, it says "I've seen a new network connection, give it a name and I'll sort out the keys in the background for you". And then I'd like it to maintain that information so that, just as Pekka was saying, when it sees the network again it will reauthenticate automatically. Basically I want to hide these keys from the user.

Let's go back to the system that I'm using. I notice it has a tendency to give these wonderfully friendly messages, unknown error, and they're usually something like this. (Laughter)

I've found, using Google, that the Microsoft knowledge base often has explanations for many of these errors. This is very helpful, particularly if the error message is actually trying to tell you why you can't get a network connection at the moment.

Richard Clayton: The actual Microsoft error code is made up of several different parts, and bits are stuck on by different levels of the system in order for you to be able to categorise the error if you have to handle it automatically. The way in which Microsoft present the errors doesn't have a direct translation for users.

The other thing is that most of these errors are not coming from Microsoft's code, they're coming from drivers.

Reply: OK, I'm not trying to attribute blame, but I'm saying that that error message isn't very helpful to me.

Richard Clayton: I would say the opposite actually, in practice that error message is extremely useful to you because it gives you a very short search string to type in the computer, and you don't even have to know about putting quotes round things.

Mike Roe: In the old days, operating system errors used to be given both unique identity numbers and also text strings, so that you could easily find in the manual the explanation of what it meant.

Bruce Christianson: Or even quickly find the piece of code where it was generated.

James Malcolm: The thing that generates the error number may well not know why it's really happened, whereas six months later when it's been fielded in the operating system and has crashed a few times, then the knowledge-base does. So there is a virtue in having the error code, although it would be nicer if the error message didn't appear at all.

Bruce Christianson: There are some stunningly unhelpful messages generated by systems which are making incorrect assumptions about what the user is trying to do.[1]

Mike Roe: It's very hard. Usually what you are generating is some invariant which should be true, but which is false. And then you try and work back through the dozen levels of software between the user and the piece of code that discovered the exact property that's not holding, and find out where it went wrong. But usually what you end up with is just: at this point in the code, this particular assertion was false, so there's something wrong.

Bruce Christianson: A deeper problem is that the error didn't usually happen at the time when the violated invariant became contingently false. The difficulty typically arose several release cycles earlier, when the relevant assertion ceased to be a logical consequence of the post-conditions of the scheduler loop[2], and so became merely contingently true, instead of logically tautologous.

Reply: May I give an example of something I've noticed which supports what Mike was saying. A large number of the times that I get one of these messages it's actually because there's been some service disabled, and the programmer had thought, oh this service is so critical nobody would ever switch it off, therefore it always works. So one thing I'd like to suggest is that programmers should be taught that even crucial services do fail sometimes.

A particular example which I remember tracking down was when I installed a service pack. Microsoft had decided that one of their services was insecure, so they disabled it, and meanwhile some other bit of the code assumed that that service was absolutely critical, and therefore it generated one of these error messages. The fix, if you go to the Microsoft knowledge base, is to re-enable the insecure service.

At a previous workshop Bob Morris said that my machine would be much more secure if I switched it off, so in order to come here I tried to do that. Nothing could go wrong with switching off a machine surely, well Windows refused to let me switch off my machine. It said that my profile exceeded quota so it couldn't flush it to the server, and therefore in order to protect the data there it would not allow the machine to be switched off.

---

[1] See Lucy Suchman, Plans and Situated Actions: The Problem of Human-Machine Communication, 1987, CUP.

[2] If p and q are pre- and post-conditions, then $CpFq$ certainly entails $CLpLFq$, but we want $CpLFq$. By the time any assertions are actually violated, it is usually too late to work out what went wrong.

Let's think about the consequences of that. Well one is, the machine stays on unnecessarily: it's sitting in my office at the moment doing, as far as I can tell, absolutely nothing. Another consequence is that the other people in the office can't use the machine while I'm away. That doesn't bother me too much but it may bother them.

But more importantly, the fact that it can't flush my profile to the server means that my profile is not part of the back-up cycle. Think about what's in your profile: the profile contains those things that you're working on at the moment, in other words the things which are not only least likely already to have been backed up, but also the things that are most critical to you at the moment. So they've carefully designed the system so that exactly what I want to be backed-up are the very things that get left out of the back-up cycle. So I go back to the original question, is my machine being friendly towards me?

If you're designing a system then I'd like you to think very carefully about the consequences of imposing a quota. I'm not saying there aren't good reasons for a quota, you may want to make sure that there's enough disk space for everyone to share so you pick some amount, but it's not just the size of the quota that matters, it's *when* you validate whether somebody's likely to exceed it. I wouldn't have minded if, while I was working, I got an error message saying, by the way your profile has now just gone past the size of the quota on the file server, I will no longer be able to flush it to the server. That would be helpful because I could do something about it then. Waiting until the very last minute and *then* saying, no you can't switch off this computer, is much less helpful, even though the same quota may be enforced.

Frank Stajano: It would be nice to have some kind of resource reservation rate: you have so much quota, therefore you would have so much profile.

Reply: Yes, that would be fine.

Pekka Nikander: There is a good book called The Design of Everyday Things by Donald Norman, which goes through many of these issues related here, including error messages and so on.

Mike Roe: In the 1970s I used a PDP11 where the logoff had an option to randomly choose some of your files to delete until you were under quota.

Reply: Well I'll show you another approach which dates back years and years. VAX/VMS had what I would call hard and soft quotas (they used the term overdraft) where they say, here is the amount of space I think you should have in your quota, but I'll give you a little bit of leeway. So if I got the error message saying I've gone over quota, I can try to write the thing again, and it will say, oh OK, I'll let you do it if you're insistent.

Richard Clayton: I think you may be being unfair to the people here. A lot of what you describe is feature interaction between two different systems. The profile system is an extremely complicated system, which is put in for large corporates who have a hotdesk scheme, and who want to do various things. Often the people who set it up don't understand that you've got to set it up differently for a laptop than you do for a big machine, for a hotdesk machine, and so forth, and therefore often set it up inappropriately. At the same time the people who designed the quota system were in a different building not talking to the profile designers. What you're describing is the resulting interaction between these two separate systems. In principle, the tension between these two ought as much to be sorted out by the system operators in the corporate user as by the software vendor.

Reply: I'm not trying to assign blame here, I'm just observing that this is the behaviour of the system as it's fielded.

In each of the cases I've shown you so far, the system didn't behave as I would expect. Well, it is actually how I'd expect, but it isn't as I'd like. And in most of the cases it generated an error message that I didn't expect, and didn't particularly appreciate. That's not to say that there isn't a place for error messages, but I think if they'd given a little more thought to what was in that message some of my complaints would no longer stand.

So one suggestion I have for the people writing this code is, trawl your source code for error messages, and then think about them. They may be perfectly appropriate, I'm not saying get rid of error messages, but just make sure you're aware of all the messages may generate.

Pekka Nikander: Some people in the HCI community say that you should get rid of the error messages, you should design your software in a way that you can't get in the situation where you get an error message

Frank Stajano: If you give that as a design rule, then when things get weird, instead of an error message the screen will just go blue.

Bruce Christianson: I think the key point here is "where practicable".

Reply: Where practicable, eliminate the cause, and if you can't eliminate it, make sure that the message is clear. And importantly, ensure that the potential for error is reported as early as you are aware that an error may occur, that's generally helpful. To appreciate this, think about when would you expect a disk full error message to be reported. Some systems, and I think this is perfectly reasonable, try and anticipate the amount of space that's needed and then give you a message saying, if I were to do that you're going to run out of disk space. I find that helpful. Others go three quarters of the way through a process and then say, you've run out of disk space, hard luck, and whoops you're now in a bad state[3].

Ben Laurie: There are two other things which you should do with error messages. One is that you should log them, so that when something goes wrong you can look at the log, and the other is that you should make error messages parsable so that log analysis tools can make sense of them.

Reply: I think those are both very good suggestions.

---

[3] And typically don't have enough free space left to run the obvious recovery process.

Frank Stajano: I think that your sequence of suggestions may not always work given current practice. Sometimes the error messages are not even in your own source code, it may be a case of what Richard describes as a feature interaction. Maybe the application really generates an error message that says disk full, but it's more likely that when you try and write the operating system pops up and says disk full.

By your argument it would be better if the application did a preliminary check to see if the error would be produced.

Reply: I agree with that.

As this is a security protocols workshop, I think that I should make one security-related suggestion. This is a very vague suggestion I'm aware, but I want to make security mechanisms as painless as possible in order that people don't object to them. People don't like having to type in long keys, they don't like being bothered about setting up the configuration file to make sure that the systems interact.

If you make security as painless as possible then people are more likely to tolerate it. If somebody is required to remember a password, or some key for synchronising systems, you can guarantee that they won't be able to remember it, so try not to force them to.

If you've got networked components, like my router and wireless LAN card, then have them authenticate each other as default, don't have the default being everything open. And encrypt absolutely everything, leave it to the knowledgeable user to turn it off rather than the normal user to have to work out how to turn it on.

Bruce Christianson: Thank you. We'll break for coffee as soon as we can turn the computer off. [Laughter]

Enhancing Privacy with Shared Pseudo Random Sequences

Jari Arkko, Pekka Nikander, and Mats Näslund

Ericsson Research
{jari.arkko,pekka.nikander,mats.naslund}@ericsson.com

Abstract. Protecting users' privacy is essential for turning networks and services into trustworthy friends. Many privacy enhancing techniques, such as anonymous e-cash and mix-nets, have been proposed to make users more comfortable in their network usage. These techniques, in turn, usually rely on very basic security mechanisms, e.g., confidentiality protection, for their realization. But these mechanisms are also used for other security related reasons.

In this paper, we make some new observations on how security can degrade privacy. For example, using security as a component of an advanced privacy enhancing technique may not have the effect we expect; i.e., too careless application of security may defeat the assumed privacy gains. In particular, introducing new identifiers may make it *easier* to track users. This effect is especially harmful to mobile users. Even in cases when privacy is not the main driver for the use of security, we believe that identifiers require special attention in some circumstances.

We propose a mechanism, which we call to allow the communicating parties to continuously change the identifiers they use, without any signalling and without adverse affects on realibility or security.

1 Introduction

In communication systems where the user terminals and/or the users are mobile, preventing tracking of users and equipment is important for privacy reasons. The main challenge in preventing tracking is to avoid the use of long-term or easy-to-correlate protocol information that constitutes explicit "identifiers" or otherwise allows users to be identified. Even if the identifiers cannot be tied to a physical entity, they may make possible to follow the same entity as it moves from one place to another (where the "place" may be geographical, i.e. physical, or logical, e.g. a network address).

Some telecommunications mechanisms take this into account already now, and can use frequently and/or randomly changing identifiers. For example, in GSM, the so-called TIMSI, Temporary IMSI (International Mobile Subscriber Identifier), is used to hide the true IMSI. However, in general, such techniques are not useful unless they are enforced *throughout the protocol stack*. For instance, while Wireless LAN authentication mechanisms can employ pseudonyms, see [5,2], or

B. Christianson et al. (Eds.): Security Protocols 2005, LNCS 4631, pp. 187–196, 2007.

even completely hide the authentication exchange from others [6], this is of limited value as long as fixed link layer identifiers (e.g. MAC addresses) are used at a lower layer.

The problem exists in many forms. A particularly visible example is the transmission of cleartext, human-readable user identities such as Network Access Identifiers (NAIs) [1]. Similar problems appear for the transmission of stable but "meaningless" identifiers, such as IP addresses [10]. A less known problem is that even data that is completely independent of any real "identifier" can be used to track users. For instance, an IPsec SPI [8] can reveal that a node in one place is the same node as a node that appears later in another location, if the SPI value has not changed even though the IP addresses are no longer the same. For example, with a 32-bit SPI, the chance is about 1 in 4 billion that it is not the same user if the SPIs are the same. This is particularly problematic for Internet Key Exchange (IKE) Security Parameter Indices (SPIs), as there is no possibility for efficiently renegotiating IKE SPIs without revealing the previous SPIs in the process. For IPsec SPIs this is less of a problem, as the SPIs can be re-negotiated within the protection of the IKE SA, hence hiding the change from outsiders. Nonetheless, the problem remains that privacy enhancing measures can sometimes be defeated by unexpected factors.

The same problem arises in certain authentication mechanisms. For authentication purposes, a popular techniques is the use of public key cryptography. For efficiency reasons, symmetric cryptography based counterparts are gaining popularity in the form of so-called hash chains. A quite well-known problem with public keys is that the key, even if not tied to an identity, leaves "traces" of the user, since anybody can verify authenticity using the public key. However, one easily forgets that also a hash chain is easily linkable in the forward direction by applying the hash.

Even data that changes for every packet can be used to track users. For instance, TCP or IPsec sequence numbers may in some cases be sufficient for the identification of equipment even if no other stable identifiers are present. As long as the sequence number space is sufficiently large and nodes distributed along to a sufficient degree, a node that presents a sequence number N in one place and $N + 1$ (or something close to it) in another place shortly thereafter is likely to be the same node.

1.1   Related Work

Hiding identifiers and other communications inside a protected tunnel or tunnels is used in protocols such as TLS or IPsec. The drawback of this solution is that often other identifiers still remain visible outside the "tunnel".

Another approach is the use of "pseudonyms". This approach is used in GSM [12], among others. In this technique, an identifier is used for login to a service, and the service returns an encrypted token that the client can decrypt and use as the identifier for logging into the service the next time. A drawback of this scheme is that the new pseudonym has to be returned, which adds to the amount of signalling necessary. In any case, this solution may not be possible in all situations. For instance, the protection of sequence numbers in this manner would be possible in TCP as there are ACKs, but would be hard in IPsec because there may not be traffic in the return direction before a new packet needs to be sent. In any case, waiting for the new pseudonym before a second packet can be sent is inefficient.

Removing sequence numbers (and thereby linkability) may be considered as an option. However, with present art this is not a universally viable, as it creates a sender/receiver synchronisation problem, at least when used with unreliable data transport mechanisms such as IP.

For public keys and hash chains, an available method to improve privacy is to frequently generate new public keys/hash chains. However, this is computationally quite expensive.

Recently, [9] proposes some mechanisms for address location privacy in MIPv6.

As mentioned in the abstract, some very sophisticated techniques for sender-receiver untraceability have been proposed, e.g. Chaum's mix-nets [3]. However, such mechanisms are far too cumbersome to use for "everyday" communication, and relies on the help of "mixing nodes".

2   A Practical Example

Let us consider an example where Alice and Bob are communicating over the Internet, using IPsec to protect their connection[1]. Initially, Alice learns Bob's IP address from the DNS, and she initiates IKE by sending an UDP packet to Bob. Bob learns her current IP address from the received UDP packet. As a result of running IKE, Alice and Bob agree upon an IKE SPI, a pair of Encapsulated Security Payload (ESP) SPIs, and ESP sequence numbers[2]. With the IP addresses, SPIs, and sequences numbers both Alice and Bob and any outsiders can easily keep track of the ongoing conversation. Furthermore, the IP addresses reveal the approximate location of the parties.

Now consider a situation where Alice moves to another location. As a consequence, her IP address is changed. This requires some action from her in order to inform Bob about the new address. One option is to run IKE again, and create new Security Assocatiations (SAs) and corresponding SPIs. Unfortunately, this is pretty costly, may involve user interaction with token cards, and with frequent movements would cause disruptions to the connection. Another option would be to use an underlying mobility service such as Mobile IP [4]. All traffic now flows through Alice's home agent, hiding her new IP address but allowing outsiders to easily link her communications from different places. If an advanced form of mobility, route optimization, is used then all packets carry a new identifier, Alice's home address. This can then be used to link different packets, even if sent from different places.

---

[1] For brevity, we ignore the link layer and physical aspects, but the principles presented in this paper could be equally applied there.

[2] IKE protects the public keys against passive attackers; we don't need to consider them here.

A third option is the use of IKE extensions (such as NAT traversal or MO-BIKE) that allow hosts to change their IP address without requiring IKE to reauthentication. Presumably, at the same time she could negotiate new ESP SPIs. Unfortunately, the IKE SPI would still reveal her identity, allowing our eavesdropper to continue tracking the connection and to learn the new IP address (and approximate location).

To summarise the current situation, Alice has basically two options: either she can gain some privacy at a computational or routing cost, by re-running IKE or using Mobile IP without route optimisation, respectively, or alternatively she can suffer a privacy loss with the gain of not needing to re-run IKE or suffer sub-optimal routing.

3   Identification Via Pseudo Random Sequences

To overcome the privacy problems caused by identifiers and other easily trackable protocol values, we propose a method where the constant identifiers or easily predicatable protocol values are replaced with values drawn from a number of shared, secretly agreed pseudo-random sequences. That is, as the parties initiate a shared communication context they agree on a number of pseudo-random sequences, constituting a sequence of sets of identifiers, in addition to the usual session keys and other protocol state.

Whenever the sending party wants to avoid identity tracking, it draws the next set of identifiers in the sequence and uses those identifier values in the outgoing messages instead of the previous values. This practise works best whenever there would be a natural rupture in the tracking sequence anyway, e.g., when the sending party has just changed its location or has been inactive for a while. This could even happen for every packet. For full privacy, it is crucial that the sending party replaces the identifiers (and other trackable values) at all protocol layers at the same time, to prevent linkage across layers.

3.1   Example: Adding Privacy to the MOBIKE Protocol

Let us reconsider the example above. With the proposed MOBIKE protocol in place, the only value that revealed Alice's identity was the IKE SPI, s. With our new mechanism in place, instead of agreeing on just a single fixed SPI value, s, Alice and Bob would agree on a *sequence* of SPI values, s^0, s^1, s^2, etc, denoted as $\{s\}^*$. The intial IKE negotiation would use the first value from this sequence, s^0, in the place of the original fixed value. Now, when Alice has moved and received a new IP address, she would use the next value in the sequence, s^1. As this value belongs to the sequence that Bob has agreed with Alice, he would still recognize the message being sent by Alice[3]. However, any outsiders that do not have access to the sequence cannot link the SPI values together.

---

[3] Message integrity and originality is still protected by the same session key.

To generate the sequence, Alice and Bob can simply use a keyed pseudo random number generator with a shared key K derived from the keying material created during the initial IKE negotiation. Two basic approaches are discussed below:

Pseudo-random Function: Alice and Bob use a keyed pseudo-random function (not necessarily invertible), f, and the jth identifier ID^j is simply $f(K, j)$, or more generally $f(K, j\|\text{IDtype})$. In practice, a cryptographic hash such as SHA-256 can be used as f.

Pseudo-random Permutation: Alice and Bob use a keyed pseudo-random permutation (i.e. an invertible function), π, and the jth identifier ID^j is simply $\pi(K, j)$, or, $\pi(K, j\|\text{baseID})$. This enables authorized receiver to reconstruct the baseID, which could be advantageous in some cases. The permutation π could be instantiated using a block cipher with apropriate block size, or, using a stream cipher $ID^j = s(k, j)$ xor baseID.

Using the method requires no protocol changes; it is enough that Alice and Bob mutually agree on the pseudo random number generator and how to derive the shared key from the keying material. Such an agreement could be provided out-of-band. However, if Internet-wide deployment is desired, a simple extension can be defined to IKE in order to negotiate the parameters; see Appendix **??**.

3.2   Avoiding Cross-Layer Correlation

In order to be effective, the method should be applied to all visible identifiers and other linkable protocol fields. Furthermore, moving from one set of values to a next set must be properly synchronized through the stack so that no value can be used to link the value sets together. For example, consider a complete protocol stack that includes the link, internetworking, transport, and application layers protocols L, I, T and A, with linkable identifiers and values ID_L^A, ID_I^A, ID_I^B, ID_T^A, ID_T^B, SN_T^A, SN_T^B, VAL_{A1}, VAL_{A2}, corresponding to the Alice's link layer address, Alice's and Bob's IP addresses, the transport layer port and sequence numbers, and some application layer values. Alice would then define pseudo random number sequences for each of these values. The first sequence, $\{ID_L^A\}^*$, need not be communicated to Bob as it is only used locally. However, it needs to be changed in synchrony with the other values to prevent correlation. The second and third sequences, the IP addresses, may not be fully known at the time the connection is initiated due to movements of the hosts[4]. All the other sequences, end-to-end in nature, Alice and Bob need to agree upon.

3.3   Sending Packets

In general, our method does not require any changes to existing protocols, other than providing a mechanisms for the parties to agree on using the method. All modifications are local to the parties.

---

[4] However, in IPv6 it would be possible for the two nodes to agree on the interface identifier parts of their IP addresses. This resembles the idea of cryptographically generated addresses [11], but instead of address ownership these interface identifiers would be used for privacy purposes, and be dynamic.

The changes at the sending end are fairly simple. When the sending party decides to move from one set of identifiers to the next set, it simply does so. That is, when Alice wants to break any on-going linkage, she moves to the next element all of the above mentioned sequences $\{ID_L^A\}^* \dots \{VAL_{A2}\}^*$, and sends the next packet using the new values. Typically, such a change would be triggered by a natural change of some value, e.g., the IP address, but in principle it can also be initiated at any time. Apart from any local means needed to associate any lower layer addresses together (such as ARP or IPv6 Neighbor Discovery), no other action is needed by Alice as the sender.

3.4   Matching Received Packets

At the receiving end the situation is more complex. In general, the receiver must be prepared not only receive packets using the current identifier values, but in case of reordering or packet loss, also some past and future values.

In an unmodified protocol, the receiver would accept packets that are identified with a set of identifiers $ID_L \dots ID_A$, corresponding to different protocol layers, and a serial number that fits in the window $SN_T^A \dots SN_T^A + \delta$. In our method, the identifiers would follow the sequences $\{ID_L\}^* \dots \{ID_A\}^*$ and, depending on the use of the serial numbers, the serial numbers would not be communicated at all or would be periodically changed by drawing new values from a corresponding sequence. If the receiver currently expects the jth set of identifiers, then it would accept any identifier sets within the range $f(K, j), f(K, j + 1), \dots f(K, j + k)$, and update j accordingly. Alternatively, with the pseudo-random permutation approach, the receiver would retrieve the sender's j from $\pi^{-1}(K, j)$.

In a typical hash-table based packet demultiplexing system, the added processing cost is neglible. In the case of receiving a packet with the expected jth set of identifiers, the code basically works just like today. In the case of identifiers that the hosts have full control over, the situation is simple: instead of accepting packets only at the jth set of identifiers, the host also accepts packets on the next k identifier sets.

In some cases accepting packets simultaneously on several identifier sets may lead to collisions. Typically, the packet hash table lists identifiers for all active remote peers. In an unmodified system, the identifiers are allocated in a manner that makes sure that there are no collisions between any identifier sets in use. When identifier sequences are used, there is the possibility that the ith identifier set for one peer may completely or partially collide with the jth set of another peer; in section 3.5 we analyse this in more detail for TCP.

Generalising, the receiver needs to allocate some additional memory for matching received packets, and possibly need to be prepared to resolve some collisions. For most modern computers, such an increase in memory and CPU use is neglible. The actual cost of collision resolution depends on the protocol, but appears to be relatively simple in the typical cases.

3.5   Example: Collisions in TCP

Considering the Transmission Control Protcol (TCP), the receiver is normally prepared to accept packets that are identified with the identifier quadruple $\langle ID_I^A, ID_I^B, ID_T^A, ID_T^B \rangle$, where ID_I^A is the sender's IP address, ID_I^B is the receiver's IP address, ID_T^A is the source port, and ID_T^B is the destination port. Furthermore, the packet must match the TCP sequence number window $SN_T^A \ldots SN_T^A + \delta$. In the current stacks, TCP acknowledgements outside of the expected window are simply discarded but the packet is otherwise processed.

To be prepared to receive packets using identifier sets $j + 1 \ldots j + k$, in addition to the jth expected set, the situation becomes somewhat more complex. In the IPv4 world, an additional source of complexity is the inability to know beforehand what the next IP address will be. As a consequence, the receiver must be prepared to accept packets that are identified with any source IP address, the current local IP address, and the TCP ports matching any of the identifier sets $j + 1 \ldots j + k$. In other words, in addition to the expected jth identifier set, it must be prepared to accept packets that are identified by the quadruple template $\langle any, ID_T^B, \{ID_T^A\}^{j+1\ldots j+k}, \{ID_T^B\}^{j+1\ldots j+k} \rangle$. The existing TCP code can be reused to find these potential "shadow" transmission control block (tcb) candidates for any non-matched packet, at the cost of at most a few hundred machine instructions.

The sequence and acknowledgement number checks become slightly more complex. In TCP, the sequence and acknowledgement numbers do not count packets but bytes. Consequently, the window sizes are typically so large that we cannot use the pseudo-random sequences directly for them. Instead, a plausible way seems to keep updating them just as today as long as the jth identifier set is used, and to add the next value to them as the host moves to $j + k$th identifier set.

In more practical terms, for each candidate "shadow" tcb

$$\langle any, ID_I^B, \{ID_T^A\}^{j+i}, \{ID_T^B\}^{j+i} \rangle$$

the corresponding acceptable sequence number window is

$$(SN_T^A + \{SN_T^A\}^{j+i}) \ldots (SN_T^A + \{SN_T^A\}^{j+i}) + \delta_A$$

where SN_T^A is the current TCP sequence number as maintained by TCP, $\{SN_T^A\}^{j+i}$ is the $j + i$th element from the generated pseudo-random sequence, and δ_A is the receive window size. Similarly, the acceptable range of acknowledgements numbers is

$$(SN_T^B + \{SN_T^B\}^{j+i}) \ldots (SN_T^B + \{SN_T^B\}^{j+i}) + \delta_B$$

where δ_B is the number of sent but unacknowledged bytes.

When receiving a new packet, the TCP stack would first look for a perfect match. If it finds one, there is little to worry as the tcb is fully qualified by the sender's IP address. However, if the packet does not match any existing tcbs, the stack next needs to look for candidate "shadow" tcbs[5]. Because the

---

[5] In the current stack a packet that does not match any existing connection is dropped.

source IP address does not qualify the "shadow" tcbs, it is possible that a packet matches more than one. In that case we have a collision; the identifiers alone are insufficient for determining which of the remote peers have moved to use a next identifier set.

To resolve collisions, and to make sure that a candidate "shadow" tcb is really the right one, the receiving host can next check the sequence and acknowledgement windows. If the sequence and acknowledgement numbers in the packet fall within the updated sequence and acknowledgement windows, the right session for the packet is likely to be found. However, as the TCP window sizes can be fairly large, it is possible that the collision cannot be resolved even with the help of sequence numbers.

If there was a collision, the receiving host may want to verify that it has found the right "shadow" tcb. To do so, the receiver can send, using the new identifier set, a TCP packet that carries no data and acknowledges zero new bytes. The packet triggers retransmission, thereby confirming that the session is indeed the correct one. Such practise does not appear any more vulnerable than the current TCP. This optional verification requires the exchange of two packets.

To quantify the situation, we should estimate the probability of two "shadow" tcbs to collide. In TCP, the port numbers are 16-bit values and the sequence and acknowledgement numbers 32-bit values. A typical receive window, δ_A, is in the order of 64 kilobytes or less. For the output window δ_B, we conservatively estimate that its size is equal to the receive window size; usually it is less. Consequently, the probability of a randomly generated packet matching with a given "shadow" (tcb) is (at most)

$$\frac{\delta_A \cdot \delta_B}{|ID_T^A| \cdot |ID_T^B| \cdot |SN_T^A| \cdot |SN_T^B|} = \frac{2^{16} \cdot 2^{16}}{2^{16} \cdot 2^{16} \cdot 2^{32} \cdot 2^{32}} = 2^{-64} \approx 10^{-19}.$$

The probability of a collision between two existing TCP connections depends on the number of simultaneous active TCP connections. Let us consider a host that maintains N active TCP connections, holds state for the sequence values $j \cdots j + k$, and initiates TCP sequence numbers randomly. The probability of having a "shadow" tcb collision between any given two TCP connections (assuming $\delta_A = \delta_b = \delta$) is

$$\frac{\delta^2}{|ID_T^A| \cdot |ID_T^B| \cdot |SN_T^A| \cdot |SN_T^B|}.$$

Consequently, the probability that there will be no collisions with any of the $(N-1)k$ incorrect shadows is (at least)

$$\left(1 - \frac{\delta^2}{|ID_T^A| \cdot |ID_T^B| \cdot |SN_T^A| \cdot |SN_T^B|}\right)^{(N-1)k}.$$

As our analysis shows, for most protocols the probability of a packet being falsely accepted or there being a collision between two existing connections is relatively low. In the cases we have analysed, it is trivial to compensate for the collisions by reusing existing protocol mechanisms. For example, if there is a collision between two integrity protected sessions, attempting to verify the message authentication code with both of the possible session keys will determine the right session.

3.6 Network Impacts

The proposed method is end-to-end in nature, and in general does not impact other nodes, as long as packets can be freely sent to their destinations. However, it is fair to note that changing identifiers such as addresses or port numbers can be problematic from the point of view of firewalls, NATs, and network access control tools such as 802.1X, all of which may keep state related to the identifiers. In addition, the efficiency of bridge learning protocols may be impacted by frequent change of MAC addresses.

4 Protecting Other Parameters

4.1 Public Key Traceability

In the introduction, we mentioned problems with the traces left by public keys, which we have not really delt with so far. As mentioned, we do not want to frequently generate completely new keys, using expensive number theoretic operations. The main use of public keys in security protocols are for key exchange, and here there are some well-known hybrids between asymmetric and symmetric cryptography that we can use. Specifically, one could use Diffie-Hellman key exchange, authenticated by the shared symmetric key and a MIC, rather than using, say RSA signatures. Since the DH values g^x, g^y are random for each protocol execution, there is no useful information extractable from these and the corresponding MIC values.

4.2 Hash Chains

Hash chains may also need to be made unlinkable. This is easily achieved by, instead of using $h_j = H(h_{j-1})$, taking a keyed variant $h_j = H(K||h_{j-1})$. The chain is still easily forwards verifiable, but only by parties sharing K. Note that here, it is important that H is a one-way function, i.e. using a pseudo-random permutation $h_j = \pi(K, h_{j-1})$, would defeat security as the chain then becomes reversible.

4.3 Mobility Parameters

Mobile IP home addresses could be pseudo-random sequences instead of current stable, real IP addresses.

5 Summary

In this paper we have outlined a generic method where fixed or easily predictable identifiers and protocol field values are replaced with values drawn from a set of mutually agreed pseudo-random number sequences. The resulting sequence of protocol packets can be easily processed by the receiving party with modest requirements for additional memory and processing, while being completely untraceable by any outsider observers.

References

1. Aboba, B., Beadles, M.: The Network Access Identifier. RFC 2486, IETF (January 1999)
2. Arkko, J., Haverinen, H.: Extensible Authentication Protocol Method for 3rd Generation Authentication and Key Agreement (EAP-AKA). Internet Draft draft-arkko-pppext-eap-aka-15.txt (Work In Progress), IETF (December 2004)
3. Chaum, D.: The Dining Cryptographers Problem: Unconditional Sender and Receiver Untraceability. J. of Cryptology 1, 65–75 (1988)
4. Johnson, D., Perkins, C., Arkko, J.: Mobility Support in IPv6. RFC 3775, IETF (June 2004)
5. Haverinen, H., Salowey, J.: Extensible Authentication Protocol Method for GSM Subscriber Identity Modules (EAP-SIM). Internet Draft draft-haverinen-pppext-eap-sim-16.txt (Work In Progress), IETF (December 2004)
6. Josefsson, S., Palekar, A., Simon, D., Zorn, G.: Protected EAP Protocol (PEAP). Internet Draft draft-josefsson-pppext-eap-tls-eap-07.txt (Work In Progress), IETF (October 2003)
7. Kaufman, C. (ed.): Internet Key Exchange (IKEv2) Protocol. Internet Draft draft-ietf-ipsec-ikev2-14.txt (Work In Progress), IETF (May 2004)
8. Kent, S., Atkinson, R.: Security Architecture for the Internet Protocol RFC 2401, IETF (November 1998)
9. Koodli, R., Devarapalli, V., Flinck, H., Perkins, C.: Solutions for IP Address Location Privacy in the presence of IP Mobility. Internet Drafy draft-koodli-mip6-location-privacy-solutions-00.txt (Work in Progress), IETF (February 2005)
10. Narten, T., Draves, R.: Privacy Extensions for Stateless Address Autoconfiguration in IPv6 RFC 3041, IETF (January 2001)
11. Nikander, P.: Denial-of-Service, Address Ownership, and Early Authentication in the IPv6 World. In: Christianson, B., Crispo, B., Malcolm, J.A., Roe, M. (eds.) Security Protocols. LNCS, vol. 2467, pp. 12–26. Springer, Heidelberg (2002)
12. European Telecommunications Standards Institute. Digital cellular telecommunication system (Phase 2); Security related network functions. GSM Technical Specification GSM 03.20 (ETS 300 534) (August 1997)

Enhancing Privacy with Shared Pseudo Random Sequences
(Transcript of Discussion)

Pekka Nikander

Ericsson Research

As a number of times before, I'm trying to make a very simple presentation, to present a very simple idea. To me, this one looks almost too simple; maybe somebody else has already made this observation, and if so I'd like to hear about that. I'm diverging from this year's theme and what I'm going to say is that, at least in some cases, security can be the system's friend. So, in this case instead of the system is being your friend, security is now going to be the system's friend, more or less.

Outline: Why do we have identifiers in protocols in the first place? What happens if, instead of having constant identifiers, we have pseudo random sequences of identifiers? What happens to mobility? Finally, a summary.

If we think about protocols, we have identifiers; and I'm not speaking only about security protocols but of any kind of communication protocols, all the protocols are full of identifiers. Many of these identifiers are globally visible, in the actual data packets in the network. There are all kinds of identifiers: IP addresses, protocol numbers, TCP port numbers, IPsec SPIs, and so on, including public keys, sent as clear text in packets. This forms a huge privacy problem, especially if you think about mobile users. When mobile users move from one location to another location, if they keep using the same identifiers, then anybody who has access to a server, or who has access to eavesdrop the network – and that's a lot of people in practice – can track the user. Given the geographical trackability of IP addresses, they can tell fairly well where you are, just by observing the traffic between you and some of the servers that you're using, such as your email server. These eavesdroppers can basically tell where in the world you are.

Why do we have these privacy-threatening identifiers, then? Well, there is an actual, practical need for all these identifiers. These identifiers are needed for de-multiplexing. When a sender sends a message containing these identifiers, the receiver does need these identifiers to determine what to do with the message, or how to de-multiplex the message. In the receiver computer, there are typically several parallel protocol states; for example, you may have multiple TCP sessions, several parallel IPsec security associations, or whatever, and the receiver must be able to tell to which session or protocol state-machine the received message belongs to. That is the reason we have the identifiers there in the first place. Well, some of the identifiers are needed for the network layer, like the IP addresses, and you can't do much about them, but everything higher in the stack than in the network layer, everything that is end-to-end, is basically needed only for de-multiplexing; that is, if it's a fixed identifier.

B. Christianson et al. (Eds.): Security Protocols 2005, LNCS 4631, pp. 197–203, 2007.

We have to also remember that there are also other data that are used in a more or less the same fashion; for example, in the TCP protocol we have sequence numbers, in IPsec we also have sequence numbers, and so on. These data are not fixed identifiers, but they are predictable data. In addition to fixed identifiers, they also form a problem. The eavesdropper can combine some identifiers and then these predictable data, and get fairly high assurance that it's the same session even if the user is using some mobility protocol underneath, like changing IP addresses, or whatever.

So, the idea is very simple: instead of having a single identifier, what happens if we use a sequence of identifiers, that is, a pseudo random sequence of identifiers. In practise, we would first use an initial identifier, then a next one, and so on. The identifier sequences are generated by using some fairly lightweight method, such as using a shared key between the sender and receiver to generate a pseudo-random sequence.

This shift from fixed identifiers to identifier sequences must be done for all of the identifiers in the protocol that we have, including the protocol numbers, the TCP port numbers, and anything on the application level, unless we use encryption. If we are using IPsec ESP, we have to do that for the SPIs, and for the sequence number. It is really important that we apply the method for all of the identifiers, that is, if we care about privacy, because if we fail to apply this idea for any of the things, then we will still remain trackable. An observer would see the incoming traffic with these unchanged identifiers, but some other identifiers being changed. Thus, they could do the correlation between the identifier spaces and find that identifier set K actually belongs to the same user as the identifier set K+1. So, we are going to generate these sequences, and then change all the identifiers in the protocols, and other similar data, at the same time in synchrony.

The practical problem here is, of course, when to do this change. One possibility would be that you do it for every packet so that whenever we send a packet, we actually take the next identifiers from the sequences.

Mike Roe: I thought the University did something similar to prevent network address correlation?

Reply: There has been work on the MAC and IP addresses, but what I haven't seen is work that goes all through the protocol stack, so that you actually do that also for the application level things. If you implement that then you need to have some, to hide it from the applications you need to have some kind of application-level identifier rewriting on both ends, and you need to know where in the application protocol the identifiers actually are.

George Danezis: For some applications this is a well understood problem: for http, for example, where a lot of the privacy concerns come from, there is software, which pretty much does that, you know, stores your cookies, and all the other identifiers. The problem is that even for http it is extremely difficult to do, because as proxy, or even as a client, you are not really sure what is a random identifier, and what is not. For example, if you see a URL that has a particular number in it, you don't know if this is actually a directory, or the name of a file, or if it is something specially designed for use with identifiers.

Reply: Yes, right, but from the practical point of view where this is really usable, this is in security protocols: if you consider IPSec ESP, where everything from the application level down to TCP, and so on, are encrypted, if you are able to apply this idea to your MAC addresses, your IP addresses, and your ESP SPIs, and sequence numbers, you're doing pretty well.

George Danezis: What I'm trying to say is that, sometimes we think of the application stack as starting at our hardware, and continuing up to the application, while actually it's infinite, it runs through layer after layer, and you never know what is on top.

Ben Laurie: Well it's defending you against the situation where you think the attacker is the server you're connected to. Otherwise you just SSL that connection, you don't care about the stuff that's inside the application stuff, you only care about your wrapper.

Reply: Yes, yes, exactly. So, in practice, you want to replace the externally visible identifiers every now and then, and at least whenever you change your IP address because of mobility. There is a practical problem related to that, namely the functionality that you want to get from the identifiers in the first place, the de-multiplexing thing.

The identifiers are used for finding out the context, the protocol stack matches that with where this particular packet belongs to. So for IPSec, for example, you have the destination IP address, and the SPI number, which identify the security association that you use to actually verify and decrypt the packet. For TCP, you have the source and destination IP addresses, source and destination protocol numbers that you used to find the TCP, the TCP ports to find the task to process the packet. In general, you use some of the identifiers in the packet to find the state at the end point at the receiver end.

So when you decide to have these sequences of identifiers instead of having fixed identifiers, you need to create several de-multiplexing mappings at the same time. Because of unreliability, some of the packets will get lost in the network. So, if you're expecting data under one set of identifiers, you also have to be ready to accept that data on the next set of identifiers, and maybe a number of identifiers after that, too, depending on your network conditions. And there is the further problem that some of the identifiers are not really controlled by you; for example, the IP address. So, instead of listening to some new source IP address for TCP, you actually need to be ready to receive on any new IP address, because you don't know what the next IP address is going to be. However, you typically know what the next destination address as it's the same as it was before. The port numbers are going to change, and the sequence numbers, and so on.

There is another problem related to the fact that you're listening to multiple sets of identifiers. You may have conflicts if your de-multiplex mapping is not unique anymore, but, for example, the next sets of two different SPIs happen to map to the same destination addresses. This happens sometimes basically because you have a set of IP addresses that map to just a single IP address, so that the SPIs will collide at some point in time.

Obviously, the more bits you have in your identifier space, the less often you will have these collisions, and many collisions will never happen, they are just potential collisions. Especially in the case of protocols where you have sequence numbers like in TCP or even in IPSec, the sequence numbers move and then the sequence numbers don't collide even though they might have. So, if you add to the state not only the SPI but also the sequence number window where you are waiting for new packets to the state, and when the sequence number windows don't collide anymore you no longer have even that potential collision. Hence, many of these collisions really are only potential; they will never take place.

Maybe surprisingly, you can actually resolve these conflicts, in most cases, fairly easy; for example, in IPSec, if you do have a collision, you have a single SPI and sequence number that maps to two different SAs. You can easily compute the message authentication code using both keys, from both of the SAs, and then you get two different results. You will immediately know which one is correct, so you burn some more CPU, but not that much, to resolve the conflict. And if the conflict persists; for example, if you anticipate that your sequence numbers are going to collide for the next packets, you can just move to the next set of identifiers, which is likely to remove the conflict.

In TCP, it's more or less similar. A collision in TCP requires that the port numbers, the sequence numbers, and the acknowledgement numbers all collide. The probability of them all colliding is fairly small, something like 10^{-19}, in a typical situation. So, what you do is to send acknowledgements to both of the TCP sessions. That generates one spurious acknowledgement, which happens to be perfectly legal in the TCP protocol. Then you move to the next set of identifiers to resolve the conflict. The protocols that we had a look at all had some kind of mechanism that you really could use for resolving the actual conflicts.

Ross Anderson: What happens if you do re-sending of a lost packet, let's say in TCP, and go back N. Would you re-use the identifiers, so you'd basically send the same packets, or will the IP address change.

Reply: If you have changed your IP address and you are re-sending the packet, you can't use the previous identifiers because then you would allow this correlation, so you're right. There are these kinds of technical problems when we go into the actual implementation details.

Tuomas Aura: If you have replaced all identifiers when you are re-sending then the protocol becomes much more fragile because losing enough packets will lose the connections.

Reply: Not really, because underneath the protocol works just as before. What happens is that the actual bit patterns that you are sending in the packet are different, but the semantics are exactly the same, you still have the same identifiers, although the bit patterns are different, and the sequence of identifiers have the semantics that the fixed identifier had before.

Tuomas Aura: But the receiver can only recognise identifiers that are in some window from the senders.

Reply: Sure, yes, it depends on the windows.

Tuomas Aura: In TCP if you re-send the same packets then you get the correlation from it.

Virgil Gligor: There are modes of encryption where you actually keep an increasing counter and you generate the next pseudo random number, by encrypting the counter. You could do the same thing here. The objection that has been raised is that now you have to have stable storage for those counters because you cannot go back to the original value, and if you have, for example, a break or a failure, then everything has to be in stable storage, and you have to recover the counter at the position where it was last.

Reply: Well the idea here is that you have a session key, which you agree on before you start using this.

Virgil Gligor: That's correct, there is no problem with the session key because you always recover the session key, the session key is usually on a stable storage. But now you have to add more stable state because you don't want to start with the same session key and initial value on the counter again.

Ben Laurie: If you start again the two sessions are linkable and the point is that they should be unlinkable, so how are you going to fix that?

Reply: If you lose your state you basically crash.

Ben Laurie: I don't care about the failure of the protocol, what I'm trying to avoid is linkability between two different sessions.

Reply: What I'm saying is that if you lose your session, then you restart, you have a different session key completing your state.

Ben Laurie: Where do I get the new key from?

Reply: Well that's outside the scope of this talk.

OK, what was surprising, is that when you actually implement this you seem to get mobility support for your protocol in some sense for free. So what is network layer mobility anyway?

Network layer mobility basically solves three problems. The first problem is how do you find the address of your peer that you want to communicate with so that you can initiate the connection in the first place. After you have solved that the second problem is how do you keep track of the address of your peer. Then the third problem is what if you lose the correct address of your peer, how do you continue keeping track, what if both of you are moving at the same time, how do they synchronise? And we are now only focussing on the second problem, the first and third ones are outside of this talk.

The usual way of solving the second problem is to have some local state for keeping track of the address, like in mobile IP you have the binding between the roam address and home address. When you maintain this state you have two problems to solve, if somebody's sending me information saying that my peer has moved, it has a new address, I have to know that it's really my peer who send me the information; and I also need to know that my peer really is in the new address, so that my peer is not lying to me, because otherwise there would be possibilities for some bumping attacks.

What appears to be the case is that we can solve these two problems using these pseudo random sequences without adding any bits to any protocol. So you have a mobile host, you have the peer which seems to be stationary at this point of time, remember we are not trying to solve the simultaneous movement problem, the peer is listening to a number of identifier sets, it's listening to set i and set i + 1, in the direction from the mobile to peer. The mobile host gets a new IP address so it moves over to set i + 1, and sends a new packet, so the packet comes now from the new IP address of the mobile to the old IP address of the peer, using the new identifier set, and if there is enough entropy in the identifier set, and not too many collisions (and typically that's the case), then the peer can be sure that this packet was actually sent by the mobile host because nobody else knows the next values in the identifier sequences. Then we can also have a simple verification about the other property, that the mobile host actually is on the new address: the peer moves also to the next set and sends a packet to the new IP address using the next set of identifiers, and the mobile host replies using the next set of identifiers, the set i + 2 in this case, so we get actually verification that the mobile host is at the new IP address because only the mobile host is able to answer using the next set.

This is supposed to solve bumping attacks. There is a weakness because the mobile hosts can anticipate, and predict that this packet is coming, and respond with this packet without seeing the prompt, so there is that problem, but it's easy to solve.

So the idea is basically very simple, you replace the static identifiers with sequences based on some key, for example, if you're using IPsec you get it from the key management protocol, but I agree with Ben, if you don't have that kind of a system then you may have a problem with the linkability of the sequences. The receiver accepts data on several identifier sets from the sequences, and so there is the possibility of conflicts, but the probability of them is usually fairly low, and most protocols have some mechanism that can be used to solve the conflicts. And what was surprising to us, is that you get implicit origin authentication for your packets, and that allows you to do mobility without adding any bits to the messages. And maybe you could use this for creating security for other kinds of protocols, even for TCP. If you apply this to all TCP packets, instead of when you change your IP address, you get this kind of a weird security based on the predictability and unpredictability by the outsiders of the identifier sets, so that you always know what are the quad numbers and sequence numbers that you're listening to, and the next packets in the TCP. Of course you have to have a fairly wide window because of the possibility of dropped packets and so on, and you may run out of bits in your identifier space and get too many collisions, but at least for those protocols which are most problematic today, where you have a large identifier set, you get this kind of implicit original authentication for your protocol if you apply this idea to it.

Richard Clayton: I think you are going to say this is outside of the scope, but the port numbers and so forth actually do two things for you. They do the de-multiplexing once you get going, but they also mean that you don't have to have a rendezvous service at the beginning because the port numbers are "well known", like server names are well known, and therefore you get session establishment at the beginning for free. So to do what you're suggesting here may require you to run a rendezvous service even for a non-mobile system.

Reply: You don't need to do anything for the initial connection. When the mobile host opens a new TCP connection it can just open it to the one port, and the only information that any outside observers get is that there is now a new TCP connection. After that if you keep changing the port numbers for all of the next packets, you can't keep track of which packet is in which TCP sequence.

Richard Clayton: But it worries me that, if you're in California and talking to your machine at home, and I'm sitting in Washington watching all the traffic going across the Atlantic, supposing that I could do that sort of thing, then surely I'm going to see a flow which suddenly stops and another one starts off to the same IP network layer destination, and I'm going to be able to tie those two things together because of the time sequencing between them. I'm not necessarily going to be able to match up what's in them, but there are relatively few flows across the Atlantic to that particular destination.

Reply: Yes. From the privacy point of view there is not a cause for panic here. We are just solving a part of the privacy problem, but quite a lot depends on your traffic patterns, and everyone more or less assumes that you have enough traffic in the network so that your traffic in a way disappears among the rest of the traffic, and that enough people are actually using this scheme. If you're the only one who is using this scheme, then it doesn't help you.

Frank Stajano: Even if other people use the same scheme, you only mix with them if they use it at same time as you. There's also an issue about the same traffic pattern; if you are watching a movie and you are 20 times bigger than all the other people around you, you can be distinguished from them.

Reply: Sure. This scheme is probably more useful in the IPv6 world where you can basically change your IP address for each packet. You don't change your prefix so you're still trackable by the prefix of the IP address, but you can change the host identity part of the IP address.

Bruce Christianson: That's a good point because if you have more frequent changes then you can't really tell the difference between one fat pipe and a large number of thin pipes. Does this have a potential application for anonymising traffic coming from behind a firewall? One of the problems with a virus is the attack is spread easily behind the firewall, but with a mechanism like this they really don't know which IP address to try and send to.

Reply: Yes, if you think of NAT boxes with a lot of traffic.

Bruce Christianson: Yes, that's a good example.

Reply: You then need to have a protocol which tells the NAT boxes the sequences, so that the NAT box can keep updating the mappings that it has.

Non-repudiation and the Metaphysics of Presence

(Extended Abstract)

Michael Roe

Microsoft Research Limited, Cambridge

J. L. Austin's theory of speech acts [1] identifies two classes of utterance:

- Constative statements, which can be either true or false.
- Performatives, which are neither true nor false but instead *do* something. Performatives can *misfire* (fail to have their conventional effect) if they are invoked by an inappropriate person or in inappropriate circumstances (*e.g.* a ship's purser cannot validly marry two people; a priest cannot validly baptize a penguin).

A revised version of his theory recogised that some utterances can belong to both classes simultaneously. In this revised theory, locutions can have a illocutory aspect (doing something) and a perlocutory aspect (changing the recipients' emotions or state of mind, *e.g.* by persuading them).

If we regard the messages in a computer communications protocol as speech acts, what kind of speech acts are they?

Here, I am particularly interested in non-repudiation protocols using public-key cryptography. An example might be the following:

$$A \rightarrow B : \{m, t_A\}K_A^{-1}, \{A, K_A, t_C\}K_C^{-1}$$

A typical use of this protocol is in e-commerce, where the message m from customer to merchant instructs the merchant to supply certain goods and authorises them to charge a certain amount of money to the customer's credit card. This is very clearly a performative. m is neither true nor false, but rather does something – buying the goods. Non-repudiation protocols are particularly useful for protecting performatives. If m is a constative statement, it might be possible to establish its truth or falsity by various different means, but if m is a performative we need to know whether A said it or not.

The second part of the protocol, the certificate $\{A, K_A, t_C\}K_C^{-1}$, is more troublesome. We can view it in two ways:

- A (quoted) constative statement
  A is quoting C saying that the entity known as A is the only entity that has possession of the inverse of K_A. This is a statement of fact, and could be either true or false. C might be lying, or might have been deceived.

B. Christianson et al. (Eds.): Security Protocols 2005, LNCS 4631, pp. 204–206, 2007.

- A (quoted) performative
  A is quoting C declaring that whoever or whatever is in possession of the inverse of K_A shall be known as A. This is not a statement of fact, and cannot be either true or false.

In non-repudiation protocols of this type, only some entities (and not others) can play the role of C. The usual shorthand expression for this is to say that C is *trusted*. There are two possible interpretations of what "trusted" means in this context, depending on whether the certificate is viewed as constative or performative:

- (Constative)
  C is both honest (unlikely to lie) and competent (unlikely to be mistaken) with respect to the constative statement $\{A, K_A, t_C\}K_C^{-1}$.
- (Performative)
  C is one of the entities who can validly perform $\{A, K_A, t_C\}K_C^{-1}$.

Austin explicitly states that his theory does not cover the use of language in poems, theatre, and jokes. This is a problem for those who would like to use his theory in literary criticism, because the specifically excluded poems and plays form a substantial part of literary criticism's traditional subject matter. Jacques Derrida's modification of Austin's theory [2, 3] places greater emphasis on the role of context and quotation.

In the non-repudiation protocol shown above, A is quoting C. In addition to the possibility that C might be lying or mistaken, we should also consider the possibility that A is quoting C out of context. C might have really made the utterance $\{A, K_A, t_C\}K_C^{-1}$, but in a context where it had a different performative effect.

We have traditionally made a distinction between data origin authentication and non-repudiation. In authentication, B is convinced that the message m was sent by A, but is not necessarily able to convince anyone else. In non-repudiation, B can convince a third party, at a later point in time, that A sent m. Authentication protocols only involve parties who are "present", in the sense that they are involved in the protocol run. Non-repudiation protocols involve parties who are "absent" – the eventual verifier of the message can be absent when A creates it, and A can be absent when the message is later verified.

Derrida's work explores the connections between speech/writing and presence/ absence. With speech, the speaker is physically present, but with writing they can be absent. Derrida shows that these two poles are not as different as they might at first appear. We can say similar things about the authentication/nonrepudiation distinction:

- Authentication protocols can be vulnerable to their messages being read in the wrong context.
- Non-repudiation protocols always make some assumptions about the verifier's context, *e.g.* that the verifier knows K_C and considers $\{A, K_A, t_C\}K_C^{-1}$ to be a valid performative.

References

[1] Austin, J.L.: How to do things with words. In: Urmson, J.O., Sbisà, M. (eds.) Oxford Paperbacks (2004)

[2] Derrida, J.: Signature, event, context. In: Margins of Philosophy, pp. 307–330. University of Chicago Press, Translated by Alan Bass (1984)

[3] Howells, C.: Derrida: Deconstruction from Phenomenology to Ethics, ch. 3. Polity Press, Cambridge (1998)

Non-repudiation and the Metaphysics of Presence

(Transcript of Discussion)

Michael Roe

Microsoft Research

Way back in the 1950s, when computer science and communications engineering were really just beginning, there was a great deal of enthusiasm for treating human beings as if they were machines. There was Alan Turing's work on the Turing Test, and there was Norbert Weiner's work on cybernetics. Claude Lévi-Strauss, the anthropologist, was inspired by all of this to go and use some stolen computer science and communications engineering ideas in anthropology. To do that you need to bash the concepts about so much that they're barely recognisable. After its success in anthropology, Lévi-Stauss's approach – by then known as "structuralism" – was applied to literary criticism. And then a certain amount of scepticism set in that this didn't quite work or wasn't quite right.

Fifty years later both sides know better. Computer science and communications engineering looks very different now than it did back in 1950, as does literary criticism. Some of the things that went wrong on our side: (a) Artificial intelligence didn't happen. I mean, OK, there are plenty of good algorithms for doing things, and search engines like Google work, but Alan Turing style artificial intelligence simply didn't happen. (b) Bug-free computer programmes turned out to be somewhat harder to write than you might have thought. (c) Various security problems have become critical. Many of these security problems are to do with quoting, and for reasons I'll come to later this is interesting.

OK, so here is the research question. Given that both of these fields started off at the same place back in the 1950s, is there some connection between what we didn't manage to get to work in computer science, and what the structuralists didn't manage to get to work in literary criticism and anthropology, and do they have any useful ideas which we could steal back? Given that the ideas needed to be bashed about quite a bit to take them from computer science to anthropology, you might have to bash them about some more to move back in the reverse direction.

This a very big question with lots of aspects. One part of it that I won't talk about here: you might try and link up what sociologists talk about when they're talking about privacy with what computer scientists talk about when they're talking about privacy. For example, the work of Michel Foucault has influenced sociological ideas about privacy and control, and at these workshops we're always talking about privacy and control, and they both have a common history, and yet the terminology has completely diverged, and we can't really map what one person is talking about to what the other person is talking about – even

B. Christianson et al. (Eds.): Security Protocols 2005, LNCS 4631, pp. 207–214, 2007.

though we even refer to some of the same texts. Jeremy Bentham's Panopticon features a lot in Foucault's "Discipline and Punish", and last year at the Protocols Workshop, when we were talking about privacy, once again, the Panopticon and surveillance technology comes up as being relevant to what we're doing here.[1] So there's an interesting piece of work to be done, working out how we can connect these things together.

I want to look at a small piece of the puzzle, starting out with non-repudiation, because that's something I'm particularly interested in. We've traditionally distinguished two different properties of protocols, one of which we've called authentication, and the other of which we've called non-repudiation. As an example of the difference (with a deliberate connection to literary criticism) you can imagine Jacques Derrida sending an email to his wife Marguerite. The authentication property would be that she knows that it really came from him, non-repudiation with proof of origin would be that she could then go and convince someone else that the letter she's received really did come from him, and non-repudiation with proof of delivery would be that he can convince someone else that she really did get it.

Bruce Christianson: That she understood the joke, or simply that she got a piece of paper?

Reply: Well that's one of the issues. This is one of the problems with non-repudiation. Another is whether Jacques and Margueritte were just putting on a performance for the audience, or did they really mean what they said?

A piece of theory we have is that proof of origin is not the same as proof of receipt; messages can get dropped on the floor by message transfer agents, so the fact that you sent something isn't the same as the fact that it was received. You'll see in Derrida a kind of reference to Jacques Lacan: "The letter might not reach its destination"[2]. Now when Lacan originally said that, it might have had a psychoanalytic meaning that didn't really relate to communications protocols, but when Derrida misquotes Lacan, it really does have something like its meaning in communications protocols: the letter might get dropped on the floor. And that's because the communications model that Derrida is using, or at least taking apart, was borrowed from us via Lévi-Strauss.

So, to continue with this example, some people's private correspondence sometimes ends up being published in books of letters — T. S. Eliot, for example. If you, the reader of the published book, want to convince yourself that those letters really were written by the famous person they were allegedly written by, that's a form of non-repudiation. It's not quite email non-repudiation, but it's physical paper letter non-repudiation. So... Jacques Derrida's *The Post Card* contains transcripts of a collection of postcards, exchanged between someone with a suspicious resemblance to Jacques Derrida and someone with a suspicious resemblance to his wife Margueritte. This could be read as a famous person's collected letters, as fiction (a campus novel), or as a demonstration of what can

---

[1] See Bruce Christianson, *Authentic Privacy*, LNCS 3957, pp1–2.

[2] In *Seminar on "The Purloined Letter"* Jacques Lacan said the opposite: "...a letter always arrives at its destination".

go wrong when you don't have non-repudiation. In the book the sender and receiver information has deliberated been stripped from the postcards. From what they say you can guess who the people writing them might be, but that's not proof. From reading their contents you can see there's complaints about, did you receive it, no I didn't receive it. So whilst you're monitoring, things are getting dropped on the floor. They're postcards so anybody can read them: there's no assumed confidentiality of the channel. And some contain cryptograms to which the key isn't provided. So from the point of view of authentication all was fine, whoever really received these postcards probably knew whom they were from, and what they meant by them, but you as the reader of the book, the third party being presented with them, are really in a very different position.

A second example, borrowed from *film noir*. Brigid O'Shaughnessy goes and hires private investigator Sam Spade, and she tells him about a conversation that she had with Kasper Gutman. Of course Kasper isn't there to be dragged along with her down to Sam Spade's office to confirm or deny what he said to her. So, does Sam believe her? Of course, if this had all been by email, then a non-repudiation protocol would have done: She could have convinced Sam that that really was the conversation she had. And the interesting thing about this, in this context, is that Sam Spade isn't a cop, although he's a private detective, so he's a bit like a policeman. Sometimes in the security literature it's built into the definition of non-repudiation that the third party you're going to convince is a policeman — frequently, a German policeman. But that's not really a necessary part of the service. You can find corresponding things in post-structuralism: Who is the third party? Do they have to have some kind of police authority?

Frank Stajano: So when you make this distinction, are you pointing out that one of the parties, whether it's a policeman or not, is therefore more or less smart, or has access to extracting other information? What's the difference between when they are or they aren't the police?

Reply: I think what I'm saying is that for it to be non-repudiation all we have to have is somebody who's interested in finding out whether the message was sent or not, they don't necessarily have to have any particular power to do anything.

Frank Stajano: So the difference is the police could actually summon up the person and check?[3]

Reply: Often you hear people talking about non-repudiation protocols as if the only possible use of them was in the courts and in the legal systems, but that's never relied on anywhere in the crypto. The fact that the third party might be a policeman is entirely irrelevant from the point of view of the protocol.

Ben Laurie: Non-repudiation is actually a legal term. Legally, it means a situation in which the law prevents you from denying, which has got nothing to do with 'non-repudiation' protocols.

---

[3] In one view, the difference is that a court has the power to punish someone if it is convinced (by the non-repudiation protocol) that they actually said some particular thing.

Bruce Christianson: You can imagine circumstances where syndicates of drug-dealers (or literary critics) also wanted to be able to convince their community that a message was sent.

Richard Clayton: No, non-repudiation in this community means, I don't know how to break it, because if I run a non-repudiation protocol, and this demonstrates at the end that I have written the next Harry Potter book, you will not say to me, "A ha! You have written the next Harry Potter book and are due royalties." You will say, "A ha! You know how to break this don't you?"

Bruce Christianson: Yes, but that's because we're in this community and not somewhere else.

Reply: Yes, I'd say OK to that, but another interesting thing is that the third party can't be just anyone. If you could imagine this being electro magnetically radiated out into space, and aliens in another star system intercept this, the non-repudiation protocols don't work for them, because things like bindings between public keys and authorities that you know to be trusted, don't apply for these space aliens on a distant planet. So although the third party doesn't have to be policemen, they didn't have to have some kind of legally recognized authority, they really did have to be a member of some community that's got some shared knowledge, such as that this particular product of two large prime numbers is special, and the factors are known by some person that you have reason to trust. All that kind of context really has to be had by the third party for it to work.

Going back to this metaphysics of presence phrase that I have in the title, roughly speaking and possibly to slightly abuse it, the idea is that in Western philosophy rather too much is made of the distinction between what is spoken and what is written. Yes, there is a difference, but it's more a difference of degree rather than of kind. So you can imagine when you're speaking to someone that you know who the other person is because they're in the room with you, they're physically present, and you sort of know their context, so you know how they're going to interpret what you're going to say, except really you don't, because you don't know somebody else's mind exactly[4]. Conversely, with writing, you write a book, it goes in the library, and in the future anybody at all could read it. You as the writer don't know what the reader's context is going to be. But there again, you actually do have to know something about their presumptions, because if you go outside that they just won't know what the bits mean. So you can see it just there that the speech/writing distinction turns out to be more a matter of degree than kind, and also the authentication/non-repudiation distinction is more a matter of degree than kind.

A non-repudiation protocol is a kind of very slow authentication protocol. Just like an ordinary authentication protocol, at the start when you create a digitally signed object, you have some idea of the set of verifiers that are going to be able to verify it, and it's just a rather longer time later that they get round to verifying it.

---

[4] But at least you can (sometimes) tell how they are interpreting what you say in time for this to have an effect on what you say next.

Being Internet people we're less likely to get caught up into believing that speech and writing are fundamentally different things, because whether it's a voice over IP phone call, or a written email letter, we know exactly what we're going to do with it, we're going to encode it into bits, and put it into packets, and stuff it down exactly the same wires. And so from that point of view we're quite happy with thinking, oh yes, these are clearly the same thing – but they might have different requirements. People might expect the communication protocols to behave in a way they think speech ought to behave when you put speech down wires, and they might expect writing to behave in the way they expect writing to behave when you put writing down wires. And so from that point of view you can see that this distinction between speech and writing might actually reflect a difference in requirements, and we might want to have two different protocols that do these two different things, to actually artificially create a distinction between two things that aren't really different.

One final thing to wind up on. If you actually have a protocol that provides non-repudiation, it's like writing; you're creating something like a written document that can be shown to somebody else, and they can know you've written it because they can see the signature. And if you're doing the thing we're calling plausible deniability, where you just have authentication, but don't have non-repudiation, then you're doing something a bit like having a private conversation: the person you're speaking to knows you're speaking to them, but they've got nothing at the end of it that they can go and give to someone else and prove that you said it.

So, I think there's some interesting connections to be made here between two fields that apparently look quite different. I'm going to stop on that, I think I've silenced everybody with such a weird talk.

George Danezis: The discussion about this might seem a bit strange in this forum, but I think it's quite relevant. I think structuralism is a big problem in the way we think about computer security, in that it really tried to cut things into very specific categories that have very fixed relationships between them. This is very much how we traditionally think about principals, and what they can access, and the actions. But actually what we end up with is that a principal is not just a clerk, or just a secretary, or just a bank manager. They might take different roles at different times, they're a bit of everything at different times, and it's all a little more fluid. So the shift that has happened in thinking in social sciences in terms of not really assigning a very fixed role or fixed categories to people or processes is really relevant to us now, and that relates quite well to what you were saying.

Reply: Another way of talking about it is that at least part of what we're doing is, or ought to be, social science because these computer systems that we're trying to make secure are actually going to be used by real people and to understand those requirements we have to understand what people want them to do. All these concerns that the social scientists have now realised are issues which we have to wake up to as well.

Bruce Christianson: What sort of thing do you have in mind to steal back from them? These notions of communication channels, and theories of semantics used by the early structuralists were lifted from a misunderstanding of Wheeler, Shannon and Turing. But now structuralism has eaten itself, it has applied its own reasoning to itself as subject matter and disintegrated. What's left for us to pick up, or is computer science about to self-destruct in a similar manner.

Reply: Every time I see the list of new security exploits against everybody's favourite operating system, I feel this whole field is self-destructing. But, seriously, one place where it might help is understanding privacy some more. We've got a real problem in translating the social scientists' notion of privacy to our protocols notion of privacy, and something that would help there would be greatly useful. These ideas of power and authority that we talk about a great deal — I think we're often being somewhat naïve when we draw nice hierarchical pictures of authorities with some king at the top. It would be good to get notions from the social scientists so as to be able to talk about the real power relations between individuals in a more sensible manner. Also I made brief references to quoting, I don't have time to go into it here, but a lot of these bugs, like buffer overflows, and cross site scripting, are to do with things inside quotation marks escaping outside the quotation marks and having effects you didn't expect. And there's similar things going on in the literary criticism with respect with how you talk about quotation, so maybe something from there might help us talk about those properties of programs in a more sensible manner.

Alf Zugenmaier: Some of the words that we already stole back from them have been misused so much that nobody knows what it means anymore when they talk about trust measures, and trusted paths, and whatever. Trust changes its meaning whenever it is applied to a different thing, and do you think that it may actually be worse if we try to take concepts, not just words.

Reply: I think there is that danger. One way I thought of doing this talk was starting off with a whole list of terms which are used in literary criticism, and also in computer science, which have almost, but not quite the same, meaning – like signature. Trace is absolutely the worst one because it really doesn't mean what you might think it means from protocols.

Yvo Desmedt: Then there was the difference between an electronic signature and manual signature. But you don't have a legal meaning for electronic signature.

Reply: Right, yes, so there's a legal notion of what a signature is, and then there's what we're calling a signature. Another thing you can learn from the post-structuralists is that language is like that and you just have to deal with it. You're not going to solve this problem of making sure that every distinct meaning gets a globally unique word for it, you just have to deal with this problem.

Ben Laurie: We can attach the hash for a public key in front of every word so we know whose version we're reading.

Matt Blaze: In fact a digital signature is a security mechanism that has certain abstract properties that we kind of understand how to use with other security mechanisms, but it's not in any sense a signature in any legal or social sense. And in fact if we look at the legal requirements for establishing evidence, at least in the United States, they're completely unconcerned with technical matters about the feasibility of forging them, you can raise those issues in challenging evidence in a case, but almost never in law is there anything near the kind of requirement for specific mechanisms that we take for granted.

Reply: Another way you could make the connection is, we don't just write computer programs, we have texts that talk about computer programs – like the publications we produce. You can apply these notions of literary criticism to our published papers. For example, you have words like digital signature not meaning the same thing as signatures mean elsewhere.

One of the things that you might take from Wittgenstein and apply to this is that non-repudiation isn't about giving you proofs that start from the axioms of set theory and end up proving that you went into Wal-Mart and bought a can of coke. Such things are clearly impossible; no amount of mathematics, no matter how clever it is, could possibly ever produce such a thing.

Yvo Desmedt: Another problem is that these laws do not necessarily originate from rule makers, they originate from lobbyists. So it's more than just two levels of difference.

Reply: Yes, yes, I know, I agree, but there's an interesting effect there, that the misunderstandings produced by the terms we've produced, then ended up getting enshrined in law.

Yvo Desmedt: The electronic signatures was not lobbied by information security people, it was lobbied by groups of, for example, thieves, who wanted to make sure they were actually scanning in your signature while you were at the signing desk.

Reply: I've not seen that, but I know now in the UK we have just gone to chip and PIN for credit cards, where previously you would get a piece of paper which you would sign with your handwritten signature to prove that you'd made the transaction. Previously if anything went wrong with the computer system they'd have to produce the piece of paper with your signature on it, or refund you the money, now there's only the bits, so you're much more reliant now on the electronic computer system not having any bugs in it. Ross can doubtless tell you a great deal more about this.

Ross Anderson: There are some electronic systems which, probably more by oversight than design, give the customer a reasonable option. A rather beautiful example, there's a supermarket in London where when you do a credit card transaction there's a little signature tablet, and you scribe your signature on the tablet, and press the button, and it then lets you take the goods away. Someone said to me, surely this is insecure because it can't check the signature and I can just draw a smiley face there as my signature. My response was, well that binds you, if you went to the shop, you take goods, and you make a little smiley on the signature tablet, that is in law your signature, you signed it. But from the point of view of the user it's absolutely brilliant, because if somebody else, having stolen your credit card, then takes it to a conventional outlet and tries to sign with the signature on the card, instead of the little smiley face, it's off to jail with him. An accidentally secure system.

Reply: At the end of Jacques Derrida's paper, Signature, event, context, as well as typing his name there's a printed copy of what his signature looks like. I'm told that that's not actually the signature he used on cheques.

Bruce Christianson: Is there any mileage in using the programs themselves as texts and attempting to deconstruct them?

I'm used to taking programmes and running them on machines that they weren't originally written to be run on.

Kamil Kulesza: Oh, you're saying the same speech act could lead to very complex webs of different semantics.

Bruce Christianson: Exactly, you would have no control over the text, but the context you can change.

Understanding Why Some Network Protocols Are User-Unfriendly

Yvo Desmedt*

Department of Computer Science
University College London, UK

Abstract. Some are wondering whether due to the appearance of spyware, insecure wireless LAN, the increase in spam, the persistence of computer viruses and worms, home users may renounce on PCs. They state, for example, that setting up a secure wireless LAN is not trivial for many users, or that users are unaware since the default comes without security.

Anderson gave an economic reason why Microsoft gave information security a low priority. In this paper we analyze some scenarios where users want userfriendly security and setting it up is far from trivial. We try to find technical reasons and folklore scientific explanations why some security problems have either not been taken into account, or why, when they have, they are not doing the best job, or why they are so user-unfriendly.

1 Introduction

The cost of having system managers spend a large fraction of their time on updating software, downloading patches, is unacceptable.

The situation for home users is much worse. In the last year, we have seen an explosion of spyware, which makes many home users' computers become excessively slow. The problem is so wide spread, that lately when visiting friends and family, the author has been confronted frequently with this phenomenon. The removal of the spyware brought back the performance of the computer to the expected level. It was clear that not all home users know how to avoid spyware, remove it, or are even aware of its existence.

In contrast with large organizations, most home users do not have access to a daily available system manager, or cannot afford the service even on a monthly basis. Worse, many system managers do not have the skills to set up the security appropriately. Examples of this, and their impact on security are given in Section 2. Observe that this is not the main goal of this paper.

Information security experts may be more aware than the average user of when they want to use network security protocols. However, as we will see, there are circumstances where their expectations cannot be fulfilled easily by the current

---

* The author is BT chair of information security. He is also a courtesy professor at Florida State University, USA.

B. Christianson et al. (Eds.): Security Protocols 2005, LNCS 4631, pp. 215–219, 2007.

implemented network security protocols. We will discuss some of the technical reasons why a userfriendly security level is not achieved. Moreover, we see how folklore scientific arguments have lead to a less secure internet than one might expect. Examples are discussed in Section 3.

2   Security Which Is User-Unfriendly Even for System Managers

The story that President Bush (the father of the current one) could not program his VCR is a well known one. So an issue since the use of VCR has been userfriendlyness. Having the Microsoft operating system preinstalled on many PC has been a big boost to the popularity of the Microsoft products. Although Windows XP came with a firewall, originally it was not enabled. Only after the spread of Blaster did Microsoft change this policy. Evidently, many users did not enable Microsoft's software firewall when installing their machine. The average user expects that the security is set up correctly when buying a system. Currently, this is in particular a problem with wireless LAN.

When buying a wireless LAN, it comes default with the wepmode and WPA off. The reason is quite clear. Imagine vendors would, then users need to set the keys for the wepkey on the clients in the network. Since users may not know how to set this up, vendors can guarantee users can test the availability of the network when the wepmode and WPA is off. So, the risk of an unsatisfied customer bringing back to the shop the wireless LAN is small. So, the approach makes economic sense taking into account the expected market. However, more troublesome is that some system managers do not know how to set it up either (for example, some have asked the author's help). Some set it up with too low security.

We may expect that system managers would be skilled and deal appropriately with security. Unfortunately, this is not the case. Worse, they often do not understand what is at stake. We give two illustrations.

Example 1. The author knows personally of some CS departments where the
system manager when upgrading the hardware/software of a unix
machine, did not copy the keys ssh_host_key, ssh_host_dsa_key, and
ssh_host_rsa_key. The fact that users were often not informed about
the changes in hardware/software, implied that such events looked
to the user as unexpected. A user (e.g. on a trip), would then find
that:
  – using tramp in emacs to the name of the machine no longer
    works,
  – when using ssh, ssh2 or sftp, one is prompted with the question
    whether one accepts the public key.
When a security aware user sees that a host public key that has been
used many times no longer works, a user may expect a man-in-the-
middle attack, and so prefer to avoid accepting the new public key.

Example 2. At a CS department for a long time the firewall was set up preventing users inside CS to use outside DNS servers, even the main one from the university. So users were forced to use the one of CS, which was just a clone of the university one! This implied that when the DNS server went down, and this did happen more than once, the whole CS network just hanged. The people responsible for the computer network at the university level told the author that many firewalls inside the university were completely misconfigured!

So, if the setup of a network to guarantee an acceptable availability and security is too complex for system managers, how can one expect it to be for the home user?

A question evidently is why system managers have the problem. A speculative answer to this question is that system managers do not understand the consequences of their actions and may not know of, for example, man-in-the-middle attacks or understand these correctly. Moreover, it may seem that blocking as much as possible (e.g. as many ports) with a firewall is the most secure approach, without realizing the implications on availability.

3 Security Products That May Be User Unfriendly Even for the Security Expert

The goal of this section is to analyze some technical and folklore scientific arguments why some security products do not achieve what one would expect. In this extended abstract we only give one example, based on a true story.

3.1 The Example

Today many scientists use wireless while attending workshops and conferences. Suppose Alice, while listening to a paper may be inspired. This may allow her to apply for a patent or to submit a new scientific paper. To make certain the idea is new she may want to use a search engine, such as Google or Yahoo. Another attendee, Eve who uses the wireless network and has set up a sniffer, may find the thought pattern of Alice and beat her in the patent application or the release of the scientific paper.

If the wireless connection would be fast the user could just open an ssh connection to a server on a wired network, which is much harder to eavesdrop for Eve and then launch a browser on that server. When using a properly set up Unix computer this browser will be tunneled through the ssh connection. However, modern wireless LAN are too slow to make above approach practical. Indeed, not only must all the http traffic get through the tunnel, but also all the browser related mouse movements, all the browser commands, etc.

A test demonstrates that the use of a browser tunneled through ssh, is significantly slower than just launching a browser on the local machine. The question in the last case is how to set up the security. A solution which seems should work is to forward port 80 from the local host (the laptop) to port 80 on the server, e.g. in FreeBSD this could be done using a command as:

ssh2 -S -f user@machine.domain -L 80:localhost:80

However, it turns out that this is not secure. A test revealed that e.g. running a sniffer in passive mode (so the sniffers sends no packets) and only sniffing traffic to the laptop, that above fails. (This can be tested running for example "urlsnarf," which will show in the clear the URL pages one is requesting.)

The purpose of the example was to state that the expected security is not achieved. Note that it is possible to achieve the protection, using a more complex method based on a proxy server. However, some universities, e.g. University College London, do not have a proxy server.

3.2   Technical Analysis

What Alice ideally wants to achieve is that *all* wireless traffic is tunneled through a secure link. The problem is that ssh runs at a high layer, i.e. the application layer. What Alice needs is a secure link at a lower layer. One may wonder why ssh works primarily at the application layer. We now explain why.

Before the paper by Diffie-Hellman [2] one distinguished between *link-encryption* and *end-to-end encryption*. A possible problem with link-encryption is that the hops in the communication path see the text in the clear. Since these may be corrupted, end-to-end encryption was preferred. For a while text books on cryptography explained both terminologies. Many modern textbooks and scientific papers speak about Alice sending information to Bob and no longer talk about link-encryption. This has created the folklore believe that link-encryption is bad. We now explain why this is not necessarily true.

One of the main advantages of link-encryption is that the key distribution problem is much easier. When a connection is established the parties exchange a secret key for that link. So in a wired network the complexity of the key distribution of link-encryption is linear in the degree of each node. In a large network, this is usually a small fraction of the number of nodes. This is in sharp contrast with end-to-end encryption. Kohnfelder [3] realized the need for a PKI. Unfortunately today a world-wide PKI is non-existent and industry has realized several problems with PKI: economic, irresponsible CA(s), reliability, lack of trust, etc. For this and many more reasons we do not have a secure network. For example, surveying the WWW truly anonymously against a powerful enemy is not solved by any current implementations, including anonymizers and onion routing. A problem with link-encryption is that if one does not use end-to-end encryption on top, one depends on the managers of the link to set it up. However, as we discussed in Sections 1 and 2, the system manager may not have the required knowhow.

When using a media as wireless, we are dealing with a broadcast environment. However, the client of the IEEE 802.11 wireless interface does usually not exploit the broadcast properties. Therefore it would be *ideal if one would have a different key for each client,* which is usually not the case. This means that one is faced with a situation the provider of the link does not offer the appropriate link-encryption.

To analyze an alternative, consider the OSI layered network architecture. It seems that the best one can hope for is encryption/authentication at the transport layer. However, ssh does not provide such a service.

3.3 Lessons

The example demonstrates the challenge changing technologies imply. ssh was primarily designed as a "secure shell client (remote login program)." Its tunneling features are clearly applications oriented. One should not be in a situation where security is a burden and setting it up is extremely userunfriendly. Folk science and technology is not helpful to achieve this goal. Security engineers should consider how to obtain security in an insecure environment, without relying on the hope that infrastructures such as PKI will be available soon.

Acknowledgments

The author thanks James Hughes for discussions.

References

1. Anderson, R.: Why information security is hard-an economic perspective. In: Proceedings of the 17th Annual Computer Security Applications Conference, p. 358. IEEE Computer Society Press, Los Alamitos (2001)
2. Diffie, W., Hellman, M.E.: New directions in cryptography. IEEE Trans. Inform. Theory IT–22(6), 644–654 (1976)
3. Kohnfelder, L.M.: BSC, MIT Department of Electronical Engineering. Toward a practical public-key cryptosystem (1978)
4. Odlyzko, A.: Economics and cryptography. In: Pfitzmann, B. (ed.) EUROCRYPT 2001. LNCS, vol. 2045, Springer, Heidelberg (2001)

Understanding Why Some Network Protocols Are User-Unfriendly
(Transcript of Discussion)

Yvo Desmedt

Department of Computer Science
University College London, UK

When I saw the call for papers for this workshop, I said, no, computers do not love us, and we don't love computers, in particular when we're looking from the viewpoint of information security. If we would love computers they would be much nore user-friendly, and so that's why I'm talking about understanding why some network protocols are user-unfriendly.

We can see that security products may be user-unfriendly for the average user, but what's more surprising to see is that security products today are even user-unfriendly for system managers, and I will give some examples of that.

So what are the problems with security products? I claim that security experts also have problems with security products, and we heard this morning from Mark Lomas[1], who basically had similar feelings about that as myself. So, that's a problem. I'm going to describe some problems, and then I'm going to describe what the possible technical reasons are that some of these problems pop up. And then we need to learn the lessons from that, and that's how we'll conclude.

Information security is an applied discipline, that means that we need to have a balance between the theoretical world and the practical world. If things do not work we better try to understand why they don't work, a nice ongoing example of that is Ross Anderson's work on why cryptosystems fail. In order to understand whether systems will work or not work we may have to do white hacking, because hacking tools are useful to detect why things do not always work as we expect them to work. So I would like to use this occasion to give my personal feeling that we should teach post-graduate students about white hacking if they desire to learn about it, and this without turning computer courses into hacking classes. My viewpoint is very different from, for example, the one from Gene Spafford, who said that this should not be done. I think if you want to evaluate security products we have no choice, and we want to make sure that students who are on your courses are prepared to do white hacking in the future, and know about it.

Who are primarily today's users, and what impact has that on security? Many system managers today actually are home users. When you have, let's say, a Windows machine at home, then you are the system manager of that machine, within all your cases, probably not such a dramatic consequence, but if you take an average user it may have quite some dramatic consequences. So it's no surprise that one finds many home users have Spyware on their machines, etc.

---

[1] These proceedings.

B. Christianson et al. (Eds.): Security Protocols 2005, LNCS 4631, pp. 220–227, 2007.
© Springer-Verlag Berlin Heidelberg 2007

We find many who don't even know what Spyware is, many don't know how to get it off, etc. Should I call these people system managers, I think I should not, OK, so I'm no longer going to call them system managers, but they are in fact managing their own computer.

If we really care about information security for most users, then it's clear that it must be user-friendly, in particular when we think about these home users, but since we are so far from making security products user friendly for the average user, we will only focus on trained system managers, and others.

President Bush (I'm not talking about the current one, I'm talking about his father who was also President) made no secret that he couldn't programme his own VCR. So, basically this set the feeling one needs to make user-friendly products. If you look at the Microsoft operating system, if you compare it to how operating systems had to be installed before, one can view it as quite a success for Microsoft. Moreover they were able to convince PC manufacturers to pre-install Microsoft operating system. This has been a big boost for the popularity of the product, but also has brought down the expected knowledge of the user. So what we now see is that Microsoft has not followed this philosophy for their information security tools. Indeed, Windows XP came with a firewall, but it was not enabled. So, all these things are pre-installed basically, but the average user doesn't expect to set anything. Many users did not enable Microsoft's software firewall. After the spread of Blaster, Microsoft changed the policy.

It's actually quite amazing when you see that this comes from a company as Microsoft that was so successful in pre-installation. The lesson from that is that the average user expects that the security is set up correctly when buying a system. Is this expectation reasonable? The answer is, no, evidently not. Think about a wireless LAN (for details see Section 2 of the position paper).

There are several system managers who actually do not know how to set up a secure wireless LAN either. I have seen some that actually know how to set it up, and have set up using a very "wrong" key, it had an extremely low Kolmogorov complexity. So it was really easy to guess it.

I'm going to give you two examples that illustrate why system managers do not understand what's at stake. As an example, some system manager when upgrading the hardware/software of a Unix machine, did not copy the keys ssh_host_key, etc, into the new machine. (For details of the impact of this see Example 1 in Section 2 of the position paper.)

Mike Roe: It's very easily done though, when you re-install your operating system, and then suddenly realise, oh yes, I should have backed up that private key.

Reply: Here is another example. At some CS department the firewall was set up for a long time preventing users inside the CS to use the outside DNS servers. (For details see Example 2 in Section 2 of the position paper.) People responsible at the same University for the computer network at University level told me that many firewalls inside the University were completely misconfigured.

So if for a system manager it is too hard to guarantee an acceptable availability and security, if that's too complex for the system managers, how can we expect them to be for the average home user. So what's the lesson that we can learn? You can say: "it's easy to make mistakes", but that's exactly what should not be the case when you're dealing with security. Another lesson is that many system managers never followed a course on computer security, or any information security course whatsoever. I also think that they often do not understand information security, and if they start worrying about it, they start to over-protect with all the bad consequences. So they may be blocking as much as possible, having the impression that must be better than not blocking, without realising the implications on availability.

Tuomas Aura: But really lots of system administrators do not understand how the system works. They know some set of tasks that they do to keep it running, and where to go to read something, they learn new tricks and new tasks that they remember to do at the right time, but in general they don't understand how the computers work, and it's not just limited to security. Security is just one factor.

Reply: Exactly, but in the case of security it makes things worse.

Pekka Nikander: It's not only the system managers who don't understand how the system works, usually also many of the programmers.

Reply: Yes, some programmers don't understand and that's why we get all these problems.

Marcus Grenado: The burden should be with the protocol designers because...

Reply: OK, good. I'm going to talk about protocol designers next.

So let me talk about ssh designers. The next statement I'm going to make is that products are even user-unfriendly for security experts, not just the system managers, but for security experts. Imagine the situation Alice is attending a workshop and there is wireless available. (For details see Section 3.1.)

OK, so what are possible solutions. If the wireless connection would be fast, but we know that usually it's not the case, but if it would be, then what the user just could do is open an ssh connection to a server. She could then just launch a browser on that server. When using a properly set up Unix computer that will be automatically tunneled through the ssh connection. So fine. Have you ever tried to do that? I've tried to do that, it's awful.

Pekka Nikander: There is a way you can do that easily, you just set up a web proxy on your remote server, and then you configure your browser on a local machine to use the ssh connection to connect to the web proxy.

Reply: OK, I'm going to give some examples and say why they're not good. I know they're a solution that works. But most wireless LANs are too slow for this to be a good solution.

Pekka Nikander: It is not really the wireless LAN that is slow, it is the Intranet which is slow.

Reply: That also depends. The problem that happens is you have this mouse movement, and rows of commands, it is much more than just the http traffic that actually is going over the connection.

Ben Laurie: Can you perhaps have all your traffic on the laptop getting sent back through an encrypted tunnel to your own corporate server?

Reply: OK, let me talk about that right now, because that was my next slide.

Richard Clayton: Let us talk about that because that doesn't do what you think it does.

Reply: Exactly. A solution that it seems should work is to forward port 80 from the local host, the laptop, to port 80 on the server.

Audience: I don't understand why anybody would think that would work.

Reply: Because the same thing works for port 25. If you start reading the manual of ssh you can tell that they expect that to work, and indeed it does not work.

Pekka Nikander: But what you are proving is only that the security people don't understand how networking works.

Reply: Yes, that's correct.

Ben Laurie: But why doesn't that work if you correctly configure your browser?

Pekka Nikander: You have to have a proxy there.

Bruce Christianson: Yes, you have to have a proxy sitting at port 80 at the other end, because what that does is it tunnels port 80 at localhost to the far ends port 80, so if you connect to localhost in your browser you will get localhost at the far end, if you do anything else it will just go straight to wherever you want it to go.

Reply: So I'm quite glad that I'm not the only one who sees that doesn't work. So how did I find out that this thing does not work? Basically by running a sniffer in passive mode (I don't want to run it in active mode) and then checking on the IP address that's actually being used, and you could use something for example, urlsnarf, and get the shock to see that all this won't actually work. Indeed, the URLs show up.

Are there solutions that work, yes there are solutions that work, OK. But the purpose of this example is to state that the expected security is not achieved. Your argument is correct, people may not understand the networking behind it, and the people who are security experts are not necessarily network experts. But again, it demonstrates the main thing that I wanted to make clear, which is that security products are not necessarily user-friendly, and so computers do not love us, and we do not love computers.

So what Alice evidentally wants to achieve is that all the wireless traffic is tunnelled through a secure link.

Alf Zugenmaier: No, that's not what she wants, she wants to have all the traffic secure against eavesdropping, so what she basically wants to have is that all traffic, independent of where it goes, is encrypted. You don't need to have unnecessary tunnelling, so tunnelling is bad in general.

Audience: Why?

Alf Zugenmaier: It's inefficient. It creates delay and it creates actual overhead. It adds about fifty percent to the network traffic over the global scale which means that network will be roughly fifty percent more, if everybody's using tunnelling.

Reply: So what Alice really needs is a secure link at a lower layer, and consequently one may wonder why ssh works primarily at the application layer. One of the reasons is that if you look at the main use of ssh is it was basically designed as a secure shell client primarily for remote login.

Link encryption may be an alternative solution (for details see Section 3.2 of the position paper). History has created the folklore belief that link-encryption is bad.

Ben Laurie: That's because it is bad.

Reply: It is not bad if properly used, and if you are aware of what you can do with it. It's more limited than end-to-end, but with end-to-end you then get all the problems that we are in today. One of the main advantages of link-encryption is that the key distribution problem becomes much easier.

Pekka Nikander: You just said in the beginning that people can't organize link-encryption.

Reply: I know, so you could view this as a third solution: what would happen is that now when you use an encryption mode of your wireless you would have a unique key, and then the wireless who set it up, basically provides every person in this room with a unique key, OK. Is it perfectly secure? No it's not perfectly secure, but it is better.

Audience: Is it much easier?

Reply: It's much easier, yes. If you look at using end-to-end encryption, people usually end up with PKI.

Pekka Nikander: There is an easier way, which is to create a new namespace. You basically use the public keys to set primary names, so everybody in the network is identified by their public key.

Reply: That does not work. Mike Burmester and myself wrote a paper about it at IFIP 2004[2], and explained it doesn't work, and the reason is revocation.

---

[2] Desmedt and Burmester, Identity-Based Key Infrastructure (IKI), Sec 2004, pp167–176.

Pekka Nikander: It depends on your revocation requirements I agree.

Reply: With PKI the problem is, as many people have figured out, that there are irresponsible CAs, there are reliability issues, lack of trust, etc. So for this and many more reasons we do not have a secure network. So, in this context, link-encryption may not be as bad as it sounds. I'm not saying it's perfect, OK.

Now to come back to what we were saying, indeed a problem with link-encryption is how can we trust it if we have to rely on system managers who may not have the required background? It would be ideal if it would have a different key for each client, which is unfortunately usually not the case for obvious reasons. So we clearly see that these things are not as user-friendly as people expect.

I believe one of the main reasons is that it's quite a challenge to change technologies. So take two examples. First, ssh was designed for limited settings with a secure login which was then slightly generalised. It's not straightforward to apply that for applications such as, for example, http. Second, if you look at what security experts do, they design for a completely new world. After the work by Diffie-Hellman, and the invention of public key, then link encryption died, people said. But there is no world-wide PKI. It's kind of saying, we're going to replace modern plane-based travel, by space-based travel. People have been talking about it for a long time, that going outside the atmosphere speeds up travel, and we hope that this all will work. Then we start abolishing planes, etc. However, you can only start doing that once you have built up this new infrastructure, and then very carefully you can demolish the other infrastructure. We have designed PKI as something which will be there tomorrow. If you look at the talk that was given yesterday by Tuomas Aura[3], some of the issues that he mentioned actually are also a consequence of this: we are not planning for transition, we're planning for tomorrow. What we have today is insecure, tomorrow we will go to completely secure. And what happens in the meanwhile? While PKI is being built up, you see all these problems appear.

Tuomas Aura: The recent idea called Better than Nothing Security[4] defines the way you can use IPsec without doing any key distribution before. There are also some projects going on, for example, there is a project at Boeing called the Secure Mobile Architecture, which is basically trying to address any of the practical problems related to deploying security on a corporate network, and the Boeing network is huge, they have more than four hundred thousand nodes in their network, and they have, if I remember correctly, something like, 700 firewalls within that corporate network, and so they really, hit the practical problems of deploying security, and there are practical attempts to address many of these things. But in my opinion, and looking at what was happening in the industry, people are gradually starting to understand that there are these transition issues, and they are gradually starting to address some of them, maybe not all, but some of them.

---

[3] These proceedings.
[4] See e.g. www.ieff.org/html.charters/btns-charter.html

Reply: Yes, the transition issue is a very important one. And so meanwhile we should have scaleable security, where scaleable may imply limited, something only for a number of users. If you look for example at the work of Eschenauer-Gligor on Ad Hoc Networks[5], then basically forget about PKI, forget about public keys, just set it up for a number of users. So there are things that need to be done. And we should definitely not be in situations where security is a burden, and setting it up extremely user-unfriendly. I believe that folk science and folk technology are not helpful to achieve this goal. Security engineers should consider how to obtain security in an insecure environment without relying on the hope that infrastructures such as PKI will be available soon.

Richard Clayton: I think the examples that you give are interesting, but by putting them together you have a funny effect. At one stage you are criticising Microsoft for not having turned on the firewall, right, and then later on you're criticising your sys admin for having turned it on and blocked all of your DNS.

Reply: No, they did more than turn it on, they turned it on and then said, OK, let's change this so to increase security as much as possible, that was their belief.

Richard Clayton: Well arguably that had an effect on security by blocking DNS traffic outward because it has an effect on whether or not worms and so forth can actually exist in your environment without having to do a lot of discovery in order to work out where to find the resources which they need in order to be able to spread. It means you may have a worm problem but it doesn't get out, so no harm done.

Reply: They also blocked the DNS from the University, OK, and didn't have a backup.

Richard Clayton: What would be far more useful than turning on the firewall, which only blocks incoming connections to your feed, it would do much better to actually re-review all of the servers which are running on your machine, and turn almost all of them off, or arrange that they can only accept connections from 127001, because in practice if you're not running a server, you don't actually have a problem which that sort of firewall would solve.

Reply: I agree, I don't disagree.

Alf Zugenmaier: We have lots of people complaining that there are too many features in the program. Eventually we will have all kinds of communities, and each one of them wants to have their feature on by default, and really to build even more features in, all of which requires some user attention. We are setting security against the user.

Reply: I think that's actually a very good comment, but this is a workshop on security, I presume that that's what we want here. OK, but I agree with you, the average user does not necessarily want security, but then if we go to zero

---

[5] Eschenauer, Gligor and Baras, On Trust Establishment in Mobile Ad Hoc Networks, LNCS 2845, pp47–66.

security, then we know basically what happens. If you, for example, say, OK, let's go back to Telnet instead of ssh, then you're going to pay a price. So we need security, a good issue which I did not address is how much. How much, and how much not. So many of us are actually thinking about it in the ideal world. We think PKI will be there, etc. In reality that's not, we are far from having a world-wide PKI. We better think about this in a more limited setting. Basically what you were saying is that we really shouldn't put all the software there, we really need to think more limited, yes, that's a good comment.

Tuomas Aura: I think security mechanisms work best when the user doesn't even know about it, then it certainly doesn't hurt the user. Now maybe you can't get all the security you want that way, but that practically explains why you had such trouble setting up tunnels, and so on. Because you just want to do your job, type whatever paper, send it off, and so on, you do not want to set up the tunnel to begin with, and so users should not be doing those kinds of things. The firewall, on the other hand, I think works quite well because someone somewhere turned it on and you did not even know that they did it.

Reply: No, I did, OK.

Tuomas Aura: But that was reliability.

Reply: And the reason why I did it is that I'm system manager on my own laptop and so I always put two DNSs in case one goes down, and so that's how I found out it was blocked.

Community-Centric Vanilla-Rollback Access, or: How I Stopped Worrying and Learned to Love My Computer

Mike Burmester, Breno de Medeiros, and Alec Yasinsac

Department of Computer Science, Florida State University,
Tallahassee, FL 32306, USA
{burmester,breno,yasinsac}@cs.fsu.edu

Abstract. We propose a new framework for authentication mechanisms that seek to interact with users in a friendlier way. Human or community-centric authentication supports *vanilla access* to users who fail an initial attempt to identify themselves. This limited access enables them to communicate with their peer community to achieve authentication. The actions of users with vanilla access can be *rolled back* in case they do not progress to full authentication status.

This mechanism is supported by a peer community trust infrastructure that exploits the effectiveness that humans have in understanding their communal roles in order to mitigate their lesser skill in remembering passwords or pins. The techniques involved essentially implement a human-centric key escrow and recovery mechanism.

1 Introduction

The research and practice of user authentication techniques often contradicts human nature. Indeed, most tasks required for user authentication, such as remembering a password or a pin, are much more effectively done by machines. While machines have no difficulties in storing and perfectly reproducing any amount of data, we humans are used to committing to memory only a few private authentication values (such as an identification card number or social security number). The real security requirements of password-based authentication (frequently changeable, long and not easily guessable passwords) are not truly compatible with human behavior, if acceptable to perhaps a minority of us. Other mechanisms that underlie strong authentication protocols, such as secure tokens, often work less well in practice than might be expected because of the human tendency to think of security measures as hindrances to be tolerated as necessary evils, or because they require extra investment in hardware and system management which may not be available.

On the other hand, humans are very effective at understanding the roles they play in their community, at organizing access control to common resources and at protecting private property. This indicates that there is no intrinsic human inability to deal with the authentication problem, only human ineffectiveness at

B. Christianson et al. (Eds.): Security Protocols 2005, LNCS 4631, pp. 228–237, 2007.
© Springer-Verlag Berlin Heidelberg 2007

dealing with machine-friendly protocols. The goal of this research is to introduce a human-centric – and since authorization happens in the context of the human role within society – a community-centric approach to access control.

The premise that humans are effective at comprehending their roles is a broad one and we believe could lead to new directions and ways of thinking about security. In this position paper, we illustrate how a broad principle of community-centric security can be applied to the design of securing a particular task, namely remote login. We then broaden our scope and speculate how this approach can be used to tackle other unwieldy areas where security technology and human-behavior intersect.

Previous efforts to tailor protocols for human capabilities include the human-computer authentication techniques by Hopper and Bloom [1,2]. Our approach here differs in that it considers not the exact user-login protocol used (in particular, Hopper-Bloom protocols could be employed for that end) but an architecture to provide for alternative means to faithfully authenticate users when they have forgotten their authenticating secrets.

Our mechanism is conceptually a human-centric escrow key recovery mechanism [3,4]. Humans who forget their password can still get "vanilla" access to network services. By interacting with other users, vanilla users can leverage the peer community trust infrastructure to achieve full access to services —provided they can convince others of their true identity. Otherwise, any transactions accomplished with vanilla-access can be rolled back.

2   A Toy Example

Consider the following use-case scenario: Alice moved to a new department in her company, one that adopts a community-centric access control system. As she starts to work using her new account, she notices few differences from her previous experience, so she does not endeavor to read the tutorial recommended by her system administrator. She next proceeds to import her "address book," and she finds that the address cards display differently in the new system. Indeed, each address card has options related to being added to a *trusted peer community*. She decides to add her office-mate Marla to such peer community, which she fairly unimaginatively names "office-mate community."

The following day the most disruptive event happens. Alice forgets her new password, what with the stress of the new position. Now Alice must contact the system administrator, get him to reset her password, and then remember a new password. In a last desperate attempt to save her pride, Alice tries to login a third time. Voilà, success, or maybe not? (This is vanilla access.)

All her files and folders seem to be nowhere in sight. Her mailbox (with her name on it, for sure) seems to be empty of e-mail; quite tragic considering all the requests her new boss had sent her yesterday. On the verge of tears, Alice sends a quick e-mail to her friend Marla, asking what should she do now? A minute later, Marla sends her a reply. As Alice opens the e-mail, the most amazing thing happens –suddenly all her files are back, her e-mail, everything. Did Marla set her up on some practical joke, she wonders, but really Marla is not the type for that. As she ponders the mystery of it all, Marla steps in and says, "I am glad you trusted me in a peer community. That's how I was able to authenticate you by e-mail today." "You authenticated me by e-mail?" Alice asks. Marla responds, "That's just it. Our e-mail system uses some secret sharing technique —or maybe threshold trust, one of these buzzwords of techno-geek. What that means is that you made me a fully trusted reference by creating a peer community with only myself in it. By the way, I suggest that you add another person to the same community you added me. I don't want to be solely responsible for authenticating you, as that also means I am solely to blame if someone manages to fool me into authenticating herself as you —not very likely, but you never know. You can add our boss, he is a stickler for procedure and would never reply to an authentication request without triple checking it was indeed you beforehand." After Alice plays the tutorial, she understands the notion of a trusted peer community. Essentially all her files are encrypted under her password-derived master key. Nonetheless, when she adds persons to a trusted peer community, they automatically receive "shares" of her password-derived key by secure e-mail. If she forgets her password, she may send e-mails to all the members of one of the trusted communities and she may log in! Of course, they will have to reply and they are supposed to check to ensure that she is indeed Alice. Today this saved her from looking like a fool to the systems administrator. She was rescued by her company's community-centric vanilla-rollback access system.

3   Analyzing Community-Centric Vanilla-Rollback

A community-centric access control system recognizes that authentication is scalar rather than Boolean. For example, it assumes that when Alice cannot remember her password, she may not be Mallory, and as likely as not, just Alice on a bad day (Murphy-Alice), so it allows a limited login to occur anyway. In fact, it even allows Alice write[1] access to her file system and e-mail accounts. We call this *vanilla* access, because it provides a modest level of access. For instance, it allows vanilla-Alice to accomplish low-risk tasks, e.g. to send e-mails. [2] (The sending mail server modifies sender information to indicate that it may come from someone impersonating Alice.) In addition, if vanilla-Alice sends e-mail to Marla, a member of one of Alice's trusted-peer communities, Marla is notified that she may provide Alice with authentication credentials if she believes

---

[1] Write-only access can be quite dangerous. For instance, vanilla-Mallory might add invisible executable files to Alice's account and cause mayhem when the real Alice comes in. That's where the rollback feature plays an important part. The write access only creates "evidentiary" files that are not committed to the Alice's file system if the vanilla-logged user leaves the system without being promoted to full access status. For details, see section §5.

[2] Simple precautions would prevent spammers from using vanilla access to relay e-mail. One possible measure is to prevent sending of e-mail to a recipient outside the peer community.

vanilla-Alice is indeed the real Alice. If Marla decides to do so, a share of Alice's key is securely transmitted in the response, and in combination with other shares, it is sufficient to reconstruct Alice's key (which protects her file-encrypting key). Alice can then recover her files and other access privileges, and change her password. Conversely, if an intruder is impersonating Alice and she fails to complete the authentication, the system will roll back to its previous safe state. We call this process *Vanilla-Rollback-Access* (VRA).

The vignette in the previous section illustrates how VRA leverages the scalar properties of community-centric authentication for rollback access control. An essential notion that is a feature of human identity but that Boolean authentication overlooks, is that identity is naturally difficult or impossible to verify (or deny) conclusively. Rather, we gain confidence in someone's identity through evidence that may take many forms with widely variable strength. VRA recognizes this inconclusiveness and balances the potential damage against the level of identity confidence that the system has acquired. For example, while the password may be incorrect, the person at the keyboard at least knew their user name. Not a great source of identity confidence, but slightly greater than zero. Additional confidence may be gained if VRA can determine behavioral aspects of users, such as typing speed or other keyboarding characteristics. These offer additional confidence in the identity (or identity denial) of the user under evaluation. Beyond intrinsic identity characteristics, external socio-contextual trust evidence may also be gathered, as in the example given in Section 2.

4   Community-Centric Authentication Sequence

In order to enable sharing of user authentication tokens, it is convenient to model the authentication mechanism as a *key re-construction* step. In systems that support encrypted file systems, this key may indeed be used as a cryptographic encrypting key to protect the user's data. In regular systems, the key may be used to simply encrypt (or key-hash) a particular system object. The result is then verified against an authenticator value stored in the user database to verify the user's identity.

In the non-exceptional case – i.e., when the user remembers his password, or is in possession of the authentication tokens – the password and other authentication information is combined with user's information stored in the system database (here abstracted as a *salt*) to derive the authentication key. When the user misses authentication tokens/information, he may instead use vanilla access to the system's communication resources to request that his peers release to the system the key shares that will enable reconstruction of a *pre-key*. This pre-key can then be combined with a second pre-key from the system itself to reconstruct the user authentication key, as shown in Figure 1.

The use of a system pre-key is required to ensure that the set of shares entrusted to the community is semantically independent from any user password-derived value. This eliminates the possibility that the peer community may collude to reconstruct a password-derived value and use that to attack the user password

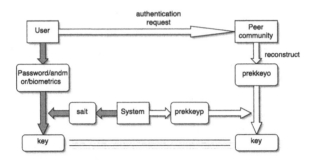

Fig. 1. Login sequence: The shaded arrows refer to the non-exceptional case. The light arrows refer to a request initiated by the user with only vanilla access.

(e.g., via off-line dictionary or brute-force attacks). A separate advantage to the use of pre-keys is that it facilitates peer community update. Whenever an update takes place, the pre-keys are also changed, ensuring that old shares from an earlier community cannot be combined with new shares from a current community to achieve user authentication in violation of the current trust infrastructure. In this fashion it is possible, for instance, to support peer community disenrollment without requiring users to update passwords, by simply distributing new key shares.

A more sophisticated authentication sequence is shown in Figure 2. Here, an additional step is introduced – the system must interact with the user to obtain additional information in order to recover the authentication key. A typical example is to require the user to answer a set of questions and verify the answers against a database. A different approach would be to use the answers directly to obtain key-like information, as in personal entropy systems [5,6].

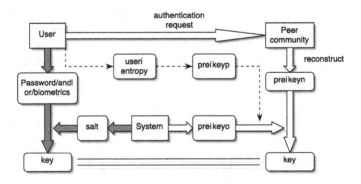

Fig. 2. Another login sequence: The dotted arrows refer to the use of a personal entropy system

The basic tools required to implement the above described authentication sequence are standard off-the-shelf tools. We require secure (private and authenticated) point-to-point channels, so that the shares of authentication keys do not leak, and techniques to derive keys from strings. In case of encrypted file systems, we may require techniques such as password-based encryption. References to all these mechanisms may be found in [9]. As for the sharing the file-encrypting master keys, there are several practical secret sharing mechanisms that can be readily used [7,8]. Finally, the peer community trust infrastructure is essentially the access control structure of a secret sharing scheme; this can be based on an unstructured trust infrastructure, such as PGP [10].

5 Vanilla-Rollback: A State of Suspension

An important enabling feature of vanilla-rollback[3] is that if a session ends before authentication is complete, the session manifestation may be suspended; neither committed nor discarded, neither alive nor dead. If the questionable session is later authenticated, manifestations can be triggered and the system state updated as though the actions were taken at the time they were initiated by vanilla-Alice. Conversely, if an impersonation attempt is recognized, Vanilla-rollback can revert the system to its original state, essentially rolling back changes that vanilla-Alice performed.

Suspended transactions are not uncommon in today's systems. For instance, journaled file systems delay the commitment of file changes for various reasons, such as reducing disk-write latency and guaranteeing atomicity of file system changes [11]. Another prevalent illustration of suspended transactions include credit card accounting. On most online credit card status systems, recent transactions reflect a temporary status. Most of these are quickly confirmed or withdrawn, but occasionally temporary transactions linger, awaiting supplementary action to become final.

5.1 Rollback Technology

The most important element of an effective rollback mechanism is partitioning. Many actions cannot be rolled back; for example, once someone has viewed a data item, we cannot make them forget it. Consequently, vanilla-access cannot grant read access, except to already world-readable data. However, there are *many* actions that every user takes that can be safely, universally allowed: Document creation and accessing some web sites are two examples of commonly allowed actions.

To protect against inappropriate access, each action taken must be identified as either: (1) Fully vanilla; (2) Vanilla-Rollback; (3) Neither. Actions in the first class need not be monitored beyond their original recognition. They pose no threat,[4] divulge no sensitive information, nor change managed state as defined by

---

[3] Rollback in SQL cancels proposed changes in a pending database transaction. In this paper we use *rollback* as both an enabling and disabling procedure.

[4] These actions potentially facilitate a denial-of-service attack by exhaustion of available resources by vanilla-users. This threat can be mitigated by restricting the number of vanilla instances of the same user within the system, and by imposing more restrictive quotas on such users.

the prevailing security policy. Opening a browser, reading a public newsgroup, or starting an SSH session are actions that fall into this class in many organizations.

Items in the second class pose no immediate threat and accomplish only actions that can be reversed. Creating a document and adding a record to a database are potential examples of vanilla-reversible actions.

The third class encompasses all actions that are not in the first two classes. At a minimum these include any action that (a) necessarily requires authenticated access (is not fully vanilla) and (b) is not reversible. These are sensitive actions that cannot be rolled back and are always prohibited to vanilla users.

5.2 Rollback Application

The reference monitor (RM) [12] is the foundation of many access control systems and can implement VRA. Action partitions must be complete and applications must be engineered to provide VRA, essentially requiring them to incorporate temporary (commit-confirm) transaction processing. Applications without such capabilities may utilize VRA, but only if they are fully vanilla. As we mentioned earlier, many computing actions are universally safe, others are somewhat dangerous, and still others are always risky. Write-only access can be quite dangerous. For instance, vanilla-Mallory might add invisible executable files to Alice's

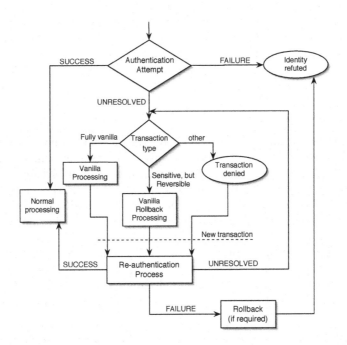

Fig. 3. Vanilla-Rollback Workflow. If the initial authentication attempt leads to an inconclusive state, transactions are either rejected (if they require authentication in an essential way), fully processed (if its execution does not require an authenticated state) or processed but not committed (to be reversed if final attempt at authentication fails).

account and cause mayhem when the real Alice comes in. Clearly, any executables installed during a vanilla session should be controlled appropriately—for instance, their execution by real users could be denied. Only after the questionable vanilla section is authenticated might such programs be executable at higher levels of privilege.

Transaction commit-confirm processing is one approach to rollback processing. An essential element for any rollback mechanism in VRA is containment. Temporary transactions must be separate from permanent state. This is essential to ensure that a vanilla process does not accomplish non-vanilla actions. For example, write access to vanilla users should create temporary files that are not committed to the user's file system if the vanilla logged user leaves the system without being promoted to full access status. This temporary file may provide forensic evidence if authentication is not completed. Whether a vanilla session was authenticated or not, the authenticated user could receive notification of the vanilla session, and could be given a choice of options -authenticate, force logout, or track the impostor, flagging her to the system administrator. Finally, once a session is purged as illegitimate, its contents are not discarded, but logged and used as evidentiary information for forensic analysis of intrusion attempts –perhaps even leading to the intruder's capture. We illustrate VRA in Figure 3.

6   Extensions

There are several ways in which our model for community-centric rollback can be extended. In this section we discuss some of them.

In our basic model, rollback is managed by the trust infrastructure of peer communities. Alice's trusted friends (e.g. Marla) have shares of her secret key, and use these to authenticate Alice, if they are convinced that she is the real Alice. Their decisions will be based on several events that partially identify Alice. For instance, Marla may remember that Alice was late and was wearing a blue sweater, and that she told her that she also loved cats. Our trust model is dynamic and context-driven: it is based on the augmentation of the (essentially static) infrastructure of the peer communities by incorporation of socio-contextual information to support trust dynamically. This information is out-of-band information and volatile. It is the kind of information that humans are ideally suited to manage and machines cannot, at least in any effective way.

A first and natural extension (from a deployment perspective) would be to use other communication media that are potentially more effective at quickly capturing socio-contextual trust data. Example of such mechanisms are video or audio chat tools. These are, in many respects, ideally suited to capture trust data which machines cannot recognize.

Another extension would be to involve enlarging the peer community, to include the system itself, with regards to the management of rollback. The system may be enabled with capabilities to monitor (human) user behavior and to develop biometric profiles of users. Profiling is a popular mechanism for supporting authentication, and has been proven to be a very effective tool. User profiling may be based on: face or voice recognition, or the recognition of keyboard stroke and other biometric patterns.

Recognition can be done by the system locally (at the host) or remotely. Both in the cases of local and remote authentication loco-temporal information can enhance the reliability of biometric profiling. For instance, vanilla-Alice is unlikely to be Mallory sitting at Alice's workstation in the mid-morning of a business day. Similarly, if the system dials Alice's home/cell phone and recognizes her voice requesting a login from home/airport —that is contextual evidence of such a nature as to be nearly impossible to forge.

7   Towards a Threat Model for Community-Centric Vanilla-Rollback Access

There is an inherent conflict between facilitating access to, and providing security for, protected computing resources. Thus, it is not surprising that an access control system with vanilla-rollback may offer intruders a fertile target for identity theft and system intrusion.

We distinguish between two types of intruders: authorized users, called *insiders*, and unauthorized users. Insiders (Mallory-Marlas) are the worst kind of intruders. In community-centric rollback systems they possess some share of the password-derived key of another user, say Alice, and will try to fool her community peers to get other shares so that they can impersonate Alice. Here we focus on such threats, since protection from these will also protect from the other threats.

Protection of a community-centric vanilla-rollback access system is achieved by: (1) Requiring that entities distribute shares of their password-derived key to community peers; (2) Allowing entities to choose their own secret sharing access infrastructure, and; (3) Supporting the access infrastructure with out-of-band socio-contextual trust information, optionally augmented by biometric-profiling information available to the system.

The first two protection items deal with secure key recovery in the traditional model [4]. The third deals with insiders, who may try to trick Alice's trusted community peers into revealing their shares, so as to impersonate Alice. In traditional authentication systems widely prevalent today, insiders can use their knowledge of facts about Alice to social-engineer their way through, or otherwise circumvent access controls. (In other words, they may know Alice's mother's maiden name.) However, that is a less significant advantage if the intruder's task is to fool Alice's trusted circle of humans. The third item in this access-control paradigm is an essential component of a hardened (and yet more human-friendly) security environment. In conjunction with the other features it shows that the access control approach based on rollback and community-centric trust infrastructures is robust against both insider and outsider attacks.

References

1. Hopper, N., Bloom, M.: A secure human-computer authentication scheme. Technical Report CMU-CS-00-139, Carnegie Mellon University (2000)
2. Hopper, N., Bloom, M.: Secure human identification protocols. In: Boyd, C. (ed.) ASIACRYPT 2001. LNCS, vol. 2248, pp. 52–66. Springer, Heidelberg (2001)
3. Denning, D., Branstad, D.: A taxonomy of key escrow encryption. Comm. of the ACM 39, 34–40 (1996)
4. Fouquè, P., Poupard, G., Stern, J.: Recovering keys in open networks. In: ITW 1999. Proc. IEEE Information Theory and Communications Workshop, IEEE Computer Society Press, Los Alamitos (1999)
5. Ellison, C., Hall, C., Milbert, R., Schneier, B.: Protecting secret keys with personal entropy. J. of Future Generation Computer Systems 16, 311–318 (2000)
6. Frykholm, N., Juels, A.: Error-tolerant password recovery. In: Proc. of the 8th ACM Conference on Computer and Communications Security, pp. 1–9. ACM Press, New York (2001)
7. Blakley, G.R.: Safeguarding cryptographic keys. In: Proc. of the National Computer Conference, vol. 48, pp. 242–268 (1979)
8. Shamir, A.: How to share a secret. Comm. of the ACM 22, 612–613 (1979)
9. Menezes, A., van Oorschot, P., Vanstone, S.: Handbook of Applied Cryptography. CRC Press, Boca Raton, USA (1997)
10. Zimmermann, P.: The Official PGP Guide. MIT Press, Cambridge, MA, USA (1995)
11. Seltzer, M.I., Granger, G.R., McKusick, M.K., Smith, K.A., Soules, C.A.N., Stein, C.A.: Journaling versus soft updates: Asynchronous meta-data protection in file systems. In: Proc. of the 2000 USENIX Annual Conference, General Session, USENIX, the Advanced Computer Systems Association (2000)
12. Anderson, J.P.: Computer security technology planning study. Technical Report ESD-TR-73-51, Air Force Electronic Systems Division, Hanscom AFB, Bedford, MA (1972)

Community-Centric Vanilla-Rollback Access, or: How I Stopped Worrying and Learned to Love My Computer

(Transcript of Discussion)

Breno de Medeiros

Department of Computer Science, Florida State University

This is a story of Alice, and she just got transferred to a new department. She was warned not to use a computer system but since it looked familiar enough, I mean, a computer system is just another computer system, she of course didn't read the manual, she probably wouldn't be holding the job if every time she needed to learn something else she had to look at the manual. So the address book has a very different feature, it has something called a trusted circle, and because it was the first time that Alice was learning the software, she was prompted to add persons to her circle of trust, so she decided to add her friend Marla, but she didn't try to find out what that meant very carefully. She got an interesting message like this, this is the only member of your trusted circle, to have access to your computer files, OK. She didn't know what to do so she just continued, she was very busy on her first day of work, the following day she realises that with all the changes she doesn't remember her password anymore, and it is now time to contact the sys admin, and she hates to do that, because the sys admin is not very user-friendly. So she tries to guess the password, I guess all of us have one time forgot the password and tried to guess it. She logs in, but nothing is in her file system, she has no email inbox, her files have vanished, OK, so she is in a limbo. She logged in apparently, she didn't get any error messages, but nothing that she expected to see actually took place.

So what did Alice do? Her best friend was Marla, before she goes to her boss and says that she's deleted all her files, she sends an email to Marla so she knows what's happening. So while she is waiting she is looking, monitoring her screen, monitoring her phone, and hoping that Marla will have an answer to her question, OK. Well she gets a call from Marla and while they talk something magic happens and her screen refreshes, and her files are restored. Alright, so of course it wasn't magic that happened, what happened is that, she basically had shared a copy of an authentication key using cryptography, and this has all happened by email, so when she sends an email to Marla, Marla had a way to reply to her email and provide the key that she needed to login properly. So the idea here is to use humans essentially to authenticate other humans in a computer system, which is maybe the way that would happen if you arrive at your workplace and you don't have your ID, you'd probably ask some other trusted person in the system to vouch that you are authorised to come in into your cubicle.

B. Christianson et al. (Eds.): Security Protocols 2005, LNCS 4631, pp. 238–244, 2007.
© Springer-Verlag Berlin Heidelberg 2007

To make this work there are many questions, but it is basically putting together things that have done before, it might become a complicated system, but there is nothing groundbreaking here in terms of the technology. There are maybe some design choices, you might not want to have an address book being in some sense a trusted type of application in the system, or you could say that this is a bad design, but in principle there is nothing to stop anybody from constructing a system like this. And it provides an alternative type of authentication so if you think of the typical textbook definition of how a user gets authenticated, is based on something you know, or something you are, for instance, biometrics, or something you have like a token; here it's based on you being attested to by somebody else, by another authenticated entity in the system. So this, in some sense, may be another bullet in the types of the strategies that you could use to authenticate users.

Frank Stajano. Well you can still classify it under something you are.

Reply. That's right, but this something you are is coming from another user. And there is an independent channel in some sense here. The channel here is the trust that somebody else has that you are who you say you are.

Frank Stajano. This is more in the verifier than what you supply as the authenticating peer.

Richard Clayton. Simpson Garfinkel has a great description of failures of authentication which is that it's something you've forgotten, something you've lost, or something which you used to be and you're not now, but here, basically, the authentication is coming from a completely different set of people, so it's nothing to do with your failures, it's to do with their ability to still see some continuity.

Reply. The denial of this would be someone you irritated.

So this was the problem of someone forgetting the password, but what if we tried to push this further, what would we need to have a human-centric approach not only to authentication, but to security. Maybe the reason why so many protocols fail is because we don't think about how they actually work, how the user is actually going to use it everyday. Is there a simple way to patch the most common cases where it doesn't work very well.

In this case we saw that the human behaviour can be a friend, not an enemy, of effective security. Of course you might need to specify policies of how users can share keys so that you don't have a more insecure system than you start with, but it could be very effective and the reason is that we are very good at recognising other people. Once we have interacted with people in an environment, we are not easily going to be convinced of someone else claiming to be someone we know reasonably well, so this is bringing human monitoring into the system, and this is a very powerful tool. Of course, you can extend this to use video chats, or phone communication. In the phone communication you could add an element of locational element, so for instance, a computer could call Alice on her desk at work, if she's signed to login at her workstation, and she's physically present there, she could get a phone call, then in that case even if the voice biometrics is not terribly accurate, the fact that you have an extra element of locality would give you more confidence that you were really authenticating the correct person.

So I don't think here only of pure biometrics, but biometrics in this extended setting in which you take advantage of context, for instance, where you have in the database the information about the user, you have her cell phone, you can call her, and then try to match her voice patterns against the biometric readings that you have for the user.

The idea of this human-centric approach that we are looking at is to concentrate on the aspects that really involve the nature of a human being being in the loop. I mean, if you have a remote login, is this a user, or is this some process that is being run on behalf of a user, maybe it's a full automated attack. So when you are looking at security and you think about users, really we are not thinking about users, we are thinking about processes, and sometimes that might not be the right model. In some context maybe the users are just that, they are human beings, and you can take advantage of that knowledge. So the human-centric approach would try to capture the aspects of the human behaviour, or interaction with other humans. And of course you have to concentrate on the interface that you're going to provide to the users, so that it makes sense in the natural activities that humans perform. Then the correct security related behaviour would be intuitive.

So we started looking at ideas that could take advantage of this human channel. Essentially as this human behaviour is an independent channel, and it's always good to rely on independent channels for security; we have a whole line of research on this, for instance, the work of Stajano and Wong, which was presented here yesterday[1], used an independent channel, a visual channel, to provide stronger security guarantees. Physical properties of the user are very much in vogue right now, using biometrics.

One thing that was characteristic of that application, that made the whole thing work, was that Alice could still do something with her computer even when she was not really authenticated there; she could send, for instance, an email to a member of her trusted circle. So you don't have an ebullient type of authentication, you have a graded privilege style approach to authentication, and in some sense you have multiple views of the system as the user can progress through these ladders of privileges, they're going to see the system in different ways.

We use the access structures and secret sharing in the description of this protocol, and there is a twist here because the access structure is actually an access structure, in some sense, of human organisation: you're mapping the group of friends, or co-workers, or the community to which Alice belongs, to her access structure here, so it's not just an abstract access structure. And you could think about how to extend this approach, for instance, suppose Marla's not there, and Alice is logged in, she knows that if she could get hold of Marla she would be able to authenticate herself by sending her an email, but Marla is travelling, how do we go from there. You could think about monitoring the behaviour of Alice

---

[1] These proceedings.

as a user of the system, this works well perhaps with using decoy tactics; so for instance, what if instead of the system presenting an empty template for Alice, what if it presents a collection of files that really were not Alice's files. The real user would immediately know that that was not her collection of files, but an attacker is trying to guess the password, it would always login, and it would always see a collection of files, how does he know he has not guessed the right password?

So by monitoring the behaviour of the user at various levels of privilege you could maybe be able to make inferences about whether you were seeing the correct user or not. How can this be more secure than the password authentication that we have today? Well password is not secure, it has an entropy, even if you know the password and you enter it in, the system can only be so sure that you are who you say you are. Even if you've successfully completed a password authentication, which is the most common type of authentication today, it's not a hundred percent sure you are the correct user.

Ben Laurie. It sounds like your trusted circle can also impersonate you.

Reply. Yes, in this application, your trusted circle could impersonate you[2], and you could think of that as a key escrow application, and you could have to be careful about how you put in your circle of users, if it was too small you probably might feel uncomfortable with it.

Michael Burmester. You may also allow for your circle to only be part component of it so you may also have to provide something very little you never forget, you have three words one of which is relevant, or something like that.

Reply. I'm reviewing the types of work which I could say directly relates to this general framework. I've discussed already some of this, the work on independent channels, we are basically thinking of the communication between humans as an independent channel, but I also discussed other possible scenarios, for instance the computer dials the user and recognises the voice speaking on that telephone, as an independent channel. We saw the work with key exchange and the visual channel. I think the use of independent channels and security is a well established idea, and again it's just the exploitation of physical properties in a bit little bit more detail. There is a fundamental difference between trying to authenticate a user who is locally sitting at a workstation, and a remote process. The reason is that the remote process could be even some type of automated tool, there could be really no user whether legitimate or illegitimate doing this, it's a process; but if someone is typing on the keyboard, that is slightly different, you have a physical location for this entity, which can be determined by, for instance, user monitoring, or a phone call, or a similar process. We can combine different tools, again, the idea is passwords do not provide a hundred percent certainty of authentication so we can think of authentication as a process of building confidence, that you indeed are dealing with the entities that you think you are, and in that sense, since you have a level of confidence that you are dealing with

---

[2] Although not untrackably. See below.

the correct entities, you could also have a gradation of privileges that these users enjoy other different levels of confidence.

So all types of interesting questions can be asked, for instance, what happens if you are dealing with an emergency case, what happens if a user changes roles, or changes tasks, and requires a new set of privileges, so when you make this transformation, if you were secure before are you still secure. Ideally one could think about having file systems based on, transaction oriented, and non-monotonic, so you could recover the privileged state, so if you were monitoring the behaviour of the user and you were convinced now that the user should not be enjoying the privileges that it has been afforded, maybe you actually want to go back in time and revoke it somewhat before, maybe there were some actions that happened just before you decided that the user is not trustworthy that you want to cancel.

Bruce Christianson. On a statistical basis you would just roll back.

Reply. I'm sorry? Oh, I would be right unless, OK. And you could think of this not only in the context of authentication, one interesting idea would be you extend this to group controlled objects, so here you are not trying to authenticate users *per se*, but try to control ways in which certain objects can be manipulated, maybe only certain combination of privileges are present, then that the objects can be operated on. So there's a lot of work to be done of course, this is essentially just a framework of how to look at things. I cannot say anything meaningful in terms of theoretical models, or even simulation models, about what the security means in this setting, and what is the scope of human-centric security or authentication.

Initial directions that we have in terms of modelling this confidence infrastructure would be, for instance, thinking in terms of traditional confidence reasoning that you see in relation with traditional authentication infrastructures such as PKIs.

Michael Burmester. But the idea is to somehow go back and formalise, a model similar to the PGP model, a trust, or in this case, a confidence model. The difference is usually each subject is defined by the trust the others in the system have for it, and here it is dynamic, the trust changes all the time. So you have a certain threshold of confidence, and you're allowed to do certain things, then something happens in the system, and your trust level drops down, and then you're blocked out. The system may have to go back to the state it was in much earlier on. And it uses behavioural temporaral location, or perhaps history.

Frank Stajano. The trust that Alice is putting in Marla is about two things, she trusts her first for delivering Alice's key when she requires it, and not denying it and saying, well I really don't know you.

Michael Burmester. Ideally you go for a group, and only three or four of them would be needed.

Frank Stajano. The second thing is trusting her not to abuse the rights she has to access all these files. These two things are separate, but how do you deal with them?

Reply. A system like that would require some form of accountability, so it is a different event that Alice authenticated herself without the contribution of anybody else, from Alice got authenticated because Marla helped her.

Frank Stajano. If Alice has forgotten her password, what makes her different from Marla impersonating her.

Reply. That doesn't make any difference for Marla, but it makes Marla accountable for that, so the fact that Marla impersonated Alice can actually be tracked.

It's a kind of proxy, but it's human-centric. The human-centric aspect is where one human gives to another human certain privileges.

In a very simple scenario, you have a computer system, every security related operation gets logged somewhere, so when I log in with my password it gets logged somewhere, if I logged in because Marla helped me to login, that should be logged somewhere, OK, that is a universal task.

Frank Stajano. You can detect it after the fact, but it won't stop Marla doing whatever evil thing she might do.

Ben Laurie. It's too late, because Marla could actually still blame Alice. What Marla does is go to Alice and confuse her system personally, and sends herself an email saying, help, I've lost my password, and goes back to her own system, re-enables Alice's system, then goes back to it, screws around with it, and then blames Alice.

Frank Stajano. That's exactly what I said, to impersonate Alice.

Ben Laurie. The point is that she is pretending to be Alice.

Richard Clayton. No, I think you've got it entirely wrong. This is a human system, you don't need all of these things because Marla is a group person, there are keys to my house, right, my neighbour has a key to my house, he can be right in there even as we speak. My next-door neighbour has a key to my house so that when I lock myself out I can go and knock on her door and let myself in. If you want a key to my house so you don't have to come back from dinner this evening, you can have a key to my house this evening, because I trust you with it.

Audience. That's human-centric, you've captured the human-centric.

Yvo Desmedt. If you look at what happens today, if you forget your password you go to the system manager, and the system manager changes it. The system manager does not know your password, so the only thing you need to do is to share that capability. It means that now the system manager cannot change your password, and everyone in the whole neighbourhood does not know your password, but what they can do, your friends can change your password, that means that if you not request that, you will detect it. This is very different from what you're proposing.

Reply. I didn't say that Marla knew Alice's password. Not even the whole group will know her password. It's a different key based authentication.

Mike Roe. The point being made is that you don't want to put the system back to the way Alice had it before, because if the password is changed Alice would notice.

Jun Li. There's a thing you can do. I only give my key to my neighbour if he gives his key to me, it's like two ways: I can get your password but you can get my password as well.

Michael Burmester. So yes, in the trust you balance out, in other words, if I do you harm, you do me harm. That would have a kind of reflection in the trust infrastructure. But that I think is outside the scope of it, I mean, if I trust you, you're my friend, I give you certain privileges.

I think if you look at the users, in the human-centric environment we do business all the time with some person, and if they want to abuse that then of course they can. Whenever you give some proxy power, to some other person to do things for you, that other person can abuse your proxy power.

Listen Too Closely and You May Be Confused

Eric Cronin, Micah Sherr, and Matt Blaze

Department of Computer and Information Science
University of Pennsylvania
{ecronin,msherr,blaze}@cis.upenn.edu

1 Introduction

Among the most basic simplifying assumptions of modern communications security is the notion that most communication channels should, by their very nature, be considered vulnerable to interception. It has long been considered almost reckless to suggest depending on any supposed intrinsic security properties of the network itself[1], and especially foolish in complex, decentralized, heterogeneously-controlled networks such as the modern Internet. Orthodox doctrine is that any security must be either end-to-end (as with cryptography), or not considered to exist at all.

While this heuristic well serves cautious confidential communicators, it is unsatisfying from the point of view of the *eavesdropper*. Paradoxically, while end-to-end security may be a prerequisite to robust confidentiality in most networks, it does not follow that a *lack* of end-to-end security always makes it possible to eavesdrop.

In this position paper, we investigate whether the very properties that make it unwise to depend on the network for security can be turned on their head to effectively frustrate eavesdropping. We observe that while the Internet protocol stack and architecture make no confidentiality or authenticity guarantees regarding the traffic that passes across it, neither do they make any guarantees to those who wish to intercept this traffic (whether authorized to do so or not). While interception is often feasible on a benign network if performed with some care, we propose that it may be possible to artificially exacerbate the eavesdropper's problem, to the point of introducing ambiguities that make it unclear how to reconstruct the actual messages passed between targeted parties even when the cleartext is accurately captured.

In particular, at least six properties of the Internet protocol stack and architecture might make it difficult for an eavesdropper to reconstruct a data stream: decentralized control and heterogeneous implementations; "best effort," as opposed to reliable, message delivery that allows data to be re-ordered, duplicated or dropped in transit; shared state and context between communicating parties (e.g., in TCP, and particularly end-to-end error correction); dynamic (and often asymmetric) routing that can change during a flow's lifetime; lack of sender and receiver authentication; and ambiguities in protocols, implementations, and configurations.

---

[1] Quantum cryptography represents a respectable counterexample, of course.

B. Christianson et al. (Eds.): Security Protocols 2005, LNCS 4631, pp. 245–249, 2007.

These properties mean that a great deal of state information is involved in the correct interpretation of any given packet, and this state is spread across many places, including each of the communicating parties and the network itself. Without complete knowledge of this state, the mere presence of a packet somewhere on the network does not automatically imply that it will be accepted by the recipient given in its header, that it came from the supposed sender, or that it has not been (or will not be) altered, duplicated, or deleted somewhere along its path.

Any intercept system must take into account these properties (and all the corresponding state) in order to ensure not only that it is sufficiently *sensitive* (that it receives all data exchanged between the targets), but also that it is sufficiently *selective* (that it rejects spurious data that is not actually part of the targets' exchange). There are quite a few degrees of freedom that affect how intercepts must be performed. The figure of merit most often considered in judging intercept systems is sensitivity; adequate selectivity, on the other hand, is generally thought to be easily achieved by cursory examination of, e.g., packet headers. In fact, selectivity may be a far more difficult problem than most intercept systems recognize, especially in the presence of deliberate countermeasures.

Depending on the network configuration, many ambiguities can be easily induced, either by one of the communicating parties or by a third party altogether. In fact, as we look at in detail in a forthcoming companion work [8], across much of the protocol stack, from the physical layer to the applications, it is surprisingly simple to introduce data that appears entirely valid but that might not be received and processed by the purported recipient. The Internet appears almost to have been designed to maximize uncertainty from the point of view of those eavesdropping on it.

We believe these properties can be formalized, and, furthermore, that they can often be exploited quite effectively to render it difficult for many interception configurations to obtain reliable transcripts of networked sessions, even when no end-to-end security is employed. Surprisingly, this does not appear to require any bilateral countermeasures to be employed by the communicants, and in some cases, can be performed entirely by a third party.

In particular, we observe that a single party, which we call a *confuser*, can introduce traffic directed at an eavesdropper but that is never actually received (or if received, is rejected) by the ostensible recipient. Depending on the eavesdropper's configuration, and, especially, its position on the network, this traffic can be made indistinguishable from legitimate traffic. In the presence of sufficient confusion, an eavesdropper may be able to be made arbitrarily uncertain as to whether a given intercepted message was real or spurious. We call this indistinguishable-but-spurious traffic *confusion*.

1.1   Related Literature

Investigating the problems associated with electronic eavesdropping is not a new area of research. However, most work in this area has focused on narrow subdomains of the problem space, especially Network Intrusion Detection Systems

(NIDS) [13,14,10,18]. Other related work is found in the field of privacy enhancing technologies, which obscure endpoint identity and evade traffic analysis (but where the content is generally encrypted end-to-end) [15,9]. Both commercial and open source developers have produced a number of tools for eavesdropping, and we look to these as example practical adversaries for evaluation [1,2,11,19,12]. Finally, it is instructive to examine how some of the most important users of eavesdropping, law enforcement and the courts, view the potential for problems with intercepted communications [3,6]. But again, there has been surprisingly little investigation of the relationship between eavesdropping and active third parties, and little work on the "fidelity" of intercepted traffic.

Finally, Rivest's work on Winnowing and Chaffing [16], which uses chaff "noise" to create privacy without encryption is fundamentally related to confusion, albeit in a different context. There, a cooperating sender and receiver achieve end-to-end confidentiality without the use of encryption by sending noise data that is rejected by the receiver by failing a cryptographic checksum that cannot be computed by an eavesdropper. In this proposal, on the other hand, the sender and receiver need not themselves participate in the scheme, and the network topology and protocols themselves frustrate the eavesdropper's ability to distinguish real data from noise.

2   Confusion and Interception Fidelity

Any communications interception system must deliver a sufficiently accurate reproduction of the communications between the targeted parties to satisfy its requirements. That is, the quality of an interception must be of sufficient "fidelity" to be useful, much as the quality of an audio recording must be of high enough fidelity to satisfy its listener. How high the fidelity must be depends on the application; in a non-targeted diagnostic system, such as might be used in a network operations center, low fidelity may be acceptable, while in a law enforcement intercept conducted under a court order intended for producing legal evidence, higher fidelity (and with known properties) may be required.

In a digital network, several factors affect interception fidelity, including whether the relevant data are captured ("sensitivity") and whether irrelevant noise is correctly discarded ("selectivity").

The fidelity of eavesdropping systems, especially those operating in the presence of active attacks, has not been extensively investigated[2]. Instead, much of the prior work relating to electronic eavesdropping has focused on the problem of sensitivity; that is, how to adequately capture the data that is transported across the communication medium. In particular, much attention has been made to preventing *evasion* attacks [14,17] in which an attacker attempts to bypass an electronic wiretap by crafting abnormal traffic that escapes interception.

Our focus is on analyzing and developing attacks (and countermeasures to attacks) against selectivity, rather than simply evasion. An interception system

---

[2] We are not, however, the first to question the reliability of eavesdropping systems. See [4,5].

is susceptible to *confusion* if it is possible to direct apparently valid traffic to the eavesdropper that is not detected (or, if detected, is rejected) by the targeted receiver. In fact, across much of the protocol stack, from the physical layer to the applications, it is surprisingly simple to introduce data that appears entirely valid but that might, or might not, be received and processed by the intended recipient.

3 Preliminary Steps

Our exploration into confusion to date has just scratched the surface, but already we have seen interesting and confirming results [8]. We have developed a basic model of confusion, and used this to analyze how "confusable" different protocols are. To explore the more practical side of confusion, we have also constructed several confusion generators for Internet communications. Surprisingly, even the least confusable of protocols contains enough ambiguity to thwart current eavesdropping tools.

4 Conclusion

As we have seen, accurate capture of all cleartext is not by itself sufficient to ensure accurate message reconstruction by an eavesdropper, and rejection of spurious traffic is not a trivial problem. To build an accurate and reliable message stream, an eavesdropper must simulate correctly the entire delivery process, about which there can be significant uncertainty in real networks.

Our analysis and preliminary experimental work suggest that unilateral and third party countermeasures can greatly increase this uncertainty, and relatively simple confusion injection techniques can effectively thwart many Internet interception systems.

There has been remarkably little research investigating the fidelity that can be achieved in eavesdropping on digital networks, and existing work does not consider second- and third-party active countermeasures that thwart the eavesdropper without the use of end-to-end techniques.

From a communications security standpoint, confusion is a potentially interesting "third" technique, alongside cryptography and steganography for increasing confidentiality. Current network architectures, exemplified by the Internet and many sensor network systems, appear to have structures that make eavesdropping vulnerable to our approaches.

Confusion may also have legal and public policy implications. Network-based interceptions are said to be increasingly important as evidence in (criminal and civil) legal cases and as an intelligence tool for law enforcement and national security. But how reliable are network wiretaps? Can they be thwarted by active techniques such as confusion? Are there systematic techniques for analyzing an interception system to measure is reliability and fidelity? How should the courts treat interception evidence?

Current US law on the treatment of electronic evidence is remarkably inconsistent; depending on context, computer-based data is either accepted almost uncritically or rejected out-of-hand as unreliable. For example, the Department of Justice prosecutor's manual on computer evidence [7] cites at least four contradictory, yet controlling, cases on this issue. Well-understood answers to the questions above could help inform the increasingly important legal and policy debate on wiretap evidence and how it should be collected and treated.

References

1. NetIntercept. http://www.sandstorm.net/products/netintercept/
2. NetWitness. http://www.forensicsexplorers.com/
3. Electronic Crime Scene Investigation: A Guide for First Responders (July 2002), http://www.ojp.usdoj.gov/nij/pubs-sum/187736.htm
4. Bellovin, S.M.: Wiretapping the net. The Bridge 20(2), 21–26 (2002)
5. Blaze, M., Bellovin, S.M.: Inside RISKS: Tapping, tapping on my network door. Communications of the ACM 43(10) (December 2000)
6. Casey, E.: Digital Evidence and Computer Crime: Forensic Science, Computers and the Internet (2004)
7. Computer Crime and Intellectual Property Section. Criminal Division. United States Department of Justice. Searching and Seizing Computers and Obtaining Electronic Evidence in Criminal Investigations (July 2002), http://www.cybercrime.gov/s&smanual2002.htm
8. Cronin, E., Sherr, M., Blaze, M.: On the reliability of Internet eavesdropping. (submitted for publication, February 2005)
9. Dingledine, R., Mathewson, N., Syverson, P.: Tor: The Second-Generation Onion Router. In: Proc. of the 13th Usenix Security Symposium, pp. 303–320 (August 2004)
10. Handley, M., Kreibich, C., Paxson, V.: Network intrusion detection: Evasion, traffic normalization, and end-to-end protocol semantics. In: Proc. of the 10th Usenix Security Symposium (August 2001)
11. Jacobson, V., Leres, C., McCanne, S.: tcpdump. http://www.tcpdump.org/
12. Lightfoot, C.: Driftnet. http://www.ex-parrot.com/~chris/driftnet/
13. Paxson, V.: Bro: a system for detecting network intruders in real-time. Computer Networks (Amsterdam, Netherlands: 1999) 31(23–24), 2435–2463 (1999)
14. Ptacek, T., Newsham, T.: Insertion, evasion, and denial of service: Eluding network intrusion detection. Technical report, Secure Networks, Inc. (1998)
15. Reiter, M.K., Rubin, A.D.: Crowds: Anonymity for web transactions (1998)
16. Rivest, R.: Chaffing and winnowing: Confidentiality without encryption (March 1998), http://theory.lcs.mit.edu/~rivest/chaffing.txt
17. SANS. Intrusion detection FAQ: How does fragroute evade NIDS detection? (2002), http://www.sans.org/resources/idfaq/fragroute.php
18. Shankar, U., Paxson, V.: Active mapping: Resisting NIDS evasion without altering traffic. In: Proc. of the 2003 IEEE Symposium on Security and Privacy, IEEE Computer Society Press, Los Alamitos (2003)
19. The Ethereal Project. Ethereal: A network protocol analyzer. http://www.ethereal.com/

Listen Too Closely and You May Be Confused

(Transcript of Discussion)

Matt Blaze

Department of Computer and Information Science
University of Pennsylvania

I'd like to shift views a little bit, and think about the problem that we usually focus on, which is building good defences, from the point of view of how to attack effectively. We tend to focus on the defending problem, for example, the confidentiality of my traffic, and in the mainstream and conservative approach to security that we all know and love we make very generous assumptions about the adversary: we are willing to assume that the adversary gets a copy of every packet we send, it can alter some of the bits in real time, and has unlimited computational power, etc. As a result of that conservative assumption, we ask to have solutions that assume that the network is unlimitedly hostile. And, if you want security, we must accept nothing less than end-to-end security, and if we don't have to end-to-end security we simply assume that it is insecure, because it would be very silly to depend on anything less than this very reasonable conservative assumption.

Now if we switch viewpoints and think about this problem from the point of view of the attacker, the law of the excluded middle stops working. When we change the problem from how do I prevent eavesdropping on my traffic into how do I eavesdrop on your traffic. Now obviously the conservative people who employ end-to-end security will thwart us in doing that, but they're not the only obstacles. Someone who wants to eavesdrop on network traffic has to deal with all sorts of potential problems that might come up: they might not be able to capture the signals, there might be noise on the network, the routing system might route the packets away from where their network is, the protocols might have state in them that you can't figure out just by reading what's happening, you might not have the same implementations of the protocol stack as the end users, you have a long checklist of problems. It's not the case that people who fail to install the crypto modules automatically have everything they transmit and receive sent to anybody that wants it, the attacker has many problems to solve beyond discouraging users from deploying end-to-end security. So the failure of Alice and Bob to protect themselves is not sufficient to guarantee the eavesdropper's success.

So let's think about why we, as sensible security practitioners, suggest that people use cryptography. Well we suggest that they use it because we assume that the network is hostile, and the reason we make that assumption is because networks like the Internet are allowed to do things such as route packets via unspecified places, that in fact might change dynamically throughout the lifetime of a stream. In fact we explicitly allow the network, if it feels like it, to duplicate

B. Christianson et al. (Eds.): Security Protocols 2005, LNCS 4631, pp. 250–257, 2007.

a packet, drop a packet, deliver packets out of the order that they're sent in, interleave one screen's packets with another, corrupt data whenever it likes, and it's not required to even apologise to us when it does that. Anybody can forge traffic, there's no inherent restriction on what you put in the source field of something that you send, the network's only guarantee is that it will make some sort of effort to deliver it to the destination, it doesn't really tell us anything about who the source is. End-points are expected to maintain all of the state associated with correcting for these things, not the network. The fundamental rule of modern networking is, make the network really dumb and allow the network to be as cranky as you like, and of course wireless networks, such as the one we have here at our security workshop, exacerbate this, and encourage us to embarrass our colleagues who didn't get the end-to-end security message. So essentially there's this kind of best effort, but no guarantee, model: a really good network will nearly fail to corrupt your data very often, but no network, well, no economical network – and I'm a former telephone company employee – says that it will never corrupt your data.

So, well why might the eavesdropper's problem be hard? You need cryptography because you can't depend on the network, but what about from the eavesdropper's point of view? This is a very different list of problems. The network has to be assumed to be hostile to the eavesdropper, it's allowed to route packets via unspecified places, and it's allowed to change this route dynamically, the network's allowed to duplicate, drop, re-order and corrupt data whenever it feels like it, anyone's allowed to forge data to the eavesdropper and make it look like it's part of a communication stream, the state is maintained in the end points, not the networks, so you have to ask the people that you're eavesdropping on to tell you what their state is, and wireless networks make this all worse and confusing, they have variable signal levels, and power levels, and so on. The network just makes no guarantees whatsoever to the eavesdropper.

So, we can turn things around and make a kind of trivial, but maybe interesting observation, that the very same reasons that we advocate the use of cryptography and end-to-end solutions are the reasons that an eavesdropper might not be successful. And it might be worth asking, just how vulnerable is network traffic in the kinds of networks where we insist on end-to-end security, and maybe cryptography isn't required at all. Now, before you point out what an idiot I am, I agree that depending on the network to protect us is dumb, I agree that at best the title of this workshop, that The Network is Your Friend, is a speculative and ironic one, but in fact sometimes we have no choice at all about depending on the network for security. End-to-end security requires that the two end-points agree on what the security policy should be, and have some capacity to secure each other. So if either party drops the ball with respect to end-to-end security, we're screwed, and not everybody has the capacity to manage things like cryptography and keys. Certainly my laptop has the capability to do encryption, but I, like you, I have no idea how to actually run it most of the time, and, things like sensor networks and very lower power devices may still be computationally constrained.

Another reason to look at this question is, we're relying on intercepts in important contexts, right. Law enforcement and intelligence agencies intercept traffic, and they think they know how to do it, and they may or may not be able to do this as reliably as they think they can, in the context of these networks. Just how much faith should we put in an intercepted and reconstructed stream that was performed by a passive eavesdropper.? I'd like to advocate that we turn the problem on its head and study this from the point of view of the attacker. What does it take to produce an intercept of high fidelity, that is one that faithfully reproduces the stream between Alice and Bob, in a way that we can have real confidence? Then let us ask the question, in an eavesdropping system, what are the equivalent from the attacker's point of view of the conservative assumptions that we make in inventing end-to-end solutions.

There's some other interesting questions that we might think about. How can current interception architectures be attacked? Maybe we can look at the answer to this question, and design networks that have different properties. In particular, if we design a network that's intended to be very, very difficult from the point of view of the eavesdropper, maybe we could relax the requirement for end-to-end security. Similarly, maybe if we wanted to move to some fascist police state we could design networks that were very difficult to prevent eavesdropping on, or we could learn that such networks would be so difficult and expensive to build that they're infeasible, but as it is now we don't have way of answering that question.

So let's identify the properties that a network might have, that could make life difficult for an eavesdropper. One is very familiar to us which is that you might be prevented as the eavesdropper from interpreting what you see, obfuscation of the data in some way. This is part of the standard conservative approach that assumes bi-lateral end-to-end cooperation, and things like encryption and steganography fall into the obfuscation category, you can see the data but you can't make any sense of it for your purposes. That's the property we traditionally focus on, we say, if you don't have obfuscation then you do have eavesdropping. But in fact there are two other possibilities.

One is that the traffic might never make it to Eve's interception system, that is, there might be *evasion* in addition to obfuscation, where essentially Eve's receiver is insufficiently sensitive to pick up the traffic that's been sent from Alice to Bob, it may never actually be demodulated at one layer or another by Eve. Now this has the interesting property that, for evasion to occur, you don't necessarily need bilateral cooperation between Alice and Bob. If Alice, for example, can whisper at a level that she has confidence that only Bob can hear and that Eve cannot hear, it's sufficient for Alice, the sender, to implement everything necessary for evasion. This is an interesting property from our point of view of securing a network, because you no longer need all of the baggage of end-to-end security, you just need one end-point.

Now evasion has been studied fairly effectively, but I'd like to introduce a second possibility, which is that Eve is induced to accept noise as part of the traffic. Eve is insufficiently selective in what she includes in the intercepted stream, and becomes confused by what she sees: she sees all the traffic, but she also sees other stuff that she assumes is part of the communication, and these spurious bits never actually made it from Alice to Bob, but Eve thinks that they did. Now *confusion*, as I'm calling this category, has the property that it might be caused, not by Alice or by Bob, but by a third party. These bits might be generated anywhere, they might be generated by the network itself, they might be generated by Alice, they might be generated by Bob, or they might be generated by Eric, in fact maybe they are being generated by Eric right now, I don't know.

Most research from people like us has been focused on how to achieve better obfuscation, and from the point of view of communication security, this is a very sensible approach, but it doesn't tell us the whole picture. The people interested in interception in the research community have mostly focused on evasion, and how to prevent evasion. Most of that work is done in the context of intrusion protection systems, how do you make sure that the evil bits don't get ignored by your intrusion detection system and passed without setting off an alarm. There's been surprisingly little attention paid to the possibility of confusion, and there doesn't seem to be any formalisation of confusion at nearly the same level of obfuscation, or anywhere close to the level of work on evasion, but in fact it may be a more serious threat to the eavesdropper than evasion, or obfuscation.

Ross Anderson. Matt, in which of these categories would you put the use of temporary addresses, for example, Osama bin Laden may currently be Alice165.

Reply. Well that could actually fall into both categories because that address – let's imagine it's a reused IP address that's going to be reassigned to someone else – is going to generate traffic from some new person who's going to have the police show up at their house. So there's some confusion thrown in there, but it also obviously has the effect of evasion until you learn what the new address is, so that falls into both categories.

Let's look at a simple example where you might have both evasion and confusion. Imagine a really simple local area network, we established at lunch that I'm not an electrical engineer, so a shared network where there's a wire running around that we're all hooked up to, Alice, Bob, the eavesdropper, everyone, and anyone can transmit and receive on this wire. And there's some laughably simple version of Ethernet with collision detection, and some framing, and some media access thrown in there, so that you make sense of packets on this thing. But underlying this the bits are represented in a three state system: there's no bit being transmitted when there's zero volts on the wire, positive five volts represents a 1, and negative five volts represents a zero. And there's some self-synchronisation where you have to have a zero volts after a pulse happens, or something like that, the simplest encoding you can imagine, even a computer scientist can figure out how that works, or at least even I can.

Whether this channel is analogue or digital depends on when you're looking, it's not a clear answer. The senders and receivers are using this as a two-state binary system to send digital data, but underlying that the channel is implemented with analogue components that have infinitely many states associated with them: at any give time there might be three and a half volts on this network, not zero volts, positive five or negative five, you can put any voltage you want on it, you put too much things will start exploding, but there are infinitely many gradations between. Now the standard says positive five volts for a 1, and negative five volts for a zero, but every receiver is going to choose a different threshold. Somebody's going to implement this so anything above 4.7 volts will be a 1, and someone else will say, I'll take anything above 4.8. Everybody's going to be just slightly different because analogue components are never identical.

Now if the eavesdropper wants to faithfully reproduce what somebody is receiving on this network, then they have to guess exactly the threshold of the target that they're trying to reproduce, and this is not quite so easy. So let's look at three packets on this network, and let's imagine a network with Alice, a sender, and Bob, a receiver, and two eavesdroppers, Eve1 and Eve2, and Bob has his threshold set at whatever this is. Eve1 has her threshold set above that, and Eve2 has her threshold set below Bob. Now packet A, this little pulse stream here, comes in and Eve2 receives it but Bob doesn't, so we can say that packet A confuses Eve2 because she regards it as having been received but Bob doesn't. Now packet B, on the other hand, was received by Bob but Eve2's threshold was above Bob's, and so it evaded her. And packet C ends up being received by all, but, Eve2 got more than Bob, and Eve1 got less than Bob, neither produced a faithful reproduction of Bob's traffic. So we can think of the little region below Bob as the confusion zone, and the little region above Bob as the evasion zone, and we can trivially say that in an analogue system an eavesdropper is going to be vulnerable to one or the other because thus you can never get Bob's signal exactly, and they can never know that you've gotten it exactly.

In fact, it's even worse than this, because real eavesdropping systems often have no chance of learning much more about the network than they started out knowing. They're usually completely passive, they can't transmit, they're not allowed to contribute state to the exchanges, they have to make guesses about the state, they generally tap in at a single place in the network and so they can't figure out directionality, they can't correlate events in different parts of the network.

Richard Clayton. That may depend on the technology, because if they tap at a single point in an Ethernet, which is one wire in one direction and one wire in the other direction, that together with timing information will suffice to do correlate events.

Reply. Yes, that's why I said other parts of the network: not the part into which you tapped. I'm now going out of this analogue system and back into the digital domain. In general we depend on an eavesdropping system to be passive, and we generally stick it in one place, where you don't know anything about what's going on elsewhere on the network. And, most importantly, they generally pick a layer of the protocol stack and record at that one, and the consequence of doing this is that you throw out a lot of data that you don't need, but you have no chance of altering your assumptions about what went on at that lower level later. So you can't change your assumptions about what the thresholds were at level 1 if you are recording up at level 3.

Now in fact on the Internet, not on the simple dumb three state Ethernet, it seems that there's a potential for both confusion and evasion at just about any layer you'd like. A very simple example is to consider the TTL field in an IT packet. If Eve is sitting somewhere between Alice and Bob, it's trivial to direct packets to Eve that Bob will never see simply by setting the TTL a little bit too low. Now Eve, if she's using a standard implementation of the protocol stack, is almost certainly going to engage in the behaviour of seeing a packet with a new sequence number, and subsequently rejecting any future packets that have the same sequence number even if they're sent at a higher TTL, because obviously a packet with the same sequence number is a duplicate. You can combine these techniques at different layers of the stack to make it very difficult for many eavesdroppers to really have any confidence at all in what they're doing. And remember, it doesn't have to be Alice and Bob doing this, it can be some completely third party that Alice and Bob don't even know about. So the Internet architecture seems to be somewhat ripe for this. Alice and Bob might cooperate to add to the confusion, but if they can cooperate they might as well use crypto. The interesting case is unilateral confusion by Alice, or Bob, without the other's cooperation, or third party confusion as a service of a third party: if somebody's angry at the authorities, they might send out packets just to make it hard to intercept. So there's this trade-off for the eavesdropper, they've got to choose between vulnerability to evasion, and vulnerability of confusion, and in picking their threshold they pretty much have to pick the lesser of the two evils for their purposes.

We can think of the state that's required in order to to make the correct choice as being like a distributed cryptographic keyspace that's out there in the network, implicit in the design of the protocols and the network architecture, and that's difficult to reconstruct enough information about. It looks like the internet is neither optimal, nor pessimal, from the point of view of eavesdropping, but it almost certainly is the case that the presence of these techniques can really cast doubt about whether or not an intercept really reflects what happened between two parties. I think that's interesting, but I think more interesting is the possibility of designing networks specifically to make confusion and evasion simple to do: the internet has this property accidentally, what if we really set out to make it easy.

So we did some preliminary experiments. I should point out this is joint work with Eric Cronin and Micah Sherr, who are sitting in the back conspiring, and by we I mean they. We have built little tools that appear to be able to confuse every internet moderating tool that we know of, by using very simple unilateral and third party techniques. Their effectiveness, and which effect or technique you want to choose, depends on the network topology that you've got, but under different circumstances, and different topologies, you can pretty much confuse everything that's out there. Some of these are techniques that you could develop countermeasures against by going to a lower level, or by having the ability to alter your assumptions, but others are just properties of the network where if you're in a particular place you cannot distinguish between the confused traffic, and the real traffic.

Frank Stajano. In this situation I can easily imagine cases where if you know where Eve is you can do things that would confuse her. Are you also suggesting that you have developed techniques such that if you have an eavesdropper you don't even know they're there, let alone where they are, they're still going to be confused?

Reply. Under some circumstances, yes. Depending on where the confuser is, and where the eavesdropper is, maybe yes, maybe no. The interesting question is, if you present an interception, you have to know an awful lot about the topology of the network in order to be able to even make statements about how much confidence you should have in that interception: who else was upstream, who else was downstream, what ingress filtering was happening, where, these are things that are outside the scope of the interception system itself. But, I think the question about how vulnerable the current internet is to this is somewhat less interesting than the question of, could you design a network that moves this balance in one direction or the other.

Tuomas Aura. At what level in the protocol stack are you confusing the eavesdropper? If the eavesdropper's goal is just to collect all the packets that were sent on the network, then obviously you can't do anything about that, but if the eavesdropper's goal is to assemble IP packets, or to a data stream. . .

Reply. Right, we're assuming the goal of the eavesdropper is produce a transcript of the data sent between two parties.

Tuomas Aura. But at which protocol level?

Reply. Yes. We've got techniques at a variety of layers of the protocol stack, and we've implemented them at a few of those layers. This seems to be a promising thing to look at, and it's a surprisingly ignored area.

Richard Clayton. Well it's not totally ignored because the intrusion detection people are looking at evasion techniques, the fragmentation and so forth. The claim you're making is that you can evade all these things, in practice if you just collect everything that the Internet gives you then basically you have to say, I have been confused. But if you have a proper model of what Bob looks like then you can make a correct selection from your large number of packets as to which is correct.

Reply. I disagree with your assertion that if you know Bob's state you can necessarily reconstruct this. You might be left with multiple possible interpretations of this stream, and without knowing everything about the state of the network at a given time, be unable to choose which one is actually the true one. Now you might be able to make good guesses, if one of them says, I'd like a pizza, and the other one says, I need you to shoot Vinny, then depending on the symmetric model you have of the two endpoints, you may or may not be able to reach persuasive conclusions about that. But we've definitely got techniques depending on where the eavesdropper's located that leave you unable, regardless of what you've collected, to distinguish between the two streams.

George Danezis. I'm not really sure if this has not already been the subject of quite a lot of research. The whole topic of electronic warfare is about jamming, and confusing signals, and sending things to the wrong place, but also in the field of anonymous communications, it has been known for a while that we should start looking at models of eavesdroppers and not actually look everywhere. The problem with these things is that they usually make quite heavy assumptions, well some assumptions that are not verifiable so, for example, I cannot really say what percent of my network can be observed reliably or not. If I say all of it then I am erring deliberately on the safe side.

Reply. Yes, one of the properties of anonymous communication networks is that they generally require cooperation of at least the sender, or the receiver. But an interesting question is, when nobody involved in the communication is trying to hide, let's look at the simplest case, there's somebody malicious out there somewhere on the net who wants to prevent eavesdropping, can they be successful? Surprisingly, sometimes they can be, and I think maybe using that observation to build networks that make this more amenable is potentially fruitful.

Yvo Desmedt. Preventing eavesdropping is actually not that new because if you look at quantum cryptography that's exactly what it does.

Reply. Yes, if you look at the first footnote in my position paper I point out that the only respectable example that one can come up with, where we can depend on the network for security, is quantum crypto.

Yvo Desmedt. The problem with that, as we know, is that in order for it to work over the network you need to basically change all the routers and the switches, etc, so the question is, can you extend your technique so that you could actually use all the maths from quantum crypto, but using not the quantum, but ordinary bits, that's one thing which I think is worth looking at.

The second question is, do you see how this can be extended to deal with basically insider attacks instead of just outside things?

Reply. I'll have to think about that. I'm not sure how much time, OK, so if you can speak with time travel.

Alf Zugenmaier. Suppose you had traffic normalisers which try to reduce the confusion by setting bits back to their normal state. If you have one of these sitting on the path then you have to make sure that your confusion can get through.

Reply. Right, so that would be an example of a network that tries to prevent confusion and evasion as a specific service, but the current internet does not fall into that category.

Bruce Christianson. Then you would create a market for de-normalizers.

The Dining Freemasons
(Security Protocols for Secret Societies)

Mike Bond and George Danezis

Computer Laboratory, University of Cambridge,
JJ Thompson Av., CB3 0FD, UK
{Mike.Bond, George.Danezis}@cl.cam.ac.uk

Abstract. We continue the popular theme of offline security by considering how computer security might be applied to the challenges presented in running a secret society. We discuss membership testing problems and solutions, set in the context of security authentication protocols, and present new building blocks which could be used to generate secret society protocols more robustly and generically, including the *lie channel* and the *compulsory arbitrary decision* model.

1 Introduction

Offline security has become a matter of study and interest in the academic computer security community, with aspects of physical lock and safe security being presented by Matt Blaze [1] and air travel security by Bruce Schneier [2]. They have argued quite convincingly, that that security outside the computer world, would benefit from the methodology, analysis and techniques that have been developed to protect computer systems, such as the careful threat modelling, security policies, understanding the strength of mechanism, and relying on small secrets rather than obscurity, as well as these worlds having a few lessons for computer security too.

In this paper we consider the *secret society* – an enterprise in which there has been much security-related innovation historically, but is largely overlooked. We present and categorise techniques that can be used by people, without the assistance of a computer, to authenticate their membership of a secret society and discretely exchange information past a warden. We link these real-word applications with the corresponding fields of authentication protocols and steganography models, but also embrace the constraints of the physical world – which sometimes leads to more elegant solutions.

Secret societies are a common subject matter of fiction novels[1], but of course many secret societies do exist in real life. Other closed-membership associations, from spy rings to the mafia, share the need for secrecy and covert authentication and communication, and would benefit from a more principled approach to security. To a first approximation, a secret society has three functions:

---

[1] For instance consider Dan Brown's recent bestseller "The Da Vinci Code".

B. Christianson et al. (Eds.): Security Protocols 2005, LNCS 4631, pp. 258–265, 2007.
© Springer-Verlag Berlin Heidelberg 2007

- to recruit the worthy,
- to pass on a secret doctrine,
- and to reward its members.

Each area presents intruiging challenges, but cruicial to each aspect is membership testing – society members must be able to identify each other in order to pass on the doctrine, to confer rewards and to consider new applicants.

2 Membership Testing

How do you determine if someone is a member of your society? Societies with cell structures preclude full knowledge of membership; a member might have to search for another member when travelling in a new region. Alternatively there may be a full membership list, but a given member may not have full access, or the authentication might need to be performed in anonymous circumstances.

The simplest technique is *broadcast*. Each member of the society advertises their membership in a straightforward way to all who care to hear: overt societies use uniform or insignia to achieve this very purpose. Secret societies do the same, but attempt to to hide their broadcast.

2.1 Steganographic Broadcast

A *steganographic broadcast* is a signal visible to all but understood by few. In our model it requires no challenge whether issued deliberately by another member, or conincidentally by a stranger. In Roman times Christians doodled the sign of the fish in the sand to broadcast their membership; done casually with the sandal this is covert. For the signal to remain hidden even when repeated, it must have a low information content. The secret society must make a trade-off in their signal S between certainty of authentication and probability of discovery[2], or in other words choose between false positives and plausible deniability.

However, steganographic broadcasts can conceivably be replayed: the outsider carefully observes a suspected member, then repeats their set of actions exactly. Should the secret signal be discovered, all members of the society are quickly exposed and the society cannot observe that they are under attack.

To overcome the shortcomings of steganographic broadcast, we next consider what can be gained from adding interactivity, and in this case the verbal channel rather than the physical channel is better suited, and will be the focus of our discussion.

2.2 Interactive Authentication

Suppose we permit interaction between the prover and the verifier. Interactive proof is appealing as it reduces the workload on society members who need not

---

[2] Equally important in broadcast signal design is the standard deviation of the information content in the signal. A well designed signal cannot be poorly executed thus confirming membership with high certainty, but revealing the signal to all. The fish in the sand unfortunately has a high standard deviation.

keep up the effort of a constant broadcast. It is natural to apply this extension symmetrically, thus we arrive at a *steganographic simultaneous interactive proof*. The verifier uses a key phrase within conversation and the prover then must formulate the correct reponse. The trick of course is to design code phrases effectively, to achieve the usual balance between false positives and deniability. At one end of the scale, in WW2 British Sitcom *'Allo 'Allo* a member of the french resistance plans to authenticate himself to a cafe owner with the following exchange:

LeClerc: "Do you have a light?"
Artois: "I have no matches"
('Allo 'Allo, Pilot Episode)

When a fellow cafe customer lights LeClerc's cigarette before he can utter the first phrase, then leaves his matches at the bar, confusion ensues! An alternative is to use a signal with high information content, for instance when Bond authenticates a CIA agent:

Bond: "In Moscow, April is a spring month."
CIA Agent: "Where as here in St. Petersburg, we're freezing our asses off."
(James Bond, "Goldeneye")

Here the phrase is innocuous, as the high information content is in the exact wording. However, demanding exact wording on repeated authentications quickly damanges deniability, so here the phrase is a session authentication key rather than a long term one. A better approach for repeated authentication is to use multiple rounds of low-information response each slowly adding to the certainty of authentication for both parties.

Interestingly, bi-directional interactive authentication seems more natural to conceive here than the uni-directional counterpart. Uni-directional authentication differs from broadcast as it requires a challenge from the verifier. In fact, totally uni-directional interactive authentication is pointless – the challenges must yield no information as to whether the verifier is a member, thus there will be excessive false positives. However, partially balanced authentication may be a useful primitive: the goal of such an interaction could be for the verifier to deduce that the prover was a member with high probability, whilst the prover may only be able to authenticate the verifier with low probability. The prover enjoys knowledge that someone is *probably* testing their membership, but cannot achieve certainty.

Finally, mixing broadcast and authentication strategies will further reduce the workload on a society member. A well-crafted steganographic broadcast could reduce the number of candidates a member considers for performing full authentication, whilst not marking anyone definititively as a member of the society.

2.3   The Lie Channel

We have summarised the basic structure of steganographic mutual authentication protocols, but an important practical question remains open: how can one design a robust set of hidden phrases for gradual authentication which will work for repeatedly, and endure over a considerable period of time? Furthermore, how can the members commit this to memory?

We suggest exploiting the ability of the human brain to detect lies – to rapidly match a statement against a body of knowledge and determine whether or not it is contradictory. A concrete protocol for gradual mutual authentication can be built as follows. Assume the members of the society share a key, in the form of a 'holy' book B that is only known to the members of the society. Any such book can be used to provide authentication, yet to maintain deniability its subject matter should be appropriate to discuss over dinner (A cooking book, might be perfect, although a play by Shakespeare, or a crime fiction, could also be fine). Let B contains a set of true statements denoted $F_1, F_2, \ldots, F_n$. In the case of *Macbeth* some true statements could be:

> The characters are Macbeth, Lady-Macbeth, Duncan and Macduff. Macbeth is an evil noble[0]. Lady-Macbeth is a greedy ambitious woman[1]. Duncan is a king[2]. Macduff is a loyal noble[3]. Macbeth is weak because Macbeth married Lady-Macbeth and because Lady-Macbeth is greedy[4]. Lady-Macbeth persuades Macbeth to want to be king.[5] Macbeth murders Duncan using a knife because Macbeth wants to be king and because Macbeth is evil.[6] Lady-Macbeth kills Lady-Macbeth.[7] Macduff is angry because Macbeth murdered Duncan and because Macduff is loyal to Duncan.[8] Macduff kills Macbeth.[9] [4]

To initiate the authentication protocol Alice states a true or false fact C_0 from the set of facts $F_{0...n}$. Bob has to reply with a true or false fact R_0, matching the challenge, and provide a second challenge C_1. Alice replies with a true or false fact matching the second challenge. As an example:

Alice: How is Duncan?
I hear he was the king of the casino last night! ($C_0 = F_2 = $ True)
Bob: Another player has come to town, and he is the king now.
But he dominates his wife completely, won't let her play at all.
($R_0 = F_6 = $ True, $C_1 = \neg F_4 = $ False)
Alice: Yes I know her, she's so generous though – she'd be useless
as a gambler! ($R_1 = \neg F_1 = $ False)

Alice and Bob simply repeat this protocol until they are certain that the answers they got match, or do not match, the statements in B. Alice could include a new challenge in the third step, making the repeated protocol take on average two steps per round. Their certainty increases exponentially with each round. Note also that it is quite difficult to replay the conversation, since the challenges that the parties are exchanging are fresh, and will on average require good knowledge of B to determine if they are true or false and answer correctly.

Note also that the protocol, correctly executed, protects the key B. An adversary observing the conversation does not know if a statement is true or false, and often will hear contradictory statements in different conversations. Therefore it is not trivial to reconstruct B fully. In practice marshalling the set of facts from B might seem cumbersome, but indeed many secret (and not-so-secret) societies to require their members to committ to memory large parts of their doctrine. It can often be part of a rite of initiation to recite some true facts, or even to participate in a ritualised (non-steganographic) authentication protocol similar to the above above. Learning a set of true statements along with a set of false statements also seems to be common practice according to the Fishman affidavit [3].

2.4   Deniable Authentication

The basic authentication methods described above are straightforward and have certainly been used in practice. However, some situations demand an extra component from the authentication process – forward plausible deniability. Consider a defendant in court who might broadcast his membership of the secret society in the hope that jury or judge would hear. If the key has already leaked outside the society or some member chooses to leak it subsequent to his broadcast, then this broadcast could be used against him. Furthermore if it is the judge or jury members themselves who wish to reassure the defendant that they will support him, how can they do this and not risk incriminating themselves in the event of key compromise?

The solution we require is a *steganographic deniable authentication*: a judge can then authenticate himself to the defendant, but neither defendant nor outsider can ever prove that the authentication took place. If we assume the existence of a *deniable* covert channel – that is a channel that neither party can prove exists – the protocol becomes relatively straightforward.

$$A \xrightarrow[\text{covert}]{} B: \quad N_A$$
$$B \xrightarrow[\text{covert}]{} A: \quad N_B \tag{1}$$
$$A \xrightarrow[\text{deniable}]{} B: N_A \oplus N_B$$

Deniable channels generally have very limited bandwidth, and may not be covert, so if some static secret K is transmitted, a replay attack on the channel would be easy. Provision of a challenge by B prevents an attacker recording A's actions in minute detail then performing a replay attack. A's challenge ensures suspected members cannot be linked through giving the same response to sending of a fixed challenge if the attacker repeats B's actions in minute detail. A is authenticated to B as A proves the ability to recover B's nonce. To gain a concrete implementation of this protocol we next need to consider some real world covert and deniable channels.

3   Covert and Deniable Channels

If a channel between two parties cannot be observed by others or provably recorded by either party, then it is a *deniable channel*. Such channels are sometimes *covert channels* in that their existence is not known, but as deniable channels are harder to create than covert channels, a small number of well-known (ie. no longer covert) deniable channels may have to suffice for creation of the protocol.

3.1   The Compulsory Arbitrary Decision Model

The *Compulsory Arbitrary Decision (CAD) Model* is a generic template for creating covert and deniable channels. It carries only a single bit, and this represents a decision chosen, or within reasonable control of the sender, which is *compulsory* – it has to happen one way or the other, and *arbitrary* – the sender might reasonably be expected to choose either way.

This model contrasts building protocols on arbitrary inclusion models, where a particular phrase is said or not said, or where an action is performed or not performed. It is much more difficult to bound the information content of the inclusion of phrases within a conversation, so it is a poorer choice as a building block for secret society protocols.

A good example of a compulsory arbitrary decision (CAD) is when two people leave a room: one of them must walk through the door first. It is quite reasonable for one of the parties to be able to control this, and individuals are unlikely to have strong preferences either way. Interestingly, this channel can be duplex, but collisions will occur if both parties try to transmit the same bit value at once. This channel is covert, but in the presence of a video camera is not deniable.

Other examples of channels with similar characteristics include:

The Chinese Menu Channel. High-capacity CADs are also conceivable, for instance, the choice of item on a menu. When seated at a restaurant, ordering food is as good as compulsory, and if a dish is chosen by number at a chinese restaurant from a selection of maybe one hundred dishes, this could contain at least six bits of information. The channel may be covert, but as the request is verbal, and an itemised receipt is provided it is not deniable.

The Handshake Channel. The most imfamous deniable channel is the *handshake channel*, through which the freemasons allegedly signal their membership through adding pressure with their thumbs on or between particular knuckles of the recipient during a handshake. The appeal of using skin-to-skin contact is that modest pressure applied is easily detected, but difficult to observe through even close visual surveillance. This means that only the giver and the receiver can observe the channel, thus one could easily frame the other. Direct measuring of the handshake pressure would require equipment difficult to conceal on the hand. The handshake is thus an excellent deniable channel, though these days it is not particularly covert. Determining the practical information capacity per handshake is an open question, though it seems it is at least one to two bits.

In cryptology, a quantum cryptography channel exploiting polarisation of photons transmitted down a fibre-optic link represents the ultimate deniable channel.

It is an open question whether or not a deniable channel can be created between two parties using purely verbal communication.

4   Other Challenges

Knowledge Set Bootstrapping. It is an interesting challenge to agree upon a shared key between two parties who are not already members of the same society, in the presence of a passive adversary who is observing the entire conversation. Whilst cryptographic solutions involving number theory such as Diffie-Hellman key exchange are fine for computers, they are not much good for humans.

The NSA may be able to intercept any US phonecall, and they may have formidable computing facilities, but if the computation lies in the human world, then their computational bounds are severely reduced.

Two parties can discuss their common knowledge, wheeling through books, moveies, music, religious texts, cryptographic standards – flagging each time when they hit a common area of knowledge. Key material can be efficiently collected from this area using the lie channel (see section 2.3) and then combined with existing key material, for instance using XOR. If their conversation crosses outside the bounds of knowledge of the adversary even for one category, then they have a short key, which can be later used to transmit a message maybe confirming a meeting location.

Counter-Surveillance. A variation on this bootstrapping is to work in a common source of data which the attacker will find hard to record or memorise. e.g. the stream of traffic flowing past a window. Alternatively two parties under audio but not video surveillance could point at simple card with "Truth" and "Lie" printed on it to allow them to selectively mislead the eavesdropper.

Semantic Encoding. There are already plenty of adequate proposals for hiding information within text, which are of use to those trying to transmit data across a monitored channel [5]. In interesting question is to consider what steganographic techniques could encode a very small amount of data in a body of text that will persist despite radical transforms which only preserve top-level semantics. For instance, suppose the doctrine of the secret society contains a parable. How can we encode in the detail of the story a byte of information in such a way that it will survive translation, summarisation, and incidental errors in the telling of the story, even exaggeration? A parable is an interesting choice as it is clearly an arbitrary story made to illustrate a point, yet because it can be read on many levels details which are not understood are not necessarily perceived as inconsequential by the storyteller.

5   Conclusions

Just as principles of computer security can teach offline security a lot, we have plenty to learn from the offline world too. We believe a study of secret societies performed in greater depth would reveal some interesting new protocol challenges, and some real-world tools and constraints for which there may not yet be a cryptographic analogue. Furthermore, developing a full set of practical primitives for constructing secret society protocols would be of some use to todays existing secret societies in this age of increasing surveillance.

References

1. Blaze, M.: Toward a Broader View of Security Protocols. In: Twelfth International Workshop on Security Protocols, Cambridge UK (April 26-28, 2004)
2. Schneier, B.: Crypto-Gram Newsletter (August 15, 2004)
3. The Fishman Affidavit, http://www.xs4all.nl/kspaink/fishman/index2.html
4. Clocksin, W.: University of Cambridge, Computer Science Tripos 2000, Paper 9, Question 9 (2000), http://www.cl.cam.ac.uk/tripos/y2000p9q9.pdf
5. Atallah, M.J., Raskin, V., Crogan, M., Hempelmann, C., Kerschbaum, F., Mohamed, D., Naik, S.: Natural Language Watermarking: Design, Analysis, and a Proof-of-Concept Implementation. In: Moskowitz, I.S. (ed.) Information Hiding. LNCS, vol. 2137, pp. 185–199. Springer, Heidelberg (2001)

The Dining Freemasons
(Security Protocols for Secret Societies)

(Transcript of Discussion)

Mike Bond

Computer Laboratory, University of Cambridge

Good afternoon everyone, I was expecting to have the last talk before dinner. [Laughter]. We're going to take a slightly less serious look at some of the work that George Danezis and myself have been doing on trying to find exciting, or at least interesting, new ways to think about security protocols, and to find environments that encourage us to find interesting new protocols. Our chosen environment is Secret Societies, and although there are all sorts of things in there, we're going to concentrate mainly on membership testing, and look at some of the algorithms that you might use to figure out whether or not somebody is a member of your secret society, or try and decode whether or not members elsewhere are members of their societies. Then we'll go on to figure out if we can take what we know from what we read in books, and stories, and history, and do it a bit better using our skills from cryptography, and we'll look at a couple of models that we have for that. And then I'll present one protocol to you, and show how we built it up, which tries to do authentication between two people in a better, more interesting way.

We're going to take a pretty crude view of a secret society: just like all societies, corporations, whatever, their aim at the end of the day is just to carry on existing. Secret societies tend to try to get new people, and have some bar that they need to jump over in order to be members; they've got some doctrine that justifies superficially their persistence, and they have some tangible rewards for the members for belonging.

Audience. You don't need the word "secret" there yet.

Reply. Yes, but it will come into play later when you'll see that people may not wish to reveal exactly what societies they're members of. There are a lot of societies which maybe do strange things but aren't secret. I've sprinkled logos and conspiracy theory images all around the presentation, although they're unfortunately not relevant to the slides.

I guess one question to ask is, are they important? Well, yes, historically, some of them have been. These days you could consider terrorists to be secret societies, but that's not what I'm asking here. I'm trying to say, is there anything that the study of them can teach us about the real world, and is there anything we can offer back to them in return. A bit like some work presented by Matt Blaze here last year saying, what can security protocols learn from looking at the real world of restaurants, and purchasing wine, this sort of thing, and vice

B. Christianson et al. (Eds.): Security Protocols 2005, LNCS 4631, pp. 266–275, 2007.
© Springer-Verlag Berlin Heidelberg 2007

versa[1]. So we're going to concentrate on membership testing first. We'll leave aside how to create interesting and compelling doctrines to keep you alive, and how to deal with all the businesses of making money illicitly and distributing it, and concentrate on membership testing.

So this is obviously necessary in order to reward new people, and there are some interesting circumstances in which you might want to authenticate, it's not simply about having a list of people. Even if you do have a list of members of your society, you might want to authenticate with someone in order to reward them, or buy them a drink, in a situation where you're not actually revealing your whole name. So sometimes, even given that there is a list, you may want to be able to authenticate anonymously. The simplest strategy for doing this sort of thing is what we call a steganographic broadcast, which is a sign that you give out that's only understood by a few people. Non-covert, the standard signs are wearing a uniform, or some sort of insignia. There are some slightly more subtle things like the Aids awareness ribbons, things like that, if you wear them people who don't know what they are will just think, oh, you're wearing a ribbon, so that's a slightly more subtle sign. You then start to go to a covert stage where there are all the sorts of things you can read about in fiction books, or you see on the X-files, where somebody broadcasts that they want to be met by their handler by putting a masking tape X in the window, the stories about how the Freemasons signal to an entire jury that they're one of the members by looking up at the ceiling at a crucial moment. The trouble with these sorts of broadcasts is that you don't know who's listening: if you're trying to make contact in a new area you have to decide, out of the people I'm considering broadcasting to, out of you all in the room, if I suspect that some people know the sign but aren't members, and some people know the sign and are members, do I risk making a broadcast. So there are issues to do with whether or not broadcast is viable.

An interesting example of a broadcast from ancient times, and again, you've got to dig into the history to find out whether this anecdote is true, is the use of Ichthus, the fish, as a sign that you might scrawl in the sand saying, hey I'm a Christian, do you want to introduce yourself to me? One of the interesting things to abstract from this is not just how deniable it is, I was just doodling in the sand rather than deliberately drawing a fish, but also the variability in a level of covertness with which you can do it. If you've got a newish initiate who's not very clever, he's just going to get out a big fat stick and go, cceerr, in the sand, and everyone will know. And you've then got a problem because you've exposed the sign, and you exposed this person, and presumably people who see this sign broadcasted so obviously would not dare to go up to this person, and would not let them join. So wouldn't it be nice if we can find ways of doing these sorts of broadcasts which are a little bit more stable, and a little bit easier for people to work with.

One way to go forward is to move to an interactive authentication, and this has various advantageous properties, basically the prover responds correctly to some challenge from the verifier, and the challenges obviously need to be chosen carefully. If you make them too general or too innocuous to fit with, let's say, taking

---

[1] Matt Blaze, Toward a Broader View of Security Protocols, LNCS 3957, 106–132.

the verbal communication channels example, they fit in with conversation really easily, then you're going to get false positives all the time, people will think you're trying to authenticate to them, or you'll think that totally innocent people are trying to authenticate to you. Intuitively speaking, an interactive authentication, if it's done in rounds, is symmetric, because every time you get a new challenge, you assume that the person before has understood the response from you, so you build up confidence in each other's membership slowly, and symmetrically.

You could also conceive imbalance systems, obviously a totally unbalanced system that's unidirectional doesn't make a lot of sense to be interactive, but something like knowing that you've had your membership tested with eighty percent probability means there's quite a good chance that the person who was enquiring wasn't deliberately enquiring, but that person now knows, say with ninety-nine percent probability, that you are a member.

Ross Anderson. It's not entirely clear that completely imbalanced systems are useless, because of the equivalence between interactive and secret key proofs, you can have means of proving yourself to somebody as a function of the secret, so there could be an algorithm for generating passwords.

Reply. Yes, I suppose so, I guess the issue there is, when does unidirectional authentication become a broadcast again, because isn't what you're describing also viewable as a broadcast?

Ross Anderson. It's viewable as a broadcast, but a broadcast with slightly less information being given because it allows revocation, or alternatively, this broadcast might be a function of some context so it can't be verified outside that context.

Tuomas Aura. It is the admit membership and the prove membership, that seems to be the symmetry, the verifier admits membership, and the prover proves membership.

Reply. Yes, in an interactive authentication like this, if you have a balance that builds up in rounds where each person learns something every single round, then they're both verifiers, they're both provers, the terminology isn't relevant, but if you put in some imbalance then you could say that the verifier is the one who has succeeded in getting a high probability, and the prover is the one who's done all the effort in giving somebody else a high probability.

Tuomas Aura. Well it's like a policeman who pretends to be a member, and he's not, he's admitting membership, he admits to being a member of the secret society, although he's not proving it.

Reply. Ah, OK. This is all within the scope of the steganographic, the hidden communication, so it's not about saying, I'm a member of the secret society, and by the way, here are all the exchanges. I don't even consider people overtly saying, I a member of this society as admission, that's outside the context of the protocols.

Bruce Christianson. But a policeman could attempt to authenticate someone else, because he's a policeman he has suggested a secret protocol and ...

Reply. Yes, that could happen in the examples that I'm working with. Anyhow, in your interactive authentication you've got challenges and responses, and it all looks great, the cryptographic protocol people are happy, but what about the actual design of responses. So let's look at some fumbled examples that show how designing the actual words that you say can be tricky. A slightly dubious comedy from the 80s, Allo Allo, has an interesting exercise here to do with authenticating two members of the French resistance, the plan sounds fairly simple, one of them enters, orders a brandy, and says the phrase, do you have a light, the other one must respond, I have no matches. As we will see, there are some shortcomings in this, even though it sounds simple. So the wrong chap comes in, orders a brandy, and the waiter, Artois says, I suppose you'd like a light, to which unfortunately he responds, yes, thank you, you're very kind, so Artois now has to say, I have no matches, so Gruber is confused, why do you ask me if I wanted a light, authentication failed. But there's a problem, Gruber, being a helpful chap of course gives him a box of matches, and now when we have the true resistance agents come up, ask for a brandy, seconds before he can utter his phrase, his cigar gets lit, so we have his challenge, do you have a light, completely out of context, and the response, I have no matches, meaningless. So two phrases, that made sense, that seemed covert, basically changed through quite logical progression.

They're all slaves to the comedy and farce, but if you pretend they were being serious, there are some questions about. If you're going to design protocols for people to authenticate, you've got to recognise they're not going to be the designers themselves, they're just going to have to use this in practice. What are they going to get wrong? Maybe they'll be confused about whether they should initiate or respond: Artois saw the guy with the brandy and thought he should push on with the protocol, then discovered retry capability was not specified. Somebody came up and tried to authenticate, how many times should he let them have a go? If LeClerc had been happy to just stop the protocol then and there, and then start again later, maybe it would have worked.

Meanwhile at the other end of the scale we've got my namesake, almost, James Bond, trying to do a similar sort of job. Bond recites a particular phrase in Goldeneye, in Moscow April is a spring month, and a CIA agent wisecracks back at him, and of course the trouble with this is that the CIA agent could have been an impostor who'd made up this wisecrack. They'd been tailing Bond from the airport, they knew that as soon as he sits down and comments about the weather, or comments about any seemingly innocuous thing, they should just try and wisecrack back. That's an interesting attack in that it does highlight the shortcoming of trying to design phrases that way, which is that basically you've only got a one-time use out of them. How can you come up with a method for having a key between people that is easy for them to memorise but gives them a whole batch of phrases to authenticate with all the time, how can you just get an algorithm that will be small enough to fit into someone's head easily. Let's consider some options.

What about taking a security professional's approach and stop thinking about ad hoc phrases. Can we do it more rigorously at bit level? Let's try and construct a primitive that transmits a sequence of single bits covertly. For instance, the idea of a compulsory arbitrary decision, if you go to a meal at a restaurant with somebody, there's going to be a doorway, the two of you will pass through in a particular order, you can control this order, presumably the other guy will have no strong opinions, so there it's something you're expected to do, you have to leave the restaurant, you have to enter the restaurant, but you've control over transmitting one bit. You could have a handshake and modestly only try and transmit a single bit with either a weak or firm handshake, or if you're say at a Chinese restaurant, you're quite reasonably expected to have to order, people can't throw you off too much at this, so maybe you've got six bits out of your choice of dish.

And building on some of the discussions that we had with Frank Stajano the day before[2] about the different channels that exist in the real world for mobile users, that might be worth considering later. We'll be looking mainly at covert and deniable channels for this discussion, but I was most intrigued by the idea of a comparison channel where you have two devices that can transmit, and they do have a sort of communication channel through one person who's able to rapidly compare their output, and it's much better to model that channel that way as a comparison rather than modelling the two people transmitting to a third party, because that way you build into the channel the limitations of the person doing the comparing, in how much information he can process, how fast he can process it. So, scope for future work there.

One channel that we struck upon, which we though might be an interesting point, would be to exploit the human's ability to detect something which is wrong, a blatant lie about a field of knowledge, so, you know, if you consider the 64-bit block size of DES compared with the 130-bit block size of AES, I've already transmitted some information to, hopefully, all of you guys here. So you can use this ability, and if you choose the right body of specialist knowledge you can do a context transplant. If you're talking about block size that's maybe a bit difficult, but if you're talking about people and their relationships, and you know a story, or you know the dynamic of a certain group of people, then it's easy to change their names and transplant them into different environments. Alternatively you can use the channel overtly and simply look for knowledge which your known eavesdropper probably won't know, and build up that way, and try and buy yourself time as they rush off to the encyclopaedia or start Googling rapidly, to try and figure out exactly what the block size of AES is.

Our example is taken from a Tripos paper in artificial intelligence where we're given ten facts about Macbeth, er, I mean the Scottish play, and this example shows a possible situation where some people sitting over a restaurant in Vegas are discussing Duncan, the king of the Casino, and his wife. As you can see, Duncan was the king of the Casino last night, Duncan is a king, true fact, so you've transmitted one bit. Another player's come to town, he's the king now, but he dominates his wife completely, so there we're saying something

---

[2] Multi-Channel Protocols, These proceedings.

false, talking about the relationship between Macbeth and Lady Macbeth. So, we're not saying that you guys can read this presentation, go off, and start authenticating straightaway, but these are starting points of building slightly more robust communication methods for secret authentication.

Ross Anderson. That's very slow, why don't you instead have a convention that whenever you tell a lie the subject in the sentence is key? Just an example, but you don't have to do it in single bits.

Frank Stajano. Except you can only make sentences out of nouns.

Ross Anderson. Well in American English any noun can be a verb.[3]

Matt Blaze. This reminds me of Leo Mark's book, Between Silk and Cyanide, inventing practical non-computerised crypto schemes for agents going into enemy lines where they might be tortured into revealing their codes. A countermeasure that they developed was that each agent was instructed to make certain errors in encoding their messages, and if they revealed the codes after being captured they would reveal the correct code.

Reply. So you've got a channel back there to show you've been compromised. What we're going to look at in the final protocol is to design a deniable protocol which will stop a particular member having say a video surveillance recording of them authenticating, from being used against them, even if the membership rules, and the secret rites of the society have subsequently been divulged.

Frank Stajano. Mike, in the previous slide you have Alice transmitting bits, Bob transmitting bits, it's not clear to me what the relationship between these bits is, it looks like there is stream dependence.

Reply. Ah yes, I've forgotten to explain part of the protocol. This was George's idea, I think. Basically the way we use the lie channel here is to match, so Alice says a truth, which is her challenge, and Bob is able to determine whether or not that's a truth, and then responds with like, so he says a true fact, and then produces a challenge which might be a true or false fact, and you continue matching people's true or falses in conversation, and if they don't spot that your lie is a lie and they respond with a truth then they've broken the stream, and then you start again, and you start building up a shared key.

George Danezis. This also protects against an extremely simplistic attack where true facts are always repeated, so we always say Duncan is the king, Duncan is the king, Duncan is the king. Probably someone who listens to many conversations will actually be able to realise this is part of the response you want, but if sometimes Duncan is going to be the king, sometimes he's not, then you actually don't know what the key is because you only see matches of true, true, false, false.

Bruce Christianson. There's an attack where the respondent simply feeds back an earlier challenge.

Tuomas Aura. You assume common knowledge here. Maybe Alice did not go to a British public school for her knowledge of Shakespeare. In this protocol any single error could break it.

---

[3] General Alexander Haig contexted such verbings outstandingwise.

Reply. Yes, but you can start again, so it depends what your retry facility is. If you want 10-bits of certainty, so one in a thousand probability, then yes, it may take a few runs through if people's knowledge of the secret rituals is not up to scratch.

Bruce Christianson. Members of the society would know the real wording in Shakespeare.[4]

Reply. And the real author as well maybe.

Frank Stajano. So what's the answer to Bruce's comment that every time Alice challenges the response is the same.

Reply. Well if you don't respond using knowledge of the doctrine, you won't build up shared key.

Frank Stajano. If I'm a malicious person who overhears and sees that they walk always together, I don't know if it's true or false, but that must be the right answer to that question.

George Danezis. The answer to that is that it's an attack, but this protocol is meant to be run by humans, who are extremely good at spotting boring people as well as attackers, so if that's the only conversation you can have, then it's becoming less credible that you are actually some part of our society. It's all about building confidence in a slightly more rigorous way than just waving a big flag saying I am one of you.

Bruce Christianson. So you have a rule, no boring members.

Mike Roe. The pairs you see would be different pairs then.

Reply. OK, just so.

Alf Zugenmaier. How do you find out which signals to try to authenticate?

Reply. That's done in the rule set of the society that you're a member of.

Alf Zugenmaier. So no two secret societies are permitted to use Shakespeare?

Reply. Well hopefully there will be enough secret rituals to go round. There is a small chance of collision between secret societies, yes, but basically the idea is that because this is all hidden conversation, you shouldn't be aware of the existence of another secret society.

Tuomas Aura. If I'm a member of ten secret societies, and you're a member of fifteen, and we only have one conversation, we will never find the code

Reply. So there you need some way to package up your credentials into one conversation. OK, let's assume exclusive secret societies from now on.

Ross Anderson. It's much easier in Mediterranean countries where it's normally enough to put your hand on another guy's shoulder, and then you could speed out Morse code.

Reply. Yes, this is one of the issues. In trying to improve these authentication protocols, we're really interested in deniable channels. Putting your hand on someone, basically any skin contact, means it is actually quite difficult to observe

---

[4] *Lay* on MacDuff.

or record what went on via visual surveillance. To be honest we have not done detailed experiments here, but the theory is that you can't tell whether or not I gave a firm, a moderate, or a weak handshake, just by a video recording, and if you're on the other end of the handshake you can say how firm my handshake was, but, you know, you could have made it up.

Yvo Desmedt. You will burn more energy to give a firm handshake, so if you try an infrared camera...

Reply. Possibly. So is this an attack against the confidentiality of the signal across the handshake, or the deniability of it? If you're watching as a third party with an infrared camera, that would be an attack against the confidentiality of the bits transmitted, whereas if you've got some ingenious way of measuring provably how firmly somebody squeezed you by looking at your electrical signals, and it can all be put back here[5], so that your hand doesn't have little sticky patches on, then possibly you can get a convincing argument to say, yes, I can prove he gave me a firm handshake.

Anyhow let's move on and see the protocol, I'm going to show you five versions. It starts off really simple, and we'll fan through the threat model. The model we considered had three major things, the danger that somebody would be impersonated, second threat is, can a member be revealed in a provable way, and thirdly, is there someway you can exploit the protocol to pull out an entire membership list. We're looking at a resourceful attacker who's got cameras, high-tech kit, we're looking at somebody who we want to prove is a member who might be a powerful and influential person, the sort of person who it would be a major issue if we did have evidence that they were a member, and we're looking in the setting of two people meeting at a meal at a restaurant, they're not in privacy, but they are expecting to be able to be, roughly speaking, left to their own devices.

In the dining freemasons protocol, we start off with the dodgy handshake. The prover sends to the verifier some key, some signal, through this deniable handshake channel. The trouble with this is that if you can play the role of verifier you can receive this key K and then you can replay it. Now you can do various things with keys of the day to solve this problem, but if the rule set is divulged you may get the keys of the day upfront as well anyway, so there are dangers with this approach of membership impersonation. We could say instead, why don't we signal it covertly? This is using something like a couple of compulsory arbitrary decisions, you signal your key, the covert channel is modulated with a particular rule set of the society, this way only the verifier who knows R will be able to receive this signal K. Trouble with this is, if this taking place in a restaurant and you were able to record the actions of some important, powerful individual who's under scrutiny all the time, then you might be able to get their actions within the restaurant in enough detail to potentially replay it, so you've got a situation where you transmit the covert key without knowing what it was just by repeating in as much detail as you can manage.

---

[5] Reveals shoulder holster.

The other problem with this is that, if in the future the authentic copy of R is revealed, you know, that's a sealed document from the society which can be proven to be authentic, then any video footage of P performing this authentication will incriminate them as a member. So, what about solving that problem by having the prover send some kind of nonce, and then send the key XORed with the nonce over the deniable channel, so they do some stuff in the way they act, and in their arbitrary decisions, and then they use the handshake to modulate in the key. Is the problem solved? Unfortunately not, because you can still record the actions of V as well as P.

So what if the verifier sends a nonce, and then the prover replies with that modulated into the handshake. We've got quite an interesting attack here which is that if you play the role of V, your verifier, and you do whatever you like, but you record what you do in minute detail, then so long as you can re-create your actions in sufficient detail at the restaurant, then you can observe whether or not the new person you're meeting gives you the same information back across the handshake. If they do, then you know that if the first guy was a member, then the second guy is too. In this way, from your suspicions about who might be a member, and observing that they all send the handshake when given the same challenge, you build up the membership set through membership linkage.

So the final iteration, which we show in the paper, is the prover supplying a nonce, the verifier supplying a nonce, and then the XOR of the two nonces, because hopefully you can just about do XOR in your head, is sent over the deniable channel. The nonce from V stops the recording of P's day, the nonce from P varies the deniable data to stop a receiver using it to link up the membership, and we don't actually bother with K now, simply knowledge of the rule set and ability to extract these nonces from the covert channel, is sufficient to prove yourself being a member. And we don't know an attack on this.

Ben Laurie. If the verifier is working for the attackers, and uses the same nonce on two occasions, and the prover doesn't, then you can extract what the two possibilities are for about half of the deniable handshake bits from that, because those bits looks different.

Reply. It can't prove that he's a member I don't think, although it may well succeed in confirming that he's a member.

Ross Anderson. You can add some broadcast measure local public data, for example, you put a newspaper down on the table and it's open at page 17, so 17 is the nonce.

Reply. The page it was opened on could be controlled I suppose. A choice which isn't under control of either of the attackers would be better. You could assume (well actually you probably can't with the Illuminati) that the front page news story is OK, you could use the first letter of the front page news story of the day.

In conclusion, there's lots of problems, lots of interesting side alleys to go down. You could look at what happens when you break the protocol, and watch how people get confused and balk like the squeezing their hand too hard attack. There are interesting things you can do with using the lie channel to build up keys when you know you're under surveillance, and you hope that you wander through enough different topics of common knowledge, but because the adversary is passive they can never interject things they know about, so hopefully you build up enough data from your common knowledge, and you know that by the time the attackers have Googled through all the knowledge, will be three hours behind, or one hour behind, and that's enough to do your cocaine exchange, or something.

There are all sorts of interesting challenges that we'd like to look such as how do you get the magical effects that are needed to make these societies work well. If you look back in Greek times, people who could do stuff with mechanics, and make cogs, and whirring things that made the temple doors open when the fire came on, succeeded in getting lots of followers. Can we use our knowledge of cryptography and security to do the same magic tricks to pull candidates into our society.

Yvo Desmedt. You had very interesting pictures. One of your pictures, was this guy who was dressed with the pants being shorter on one side. When you had that picture I thought that you would be starting to talk about actually using the clothing.

Reply. That sort of thing would be classified as a broadcast, everybody who sees you will see. You are saying to everybody by this particular button combination that you're a member of that society. All it takes is a photo of Tony Blair with his bottom button done up, and then revelation that a secret society has those rules, and then you know that he's a member.

Yvo Desmedt. No, I'm talking about inside the protocol.

Reply. So using the clothing as a communication channel? That's something we hadn't considered. Yes.

Frank Stajano. Today Mike is wearing a jacket, and yesterday George was wearing a jacket, so a very high information content.

Reply. Yes it's a very rare event for George to wear a jacket.

Ross Anderson. Well there's the other completely different question of how you make your secret society resilient against takeover, because it will be penetrated bit by bit. The use of Freemasons brings to mind that the Masons were apparently started by merchants, traders, people like that, who wished to spread the doctrine of free trade under the blankets of an opposing aristocracy four or five hundred years ago, and now of course, the Grand Master Mason in the UK is apparently the Duke of Kent, so they've clearly been taken over by the other side even now.

Reply. I guess the solution there is all in the doctrine design isn't it. Time-locked doctrine, and ever closer inner circles, and discovering that the Grand Master Mason isn't the true Grand Master Mason because there are higher degrees...

Audience. How do you know all that?

Reply. I found a web page where it explains it all.

On the Evolution of Adversary Models in Security Protocols (or Know Your Friend and Foe Alike)

(Transcript of Discussion)

Virgil Gligor

University of Maryland

When I saw the announcement of this year's workshop theme, I wondered about what I should be speaking about. [Laughter] One possibility was actually suggested by the presentations which were given before mine, particularly Yvo Desmedt's[1], which point out the unfriendliness of some of today's systems. With such "friends" who's needs "adversaries"? Well, we actually we do need adversary definitions, and my theme is that not only do you have to know your "friend" the system (using the methods that perhaps Ross is going to talk about), but you have to know your "adversary" just as much in order to design and analyse meaningful security protocols. This presentation is related to some joint work which I have done with Adrian Perrig and his two graduate students, Haowen Chan, and Bryan Parno.

The first point I'd like to make is that new technologies – and it doesn't matter in what field the new technologies appear, but we'll talk about computers in general – introduce new security vulnerabilities. New vulnerabilities sometimes require new adversary models not just new countermeasures based on old models. Of course, once we have new adversary models, we can develop new protocol analysis methods and tools. In practice, it's not clear which comes first, whether the adversary model comes first, or the analysis methods and tools come first and the adversary models get retrofit, but in any case one has to generate these two items in order to reach some level of comfort in protocol and system security. So I'd like to give some examples of this process, and then argue that there is an uncomfortable gap between the time when new technologies and vulnerabilities are introduced and the time when countermeasures (e.g., new analysis methods and tools) are found. An additional conclusion is that our adversary models need to be updated more frequently than in the past.

In the mid to late 60's researchers started talking about *computer utilities*, which basically introduced techniques of sharing user-level data and programs. Once sharing user-level data and programs becomes a practical reality, concerns of their confidentiality and integrity arise, because to some extent sharing allows the destruction of these two properties. Hence the notion of *controlled sharing* was introduced, that could enable enforcement of sharing policies for confidentiality and integrity of user-level programs and data. Design and implementation of such policies led to the introduction of security kernels, and both the

---

[1] These proceedings.

B. Christianson et al. (Eds.): Security Protocols 2005, LNCS 4631, pp. 276–283, 2007.
© Springer-Verlag Berlin Heidelberg 2007

correctness and penetration-resistance of these kernels became significant concerns. Who was our new adversary at that time? In that context, our adversary was an untrusted user and his untrusted programs that might contain carefully placed Trojan horses, which could violate the confidentiality and integrity properties of user-level shared programs and data, and penetrate operating systems kernels. Over time researchers developed analysis methods and tools for confidentiality and integrity as well as policy models, the earliest of which was Lampson's Access Matrix model (1971)[2]. System architecture techniques that emphasized kernel isolation and non-circumventability emerged in early 70's, followed by various informal penetration analysis methods, such as the Flaw Hypothesis Methodology (FHM)[3] in the mid 70's. Formal models of penetration resistance and verification tools followed FHM, the first being the penetration resistance theory and tool we built[4] at the University Maryland between 1989 and 1991.

It is important to note here that although the new controlled-sharing technologies were introduced - primarily by MIT's Multics system[5] - in the mid 60s, formal analysis methods the tools for handling the new adversary came much later. For example, formal policy models and tools for information flow analysis appeared about 1973-75 (viz., the Bell-LaPadula model and its Multics interpretation)[6]. The delay in producing formal penetration analysis models and tools was even longer: the first *formal* analyses of C language UNIX source code appeared only in 1991[7], though storage channel analysis of UNIX source code appeared in the late 80's (viz., the Secure Xenix analyses)[8]. Nearly a

[2] Lampson, B.W., "Protection," Proc. of the 5th Princeton Symp. on Information Science and Systems, pp. 437-443, Mar. 1971; reprinted in Operating Systems Review, Vol. 8, no. 1, pp. 18-24, Jan. 1974.

[3] Linde, R.R., "Operating Systems Penetration," Proceedings of the National Computer Conference, 1975.

[4] Gupta, S., and V.D. Gligor, "Experience with a Penetration Analysis Method and Tool," S. Gupta and V.D. Gligor, Proc. of the 15th National Computer Security Conference, Baltimore, Maryland, October 1992, pp. 165-183, and "Automated Penetration Analysis System and Method," *U.S. Patent Number 5,485,409,* Jan. 16, 1996.

[5] Organick, E. I., *"The Multics System: An Examination of its Structure,"* M.I.T. Press, Cambridge, Mass. 1972.

[6] Bell, D.E., and L.J, LaPadula, "Secure Computer Systems," Air Force Electronic Systems Division, Report ESD-TR-73-278, Vols. I, II and III, Nov. 1973.
Bell, D.E., and L.J, LaPadula, "Secure Computer System: Mathematical Foundations and Model," MITRE Corporation, M74-244, Bedford, Mass., Oct.. 1974.
Bell, D.E., and L.J, LaPadula, "Secure Computer System: Unified Exposition and Multics Interpretation," MITRE Corporation, MTR-2997, Rev. 1, Bedford, Mass., March, 1975 (available as NTIS AD-A023588).

[7] Gupta S., and V.D. Gligor, "Towards a Theory of Penetration-Resistant Systems," Proc. of the 4th IEEE Computer Security Foundations Workshop (CSFW), Franconia, New Hampshire, June 1991, pp. 62-78, also in *Journal of Computer Security,* Vol. 1, 2 (1992), IOS Press, pp. 133-158.

[8] Tsai, C-R., V.D. Gligor, and C.S. Chandersekaran, "A Formal Method for the Identification of Covert Storage Channels in Source Code," Proc. of the IEEE Symposium

decade passed between the understanding of the new data and program sharing techniques, and the formal definition of new adversaries and countermeasure analysis methods and tools.

Other new technologies that required rethinking of the adversary model and the introduction of new analysis methods and tools were based on *shared stateful services*, like shared database management systems and network protocols, and this of course was in the early to mid 70's. These technologies enabled a new form of attack namely *denial of service*. Interestingly enough, denial-of-service instances noticed in the Jim Anderson's U.S. Air Force report (1973)[9] and the Provably Secure Operating System (PSOS) design at SRI International (1973-1977)[10] were considered to be either a resource allocation or a system integrity problem, but *not* an independent, distinct security area such as confidentiality and integrity. No one looked at denial of service as a distinct security problem until 1983 - 1985[11], when a proper definition of the problem was given setting it apart from other security concerns. In the case of new technologies that enabled denial-of-service attacks, the delay between the technology introduction and the first formal analyses methods and tools to address denial-of-service attacks was a bit longer. For example, formal analysis of some aspects of denial of service appeared between 1988[12] and 1992[13]. Here the new adversary could exploit new techniques like concurrent access to stateful services and protocols.

Moving along in time, new technologies such as the Personal Computer (PC) and Local Area Networks (LANs) appeared in 1973-1975 and the first public-domain cryptographic standard (i.e., DES) in 1977. The new vulnerabilities introduced were in the network area: an adversary could modify, block, re-place, insert and forge messages, at will. In fact, many of us played various

---

on Security and Privacy, Oakland, California, April 1987, pp. 74-86 (also in *IEEE Transactions on Software Engineering*, Vol. SE-16, No. 6, June 1990, pp. 569-580.

[9] Anderson, J. P., "Computer Systems Technology Planning Study," Air Force Electronic Systems Division, ESD-TR-73-51, Air Force Systems Command, Hanscomb, Mass., 1973.

[10] Neumann, P., L. Robinson, K. Levitt, R. Boyer, and A. Saxena, "A Provably Secure Operating System: The System, Its Applications, and Proofs," Technical Report, SRI International, Menlo Park, CA, June 1975.

[11] Gligor, V.D., "A Note on the Denial-of-Service Problem," Proc. of the IEEE Symposium on Computer Security and Privacy, Oakland, California, April 1983 (also in *IEEE Transactions on Software Engineering*, SE-10, No. 3, (May 1984).
Gligor, V.D., "Denial-of-Service Implications for Computer Networks," Proc. of the DoD Invitational Workshop on Computer Network Security, New Orleans, LA., March 1985;
Gligor, V.D., "On Denial of Service in Computer Networks," Proc. of Int'l Conference on Data Engineering, Los Angeles, California, February 1986, pp. 608-617.

[12] Yu C-F., and V.D. Gligor, "A Formal Specification and Verification Method For the Prevention of Denial of Service," Proc. of the IEEE Symp. on Research in Security and Privacy, Oakland, Calif., April 1988, pp. 187-202; also in *IEEE Transactions on Software Engineering*, Vol. SE-16, No. 6, June 1990, pp. 581 - 592.

[13] Millen, J.K., "A Resource Allocation Model for Denial of Service," Proc. of the IEEE Symposium on Security and Privacy, Oakland, California, May 1992, pp. 137-147.

attack games with the Telnet protocol late 70's and early 80's: we set Ethernet interfaces in "promiscuous" mode and obtained Telnet packets containing clear text passwords, thereby collecting everyone's password on remote login. Clearly very potent new attacks were enabled at the time. The new network adversary was the "man in the middle," and the new crypto adversaries included active, adaptive and mobile attackers. The first formal model of the network adversary was the Dole-Yao model (1983)[14], which is still with us. A little earlier, the notion of Byzantine adversaries was introduced for consensus protocols[15]. Here we had distributed computations in which pieces of the computations could be taken over by an adversary, and in fact a lot of work to counter such adversaries was done much later, in the 1990s. The first precise models of the crypto adversary appeared in early to mid 80's[16]. The crypto adversary included adaptive chosen message attacks. Later, in 1991, Rackoff and Simon introduced the notion of chosen ciphertext attacks[17]. Refinements of these attacks followed in early and mid 90's. Once again, we notice a fairy large delay between the introduction of a new technology and, implicitly, new vulnerabilities, and that of the formal model of a new adversary, new analysis methods and tools: roughly between half a dozen years and a decade.

Of course, the Internet introduced new large-scale networking technologies and made possible new *large-scale* vulnerabilities; e.g., viruses, worms, and flooding caused by distributed denial-of-service attacks. These attacks started appearing in late 80's (e.g., R.T. Morris' November 1988 internet worm[18]) although small-scale attacks of these types were known before then. The new adversary could coordinate concurrent processes over the Internet to launch these attacks. Analysis methods like virus scans, trace backs, intrusion detection, which took hold in the mid to late 90's, were known before the late 90's but these tools were not distributed widely before then.

What can we conclude from all these examples? First, there are large time gaps between the introduction of new vulnerabilities on one hand, and new adversarial models and new formal tools on the other, and that accelerated research should shrink these gaps. Second and worse, for many years after new technologies are introduced with the related new vulnerabilities, we seem to use old adversary models and countermeasures to deal with them. Third, before we introduce a

[14] Dolev, D. and A. Yao, "On the Security of Public Key Protocols," *IEEE Transactions on Information Theory*, vol. 29, no 2., pp. 198-208, March 1983.

[15] Lamport L., R. Shostak, and M. Pease, "The Byzantine Generals Problem," *ACM Transactions on Programming Languages and Systems*, vol. 4, no. 3, July 1982, pp. 381-401.

[16] Goldwasser, S., S. Micali, and R. Rivest, "A Paradoxical Solution to the Signature Problem," Proceedings of the 25th Annual Symposium on Foundations of Computer Science (FOCS'84), West Palm Beach Florida, pp. 441-449, October 1984.

[17] Rackoff, C., and D. Simon, "Non-Interactive Zero-Knowledge Proof of Knowledge and Chose Ciphertext Attack," *Advances in Cryptology - Crypto '91* Proceedings, LNCS, Vol. 576, J. Feingenbaum, (ed.) Springer Verlag, 1991.

[18] Spafford, E., "The Internet Worm Program: An Analysis," *Computer Communication Reviews*, vol. 19, no. 1, Jan. 1989, pp. 17-57.

new technology we absolutely must investigate its security implications including the possible re-definition of the adversary model.

An example of a new technology that requires proactive re-definition of the adversary model is that of large, wireless sensor networks[19]. Such networks, which have not been deployed yet, consist of a large array of sensors, which are fairly easily dropped on a particular field, which might be a hostile area. The sensor nodes could be dropped at specific desired locations, or could be dropped randomly over an entire target area. They are connected, possibly using routing protocols, to base stations that collect data and control the sensors' operation. Node and crypto key connectivity in neighbourhoods is established at network deployment and extension, and requires neither administrative intervention nor base station interaction. This is a basic *self-organised network* using key pre-distribution protocols for key sharing between various neighbours, simple neighbour discovery protocols, and path-key setup protocols for use between neighbours that might not have a shared key. Communication is done via radio broadcast.

An additional fact about sensor networks is that the nodes comprise very low cost commodity hardware. This implies that physical node shielding (e.g., to counteract pressure changes, temperature changes, and voltage changes) is not really practical because of very high relative costs. These costs are orders of magnitude higher than the cost of the node itself and hence impractical. As a consequence it's fairly easy to get to an internal state of a captured node. This implies that captured nodes can be replicated and replicas inserted into the network. Thus we have a new kind of vulnerability and a new kind of adversary. Let us examine how replica insertion could take place in practice.

Suppose that you have the neighbourhood where sensor nodes can communicate securely with each other using shared-key cryptography. Some of these nodes, such as node 3, share keys with other nodes in distant neighbourhoods although direct communication with these nodes is not possible. However, if node 3 is captured and replicated, its replica can be inserted in one of these distant neighborhoods where it already shares at least one key. Replicas can subvert many applications such as data aggregation.

Another application that may be subverted might be distributed sensing. Here multiple sensors in a neighbourhood sense the same globally visible event. Each sensor broadcasts a 1, if it senses a global event; if it doesn't sense the event, it does nothing. That is, a node doesn't broadcast a 0, and of course does not check for the non-existence of the event. T broadcasts are needed, where T is a positive threshold value no greater than the number M of nodes in the neighbourhood.

Frank Stajano. Can these sensors detect if repeated 1s come from different nodes or from the same nodes?

Reply. Yes, in fact part of the problem is to be able to handle such a situation. Now we have some operational constraints, such as that the absence of the

---

[19] Eschenauer, L., and V. D. Gligor, "A Key-Management Scheme for Distributed Sensor Networks," Proc. of the 9th ACM Conference on Computer and Communication Security (CCS), Nov. 2002, pp. 41-47.

global event cannot be signalled. Individual broadcasts cannot be authenticated, in other words, we don't have a PKI, and in fact, it may very well be that these sensors don't even share a key with each other. So this is one significant constraint. The threshold T is a constant set by design, it's not a function necessarily of M, except that it's always no greater (and typically much smaller) than M. All broadcasts are assumed to be reliable, and counted in sessions, so we have synchronous communication that enables vote counting. Votes from one session cannot propagate to other sessions, and duplicate votes in the same session are discarded. It is required that we have a broadcast of 1s from any subset of T out of M sensors to declare a event authentic, the T votes have to be authentic, and cannot be replayed across sessions. Of course, votes issued by nodes in other neighbourhoods cannot be counted.

What do we know about distributed sensing? This is a different problem than that of Byzantine agreements; e.g., T need be neither two thirds nor a simple majority of M. The votes are only 1s, not 0s or 1s. Hence the adversary models for the two problems are different.

The new adversary model differs from Dole-Yao's. To refresh your memory, the Dolev-Yao adversary controls effectively the network operation, it performs a man-in-the-middle attack, it can send and receive any message to and from any principal, and it can act as a legitimate user of the network. However, a Dolev-Yao adversary cannot perform unbounded computations (and neither would our new adversary), and cannot discover a legitimate principal's secrets, so it cannot become an insider and capture a node which actually has secret keys. Further, it cannot take over that node, it cannot coerce the behaviour of any legitimate principal in any way, and of course it cannot replicate nodes adaptively and modify the network and trust topologies.

An important observation is that we may have to put up with new countermeasures to new adversary attacks that do not necessarily succeed with probability 1. In the case of this new adversary we might not be able to offer absolute guarantees. We need to think more in terms of *emergent properties and protocols*. That is, properties that emerge out of the collaboration of multiple parties with a certain probability which can be much less than 1, but perhaps higher than 0.5. In other words, we may have to put up with security properties that in the past we considered basically unacceptable and with security mechanisms that are not fool-proof in the case of some new and powerful adversaries.

An additional observation is that we really need to decrease the time gap between the introduction of new vulnerabilities and the introduction of the new methods and tools that we use.

Simon Foley. How the sensor network adversary behaves really depends on the context of protocol use.

Reply. What I am suggesting here is that we define adversaries for specific protocols, and we show that a specific protocol is likely to succeed when used in the presence of the adversary with a certain probability, say 64.5%. We can actually show that such properties hold via careful analysis. In fact, we have an example of such analysis in this year's IEEE Security and Privacy Symposium[20], but as in that example, one would have to carry out such analyses on a case by case basis.

Ross Anderson. Well Virgil, this isn't entirely new, because the model that the adversary can eavesdrop any communication but not all of them is something people started talking about ten years ago, or more, in the context of the layer wars. The idea that any node can be compelled, but that the adversary cannot compel all of them, is certainly there in my paper nine years ago[21], and the idea that you can subvert any node or any link by compulsion or eavesdropping, was around for some time. I will speak briefly tomorrow about some of the stuff from my ICNP paper of last year[22], where we were doing protocol security analysis by simulation and showing that 97, and 98, and 99% of the keys are secure, but this is something that has been known for some time, and it's great if the community of people who do complexity theoretic proof finally catch up with it.

Reply. So, Ross you seem to make my point very violently. We've known about these vulnerabilities for a long time yet we have not modified the Dolev-Yao model in formal analysis, and I'm talking about *formal* protocol analysis not *complexity* based analysis. So clearly I agree with you.

Ross Anderson. Well, in formal analysis people let the engineers go ahead, and *then* theoreticians come in and analyse the system.

Reply. Yes, so the question is: how large is the time gap? My point is that this gap has been uncomfortably large, and I'm very happy that we're in very full agreement in this.

Mike Bond From my experiences trying to stir up some interest in the analysis of security APIs, I'm beginning to think that there is a fundamental divide between mathematical thought and computer science thought, or any new input, which is really about how uniquely can you express the problem. What worries me is that, with this gap, we may never be able to catch up because the problems that we pose, be they in sensor networks or wherever, just simply won't be sexy to mathematicians, if their spec cannot be written in one line. And the trouble with these things is that they're important problems, but they're just getting bigger, and even if you invent really ingenious notations with all sorts of little things above, and all sorts of little things below, and using Arabic and Russian characters, the problems are getting too big to pin them on peoples' walls ...

Reply. I agree with that. However, one reason why I started talking about sensor networks as new abstractions is to give an example of an anticipated

---

[20] Parno, B., A. Perrig and V.D. Gligor, "Distributed Detection of Node Replication Attacks in Sensor Networks," Proc. of the IEEE Symposium on Security and Privacy, Berkeley, California, May 2005, pp. 49-63.

[21] Ross Anderson, 1996, "The Eternity Service", pp 242–252 in Proceedings of Pragocrypt '96, CTU Publishing, Prague, ISBN 80-01-01502-5.

[22] Anderson, R.J., H. Chan and A. Perrig, "Key Infection: Smart Trust for Smart Dust," Proc. of 12th IEEE International Conference on Network Protocols (ICNP), Berlin, Oct. 2004, pp. 206-215.

technology. In fact, we may be going in totally the wrong direction, and these networks may never materialize, but at least we envision them and their new vulnerabilities. This is actually a very positive sign, and in the past this did not happen in a timely manner. In the past, new technologies were introduced sometimes knowing that they had vulnerabilities, and yet the decision was made to market these technologies anyway. These technologies introduced positive functionality, which was demanded by the market: a very good thing. However, nothing was done about alerting users regarding the new vulnerabilities, and about new stylised ways of using the new technologies that might counter those vulnerabilities. So our next conclusion might be that those time gaps, which I pointed out above, might actually be narrowed if we start anticipating some of the new technologies and their vulnerabilities.

Yvo Desmedt. One of the things you were talking about is that when you have these sensor networks, you have what you call global authorisation, and that has not been exploited.

Reply. That's actually an instance of what I call distributed sensing.

Michael Burmester. There is another problem when one uses replicated components, namely if there is some kind of common weakness in nodes. If you break one key in one node and all replicas use the same operating system, say you found a weakness in Microsoft, then you break the security of the entire system.

Reply. Right. I looked at this problem but not in sensor networks; I looked at it in the context of system survivability in the face of insider attacks. One of the problems that you seem to point out is that most of the proactive security protocols, for example password based key exchanges (and we've seen maybe five or six papers in the crypto area about password-authenticated key exchanges), use replicated servers. Here one has to have at least three servers because they use majority-based rules, but they have no diversity. In other words, as you point out, you break one of them and you break them all, so the fact that one has multiple replicated mono-culture servers render the protocol useless.

Michael Burmester. Unless they're independent.

Reply. But they cannot be independent if they use the same operating system, for instance.

Michael Burmester. It means you would have to use independent operating systems.

Reply. Essentially to achieve independence one has to use diversity. However, diversity is expensive. The major expense does not come primarily from equipment and programming costs, but from recurrent costs; e.g., personnel costs, such as those for different types of administrative skills for managing different operating systems. Thus, practical solutions cannot use three or four types of servers, and one has to do it with, say, two. This suggests that most proactive survivable crypto protocols using replication will be impractical due to high (e.g., recurrent) costs of diversity. New technologies are needed for achieving high resiliency with only two diverse systems, in the limit. That's a slightly different problem from the one you posed but it's equally interesting.

Safer Scripting Through Precompilation

Ben Laurie

A.L. Group
ben@algroup.co.uk

1 Introduction

One of the challenges in modern systems is the conflict between the desire to run software from a wide variety of untrusted sources and the need to prevent malicious activity by those scripts.

The current standard practice is to attempt to achieve this through permissions, but this has been shown repeatedly to fail in a variety of ways. If permissions are made too granular, they become impossible to configure and so tend to become useless. If they are less granular, loopholes appear through which malicious scripts can wriggle. In either case, providing useful defaults whilst still providing security has proved to be a daunting (or, perhaps, judging on the evidence, impossible) task.

Capabilities (in the object-capabilities sense [1]) allow authorisation through designation, a paradigm that permits fine-grained security without the need for tedious configuration. For historical reasons they have largely been ignored for the last few decades, meaning that there are few platforms that support them, none in wide use[1].

It has long seemed to me that the best way to introduce capabilities into existing environments is through modified versions of widely used programming languages, for two reasons – firstly, programmers are already familiar with the language, so the learning curve is shallow, and secondly because it is then possible to leverage the large body of existing code, through the process known as "taming".

I'd made several attempts at this, with little success – until I realised that the thing to do was to compile a modified version of the language into the unmodified base language, and introduce capabilities that way.

This paper outlines an experimental implementation of this idea for Perl. It assumes familiarity with Perl.

2 Overview

There are many different ways to express capabilities, but perhaps the simplest and most easily understood is to implement them as standard objects in an object-oriented language. Of course, they are not capabilities unless some of the

---

[1] Although the AS/400 is allegedly a capability system, this is not exposed to applications, sadly.

B. Christianson et al. (Eds.): Security Protocols 2005, LNCS 4631, pp. 284–288, 2007.

standard behaviour of O-O languages is eliminated. It should not be possible to "look inside" an object. There must be a distinction between public and private methods. Global variables should be avoided.

It is also necessary to create the capabilities in the first place, either externally to the system or through the use of "trusted" code.

Perl sounds like a fantastically unsuitable language to use as a basis for this, since there are so many ways to bend the rules in Perl. Interestingly, though, the use of a precompiler can quite easily enforce these rules precisely because Perl *is* so flexible.

The approach is to use Perl's introspection in the compiled code to ensure that each package can only access its own data, to add restrictions to what can be written by only accepting a subset of Perl, and to add slight extensions to the language to enable public and private methods to be created, and to differentiate between trusted and untrusted code.

The result is surprisingly useable, even with only a subset of the compiler implemented.

3   Objects

Perl isn't *really* object oriented, instead it uses the concept of blessing to link objects to code (via their package). This makes restricting access to objects quite easy. Every time CaPerl code attempts to de-reference a blessed object, using the `->` operator, the code emitted first checks the de-referenced object using the built-in `ref` function to see whether it "belongs" to the current package. If not, then the code `croaks`.

4   Public and Private Methods

In fact, because there is also the need to distinguish between trusted and untrusted code, CaPerl introduces the concept of a "trusted" method, as well as public and private ones. These are flagged with a keyword in the `sub` declaration, for example:

```
trusted sub some_sub { ... }
```

These are checked with the built-in `caller` function. A private method can only be called from the package it is defined in, a trusted method can only be called from trusted code and a public method can, of course, be called from anywhere.

Note that because the called routine checks the caller, CaPerl makes no restrictions on calling methods on objects in untrusted code. In fact, such calls are the only thing of interest untrusted code can do with an object not its own.

5   Trusted and Untrusted Code

Trusted code is needed both to create the environment for untrusted code and to "tame" existing plain Perl code. The two are distinguished by a compile-time flag. Trusted code is allowed to do things untrusted code cannot: it can load modules written in Perl rather than CaPerl, it can call trusted methods in CaPerl code and it can use certain dangerous built-in Perl functions.

When compile CaPerl code wants to check whether its caller is trusted or untrusted it does so simply by checking for a global variable in the package, which is introduced by the compiler.

6   Global Variables

Untrusted code should not be allowed access to globals. This is accomplished by the trivial expedient of prohibiting the use of ::!

7   Built-in Functions

Perl has a large number of dangerous built-in functions, so untrusted code is only permitted to run a subset. This is achieved by prohibiting function calls (as opposed to calling methods on objects), and then permitting a few selected functions, for example `shift`.

From a capabilities perspective, the term "dangerous" does include functions that would normally be considered quite harmless, such as `print` or `fileno`, so these can only be called by trusted code.

8   Taming

Existing Perl code is not, of course, written with capability discipline in mind, so it cannot be exposed directly to untrusted CaPerl code. The process of "capability-ising" such code is known in some circles as taming. What this generally consists of is writing a very thin wrapper around the desired module in CaPerl. This is perhaps best illustrated by an example, a partial wrapper for `Term::ReadLine`.

```
package Wrap::Term::ReadLine;

use untrusted Term::ReadLine;

trusted sub new {
    my $class=shift;

    my $self={};
    bless $self,$class;

    $self->{readline}=new Term::ReadLine();

    return $self;
```

```
}

public sub readline {
    my $self=shift;
    my $prompt=shift;

    croak if ref($prompt) ne '';
    return $self->{readline}->readline($prompt);
}

1;
```

Taming can also be used to produce safer versions of built-in functions, such as `opendir` or `read`.

9   Departures from Perl

Of course, the extra keywords used are changes from Perl, but there were also syntax restrictions introduced, partly to reduce the complexity of the compiler[2] and partly to reduce the risk that cleverly written code would somehow circumvent CaPerl's security.

One of the major changes was to remove the ability to call functions without parentheses. This turns out to be surprisingly hard to support, particularly since, for example, `f g(a),b` is ambiguous: it could mean `f(g(a),b)` or `f(g((a),b))`. It may be that a future version will reintroduce this, since it was surprising how often experienced Perl authors use this facility.

Currently, string interpolation is also omitted from the language. This doesn't restrict what can be written, but does make some things rather more verbose than in standard Perl. It isn't particularly hard to get this back, by parsing interpolated strings into a series of concatenations of the contents (in fact, this is what standard Perl does anyway).

Because Perl packages can introduce global functions, and access to built-ins must be restricted, the ability to use functions which are not object methods has been completely removed for untrusted code. This is not really a great handicap – at worst, the occasional function will have an unused extra parameter.

It is not currently clear how to support inheritance, so CaPerl currently doesn't.

10   An Example of CaPerl's Use

There are clearly many environments in which a restricted language such as CaPerl could be used. The "real world" I have been using in testing is CGI

---

[2] Perl's lexer, parser and compiler are rather horribly intertwined in order to permit some of Perl's shorthands and grammatical ambiguities.

scripts. The idea is that a web-server could be run which permits arbitrary users to upload CaPerl scripts, which are then run in a restricted environment.

The version I have been running passes these scripts just two capabilities. One is a capability which can be used to write HTML back to the HTTP client[3] and the other gives each script access to a subdirectory of its own – it can list the directory (that is, get the functionality normally provided by `opendir` and `readdir`), and open (for read or write) or create any file in that directory. It cannot, however, move outside its own directory – the code implementing the capability prevents that.

Why is this useful? Even this trivial example has at least one quite profound use – imagine two mutually untrusting parties want to enter into a contract – they want to exchange two binary objects. But since they do not trust each other, each cannot be sure that the other will release his object once his own has been released. The usual answer is to use a trusted intermediary, but now we have an automated solution. The two write a simple script that takes the two objects and stores them, but won't release them until they are both present. They upload this to a trusted machine which runs it in the environment described above. They can then execute their transaction without any further help, and the owner of the trusted machine can be sure that their script can do nothing bad, even though he has no control over its content at all.

11   Future Directions

Possible future work would include supporting Perl more completely and figuring out how to manage inheritance.

It would also be interesting to apply the approach to other scripting languages, such as Python.

Reference

1. Miller, M., Yee, K.-P., Shapiro, J.: Capability myths demolished (2003), http://zesty.ca/capmyths/

---

[3] Although I currently use a version of this which gives the script a very free hand to write what it wants on the returned page, it would be quite easy to make a version that only permitted a subset of HTML to be used, for example.

Safer Scripting Through Precompilation
(Transcript of Discussion)

Ben Laurie

A.L. Group

I'm going to talk about putting capabilities into scripting languages. The reason that you might want to put capabilities into a scripting language is because it would be good if we could get a script from any old place and run it without being worried that it was going to do something nasty to us, and more than that, we would like the script to do things that were actually useful, to read and write files, and make network connections, and all the things that we expect programs to be able to do, but *only* exactly what we want it to do.

Now there are these things called capabilities, which nobody likes anymore, that let you do this. So what do I mean by a capability? It's a word that's used by lots of people to mean lots of different things. Linux has things it calls capabilities which are actually a kind of fine-grained access control. Java has things that it calls capabilities which are actually another kind of fine grained access control, *i.e.* they are things that if you hold them you can do something, like open this particular file, or send to the printer, or whatever. In order to distinguish these capabilities, people who talk about them these days have started calling them object capabilities, which means that you can think about them as standard object oriented gadgets which are objects in an object oriented language that you cannot look inside, so they're opaque, and that you can't get a reference to unless you're given it, and the general way in which you use them is that you pass them around as parameters, any function can only use the capabilities which it has been passed, or which are within data structures it already owns, functions and models as functions on objects in general, so they usually have a single capability which they can look inside, and they're the only people who can look inside that capability. And if you write your program right, capabilities correspond to things like read a particular file, write to a particular socket, give me money, that kind of thing. Give me money obviously would be a more general distributed kind of capability, not just within a particular program, so would be represented by bits on the wire as well as a capability in the program.

Capabilities has been around for a very long time, and these days people who are interested in capabilities tend to be language theorists. But I think that if you want capabilities to be *used* you should put them into a language that people already know. Obviously you're going to have to tweak it a bit, because standard languages don't do capabilities; actually somebody told me Pascal would naturally do capabilities, but I did it in Perl. I chose Perl because you cannot possibly do it in C or C++, and Perl is probably the next most widely used language. In theory, Perl is very difficult to put capabilities in because it has so many ways of doing things in an ad hoc way, it's very uncontrolled, it doesn't really have objects as we would normally understand them, though you

B. Christianson et al. (Eds.): Security Protocols 2005, LNCS 4631, pp. 289–294, 2007.
© Springer-Verlag Berlin Heidelberg 2007

can simulate them. So I think if you can do it to Perl you can probably do it to most scripting languages. I know Perl really well, I did consider doing Python but I don't know Python as well, and I also had a very bad experience trying to do it to Python the last time round, when I hadn't thought of this approach.

The problem that you're trying to solve when you add capabilities to a scripting language is, you have to prevent anyone except the owner of an object from looking inside the object; you also have to prevent any way of finding objects other than creating them yourself, or being handed them by somebody else, you want all interaction through the operating system to be mediated by capabilities so that the stuff you don't trust can't do anything you don't expect, and as I said earlier, scripting languages do not make this easy at all. When I first tried this I tried to actually change the interpreter so that it would enforce these properties, and that turned out to be very difficult. Python was the language I tried to do it to, but it turns out that the interpreter doesn't know enough inside to actually enforce this kind of stuff, and Perl looked even less likely to work, so I didn't even try. I also didn't want to rewrite the interpreter from scratch because that's a pretty big job.

But I realised one day that Perl actually gives you a lot of access in the language *itself* to the stuff I need in order to do the checks I need to do, in particular, you can find out who called you, and you can also find out who owns an object, and since pretty much what you're trying to do is say, only the owner of an object can look inside it, and that is effectively the caller, or the current module that you're running; you can find out who has something using `ref`, and you can also find out who called you using `caller`. I realised that what you wanted to do is, you wanted to take a Perl like language, you have to add a few key words because you want to add things like private functions, you want to add the concept of trusted and untrusted code, the idea there being that trusted code can load Perl libraries as opposed to CaPerl libraries, and it can call operating system functions like print, open, read, that kind of stuff, and untrusted code can only access CaPerl libraries.

People do this often these days; E, for example, is actually implemented on top of Java, and rather than rewrite all the OS interface in E, what they do is a thing called taming where you take the existing libraries and wrap them with trusted code (which checks that the parameters you've been passed are OK), and you restrict the functions that you can call to the ones that you think are safe, and so, just like that, taming is done with trusted CaPerl in my system.

Frank Stajano. At the start you said you wanted to run scripts you knew nothing about. Would these scripts be written in CaPerl, or would they be written in Perl, and then you do something with them?

Reply. They would be written in CaPerl. So what you would do is compile them, wrap them with some trusted Perl.

Frank Stajano. So these people who you don't know anything about, you still have persuaded them to write CaPerl?

Reply. Yes, on the basis that if you want me to run it, it has to be in CaPerl. If I'm the only guy who does it I'm not going to get very far, but hopefully other people will see the virtue of this approach.

CaPerl is written in Perl; the actual compiler is 1300 lines, there's a grammar, which is a Perl grammar, that's 340 lines, it doesn't do everything that Perl does, and actually the vast majority of this 1300 lines is building the parse tree, and printing it back out again, mostly without modification, but in some cases with minor modification. So basically that's as far as what I'm doing, if you want to see some CaPerl, I have some, do you want to see some CaPerl, yes, obviously you do. If you don't write Perl this might be kind of hard to read, but if you do it should look pretty standard.

So this is a function that reads a directory, it is handed a single capability, which is the directory capability, and I'll show you the wrapper for this in a minute. This is actually part of my test bed so when I run the regression tests this is supposed to produce a known result. So this is just standard, you say what the package is, which is just because you have to, CaPerl actually forces you to say the right thing there, you create an object, you bless it, Perl aficionados will notice I have not said which package I bless that in, and that's because you're not allowed to if you're untrusted code, and then you return the object. The read function is called by the wrapper, gets passed the object, so directory capability, it says, open the directory, creates an array, runs through the files in the directory, and pushes them onto the array, and then it returns to the array. Perl aficionados will also notice that I've got brackets in the push which you don't normally, and that's because I had to restrict the grammar, because Perl grammar is very much not properly parse-able, and does lots of nasty tricks inside the actual Perl interpreter to make some things work, and I decided to just drop them. Now when I first wrote this I actually printed what was in the directory, and checked the output, but of course you can't print in an untrusted code because that's an operating system call, so it died, which is what should happen, and it was good.

Here's the actual wrapper. First of all it pulls in the tamed version of `opendir`, so in other words that's been wrapped by a trusted Perl library that produces the capability that corresponds to `opendir`. This stuff is just creating the test environment: removing the test directory, creating the test directory, putting a couple of files in it. That creates the capability for this test directory, so it creates a wrapper that is on that one directory, so the wrapped code can only look at that directory, no other. It then uses the thing that I am going to test, creates an instance of it, calls it, gets the file list back, and then just checks that the file list is what it expects, and dies if it isn't, there is the regression test, and then it cleans up after itself, so that's a simple one.

My more cunning stunt is to run a CGI under Apache, because I claim I will take any script in CaPerl, and compile it, and allow you to access it over the Web, running on my computer, and this is the wrapper that goes around the script that you have given me. So, it's a little more elaborate; CGI is a Perl module that does useful stuff, so it gets parameters from the URL, it gives you functions for constructing web pages, and things like that. This construct here uses untrusted CGI, trusted code signals that it actually knows it's loading an untrusted library rather than a CaPerl library by saying, use untrusted, if you didn't say that when you try to load this it would die.

So here it creates an instance of a CGI, then it checks that the URL isn't doing anything naughty by restricting it to a safe character set, so you can't put dot dots or slashes, or anything like that in it.

So what this wrapper actually does is it takes the untrusted code and it gives us a directory, which it can use as a playground, and in that directory it can read files, it can write files, and it can scan the directory, so the untrusted thing has a long term store on my machine. So it works out where that directory's going to be, which is just the same name as the script, but in a different directory obviously, creates it, and then it creates this capability, which is not a wrapper, this is a restricted object that will allow you to scan a directory, and create files in that directory, but not directories in that directory, and you can't move out of the directory, and this is what it's all about basically. It creates an instance of that on the directory I just created that corresponds to the untrusted script, and it does something kind of strange here which is it pulls in the actual text of the untrusted code and then evaluates it, and that's just to be really sure that we're pulling in the right file, because Perl will actually go and look for it if you don't do something like this on the path, and so you might end up being fooled into running a library file if you don't do that. Then it creates an instance of the untrusted code, and it tells it to go, and it gives it just two capabilities which are the CGI wrapper, and the directory wrapper, so the only thing it can do is it can read parameters from the command line, it can write stuff to the browser's screen so it can interact with the user, and it can read and write files in that directory.

And this is an example of a wrapped CGI that creates a form which lets you enter a filename and some contents, and gives you a button that if you press it will create that filename with the content that you put into the form. So it creates the object, here's the two capabilities getting passed in, checks that it can actually open the directory (it should always be able to because the wrapper pretty much guarantees that it's able to, but that's just being thorough). This bit is what gets executed once you have pressed the button; it takes the content, tells the directory capability to create a file (again, the directory capability will check that that filename isn't anything silly, doesn't have any dot dots or slashes, or anything bad that might allow you to escape from the directory you're trying to use), writes to the file, and then tells you it did so. This bit here gives you a list of the files in the directory and it gives you a way to click on a file name, and if you do, it shows you what's in it. And that's it. And I think that's the end of my slides, so any questions.

Frank Stajano. I am not sure I really understand how unsafe operations are prevented. I assume that anything you don't wrap can still be done, otherwise you would have to find a wrapper for everything?

Reply. Only trusted codes can still do it, so all system calls are banned in untrusted code, loading of standard Perl libraries is banned in untrusted code, you can only load an untrusted code, trusted libraries, and in fact only libraries that are marked as ones that untrusted code can load, and you can only access the capabilities you were given. So we make a distinction between the stuff that I wrote, which is trusted and can do operating system calls (and I can create libraries that do operating system calls, and capabilities to those libraries), and the untrusted code, which is the stuff you wrote, and that I run. It's actually marked as trusted or untrusted when you compile it, so you give me some code, I compile it as untrusted code, and then it's unable to do system calls, or any of that stuff, and it really only has access to the ones with the capabilities that I hand it from my trusted wrapper.

Frank Stajano. So how do I know which function calls I can make?

Reply. That's defined by your environment, so the CGI in this case makes the promise that it will give you two capabilities, one of them is the CGI capability, and the other is a directory that you can read and write. If I wanted to provide an environment that was richer, for example, I might give you access to a database, let's say, then I would just add a third parameter to the call that runs the untrusted code that was a database capability. You can imagine other systems where you say there's this menu of capabilities that I am prepared to provide to you, and when you upload your untrusted scripts you also say, by the way I want a directory of my own, a database, a file open dialogue to present to the user, whatever, and obviously it would only put things on the menu that you were prepared to allow untrusted code to use, and the idea is that that's the only things it can do, nothing else.

George Danezis. I'm not sure how far the loading a library goes because in interpreted languages there is not much difference between, you know, a piece of code and a string ...

Reply. You can't run `eval` in untrusted CaPerl, so you can't execute a random string. In fact I think that you could allow `eval`, but instead of doing what Perl normally does, which is to run Perl, it would run the compiler, produce compiled CaPerl, and then `eval` that, which should be a safe thing to do; you'd run the compiler as untrusted obviously. Slightly awkward because really CaPerl needs more context than Perl does for a random piece of code.

Bruce Christianson. Are capabilities just like addresses, or do they have parameters as well?

Reply. Capabilities are like objects, so they're the address of an object, when you create it you can give it parameters certainly, and any function you call on that object you can also give parameters.

Bruce Christianson. Are there restrictions on the parameters that you can pass on?

Reply. No, anything you've got you can pass around; that's kind of the essence of capabilities.

Richard Clayton: Do you not end up having to be basically extremely clever in understanding what the script requires? Or do we have some list at the top of what capabilities it will need to run?

Reply. Yes.

Richard Clayton. Do you not also have to be moderately clever in terms of understanding the bad effects of giving it too many capabilities? What if it says, oh I'd like you to go and read /etc/password, and oh by the way, I'd like to open a socket.

Reply. Well if you had "read /etc/password" on your menu of things that it's allowed to do, then you're probably an idiot, but you might have good reason for allowing that.

Richard Clayton. Well you might turn up with something that says it pretty prints my Perl programs, but instead you're reading all my files. It seems to me that apart from a very restricted set of things like your directory example, it's hard to do anything both safe and useful. This directory thing really doesn't interact with me at all, they're all your stuff and not mine; I don't see what the value is of running that script from your machine on mine, because you're basically just providing a little bubble from your machine onto mine, so you're just using them some computing resources, and nothing else. You don't get anything useful out of this because you could leave some files behind at the end.

Reply. There are people who make pretty good business out of just giving computer resources to people, and that's GRID for example, and you know, there's a lot of money in GRID.

But secondly, a typical example of where you would have real interaction with the computer is where, exactly as you say, somebody says, I will give you this untrusted code that pretty prints your Perl, and what I would do is I would pass it a capability to a file open dialogue, which is to find the Perl that you're going to pretty print, and the user would choose a piece of Perl that they want it to be able to read through the file open dialogue, and the file open dialogue will return the capability to that file, that's actually one of the strengths of capabilities is that designation is authority, so the fact the user said it can read this file is all you need to do to give it permission to read that file, but it cannot read any other file. Does that answer your question?

Richard Clayton. It was the writing of files that was worrying me more.

Reply. Well you do the same thing, you give it a file open dialogue for writing files, and the user chooses a file it's allowed to write, and because it's the writing files file open dialogue, the user knows the file that he chooses is going to be overwritten. You already have to trust the user to not shoot themselves in the foot. But although you can do that, I was actually thinking of this system more for operating within semi-restricted environments, *i.e.* where I have an application that's running on my local machine that wants to accept scripts from other applications that it communicates with, probably the same type of application, in order to do something funky between the two copies, so things like diary synchronisation with extra bits would be an example, and yes, and I think it's an open question whether you can build arbitrarily complex systems with these kinds of capabilities, because, like I say, they've been around for 30 years, but have been pretty unpopular for that time. Nobody's really written any big stuff, though there is actually a whole capability-based operating system called KeyKOS which is used for doing real things, and apparently works pretty well; but nobody's allowed to use it.

Implementing a Multi-hat PDA

Matthew Johnson and Frank Stajano

University of Cambridge

Abstract. We describe our work in progress aimed at implementing a multi-hat PDA. Our current prototype is based on SELinux and KDE and accepts a proximity token, in the form of a Bluetooth cellphone, as an alternative authentication method. We analyse in detail the suitability of several alternatives for the graphical environment and underlying OS and we discuss a variety of interesting implementation issues that arose during development.

1 Introduction

At the previous Security Protocols workshop one of us (Stajano [13]) described a "multi-hat" PDA as a design reconciling security and usability.

The central idea of that work was that, although the PDA is the archetypal single-user machine, it may be useful for its owner to be able to assume several roles (referred to as "hats"), each with specific security requirements. Hats map naturally to operating-system-level user-ids, each with its own password—or, more generally, access credentials.

The multi-hat PDA supports several concurrent graphical sessions, only one of which is accessible at a time. It is possible to switch from one session to another without closing the first session, so long as one presents the credentials of the hat owning the second session; on coming back to the first or any other suspended session, though, one must again present the credentials for that session.

There is a special "null" hat which can be accessed without any credentials. It corresponds to a "guest" user-id or to an anonymous account. Being able to switch to the null hat session at any time with no hassle to access stateless applications or briefly to lend the machine to others is one of the features that improve the usability of the multi-hat PDA without compromising its security.

The work in progress described in this paper aims to build a multi-hat PDA. Ideally, our projected implementation target is a machine from the Sharp Zaurus SL-C family, a series of StrongARM powered devices that natively run Linux and Qtopia. In that perspective, our multi-hat PDA will have to be able to run native unmodified Zaurus applications. At the prototype stage, however, for convenience of development we have chosen to target a standard desktop or laptop PC. We are also refraining from committing prematurely to a particular graphical environment such as Qtopia, since only the experience gained while implementing the prototype will allow us to choose the technically most suitable alternative.

B. Christianson et al. (Eds.): Security Protocols 2005, LNCS 4631, pp. 295–307, 2007.
© Springer-Verlag Berlin Heidelberg 2007

2 Operating System Alternatives

2.1 Windows XP

Microsoft Windows XP was initially the closest to what we are aiming for because of its "Fast User Switching" feature [2]. This functionality—having multiple users running at the same time and being able to switch between them without having to log out or close the applications that other users are running—had been available in Linux for some time at the console level, while Richardson et al [9] extended multiple users to graphical logins in the context of the X-based Teleport System and, later, VNC [10]. The innovation introduced by Windows XP was to integrate this with the login manager, screen-saver and desktop. This has many of the features that we require such as allowing multiple users with differing permissions to run sessions simultaneously and providing a central method for changing between them. However, there is no easy method to hook our own events, such as lid closing or proximity events, into the switching system.

To implement a session for the null hat we need a system either supports users without a password, or allows logging in without having to provide the password. Windows XP supports password-less users. If the user without password is the only one then the login screen will not even be displayed: the user will be logged in directly. When there are multiple users one must still be explicitly selected, but no password will be prompted for if the user has none. Windows allows for some credentials other than passwords (for example smart cards), but the range supported is fairly small and adding support for other credentials is non-trivial.

Windows has a fairly comprehensive system of file permissions which is reasonably expressive and fine-grained—it will certainly allow us to restrict the less privileged hats as desired. We also, however, need to limit the network access of each hat. Windows XP has a built in firewall, but this is designed for a different problem. The firewall can restrict which ports and applications can access the network, but not which user can access the network, which is what we need to be able to restrict. The user and group policy editor allows an administrator to restrict many of the operating system features on a per-user basis, including remote access of the computer over the network, but cannot restrict which users can make outgoing connections.

The ultimate goal of this project is to produce a system on a PDA. Microsoft provide a version of Windows to run on PDAs, but this is Windows CE, rather than Windows XP, and doesn't support the permissions and Fast User Switching features we need. This, combined with the other problems, means that while possibly being the closest existing system to what we need, Windows cannot easily be used as the base for our initial prototype.

2.2 Linux

The free Linux operating system was the next system we looked at. Linux has the advantage that, due to its open source nature, it can be extended very easily. We looked at several methods to achieve our aims in Linux—most basic distributions are unsuitable in a couple of ways, but fortunately these have been supplemented by other projects that build on Linux. Firstly we needed to improve the permissions model that is in use by Linux. Linux uses a fairly coarse-grained POSIX discretionary access control mechanism. We looked for solutions that provided more fine-grained control over the permissions granted to the various hats and that allowed us to define other restrictions such as per-user network access, things which it is not possible to do in normal Linux. Secondly, the multi-user support is not very well integrated—there should be a centralised way to manage sessions and multiple users.

Xen. The Xen Virtual Machine Monitor [3] provides several virtual machines with strong separation between them. Each hat would be given its own virtual machine and Xen would provide the strong protection properties between hats. The idea is to offer essentially a separate machine to each hat, with a separate operating system and application suite. Network access can be restricted by using a firewall in the controlling domain. Xen would fulfil the security requirements, but has several practical disadvantages in this case. Because Xen is providing a different machine for each hat, the physical resources must be partitioned a priori. This is particularly a problem because Xen uses a static memory partitioning scheme, while PDAs usually do not have very much memory. Having an entirely separate operating system for each hat implies substantial overhead in disk, CPU and memory usage because there is very little which can be shared. It reduces the effectiveness of techniques such as shared libraries as these must be loaded separately for each domain. Xen is also currently only available on the Intel x86 and AMD-64 architectures, whereas we are intending to produce a prototype on an ARM-based PDA. Porting Xen would require significant work.

SELinux. SELinux [8] is an extra security layer for Linux, developed by the NSA and distributed in the form of patches to the Linux kernel. SELinux is a Mandatory Access Control System that uses Role-Based Access Control.

The feature we are most interested in is the role-based access control. This means that a user may have several roles, which could be shared by other users and the access permissions are defined in terms of roles. These roles are inherited even when the UNIX user may not be, which means a process started in one role always has that role associated with it when checking permissions. The idea of roles maps very closely onto the idea of hats we are using.

SELinux provides hooks for restricting the right to view or write arbitrary files, execute programs, bind to network ports and send or receive network packets. These permissions can be granted based on the user, role, program used and object type and can represent any of the protections we wish to implement. Several users can have the same role for permissions which are based on the role, while having other permissions distinct per user. These permissions are all enforced using the general SELinux mandatory access controls.

The overhead for SELinux is a lot smaller than that of Xen. Because when using SELinux all sessions use the same operating system instance, there is no need to statically partition the RAM between the security domains, the normal operating system dynamic memory allocation is sufficient. There is also no unnecessary replication of system processes across hats, whereas in Xen each operating system daemon must reappear in each hat and has to use CPU time for what is essentially duplicated effort. In addition, read only code pages can still be shared between domains which can execute the same processes.

The permissions system is also sufficiently flexible that nothing needs to be duplicated on disk because each process and user can be given access to exactly what they need.

Because SELinux is implemented as a security layer internal to Linux and uses generic extended attributes to store all the extra policy and label data, it is completely independent of the architecture and hardware that it is run on. This allows us to use SELinux on any system on which standard Linux will run. The PDAs we are using to build this system already run a port of Linux which makes SELinux an ideal candidate.

KDE. The permissions system used to govern the access given to each hat is fairly independent of the user interface used to control sessions for the hats and the method used to control switching between the sessions.

Session switching has only recently made its way into the UNIX world in a centralised and integrated way through the K Desktop Environment (KDE). The facility is functionally similar to that in Windows XP. KDE uses multiple X Window System sessions and provides integrated GUI management of the sessions. These can be queried and controlled via the K Display Manager (KDM) and widgets on the desktop allow the user to easily change between the available sessions, or create a new one. KDM provides a remote interface by means of a FIFO and that can be used to control the creation of and switching between sessions.

KDE also provides a comprehensive remote interface to all the GUI features within each session. Each application registers methods which can be called remotely with the Desktop Communications Protocol (DCOP) server, which allows these methods to be queried and executed. DCOP calls can be used to send commands to any application and also perform session management, screen blanking and locking and so on.

As regards support for a public user without credentials, Linux makes it difficult to create a user with a blank password—the standard tools for setting passwords reject a blank password. If the password is manually set to nothing, however, then logging in will not prompt for a password. We would rather not do this in general because there may be some remote interface to the PDA and only local access should be without credential. KDM provides an interface to create a session for a user which can be provided with a password. This allows our system to create the public session without requiring any credentials, but also protect the system in other ways.

Mac OS X. Recent Apple operating systems have a similar fast user switching feature to Windows. Since the Panther release you have been able to switch between simultaneously running users (with suitable Apple eye-candy), being prompted for a password as necessary. Despite this we haven't considered Mac OS X a good candidate. Mac OS is a proprietary operating system and Apple do not provide any version of it on a PDA. This may be because their graphical environment is heavily dependent on powerful graphics hardware, which is generally not found in PDAs. The lack of portability to our desired platform makes OS X a bad choice.

The system we have, therefore, chosen as the basis for the initial prototype is Linux with the NSA Security-Enhanced patches running KDE with KDM. This will allow us to run standard X-based applications. Most Linux-based PDAs don't run standard X, however, but instead run an embedded environment like Qtopia or GPE. To run applications for these PDAs unmodified we will have to produce a system which will work with those environments. This is discussed later in section 6.3.

3   The Hats

The multi-hat system is introduced primarily in order to allow easy access to the null hat that holds no secret data. A minimal multi-hat system will just have the null hat and another hat holding some secret data. The main distinction is therefore between the null hat and the others. Any further differentiations between hats will be implementation-specific and our security policy allows for this.

3.1   The Null Hat

The null hat is publicly accessible and provides services for which no credential is needed. These applications and services are ones for which the Big Stick security model [12, p. 96] is appropriate. Typical PDAs contain several applications like this, including a calendar (not diary), calculator and world time function, as well as most games. These applications are all stateless and do not use any resources which may be scarce or costly (for example, Internet access). The null hat can, therefore, always be accessed without presenting any credentials and one should be able to do this easily and simply. The default session to which the system changes if the user does not have any valid credentials is that of the null hat.

3.2   Restricted Hats

The security policy defined here will be flexible enough to allow any number of restricted hats, each of which can be given a different set of permissions. In our implementation of this we give an example set, although this is by no means canonical or the most that can be done. These hats will have access to resources that the null hat will not be able to use, such as communication over the network, or access to files on the PDA. Any stateful applications, particularly those which store credentials for other systems such as email clients, should be in a restricted hat but it is up to each implementation to assign the desired security policy for what each hat is allowed to do.

We provide as an example two forms of restricted hat. The first one contains particularly secure personal data and always requires a credential to change into. In our implementation this credential is a password. The other restricted hat contains applications with network access and that can store some state, but do not have access to the private data. This will have a more relaxed security policy which may not always require explicit passwords to access.

4   The Multi-hat Security Policy Model

The multi-hat idea is described concisely but completely in the rules of the following security policy model.

Rule 1. Hats. The machine supports a finite number of hats[1]. One of them is the special case known as the null hat[2]. Every hat, except the null hat, is associated with some credentials.

Rule 2. Sessions. The machine supports several simultaneous sessions[3], each belonging to a hat. Each session can be either active or locked[4]. At any one time, at most one session is active. The user can only interact with the active session. When the machine is in sleep mode, in hibernation mode or off, no session is active.

Rule 3. Session unicity. For each hat there is at most one session[5].

Rule 4. Hat selection. There is a convenient way[6] to select any of the hats of the machine for the purpose of switching to (or launching, if necessary) the session of that hat.

Rule 5. Switching sessions. To make a new session active, the credentials of the hat owning that session must be presented.

In this policy we do not specify what will qualify as appropriate authentication credentials, as we believe this should be both implementation-specific and also subject to change. In our prototype system, authentication credentials mainly consist of traditional user-name and password combinations, but we look forward to using other more convenient authentication methods. Some of these are discussed next.

---

[1] Hats may be considered equivalent to roles or to OS-level user-ids.

[2] The null hat, reachable without credentials, corresponds to an anonymous "guest" account.

[3] A session corresponds to a graphical login or "desktop". Within a session, the private data of the corresponding hat is accessible. The null hat has no private data.

[4] When a session is locked, all the data that is private to the hat owning that session is inaccessible to anyone without the credentials for that hat. This may be implemented by encrypting the data of a locked session with a key derived from the hat's credentials. Note that the null hat session has no private data and therefore locking it has little practical effect.

[5] This rule is not logically necessary (one could conceive opening several sessions for the same hat) but it makes the model simpler and easier to understand—and therefore more usable.

[6] This may be implemented with dedicated buttons, a scroll wheel, a top level menu or any other appropriate user interface device.

4.1   Authentication by Proximity Token

One of the methods of authentication we have investigated is the use of a locality-based token. The credential is deemed to have been presented whenever the token is within a certain distance of the PDA. We have a working prototype of a proximity-based system that tracks the position of a 'master token' using Bluetooth. The master token can be any Bluetooth-capable device: we use a mobile phone. This is done by tracking the signal strength of the Bluetooth connection between the PDA and our token. This is similar to the system implemented by Corner and Noble [6], but does not require custom hardware or protocols because it uses the existing Bluetooth protocol found in many devices.

Bluetooth provides some authentication and encryption in the protocol itself. A shared secret (PIN) which is input manually into each of the two devices the first time an encrypted connection is requested. The PIN is used, along with nonces sent in the initial handshake, to generate a shared secret. This secret is used in future connections to authenticate the devices to each other and to secure the connection. If an attacker can read the traffic during the initial handshake then the security is entirely reliant on the strength of the PIN. Ideally the initial pairing operation should be done somewhere the communications cannot be snooped. For any extra security another protocol would have to be run on top of the Bluetooth protocol, which we decided not to do because we wanted our system to be compatible with all Bluetooth devices which wouldn't need to be programmable. With recent devices such as smart phones it would be possible to implement a separate protocol using a more secure system.

This still doesn't address the Man in the Middle (MITM) attack which is possible in this system. We could envisage an attacker having stolen the PDA relaying the Bluetooth protocol to an agent standing within range of the token to cause the PDA to unlock. This is more subtle than the conventional MITM attack on key agreement protocols, because the attacker is not able to read any data. He can, however, convince the PDA that it is close to the token. Bluetooth uses pre-shared keys in the form of the PIN and this shared secret is used to bootstrap the authentication. However, the attacker does not need to be able to read the traffic: all he is interested in is relaying the authentication challenge from the PDA to the authentication token and sending the replies back. This is one of the reasons we have not used the proximity token as authentication for all of the restricted hats—even with this attack access would not be gained to personal or particularly sensitive data.

A number of people have suggested solutions to this problem. Brands and Chaum [5] proposed to calculate the maximum distance between prover and verifier given the propagation speed of the communications channel. More recently, Sastry et al [11] proposed a solution based on ultrasound echos and measuring the response time. A different solution to this problem is given by Alakassar [1]. He points out that being able to snoop the communication channel is required to perform this MITM attack and proposes a probabilistic channel hopping scheme which would require an attacker to be able to relay a large spectrum and be technically infeasible. Most of these systems have the same disadvantage as Corner and Noble's proposal because they require custom hardware.

An approach which doesn't necessarily require custom hardware was suggested in 1990 by Beth and Desmedt [4]. Their protocol requires each participant to reply at a fixed time interval agreed between the two. If the attacker requires a non-zero time to forward the signal, then the attack will be detected because responses will take too long. This protocol, unlike many others, can allow computation by both the prover and the verifier because the time delay can be set appropriately. The technical requirements for this approach are merely that the transmission time of the communications medium is already known by the participants and that the jitter in transmission times is smaller than the expected time the attacker needs to forward the signal. Unfortunately, the link layer echo times recorded vary between 26.38ms and 48.85ms at close range and up to 60.8ms at longer range. In comparison the time to transmit a packet over a fixed wired network can be as little as 0.1ms and even for a wireless network only a few ms (average 3ms in tests). Such a large variance makes this approach not applicable to a Bluetooth-based strategy.

4.2   Automatic Switching

The security policy above governs what happens when a change of hat is attempted. This can be caused by a user selecting a new hat using a keyboard combination or a menu item, or by a system event triggering a transition.

Events such as selecting sleep mode and turning the PDA off will cause active sessions to be locked following Rule 2. Other events, such as closing the PDA, might trigger other actions, for example switching to the null hat session. We have produced an extensible and configurable event handler to manage these events and associate them with actions. The event handler can also be used to manage the presence or absence of our authentication token.

Table 1 illustrates how these events cause actions to be executed on each of the sessions in our sample implementation.

Table 1. Events and Actions on Sessions in Prototype

| Event | Effect on Session: | | |
	Null Hat	Limited Hat	Restricted Hat
Power Off/On	Create Session and Activate	Create and Lock Session	Create and Lock Session
Sleep	Activate		Lock Session
Lid Close	Activate		Lock Session
Token Out Of Range	Activate	Lock Session	Lock Session
Token In Range		Unlock and Activate Session	

5   The Prototype

The prototype we have working at the moment is implemented on an Intel-based laptop using Linux and the K Desktop Environment as a basis. This prototype demonstrates the above switching policy at work controlling access to three hats.

As per our specification we have a stateless null hat offering a null hat session which has no network access. Certain events, such as closing the lid and suspending the machine, cause switching to the null hat session and locking all the other sessions.

The hats are implemented using three different users which have corresponding different SELinux roles. The null hat user/role is given permission to run only a small set of binaries, which are essentially all stateless applications. No network access is allowed, and file-system permissions are restricted to only read the programs and libraries required to run the stateless applications.

The other two hats have users/roles with progressively more permissions allowed, Both are given network access, but have separate home directories and may not read each other's. Most applications can be executed by either, but a few can be launched only by one.

We have produced an event-handling system which uses the exposed interfaces in KDE and KDM to do session management. It can switch sessions, lock sessions and automatically log a user in on a given display. The event handler has configuration files for each session, for each event the system should be able to handle and for each action that can be performed on a session. Individual event handlers can be configured to call any of the actions on any of the sessions. The event handlers get passed all of the state of the system and can query the authentication mechanisms.

The interface is managed via KDM and KDE. On boot an event is triggered which logs in each user to a new session and locks the sessions for all but the null hat. KDE has menu options which list all the open sessions (via a call to KDM) and will allow the user to change between them. Our event handler makes sure that when the session is changed all the other sessions are locked. Various other events (mainly triggered by ACPI events such as suspend and lid-closing) are passed to the event handler which may cause the computer to activate a different session (usually that of the null hat).

Checking of credentials is done by our session-switching logic which can use DCOP calls to unlock the session without providing a password if other credentials were sufficient.

Section 3.2 describes our sample policy with two types of restricted hat. This is partly to demonstrate what can be done with the system, but also to provide access to common programs using an easier authentication method than passwords while still protecting more sensitive data. The way that system events affect the sessions for the restricted hats can be seen in table 1.

The Bluetooth proximity token uses a background demon process which maintains an open connection to the token. Each Bluetooth device has a 48 bit unique public identifier. During the initial pairing procedure, the user manually gives the computer the identifier of the chosen token. The demon constantly monitors the signal strength to the token and, when the signal crosses a user-defined threshold, the demon triggers an event in the event handler. The demon can also be queried to return the current connection state. The Bluetooth monitoring demon will be released as a stand-alone program under the GPL soon.

The prototype was implemented on a laptop rather than a PDA due to ease of use and hardware availability. We have, however, been very careful to use only elements which are going to be easy to port to a PDA. We have already said that the class of PDAs we are aiming this system at have existing Linux ports and many of them support the X Window System as an option for display. Both SELinux and KDE are independent of the underlying hardware and simply work on top of Linux. Bluetooth is also hardware that is often found in modern PDAs.

6   Further Work

The prototype demonstrates that this system is possible, but there is a lot more work for us to do in this area. Our current prototype is on an Intel IA32 laptop rather than a PDA which is the ultimate aim of the project. Because of the components we have chosen it will be comparatively easy to port the current system, but just that does not fulfil our goals because we still cannot run the original PDA applications. Section 6.3 contains remarks on using graphical environments other than the X Window System.

6.1   Authentication Methods

We have in general so far only talked about "Authentication Methods" without going into more specific details. A traditional candidate for this is, as we have said, passwords. We are, however, trying to get away from using passwords as they are inconvenient for the user to remember and enter. Therefore, we continue to explore alternative types of credentials. Our system uses a proximity-based token but it would be simple to integrate a secure contact-token like the Dallas iButton, or a more traditional smart-card. Most PDAs come with a compact-flash slot which can be fitted with a smart-card reader.

It is also possible to use some sort of biometric authentication. There are a number of companies selling mice and even PDAs with built in fingerprint readers. When the user tries to change to a restricted hat, the PDA could prompt them to touch the fingerprint reader. It would even be possible to have the system monitor the fingerprint reader and cause the PDA to automatically change to the session of a different hat.

This leads to an interesting new problem with the authentication. Ideally we would simplify the user interaction as much as possible, which is one reason for introducing tokens and biometrics. This reduces the steps required to change hat to two—select session and present token—or even to one step if the action of presenting the token causes the system to change hat. Automatic switching like this is good from the point of view of simplifying the interaction, but produces the problem of knowing which session to change to. In the system we have outlined here it is possible to have several hats which require the same credentials. Therefore, if those credentials are presented, there needs to be a method of selecting which session should be activated. Also, in general it is not desirable to authenticate by taking a password (or other credential) and then searching the possible users to see which (if any) the credential matches. We have taken the view here that presenting a token like this causes an event to occur which can be configured by the user. One of our future research areas will be into how best to handle this case.

6.2   Filesystem Protection

Just restricting logical access to data through the operating system is not enough to secure the data. Because the PDA is a small, portable device we are expecting the attacker to have physical access to it for at least a small amount of time. If the attacker only has a few minutes of physical access there is not a lot which he can do to bypass the operating system security, assuming the boot loader and BIOS are protected; but, if the PDA has been stolen, the attacker has a lot more time in which to work. In that case it is not hard to remove the permanent storage from the machine and connect it to another system to read the data directly.

Because of this we are planning to use an encrypting file system which can be integrated with the authentication system, similar to that in Corner and Noble [6]. In this case rather than just linking the encryption to a proximity token we will integrate it with the switching and authentication logic. A proximity token is just one option which may be used.

6.3   Decoupling from X

The system that we have demonstrated uses multiple X sessions, one for each hat. This is a bit wasteful on resources but, more importantly, there are several methods of changing session such as the Alt-Control-F key combination which changes between virtual terminal and are handled at a much lower level than the one we are dealing with. These are hard to trap and mediate without modifying the underlying operating system. There are various approaches which can be taken to ensure that any non-active sessions are kept locked and require credentials to change into but these are all inherently fragile and susceptible to being bypassed. Directly preventing this requires a lot of low-level alteration of the Linux kernel. A much better system would be one where we control all the methods of changing between the various sessions. Modelling the sessions as different virtual desktops within the same X server would be a better approach, the window manager in this case would have to mediate the desktop-switching and check for credentials. However, if there are several applications in the same X server then they have a lot of control over each other. This is not compatible with our security policy which says that applications with different hats cannot access each other.

One possible solution to this was proposed by Kilpatrick et al [7]. This would be a system by which all the X protocol operations are mediated by SELinux-based permissions. This would allow several users to have windows in the same X server without also being able to access each other's windows. This would enable multiple users without requiring multiple X servers. Some work would have to be done on this, however, since the model that Kilpatrick is trying to implement is separating individual applications from each other—all of which may be seen by the user—and not coping with a user who may change role during the session.

The Kilpatrick approach is a very general solution with per-application granularity, which we don't necessarily need. There are some current research projects involving X proxy servers which could provide several hats and only allow one of them at a time to communicate with the X server. In both these cases we would delegate the access control to a trusted applet which would run all the time and switch between the hats.

Running in a single session would also help us to remove the dependency on X entirely. Most of the current Linux-based PDAs, while supporting X, are designed to use embedded environments such as Qtopia or GPE. Our goal is to support the original applications written for our chosen PDA and therefore we need to be able to support these environments.

Generic solutions which can use several environments need a server/client which can display on all of them. One such solution is Virtual Network Computing (VNC) [10]. VNC is a system which can run a graphical session unconnected to an actual display and has clients on most operating systems which can connect to the session and display it in a window. There are VNC clients for all of the main systems used on PDAs and therefore a system built around VNC sessions would be feasible. In this case we would have a small switching applet written for the specific platform which would switch between different VNC connections. VNC, however, introduces a lot of latency even on local connections and, because the protocol has to cope with the lowest common denominator, a lot of optimisations which can be done with the windowing system tend to be lost.

7   Conclusions

Our proof of concept prototype demonstrates that a multi-hat PDA can be implemented by combining existing software subsystems without the need for extensive modifications. Other subsystems to be integrated may include an encrypting file system and alternative mechanisms for handling the graphical sessions.

Further challenges will include reproducing the prototype's functionality on an actual PDA and being able to run native PDA applications under the multi-hat system. This porting activity may look conceptually straightforward but, as already happened during the development of the prototype, we expect that it will highlight new interesting research issues and open new avenues for investigation.

References

1. Alkassar, A., Stüble, C., Sadeghi, A.-R.: Secure object identification—or: solving the Chess Grandmaster Problem. In: NSPW 2003. Proceedings of the 2003 workshop on New security paradigms, pp. 77–85. ACM Press, New York (2003)
2. Anonymous. Windows XP Technical Overview White Paper (May 2001),
   `http://www.microsoft.com/technet/prodtechnol/winxppro/evaluate/`
   `xptechov.mspx`
3. Barham, P., Dragovic, B., Fraser, K., Hand, S., Harris, T., Ho, A., Neugebauer, R., Pratt, I., Warfield, A.: Xen and the art of virtualization. In: SOSP 2003. Proceedings of the nineteenth ACM symposium on Operating systems principles, pp. 164–177. ACM Press, New York (2003),
   `http://www.cl.cam.ac.uk/netos/papers/2003-xensosp.pdf`
4. Beth, T., Desmedt, Y.: Identification Tokens—or: Solving the Chess Grandmaster Problem. In: Menezes, A.J., Vanstone, S.A. (eds.) CRYPTO 1990. LNCS, vol. 537, pp. 11–15. Springer, Heidelberg (1991)
5. Brands, S., Chaum, D.: Distance Bounding Protocols. In: Helleseth, T. (ed.) EUROCRYPT 1993. LNCS, vol. 765, pp. 302–9743. Springer, Heidelberg (1994),
   `http://link.springer-ny.com/link/service/series/0558/papers/0765/`
   `07650344.pdf`
6. Corner, M.D., Noble, B.D.: Zero-Interaction Authentication. In: The Eighth ACM Conference on Mobile Computing and Networking, ACM Press, New York (2002),
   `http://mobility.eecs.umich.edu/papers/mobicom02.pdf`
7. Kilpatrick, D., Salamon, W., Vance, C.: Securing The X Window System With SELinux. Tech. Rep. 03-006, NAI Labs (March 2003),
   `http://www.nsa.gov/selinux/papers/X11_Study.pdf`
8. Loscocco, P., Smalley, S.: Integrating Flexible Support for Security Policies into the Linux Operating System. In: The 2001 USENIX Annual Technical Conference, USENIX Association (2001)
9. Richardson, T., Bennett, F., Hopper, A.: Teleporting in an X Window System Environment. IEEE Personal Communications Magazine 1(3), 6–12 (1994),
   `http://www.uk.research.att.com/pub/docs/att/tr.94.4.ps.Z`
10. Richardson, T., Stafford-Fraser, Q., Wood, K.R., Hopper, A.: Virtual Network Computing. IEEE Internet Computing 2(1), 33–38 (1998),
   `http://www.uk.research.att.com/pub/docs/att/tr.98.1.pdf`
11. Sastry, N., Shankar, U., Wagner, D.: Secure Verification of Location Claims. CryptoBytes 7(1), 17–29 (2004)
12. Stajano, F.: Security for Ubiquitous Computing. John Wiley and Sons, Chichester (2002), `http://www-lce.eng.cam.ac.uk/fms27/secubicomp/`
13. Stajano, F.: One user, many hats; and, sometimes, no hat—towards a secure yet usable PDA. In: The Twelfth International Workshop on Security Protocols, `http://www-lce.eng.cam.ac.uk/fms27/papers/2004-stajano-hats.pdf` (to appear, 2004)

Implementing a Multi-hat PDA
(Transcript of Discussion)

Matthew Johnson

University of Cambridge

This is work I did with Frank Stajano, which has come out of some of his stuff that he talked about at last year's workshop[1], but I'll give to anyone who wasn't here last year a brief synopsis of what he was talking about.

The problem is this: you have a PDA, and this is inherently a single-user machine, that's how it's been designed. On your PDA you have some functions which you want to protect, so you might have your diary, and your journal, and your email on it, and you'd quite like to protect this so you put a password on your PDA, but you also have some functions which don't need a password, so you have a calculator and games on your PDA, and you don't really need a password for these. But because it's a single-user machine, obviously only one person's using it, so you have a password on the whole PDA because it's all the same person. So if you want to use your calculator you still have to type your password in. The other effect of this is that if you want to lend the calculator to somebody else, demonstrate the nice screen you've got on your PDA, you have to type in your password and then you have given them access to all of it. And what we'd quite like to do is to be able to lend someone your PDA to play games on it, or use the calculator, without also giving them the ability to read your email.

So what we've said is that it's a single-user machine, but there are different policies you want to enforce in the different applications. This idea is called having many hats, this is similar to different roles, sometimes you want to be using your email, and sometimes you want to be in a mode where you don't have as many privileges, and this will require some different credentials. You also want to be able to change between the roles, without having to close down your email program just to be able to use your calculator. And one of the nice ideas is that one of the roles doesn't require any credentials at all, and you can just lend somebody your PDA, and let them use the things that you don't mind them using, without having to provide credentials.

There's five rules we've come up with. The first is that the machine supports some number of hats, and they each have a different set of credentials. We don't specify here what these are, this is left up to the implementer of the system or the user, but one of them is special, it has no credentials at all. The machine also has several sessions, each one belongs to one of the hats, and this session may be in an active state, or a locked state, and only one of them will be active

---

[1] F. Stajano, One User, Many Hats; and, Sometimes, No Hat; Towards a Secure Yet Usable PDA, LNCS 3957, 51–67.

B. Christianson et al. (Eds.): Security Protocols 2005, LNCS 4631, pp. 308–314, 2007.
© Springer-Verlag Berlin Heidelberg 2007

at once. The third rule isn't entirely necessary, but makes everything a whole lot simpler, it's possible to imagine you might want several sessions for each hat, but you can implement this with having multi-hats easily. We also want to have an easy way to select hats which will automatically work out if there's a session already running and if not it's created for you. And finally, when you do switch, then you have to present the credentials of the hat's session, again.

So there's the null hat, as we've called it, which has no credentials. It has things like a calculator, a calendar, world time function, things like this, which it can access. Then there are things like your Internet access, which on a PDA probably costs money, and you don't have very much so it's a scarce resource, so without any valid credentials you can't access any of those resources. It should always be in a state that you can do something with the PDA, and so if you haven't presented any valid credentials, the null hat is the state which you end up in.

Conversely you have restricted hats, and you can have really any number of these, the policy doesn't specify. Then you can specify what extra resources these hats can access, and they can also run applications which are stateful, and have things like Internet access. There are several ways to change between them, obviously there's a way where you can explicitly say, I would like to access this session now, there is also a shortcut to get you into the null hat really easy, so that you can just press a key and then hand over your PDA. And then there are a few things which will automatically cause the machine to change hats, so if you close the lid or you suspend the machine, it should automatically drop any credentials you've already given it, and go back to the null hat.

One of the other things that we were looking at with this is a way of providing other authenticating credentials than just passwords, because having to type in passwords all the time is very annoying. So one of the things we've come up with is authentication based on proximity: we have a token, which in this case is my mobile phone here, and the system we've got just runs on Bluetooth, so you can use any of your devices which support Bluetooth to do this, and it monitors how far away from your PDA, or in this case the laptop, the token is, and you can delegate the authority from one hat to another.

Ben Laurie: I trust you're aware that that phone is vulnerable to snarfing, so it should have Bluetooth switched on.

Reply: I know this actually, because my housemate came on IRC in the morning, and he was like, yes, I've just been using your phone to phone random people, you should probably turn it off. I'm getting a new phone shortly.

So the device reports how far away it is from the laptop, and then you can say, as long as I'm within this distance of the laptop, you should consider this an appropriate credential.

Yvo Desmedt: This was proposed 15 years ago by myself and Tuomas Aura.

Reply: Yes. I was aware of a couple of papers which did things like this with custom bits of hardware and so on. Our approach is quite nice because it works with any Bluetooth device, and just uses the standard protocol. There are still

some possible middle person attacks in this, and in a minute I'll show you that.
I don't use this to authenticate everything: because you don't have just a secure
state and an unsecure state, you can have several different states so you can say,
these things I'm happy to delegate to this authority, and other things I really
want to have password input.

Ben Laurie: Why are there middleman attacks?

Reply: The Bluetooth protocol's secured to the device: there's some crypto.
Ford was talking about how you can sniff this, and how you can fix the sniffing.
However, to do a relay attack, you don't actually need to be able to read the
protocol. The attacker just relays the signal, and the system will think that the
token is in range. There are some techniques which are being proposed to work
out how far away something is by timing the responses, and things like this.

Ben Laurie: So you're only using the presence of the device?

Reply: Yes, it has to be the presence of this device, but you can take this up
by relaying the signal and so on, most of the other solutions require separate
hardware. Bluetooth has a shared key which is established when you pair the
devices. So it has to be the device with this key, not just with the right MAC
address.

Ben Laurie: Why not use public keys, then you wouldn't have middleman
attacks?

Reply: You still have middle man attacks even with public key because all you
have to do is relay the signal from one to the other. We use the radio signal's
strength between these two devices, if I walk away the signal strength drops, but
if you have two people, one near me and one near this thing, then they can relay
the signals.

Yvo Desmedt: If you use GPS there is no possibility of error. You can usually
guess where you are within 30 centimeters then.

Reply: If you use GPS, yes, particularly if you have a GPS device in both of
them then you can cancel out the errors, so you sort of do your own DGPS
between the two.

Ben Laurie: And it only work outdoors?

Reply: You can use GPS indoors depending where you are.

Ross Anderson: There were certainly prototype system designs, the purpose
of the system was to stop US law enforcement officers being killed with their
own guns by people whom they'd apprehended, because apparently this often
happens. The proposed fix was that police officers would have a signet ring with
some kind of RFID device in it, the gun would only go off if within 30 centimetres
of the ring. I think Sandia did a study of a whole lot of different possible ways
of including security in weapons, and that's the best that they came up with.

Bruce Christianson: You just hope the criminal doesn't have grabber.

Mike Roe: It depends what your model of the attacker is. In the example Ross just gave, it's just some guy you're trying to arrest who grabbed your gun, who will not have all the kit.

Bruce Christianson: It's also a mistake if you try and take the gun back off the attacker. [Laughter]

Mike Bond: I think you need some kind of arrow protocol where you use one hand to use the gun, and the other hand to point at the target.

Tuomas Aura: Well if you actually don't want the police officer to shoot you, if you happen to be a bank robber, for example, you just buy one of these RFID taggers and challenge. [Laughter]

Reply: OK. We've built a prototype of this, which is currently running on this laptop. The environment that eventually we would target it to is PDA that also runs Linux, it's quite easy to shift things between the two, and it was easy to do development on here. When you close the lid of the laptop then you want it to change automatically to the public hat, which can do things like play games, and so on. My authentication token is in range, that's the button to switch to the limited hat. This hat has access to things like Internet access, you don't really want other people to be using it, but if people go to all the effort of performing a middle-person attack, you don't lose that much. And that, as I said, is keyed on to my Bluetooth phone, so if I disable my Bluetooth phone, then it would automatically change down quite well, because the credential has now gone away. Now, with my phone disabled, if I try and change to the hat it will prompt me to put a password, which I can still enter, if I can remember what the password is, no I can't remember what the password is. [laughter] but if I could then it will change me into the limited hat. Finally there is a third node which is where you keep anything that you think is more private, or needs to be secure, and that has to be accessed by the password even if you've got your proximity device available.

Tuomas Aura: Are the three completely separate sessions on there rather than getting more hats, so now you can't see the thing that was showing. Of course in your secret mode that gives a warning.

Reply: There's a few reasons for this. This is implemented using multiple X-servers run on different virtual terminals, this is a lot easy to implement and still works. If you want everything in same session there's a few problems, because with standard X, for example, applications that have access to the system can write to any other applications on the X server. There are some trusted X proposals where applications won't write to each other, but in that model the applications have different security levels, rather than the user changing what credentials they have half way through the session, so it's a little difficult to arrange. But I have been thinking about some ways of doing this.

Mike Roe: What about files? If you save a file in a low level, which can be run as a script with a higher hat.

Reply: Yes, that's very easy to implement. The permissions are managed by security enhanced Linux, so it has role-based access control, and has very fine grained access privileges, so you can restrict what sort of network operations you can do. I mean, on a PDA you wouldn't really run services, but if you did, you could say that only the restricted session can bind to ports, some of the other sessions can open connections to other machines, you can specify fairly arbitrary combinations, of who can access which files.

Mike Roe: Yes, trouble, where multi-level is involved, is you always end up doing something where a restricted hat is used at a high security level.

Reply: Yes, although this system I'm using at the moment is a multi-level system when it's at the most secure level, you just have all of the access rights, and it goes down, and there are subsets to each other, you don't have to do that, you can arrange things in different ways.

We started off looking to see what systems have similar features. None of them actually do what we want: with Windows, it wasn't possible to enforce all the restrictions we wanted, and integrating is a lot more difficult because you don't have as much access to changing how the system works, and Xen has quite a lot of overheads, so we eventually went with Linux SE and it's combinations. KDE is used because it had some nice session features, and you can query what session are open, and so on, very easily. So at the moment we're using a laptop with KDE on SE Linux, all the Linux stuff has already got ports to the PDAs that this would be targeted to, so it should be fairly easy to change over. I'll talk a bit later about the X server stuff, I don't actually like this very much, and there are better ways of doing it, but it still works fine. And I've written an event handler which handles all of the switching between roles, and obviously the locality system. With laptops and PDAs you have automated API events which you can use as triggers.

So, I have two restricted hats, as you see, and the null hat, and one of the hats always requires explicit password credentials, whereas the other one uses a Bluetooth proximity token. There are only the two credentials we've got implemented at the moment, the idea is to be able eventually to use lots of different credentials, we don't really want to use passwords, so there's various sorts of hardware tokens you can use, and biometrics. We really want to reduce how much the user has to do to change between sessions, because people aren't really going to want to use this if they have to type passwords in all the time, and if it's too fine grained it just becomes unusable. That's the sort of thing we're looking at next. And also, as I said, I don't really like X, one of the problems is that most PDAs don't use X, they use GPE or they use Qtopia which are embedded application type interfaces. We really want to be able to run the access we'd run on a PDA anyway, so we need to find a way of integrating it with Qtopia, or whatever. There are some things you can do like running in the VNC server, and then connecting different VNC clients, but you lose a lot when you're doing that because they cater for the lowest denominator, so they don't actually provide as many features as you would want.

That's it. Any other questions that haven't come up during the talk?

Bruce Christianson: How do you measure proximity?

Reply: At the moment I'm doing it by the Bluetooth signal strength. This is a configurable threshold, you specify what threshold you want, it depends where you're going to be using it. If you want this on your desktop computer so when you leave your office it locks, and when you come in it unlocks, then there's quite a nice threshold when you leave the room because the signal strength is a lot lower when you go outside. It's a separately configurable threshold, and it uses the signal strength to monitor it.

Bruce Christianson: Will you move on to the next step, which is where you've got some authenticator on your mobile phone?

Reply: Yes, I was wondering about doing this. You need a device which you can program stuff to talk over the Bluetooth link and all kinds of things can do this. At the moment this system just needs a Bluetooth device, it doesn't need any extra support. All it does is open the Bluetooth connection, and it uses the Bluetooth authentication system, so it works with a lot of devices. If you're willing to restrict it to, say, a smart phone which starts to become almost a PDA as it is already, then you can do some stuff over the top of that as well.

Mark Lomas: You said one of the motivations of this is that you can lend your device to somebody else with a restricted hat. Very often you want to lend something to somebody but you are not present, so you let somebody use their phone and then say, what's Fred's telephone number, and I say, I can't remember, it's in the PDA, and the only way I can give them access to this is to give them the password which then gives them access to everything.

It would be nicer to be able to give them a one-time password with which they access it.

If you set this up beforehand then you can set up one-time passwords as an authentication mechanism, but contact lists tend in most systems to be in the same place as your email, and similar things, but we were considering things like your email to be the thing you actually want to protect from other people reading it.

Bruce Christianson: You can implement a proper capability system and then just text them the capability from your mobile.

Ben Laurie: That is the correct way.

Reply: Yes, that is actually, yes.

Mike Roe: What about an audit trail, it's an audit problem. If they looked at something when you give them the password it gets recorded what they do.

Richard Clayton: Going back to the thing at the human level, you are perfectly happy to trust certain people to look at this thing, answer the query, and promise you that she'll shut it again. What you don't want to do is give away your password which will still work two days later when you goout of the office. Whereas a temporary permission only requires that you trust them for a short period.

Ross Anderson: I think we may want to give them more restricted trust. Rather than giving you access for five milliseconds to my address book, I would rather give you a capability that lets you look up precisely one address.

Frank Stajano: That's essentially Bruce's idea, that capabilities would be the right thing here. You would give fine grain access so you could do what you really want. As Ross said, you don't want to give access to the whole address book. You want to give access a capability to access the one entry that they want to look up.

Ben Laurie: If you give a capability you'd know who they looked up.

Bruce Christianson: Well a capability to call a look-up function, and you could have a one-time capability that can only be used once.

Pekka Nikander: In the light of yesterday's discussion I think it's important for us to understand that the normal users are never going to be able to manage these capabilities. So if we want to use capabilities for something like that it has to interface to user interface, so there is some user gesture, or user action, which actually creates the capability at the same time. In a way the user doesn't really know that there is this capability created, and doesn't care provided it is easy for the user.

Bruce Christianson: It is useful to let someone login once. It would also be very useful to be able to give out a phone number that would let somebody call your mobile phone once, or just during one particular day.

Frank Stajano: I remember a few years ago, it must have been around 1999, I was working in New Jersey and I had a chat with a patent lawyer and proposed a system similar to what you just described, being able to have a number that I can give to someone, and know it will just work for that time, and he came back to me after a couple of days, ah we have already actually got a patent on that. I said, why is not in common use, I'd like to used that facility.

Bruce Christianson: Has he got a patent on the idea, or has he got an implementation of this?

Frank Stajano: He told me that the company has already filed a patent.

Bruce Christianson: The point of a patent is to stop somebody else from implementing it.

Breno de Medeiros: They realise they can't do it but maybe the competition can.

Anonymous Context Based Role Activation Mechanism

Partha Das Chowdhury, Bruce Christianson, and James Malcolm

Computer Science Department
University of Hertfordshire
England
{P.Das-Chowdhury,B.Christianson,J.A.Malcolm}@herts.ac.uk

Abstract. Privacy is not an explicit goal of traditional authorisation mechanisms. The contribution of this paper is an authorisation mechanism which takes identity out of the trust management envelope. Our protocol supports weak versions of anonymity and is useful even if anonymity is not required, due to the ability to weaken trust assumptions.

1 Introduction

Authentication, authorisation and audit are three traditional concerns in building a privilege management infrastructure: the purpose of authentication is to identify a particular user and verify that a user is who he/she is claiming to be; the goal of authorisation is to provide access for certain users to certain resources based on predefined business rules; and an audit trail links actions to principals retrospectively. Traditionally, authentication is based on permanent credentials linked to a fixed long-term identity, and authorisation is linked to audit via the authentication mechanism explicitly using the same permanent credential and identity. Privacy is not an explicit goal of traditional identity based authorisation mechanisms [6,4,2].

In this paper we present an authorisation mechanism which takes identity out of the trust management envelope. We also illustrate the use of a two level authentication mechanism, using ring signature and surrogates. A two level authentication mechanism supports the concept of *activate* security [1] according to which access control decisions depend on context which is monitored *e.g.* the assignment of users to roles is handled by role activation rules which require users to activate roles on possession of valid prerequisites. If there is a change in the context in which a role was initially activated then the role is revoked. Such an approach helps to organise access control systems into an hierarchical structure.

As well as strong privacy, our protocol also supports a range of weaker versions of anonymity, and is useful even if anonymity is not required at all, because of the ability to weaken trust assumptions; the approach we present here allows users to control the risks to which they are exposed, rather than forcing them to enter into an unnecessary compulsive trust relationship with the system infrastructure.

B. Christianson et al. (Eds.): Security Protocols 2005, LNCS 4631, pp. 315–321, 2007.
© Springer-Verlag Berlin Heidelberg 2007

Similarly, services also do not need to trust the authentication mechanism of a third party.

Our protocol allows an unbiased auditor to uniquely and irrefutably link actions to individuals retrospectively, but users do not need to have trust in the honesty or competence of the auditor as the auditor cannot forge audit records.

This paper is organised as follows. In section 2 we provide an example scenario and an overview of the design goals it gives rise to, then in section 3 we describe our key and surrogate generation mechanisms. The main contribution of this paper is the protocol which we describe in section 4, and we conclude by analysing its properties in section 5.

2   Example Scenario

Members of crime syndicates need to be anonymous to the outside world but it is a requirement that they do not act against the interests of their syndicate. This motivates our example, though the details used in this paper might not be similar to any real crime syndicate. The syndicate consists of arms dealers and cocaine dealers and members post their (cocaine or arms) requirements in a bulletin board under their pseudonyms. We assume that the syndicate uses a rôle based authorisation mechanism, and that all dealers employed by the syndicate are assigned the rôle *employed_dealer*. Dealers can acess only their own account and arms dealers should not be able to masquerade as cocaine dealers. To access a specific account they have to activate the rôle *account_owner* for that account. Dealers can access only those accounts for whom they are *account_owner*, by activating the rôle *account_owner* for that account.

The policy of the syndicate is that the rôle *account_owner* can only be activated by a dealer if the dealer has already activated the rôle *employed_dealer*; which we enforce using a two level authentication mechanism. On revocation of the role *employed_dealer* the role *account_owner* is also revoked. For every session, dealers activate the rôle *employed_dealer* once but before accessing every account a dealer has to activate the rôle *account_owner* for that account. Dealers register with the administrative server (AS) and the AS assigns rôles to the dealers. Dealers authenticate to the trading server (TS) using their surrogates and access respective accounts. The TS performs eligibility authentication *i.e.* whether or not the dealer is allowed to access this account, and not authentication of the user's identity.

Only the administrative server can link the surrogates back to the owner of the surrogates, but in doing so it must apply appropriate technical and organisational security measures, and divulge the link only in circumstances specified under rules that govern the syndicate and are agreed by a majority of the members of the syndicate.

The requirements can be summarised as:

1. Un-correlatability – It should be hard for an adversary to link actions to individuals retrospectively, even if the adversary manages to obtain the surrogate used for the transaction along with the transaction details. Someone

observing the network should not be able to gain any information about the nature of the communication and the communicating parties.

2. Misuse of surrogates – Even if an adversary manages to capture and retain a surrogate used for a particular transaction it should still be hard for him to generate and use future surrogates.

3. Protection from (partially) trusted third parties – No adversary should be able to pretend to be a legitimate owner of a surrogate. Although a third party generates and issues the information users need to generate and use their surrogates, the third party should not be able to masquerade as the legitimate owner of a surrogate.

4. Audit – An unbiased auditor should be able to link actions to individuals, but only with the explicit knowledge and consent of the legitimate owner of the surrogate.

3   Generation of Keys and Surrogates

Our key generation method is similar to that described by Diffie and Hellman in [3]. Here we use Diffie-Hellman key systems modulo a composite for which factorisation of large integers is necessary to break the system. Then breaking the system would require solving two hard problems: factoring a large integer and breaking the system in two groups $GF(P)^*$ and $GF(Q)^*$. A detailed description is found in [5]. In Diffie-Hellman key systems modulo a composite, public keys are generated from a secret in a way similar to key systems modulo a large prime. The user chooses two large primes P and Q and calculates n as $n = PQ$ and $\phi(n) = (P-1)(Q-1)$. The user selects a generator $g \bmod \phi(n)$ and constructs his/her public key X from the secret $s \in 1 \ldots \phi(n)$ such that g^s and $\phi(n)$ are relatively prime.

$$X = g^s \bmod n$$

The surrogates are generated by modular exponentiation of X using an exponent τ where $\tau \in 1 \ldots (n-1)$. The secret value corresponding to a surrogate is generated by modular multiplication of the exponent τ with the secret s that was used to generate X. The initial value (τ_0) of the exponent τ is supplied by a (partially) trusted third party. The subsequent values (τ_i) of the exponent τ, used to generate the surrogates and their corresponding secret, are generated by the user using the linear congruence equation,

$$\tau_i = A\tau_{i-1} + B \bmod \phi(n) \tag{1}$$

where the constants A and B are also selected by the third party, and are unique to the user. Then the surrogates K_i^+ and the corresponding secrets K_i^- for the ith transaction are generated as:

$$K_i^- = \tau_i \cdot s \bmod \phi(n) \tag{2}$$

$$K_0^+ = X^{\tau_0} \bmod n; \qquad K_i^+ = X^B (K_{i-1}^+)^A \bmod n \qquad (3)$$

To generate the secret corresponding to a surrogate, first the exponent is calculated by equation 1 and then the secret is calculated by equation 2. Note that these calculations can only be done by the user. The surrogates themselves are generated by equation 3. Note that

$$K_i^+ = g^{K_i^-} \bmod n = X^{\tau_i} \bmod n \qquad (4)$$

The third party sends the user the constants A, B, and the initial value τ_0 of the exponent so that the user can generate his/her surrogates. The third party can also generate the surrogates, but not the exponents or secrets which correspond to them.

To use a surrogate K_i^+ for transaction i a user proves knowledge of the corresponding K_i^-. Only the legitimate owner of X and s can both generate and use surrogates corresponding to X.

4   The Protocol

4.1   Assumptions

An anonymous communication channel between the user and the server is assumed for our protocol, so that it will be hard for an adversary observing the network to gain any additional information about the communicating partners beyond its *a priori* belief. We use the symbol $\longrightarrow_m$ to represent communication over such an anonymous channel and $\longrightarrow_s$ to represent a secure authenticated channel.

4.2   Notation

Cathy is a cocaine dealer working for the syndicate. Cathy's public key is denoted by X and s denote her secret key. K_i^+ and K_i^- represents the public surrogate and its corresponding secret for the ith transaction. τ_i represents the exponent used to calculate the surrogate for the ith transaction. A and B represent the fixed value and the offset respectively in the linear congruence equation used in equation 1. σ denotes the ring signature [7] on message M.

4.3   Message Exchanges

Cathy generates her public key X using equation 1 from her secret s.

$$X = g^s \bmod n \qquad (5)$$

Cathy registers with the administrative server using her public key and the administrative server sends her the information she needs to generate her surrogates.

1. $Cathy \longrightarrow_s AS : X$

On receipt of Cathy's public key the administrative server selects $\tau_0, B, A \in Z_n^*$ as described in section 3. So that Cathy does not need to contact the administrative server before every single transaction, the administrative server sends Cathy the information she will need to prepare subsequent surrogate pairs using the equations 1, 2 and 3 and Cathy uses these surrogates serially.

2. $AS \longrightarrow_s Cathy : \prec \tau_0, B, A \succ$

For each member, the administrative server sends the trading server a group of surrogates by iterating equation 3 for each of the next several values of i. The trading server (TS) also maintains a list of the public keys of the dealers employed by the syndicate.

For the ith transaction Cathy generates the exponent τ_i, the secret corresponding to the ith surrogate K_i^- and her i^{th} surrogate K_i^+ using equations 1, 2 and 3 respectively. Cathy signs a message M using ring signatures mod n [7] and includes her i^{th} surrogate along with the transaction. Cathy sends the trading server the signed message.

3. $Cathy \longrightarrow_m TS : \sigma, M, K_i^+$ where σ is the ring signature of M.

By signing M Cathy activates her rôle of *employed_dealer* and by proving her knowledge of the secret K_i^- corresponding to K_i^+ she activates her rôle of *account_owner*. The trading server can verify σ as it knows all the public keys of the dealers employed with the syndicate. Only upon successful verification of σ and of Cathy's knowledge of the secret corresponding to K_i^+ does the trading server allow Cathy access to the accounts that she owns.

5   Analysis and Conclusions

The properties of our protocol can be summarised as:

1. Un-correlatability – Different transactions initiated by a particular principal cannot be linked to each other or back to the initiator of the transaction without the explicit consent either of the legitimate owner of the surrogate or of the administrative server. The trading server cannot guess the dealer from the ring signature with a probability more than $1/r$. Linking K_i^+ to K_{i+1}^+ and back to X would require an adversary to solve the equation:

$$\log_X K_i^+ = \tau_i \bmod n \qquad (6)$$

or to compromise the values of A and B used in equation 1. Even if the values A and B were compromised, calculating τ_i by solving equation 6 is still thought to be an intractable problem. If an adversary cannot calculate τ_i then it cannot calculate τ_{i+1} using equation 1 nor the secret corresponding to the surrogate using equation 2. Thus it is difficult for an adversary to link surrogates to each other or to the parent public key.

2. Misuse of surrogates – An adversary stealing the numbers in step 3 cannot masquerade as Cathy as he/she cannot generate K_i^- without s which is secret. Even if an adversary can steal the values that the administrative server sends to Cathy in step 2 still he/she cannot use future surrogates from K_{i+1}^+ as s is secret and known only to Cathy. Calculating s requires the adversary to solve the discrete logarithm problem.

3. Protection from (partially) trusted third party – The third party cannot masquerade as the legitimate owner of X because the corresponding s is secret. Calculating s requires an adversary to solve the equation:

$$\log_g X = s \bmod n \tag{7}$$

which is thought to be hard. Moreover even if the value of the exponent τ is known, still without the knowledge of s it is hard to generate the secret corresponding to a surrogate using equation 2. Thus the administrative server cannot masquerade as Cathy to the trading server.

4. Audit – Since ring signature makes it difficult for an adversary to masquerade as a member of a group so the trading server can be sure that it is talking to a dealer. Moreover from the surrogate the dealer uses, the administrative server can resolve disputes retrospectively. But although the administrative server can resolve disputes, it cannot masquerade as a dealer.

Dealers only reveal their permanent credential to local entities which are legally authorised to verify them *e.g.* the administrative server. Such an approach advocates a more localised trust relationship, in contradiction to a global trust relationship such as that required by a global public key infrastructure or a global pseudonym authority (both of which in any case are developments yet to come to fruition). The problem with the more usual global trust relationship is that users have no control of the risks they are exposed to, but must enter into an unnecessary compulsive trust relationship with the system: in effect they are all forced to trust the same system to protect them from the same threats.

This paper opens a way to allow clients to exercise more control over the risks to which they are exposed by bearing the cost of relevant countermeasures themselves. We regard this as preferable to the conventional approach of forcing clients to trust the entire system infrastructure, and to bear an equal share of the cost of all countermeasures, without regard to the perceived effectiveness of these countermeasures for them.

References

1. Belokosztolszki, A.: Role based access control policy administration. Technical Report 586, University of Cambridge (2004)
2. Beresnevichiene, Y.: A role and context based security model. Technical Report 558, University of Cambridge (2003)
3. Diffie, W., Hellman, M.: New Directions In Cryptography. IEEE Transactions on Information Theory 22, 472–492 (1976)

4. Ferraiolo, D., Sandhu, R., Gavrilla, S., Kuhn, R., Chandramouli, R.: Proposed NIST Standard For Role Based Access Control. ACM Transactions on Information and Systems Security 4(3), 224–274
5. McKurley, K.: A Key Distribution System Equal to Factoring. Journal of Cryptology 1, 95–105 (1988)
6. Neuman, B.C., Tso's, T.: Kerberos: An Authentication Service For Computer Networks. IEEE Communications 32(9), 33–38
7. Rivest, R., Shamir, A., Tauman, Y.: How To Leak A Secret. In: Boyd, C. (ed.) ASIACRYPT 2001. LNCS, vol. 2248, pp. 552–565. Springer, Heidelberg (2001)

Anonymous Context Based Role Activation Mechanism

(Transcript of Discussion)

Bruce Christianson

Computer Science Department
University of Hertfordshire

I'm going to talk about some of the work that Partha has done for his PhD dissertation[1]. There's lots more in there, and if you want to read the hardback edition just get in touch with Partha[2], but what I'm going to talk about today is the bit concerned with anonymous context-based role activation, and anonymous delegation. The protocols we'll be looking at use surrogates in various forms, but that's not essential to the plot. I hope to convince you that doing these things anonymously is not only feasible, but can actually be done maintaining auditability and accountability. This approach allows us to separate identity management from trust management, which has the good consequence of allowing us to localise trust in the system infrastructure. That is a good thing — and therefore these mechanisms are useful — even when anonymity isn't a requirement at all, and we all know perfectly well who everyone is.

The context we're in is some kind of hierarchical role-based access control system of a traditional form. So we have various roles like `employed_dealer`, the various dealers are employed by various syndicates, dealers can activate the role of being able to deal in various commodities, and you have the usual requirements: for example you don't want arms dealers to be able to masquerade as drugs dealers, and you may not want principals to be able to be both arms dealers and drugs dealers, or maybe not both at the same time, or maybe principals can't deal in both hard drugs and soft drugs. We want to enforce the rules for activating roles by determining whether the possessor of a particular surrogate satisfies the pre-conditions for activating the role, and the important point to note is that in order to do this the role manager doesn't need to know who somebody actually is. All the role manager needs is the certificates that say that this particular surrogate satisfies whatever the particular pre-conditions are.

So we don't actually need to base role-activation on traditional strong authentication at all. We can base role-activation upon short-term surrogates — possibly more than one, as I may not want my different transactions to be correlated, so I may want to activate several surrogates in the role, but use each one once, to do one particular transaction.

Frank Stajano. Surrogate for what?

---

[1] Partha Das Chowdhury, Anonymity and Trust in the Electronic World, PhD Thesis, STRI, University of Hertfordshire, 2005.
[2] parthadc@gmail.com

B. Christianson et al. (Eds.): Security Protocols 2005, LNCS 4631, pp. 322–328, 2007.

Reply. Think of a surrogate as being like a short-term identity.

Frank Stajano. Like a pseudonym?

Reply. Like a pseudonym, but with certain added cryptographic properties. You could think of it as being like a short-term public key that doesn't have a conventional key certificate.

Ben Laurie. Would that be like a proxies certificates in the grid thing? Although a proxy certificate in a grid isn't really a proxy.

Reply. It's not really a proxy, no. There are relations between proxies and surrogates, but the word proxy has other connotations, so I prefer to use the word surrogate. However there are all sorts of other mechanisms that can be used to implement this kind of system protocol. Once I've convinced you that it's worth implementing we can then argue about the most efficient way of doing it, and what mechanisms to use. In Partha's dissertation he deliberately uses very old-fashioned clunky mechanisms like surrogates to provide a knock-down existence proof, on the grounds that everybody else relies on these mechanisms to have those properties anyway.

So here we are, Cathy is a cocaine dealer, and her backers have set up a meeting with the backers of another syndicate, at which they're going to trade the cocaine with the armaments. This may not be a face-to-face meeting, these days it may be a virtual meeting. The backers of the other syndicate are saying, Cathy we'd like to introduce Bob the Fingers, who will be our bagman for this heist. Now Cathy has an authentication problem. The problem isn't that she doesn't know who Bob is (hi Fingers). Cathy knows perfectly well who Bob is, she may even have worked with him before, and assuming that Cathy is both competent and motivated to behave honestly for this particular transaction, there is no possibility of her actually giving the bag to anyone else. That is not the problem.

Cathy *is* concerned about certain questions to do with whether she should give the bag to Bob or not: one of these questions is, will my syndicate get the gear if I do? Because it's not enough to ask just, is Bob authorized by his syndicate. The second question is, can I prove (in some appropriate sense) to *my* syndicate that Bob's syndicate had authorised him to take the bag on their behalf? And finally, is this proof that my syndicate can give to Bob's syndicate? Will a receipt from Bob's surrogate do, and does such a receipt allow my audit record to satisfy the requirements of the inter-syndicate protocol? Basically an outside auditor, one of these inter-syndicate functionaries who doesn't have inside information about the dealings of any particular syndicate (so that he can deny it under oath), has to be able to tell whether the audit record satisfies the requirements of this handover protocol.

Provided Cathy's satisfied about those three things, she's OK to give Bob the bag.

Audience. Could you just explain again what needs to happen, what proof needs to be provided by whom, in order to make sure that the syndicate gets paid? And what are the trust assumptions?

Reply. Oh, how we map all these things onto bit patterns is on a later slide. Here you go.

Audience. But at a very high level, what needs to happen for the syndicate to get paid?

Reply. Basically Cathy has to believe that her syndicate is happy for her to hand the bag over, that's the bottom line. But that is typically the final step in some huge delegation food chain.

Questions of no interest to Cathy include, do I know who Bob really is, as distinct from the fact that he is the bagman? She does actually, they had something going once, but this is of no interest.

Ben Laurie. Does that mean that the answer no is equally satisfactory?

Reply. The answer no would be equally satisfactory, provided Cathy has the bit patterns shown in that slide, which justify the handover. It's surprising, isn't it, that it's actually really not very interesting. *Can* Cathy prove who Bob is, well that depends on to whom, and it depends on what you mean by prove. The important point to note before you get dragged into all that, is that it's not an interesting question, in the sense that the answer is not significant in this context. Cathy doesn't need to be able to prove anything about who Bob *really* is at all.

However these are questions of fascinating concern to Bob's syndicate managers, right, particularly if Bob disappears with the bag. Suddenly then these questions become very interesting: who is Bob, where is Bob, all of that stuff, but none of this should be Cathy's problem. You really do want to design your systems in such a way that Cathy does not have to depend on knowing answers to these questions. If it turns out that this cryptographic material, that was agreed as the audit trail, doesn't actually contain enough information for Bob's syndicate to work out who he is, then that should be their problem: they shouldn't have agreed to that being the handover protocol. But Cathy shouldn't be running around trying to work out what's gone wrong with the authentication mechanism in a remote domain, that's just bad system design. What we want is that the auditor who is internal to Bob's syndicate can decode the handover material and work out who Bob really was, and that way everybody ends up sleeping with the fish from their own domain.

Second example. Cathy delegates her part of the job to Alice — or was it Alex? Bob does not care whom Cathy has delegated to, so long as Bob can be sure that Cathy will accept responsibility if only he has the signature from the surrogate that Cathy has delegated to. The person whose problem it is to work out to whom she delegated, and who they really are, is Cathy. The slight catch is that you want a delegation mechanism that doesn't rely on having any shared secrets, so that Cathy and Alex can't frame each other. It's got to be clear which of them actually used the surrogate. There are some falsely so-called schemes of delegation around with surrogates where you actually share the secret which is used in order to operate the surrogate. Then it's not clear who actually did the business, nobody knows who has the bag, and this is bad, at least in some contexts.

Slightly more innocuous example. Carol is allowing one of her children to charge a video to Carol's credit card. The credit card company are not interested in which child she has given permission to, they are not concerned with Carol's domestic arrangements. They don't even care if it's not one of her children, and she's not the biological mother, they just want to know that they're going to get paid for the video. Carol is likely to be very concerned about who has got permission to watch the video, and why the four year old ended up watching an R18. You need to have an infrastructure that encourages people to sort out their own messes, by giving each of them both the motivation and the means to do so.

There are various mechanisms that can be used to build handoffs like this. Last year I talked about one that was based on linear congruences[3], which are these things where you have a Diffie-Hellman key blinded by a secret which you can then unblind. You can do Diffie-Hellman modulo the product of two primes, rather than modulo a single prime, and then the person who knows the secret can do the business and the other person can't. Another good mechanism based more on RSA is the notion of a ring signature, due to Rivest, Shamir and Tauman. I'm not going to go into the number-theoretic details.

Ben Laurie. I think I know what ring signatures are, but can I just check? They're a group of signatures which you sign with, and you don't know which one it was?

Reply. That's exactly right. The idea is you've got a group consisting of a set of public keys, and you produce a token which has the property that you can prove it was signed by someone who knew one of the private keys, but you cannot determine which one of them did it. One of the really neat things about ring signature is that you don't need to get people's consent to put them in the group. So if you want Leonardo DaVinci to have been a member of your secret society, then so long as you know his public key (which is revealed in many of his paintings) [Laughter] you can just put it in, and there you are.

Frank Stajano. Is it possible for someone to say look, I didn't sign this, I can prove it because if I sign this is what comes up, and you can check that that's not me?

Reply: Good question. No. I'm hand-waving over some of the details, because there are complications to do with extending functions to bigger domains, but basically it works like this. You have a set of public keys. To sign something you choose a random set of X_is, one X_i for each other member of the group. You apply the corresponding public key to each X_i to get Y_i. Then you choose the value of Y corresponding to your own piece of the signature, so that the values of all the Y_i (including yours) satisfy some congruence. Now, using your private key, you know which value to pick for your X_i to make your Y_i have the required

[3] P. Das Chowdhury, B. Christianson and J. Malcolm, Anonymous Authentication, LNCS 3957, 299–311.

value. Then the signature is basically the set of all the X_is. I've left out some details, for example you actually have to put the value of what you want to sign into the congruence obviously, but that's the basic idea. So it's not just that you can't work out who signed, there is no fact of the matter.

Breno de Medeiros. I think the point of the signature is that it is randomised, so that you can't just re-compute it and check.

Reply. Yes, I should have said that. You have to have a random number generator to do things this way.

Mike Roe. We could imagine a deterministic scheme where any member of the group can use their own private key to compute a signature, and the same signature is computed no matter which private key is used. This could be like Diffie-Hellman, where two parties each use their own private key to compute exactly the same session key.

Reply. Good point. Ring signatures are very neat, but I'm not saying that they are the "right" mechanism to do this particular thing. Actually you can force almost any mechanism to do what you want, but ring signatures have some nice properties. Very often it's not the membership of the secret society that's a secret, it's which members are actually doing the business, that's the secret. A lot of members never do anything at all, and some may not even know that they're in the society. A classic example is this: you are a cabinet minister, you want to leak something, you want to be able to prove it comes from a member of the cabinet, but you don't want to be able to have it traced back to you. You can include in the group members of the cabinet who are your personal enemies, and who wouldn't dream of leaking it anyway.

If you want to go down this route and have trusted hardware, you can do it somewhat like this. You begin with some hardware that you trust, or that the policy of your domain is to trust. The thing that goes wrong usually is having to trust hardware that's in other people's domains, and when you put your data into that remote hardware you're not quite clear what's going to happen to it next. So instead of doing that, you put the local authentication data that you really don't want going into remote domains into the locally trusted hardware here. Unlike Palladium, or whatever it was really called, the locally trusted hardware doesn't need to have the correct keys in it already. The hardware can be completely neutral and blank, and it can download the ring keys, including the secret ones, using something like an S3P protocol[4]. These protocols are usually used for leveraging a weak secret into a strong secret, but you don't have to start with a weak secret, you can start with a strong secret and get another strong secret.

You can put into the signature protocol the audit trail that the local auditor needs to see, the hardware can then run the code that it has downloaded, verify that this meets the local requirement, and produce the appropriate ring signature, which is what you're going to require the other domain to accept. The other domain says, yes, this is a valid ring signature from domain A, that's fine,

---

[4] See Christianson, Roe and Wheeler, "Secure Sessions from Weak Secrets", LNCS 3364, 190–212.

domain A will accept responsibility for this access, I'm covered. And, as I said, the actual group can be a subset of the apparent group.

One motivation for using this approach may be that you have a concern with privacy either in the sense that you've got data that you want to confine — you don't want the data going out of your domain — or privacy in the sense of non-correlation, where you don't want the two halves of a particular transaction to be linkable by somebody who isn't in your domain, or who isn't in a particular group.

But your motivation might be that you just don't trust the remote authentication mechanism. In this case it's not that people are private, or that they're trying to keep their identity secret: and when the Kerberos system in whichever laboratory it is says that someone is Bob, then the chances are they are Bob, but maybe they're not. You don't want to have to run around fixing any problems that the remote authentication server is having. This way you can take remote authentication out of your trust envelope.

It may even be that you think remote authentication works perfectly, but you're fairly convinced that you're not going to be able to persuade the auditor, the third party, that the remote authentication system works: they're going to say, is it orange book compliant, and you're going to say, I don't think so, and they're going to say, well these bits are not worth the paper they're not written on. And it might be that you don't trust the auditor: different domains have different auditors, you may have a protocol that says you've got to let the auditor from domain B into your system to check the audit record, but you may not trust the auditor from domain B.

George Danezis. So the auditors won't be able to tell who did it?

Reply. If it's the auditors from the other syndicate, then that is quite right, they can't. If it's the auditors from your own syndicate, then they can get access to this box, they can get access to the audit trail that's been put in there, and the point about the box is, it won't produce the ring signature unless you fed it the right authorisation.

George Danezis. So now my question is automatically transformed, to what extent can this box can be transformed into cryptography?

Reply. Oh, you want to transform metal into mathematics. If you want to protect the local domain mechanisms using cryptography rather than secure hardware, then you'd probably be better off using congruence based surrogates rather than the ring signatures. There are mechanisms where you can potentially determine by looking at the bit patterns who signed it, but in order to do that you need to know some information that is closely guarded by the local domain. But somewhere you're going to have to have a physically secure box that you keep that information in.

Ben Laurie. Does the other side care that it's been through this box?

Reply. Not if you've designed it right, all the other side should care about is that this final signature is valid.

Ben Laurie. Doesn't that mean that, even after having theoretically delegated to Alice, I could produce the ring signature myself without going through the box?

Reply. Ah, only if you knew the secret stuff that's in the box. Then yes.

Ben Laurie. Oh I see.

Reply. I should have made this point clearer. The point is that we are trusting the box here not to download the keys and use them unless the correct things have already happened locally.

The key idea of this approach is to localise trust by localising identity resolution. Whenever you have to do an identity resolution, you arrange the system of surrogates in such a way that the identities are resolved locally. If you want to do things where you need access to remote resources, then you are in effect doing remote delegation anyway, so the trick is to do this in such a way that you can localise the identity resolution. This allows you to avoid compulsive transitive-trust requirements, you know, I'm trusting Mike, Mike's trusting Mark, and therefore I end up having to trust Mark even though I don't want to.

This approach also helps us to design systems in such a way that Alice doesn't end up paying for Bob's countermeasures, or (in practice) just not enforcing the countermeasures that the system says she should enforce, because she looks at it and thinks, who benefits from me doing this, not me right, what happens if I don't do it but just say I did, in the short-term, very little, nobody will know, OK.

The idea that you've got one security policy which applies to the whole system is fine as long as you've got a single domain. As soon as you start working across domains, you've got more than one system policy, and people are not happy having to inherit the overhead of enforcing a policy that isn't theirs, and which results in them paying the cost of countermeasures that some remote domain thinks are appropriate in order to combat some risk which the remote domain perceives.

What we want is to design things in such a way as to allow individual domains to control the level of risk to which they believe they are exposed, rather than forcing them to accept some other domain's assessment of that risk.

Topology of Covert Conflict
(Transcript of Discussion)

Shishir Nagaraja

University of Cambridge

This is a short talk on topology of covert conflict, comprising joint work I've been doing with Ross Anderson. The background of this work is the following. We consider a conflict, and there are parties to the conflict. There is communication going on that can be abstracted as a network of nodes (parties) and links (social ties between the nodes). We contend that once you've got a conflict and you've got enough parties to it, these guys start communicating as a result of the conflict. They form connections, that influences the conflict, and the dynamics of the conflict in turn feeds the connectivity of the unfolding network.

Modern conflicts often turn on connectivity: consider, for instance, anything from the American army's attack on the Taleban in Afghanistan, and elsewhere, or medics who are trying to battle a disease, like Aids, or anything else. All of these turn on, making strategic decisions about which nodes to go after in the network. For instance, you could consider that a good first place to give condoms out and start any Aids programme, would be with prostitutes.

One of the first results in the area, on what happens when you consider the topology, and carry out attacks on various types of networks (random networks, scale free networks, and the like), was give by Albert and Barabasi[1]. Through simulations and analytically they determined that if you take out the top five percent of the nodes on the Internet, on the basis of their node degrees, then you can effectively break connectivity, because the largest connected cluster breaks down. They considered that to be a scale free network, and then they show an equivalent random network is fairly resilient to similar levels of attack. Other contributions to robustness have involved people going on to consider more resource-efficient attacks, but there is no talk on defence strategies.

So what we're considering here is, given a conflict and a network, what are the strategic and practical options available to combatants.

What kind of networks are we talking about? Complex networks. You have millions of nodes connected together, and the sum of all the nodes' individual actions does not account for the phenomena that one can observe at the level of the system. Indeed there is no central coordinator who can direct things because the systems are just too large for that.

So, how about having a random network as a strategy for resilience? Random networks are great as a baseline for comparision, but they're not really very efficient, and (quoting from complex networks literature), that's why you hardly

---

[1] Barabasi and Albert, Emergence of Scaling in Random Networks, 1999, Science 286, p507.

B. Christianson et al. (Eds.): Security Protocols 2005, LNCS 4631, pp. 329–332, 2007.

find any in real world networks analyzed thus far. So what you're looking for is a balance between efficiency and resilience.

We were inspired by the dining cryptographers construction by David Chaum[2], who shows how you can use a ring construction to mask the source and destination of the crypto traffic.

Consider an adversary carrying out a casual inspection of your computer network and then strategically targeting areas of it. What can one do about such an adversary? Let's construct a model. Given a fully formed network, we consider a multi-round game comprising three phases: Attack, Recruitment and Recovery. You have the American army which attacks the Taliban. After each attack the Taliban gets as many fresh recruits as those killed. These recruits attach themselves into the network, and then the Taliban relink some of their connections between themselves before the next attack. The attacker's objective is to cause the largest connected cluster to disappear, and/or an exponential increase in the average shortest path length in the networks, to make it effectively unusable for the load of the traffic on it. If you had an underground mp3 sharing network that required you to transit a hundred links to get an audio clip, you probably wouldn't use it. The defender's objective is to allow no more than a linear increase in the average shortest path length, in addition to preventing the largest connected component from falling apart into clusters.

So first we thought, hey, why don't we use rings? Now you see, going back to scale free networks, Barabasi and Albert pointed out that the reason why scale free networks fail so drastically is because you have the hubs: the hubs are directly visible to casual inspection, so just target them, right. Holme et al[3] carried it further, they said not only can you look at the vertex order, but you can also try to figure out which nodes contribute most to lowering the average shortest path between any two nodes in the graph, and you can target those nodes. But of course that's quite difficult, NS is one of the best algorithms you've got, but it's still quite tough, when you consider NS a million, or two million, it's quite a bit of work.

Right, so that's why we want to use rings. You can ask your neighbours because you're connected to them, OK, let's form a ring, so that effectively hides a bit of our vertex order information. But that doesn't do any good for your betweeness centrality information, it still contributes as much as before.

So, yes, rings help, but they're not good enough, where you've got rings under a vertex order centrality attack. The nice thing here is, whatever ring size you use, you seem to get the same result for the size of your biggest connected component, it doesn't change no matter how much effort you put into causing big ring, small ring. So rings can only do you so much good, and under a betweeness centrality attack, not much of a difference.

So let's go on to cliques and see how cliques do under these two conditions. They certainly do much better, because there seems to be a threshold value

[2] D. Chaum, The Dining Cryptographer Problem: Unconditional Sender and Recipient Untraceability, Journal of Cryptology 1(1) 65-75.

[3] http://www.cs.unm.edu/~{}holme

of clique size after which your network can get stable unlike rings. Cliques do take you a step further, and the network is actually alive, and the path length is steadily improving with the amount of effort you're putting in. And under betweeness centrality attack, you need to work harder, you need to push in more resources with cliques, and that's what the graph tells us.

The earlier idea that we convert everything into a random network is not very simple, because if you consider a scale-free network and go about randomly linking at edges, that doesn't work at all, because if you have a hub that begins randomising, it's going to end up disconnecting large portions of other nodes. So, randomisation is fine, but selective randomisation not random randomisation, which can be really counterproductive. Rings are a start, but cliques do better. So those strategic options are a start at the present. That's basically what I have to say.

We're essentially considering a node removing adversary who works on two algorithms, one, look at who has got the highest degree in the network and kick him out, two, find out which node is contributing to the lowest average shortest path, in the network, so you just kick him out. That's obviously more computationally intensive.

Ben Laurie. Why would your adversary actually give you this information?

Reply. The adversary wouldn't really give you this information, no.

Ben Laurie. Why do you think you are able to know it?

Reply. Well it's casual inspection. You have the network, and you just sit and observe, you go around, have a nice walk, and you find out that that guy is having really heavy traffic on him, so he's probably an order of high degree, just kick him out of the network and see what happens. So you find out that Ross Anderson is going on to all these committees, so you wonder like, what if I take Ross out, maybe that helps in destroying Cambridge University, or maybe not.

Ben Laurie. If I were on the other side from you, I would make the least important nodes send a great deal of traffic because then you'll take them out.

Reply. Yes, that would be another action for you to do, but the thing is that's OK in the beginning, but as your resources start going down the old Soviet doctrine of take out one third kicks in.

Alf Zugenmaier. Where are the costs of setting up the network, is it more expensive to set up a link than it is to add a node? Do you assume that you're comparing networks with an equal number of nodes with different strategies of getting the links in there, or networks with an equal number of links?

Reply. Right, good question, the cost model works as follows: within your geo-metrical construct, you are allowed to add as many links as you want. But it's really unreasonable to say that everyone can have as many links as they want, because then you can have a complete network, and that's almost unthinkable to create. So in the scale free model, Barabasi's model, each node is allowed to have a fixed number of links that it can source, but the links are bi-directional, so you are allowed to accept as many links as you want, but you create only three. The scale free model gets created by multi-round in which each node will try to create a link preferably to a node which has more links. So cliques end up with you having to have really high cost software, and yes of course that's unreasonable.

George Danezis. I think that the work that you just presented really shows the hard edge of the result of the traffic analysis basically, that if you are able to perform traffic analysis on a functional network, then you can do target selection much better than if you had no other information. You showed that if you kill nodes at random the effect is very little relative to killing the nodes that actually matter. So maybe an anonymous communications traffic analysis system for protecting against those kinds of attacks might actually be interesting in terms of privacy research.

Reply. Yes, I see your point. The follow-up work about adversaries who don't know everything because here we are assuming the global passive adversary who doesn't really exist in the world, especially when you think complex networks, ten million nodes, don't have a global passive adversary.

The Initial Costs and Maintenance Costs of Protocols

Ross Anderson

University of Cambridge

Software-engineering academics focussed for many years on the costs of developing the first version of a product, and ignored the costs of subsequent maintenance. We taught our students the 'waterfall model', and biased research towards the sort of tools and ideas that complemented it, such as formal methods. Meanwhile the economics of software had changed. Software is now so complex that the only way to build version N is to start with version N-1. Iterative development methodologies now rule, and the tools that real developers say have helped them most in the last fifteen years are not theorem provers, but automated regression-testing and bug-reporting systems. Nowadays, the maintenance is the product.

Security engineers have been falling into a similar trap. For years, we thought that the problem of authentication began and ended with trustworthy bootstrapping. Once Alice and Bob shared that elusive session key – and could prove mathematically that no-one else did – we could type up the research paper and head for the pub. Again, the real world has changed. Security maintainability is the elephant in the living room; people know there's an awful problem but are generally too polite to mention it (especially as we don't really know what to do with the beast). Vendors used to not care very much; after all, people replace their mobile phones every year, and their PCs every three to five years, so why not just wait for the vulnerable equipment to be thrown on the skip? With luck, vulnerability scares might even help stoke the upgrade cycle.

But attitudes are changing. The hassles caused by vulnerable machines (both directly and indirectly) continue to grow, and consumer expectations harden. Meanwhile, all sorts of consumer durables are acquiring CPUs and communications. If an airconditioner turns out to have a stack overflow in its TCP/IP code, how do you patch it? If you don't, then how do you deal with a virus that switches millions of airconditoners on and off simultaneously, causing a cascade failure of the power grid? And even before we get to the nirvana of pervasive computing, the economics of patching ordinary PCs has become a large and growing topic in security economics.

A number of ideas have emerged recently about designing protocols for maintainability. In [1], for example, we explored what happens when a principal deploys 'smart dust' in an area that is shortly afterwards attacked by an opponent. Assuming that ultra-low-cost dust motes cannot be made tamper-resistant, the opponent can recover shared secrets by reverse engineering a handful of motes and can then eavesdrop on any links whose communications she happens to have monitored. This turns out to be equivalent, in some sense, to a network whose

B. Christianson et al. (Eds.): Security Protocols 2005, LNCS 4631, pp. 333–335, 2007.
© Springer-Verlag Berlin Heidelberg 2007

nodes must send initial key material to each other in the clear. Does this make security impossible? Not at all. Under assumptions that are reasonable in many applications of interest, the opponent will compromise only a small proportion of the links, and this proportion can be kept both low and stable by combining such techniques as key updating and multipath key combination.

A similar situation arises in peer-to-peer systems, where one might assume that principals start out honest but that a small proportion of them may be subverted once the network becomes busy. Here, the problem is not initial key setup, but the design of mechanisms that limit the damage that a compromised node can wreak.

A third type of problem is rate limiting. Many attacks nowadays consist of the industrial-scale repetition of acts that are, on a small scale, not only harmless but encouraged. Examples include downloading a web page, opening an email account and even just sending an email. Here it is not the act that matters, so much as the aggregate, and much of the mischief is perpetrated by machines that started out honest but were subverted along the way.

Economics can give us some insight into how we should analyse and prioritise defence [2]. In the case of smart dust, for example, the game of attack and defence will depend on both the initial and marginal costs, of both the attacker and the defender. Equilibrium depends on marginal costs – attacker efforts versus defender resilience – and the usual outcome will be either that the attacker gives up, or the defender has to go all out to maintain his network. In many cases, it will be rational for the defender to invest in resilience, rather than in more secure bootstrapping. This is yet another reason why shipping an insecure system and patching it later may be rational economic behaviour (in addition to the market races that already provide one such reason in the case of industries with strong first-mover advantages, such as software [3]).

In the specific case of security protocols, there are other difficult issues. Protocol upgrades can be extremely expensive – a change to a bank card payment protocol, for example, can involve 20,000 financial institutions and dozens of software vendors. The design work for a protocol upgrade can be fraught: failures often occur when so many features are inserted that they start interacting, and from multiple backwards-compatibility modes [4]. And that's in the simple case, where the principals agree on the protocol's goals! Where some principals' interests conflict with others' interests – as happens with applications from privacy enhancement through accessory control to DRM – the protocol specification itself becomes the battlefield. How can we analyse all this?

Real-world failures of security protocols may sometimes be explained by economics. Protocols are somewhat like infrastructure, yet are generally not regulated by any government (they change too quickly). They also don't, in general, make their owner monopoly profits: recent attempts by Microsoft to capture the spillover from their server-side networking protocols have been firmly rebuffed by the competition authorities in Europe. So it's unclear that any single principal has sufficient incentive to undertake all the work (and liability) of protocol maintenance. And if one were to hope that collective effort might suffice, then beware the tragedy of the commons: each developer will add features to help its clients and ignore the side-effects on other developers and their clients. While a small number of protocol maintainers might conceivably sort out their dependencies by contract, this doesn't help as complexity explodes, as many protocols rely on other protocols, and the whole business gets tied up with business models such as aftermarket control.

At the deepest level, it's unclear what protocols are – or what they will become once computers are embedded invisibly everywhere. Are protocols more like roads, or more like laws, or more like mechanical interfaces, or more like habits? Different stakeholders will have different views, and we are likely to see some interesting tussles.

References

1. Anderson, R., Chan, H., Perrig, A.: Key Infection: Smart Trust for Smart Dust. In: Proceedings of the 2004 International Conference on Network Protocols, pp. 206–215. IEEE Computer Society Press, Los Alamitos (2004),
http://www.cl.cam.ac.uk/users/rja14/Papers/key-infection.pdf
2. Varian, H.: System Reliability and Free Riding. In: Workshop on Economics and Information Security (2002),
http://www.sims.berkeley.edu/resources/affiliates/workshops/econsecurity/econws/49.pdf
3. Anderson, R.: Why Information Security is Hard – An Economic Perspective. In: Proceedings of the 17th Computer Security Applications Conference, pp. 358–365. IEEE Computer Society Press, Los Alamitos (2001), also given as a distinguished lecture at the Symposium on Operating Systems Principles, Banff (October 2001),
http://www.cl.cam.ac.uk/ftp/users/rja14/econ.pdf
4. Anderson, R., Bond, M.: API-Level Attacks on Embedded Systems. IEEE Computer 34(10), 67–75 (2001),
http://www.cl.cam.ac.uk/users/mkb23/research/API-Attacks.pdf

The Initial Costs and Maintenance Costs of Protocols

(Transcript of Discussion)

Ross Anderson

University of Cambridge

I'd planned to talk about usability and maintainability – in my view, likely to be the two most important research topics in security over the next five years. As everybody's talked about usability, I will talk a bit more about maintainability.

In the old days we always considered that security was about bootstrapping. Once Alice and Bob could be induced to share a key, job done: we go off down the pub and the following day we write the paper. This is a bit like software engineering 30 years ago where people just studied the waterfall model. But the real world nowadays is different. Nobody's interested in waterfall; everybody's interested in evolutionary development, extreme programming and so on. The maintenance is the product – because almost all your costs fall at points in the system development lifecycle other the first one.

How is this going to affect security? Well for companies like Microsoft, the costs of patch management already dominate the security equation by orders of magnitude over the costs of designing stuff for new products. For mobile phone companies the world's about to change: in the old days they assumed that you would toss your phone away every year and buy a new one, and so phone companies, and embedded system companies, ignored maintainability. That cannot persist, because once you start giving devices like air-conditioners communications such as Bluetooth, you really need to fix vulnerabilities. Otherwise somebody will write a virus that turns on all the air-conditioning units in America at six o'clock every day and brings down the power grid.

So the big problem is how you maintain security, and that comes down to two questions: how you maintain data (in other words, cryptographic keys), and how you maintain code. Threat models include intrusions all over the network, and maybe a million nodes compromised in a hundred-million node network. You've somehow got to recover, you've got to ship new protocols, and you've got to recover key material, and you may not be able to do initial bootstrapping well or at all.

I first looked at this some time ago, and gave a talk last year at ICNP on how you distribute keys in sensor networks[1]. PKIs are too expensive, but single symmetric master keys will be compromised when a node is compromised. There are combinatorial techniques, but they're also too expensive. So the idea that I

---

[1] R. Anderson and A. Perrig, Key infection: Smart trust for smart dust. 12th IEEE International Conference on Network Protocols Berlin, Germany, October 2004.

B. Christianson et al. (Eds.): Security Protocols 2005, LNCS 4631, pp. 336–343, 2007.

came up with Adrian Perrig a couple of years ago when I was at Berkeley is that you look more carefully at the threat model.

With 'smart dust', Alice deploys the smart dust somewhere in Bob's territory. She fires an artillery round over the front line, and shhumm! There's a thousand, or a hundred thousand, nodes now scattered over a patch of Bob's territory. Bob detects this and gets his own cannon to fire – shhumm! His black dust covers Alice's white dust, and tries to disable it.

Bob's strategies then include, for example, seeing what movements give rise to sensor traffic, so he learns how capable the white dust is. His active strategies include jamming, deception, routing partition attacks, and so on. If you look at this a bit more closely, you see that Bob starts off as a partial passive defender. He only has a few motes of defensive black dust around his own area when Alice suddenly, shhumm, throws in this huge big network of white dust. This means that he can monitor some of Alice's links initially, but not all of them. After deployment of course the gloves can come off. Bob can send in little robot insects which start reverse engineering white nodes, and he starts doing what he can to monitor and disrupt.

Suppose Alice simply initialised all the nodes in her artillery shell with the same shared secret key, and they use this to bootstrap link keys once they hit the ground. So node 1 says to node 2: 'hi, I'm node 1, and here is a key to communicate with me encrypted under the master key'. Once Bob's reverse engineering ants come along and start extracting keys from the white dust, they get the master key. Now Bob can get access to all the traffic that he actually monitored when the white dust deployed. As he didn't monitor all of it, he might get a fraction of a percent. Alice's nodes will all be communicating in the same frequency, so they all interfere with each other, and Bob can't do long-range monitoring. So the functional model is that the white nodes broadcast keys here, and the black nodes manage to intercept a percent, two percent, five percent, and so on.

We built a model and ran simulations. With a naive approach, one percent of white dust compromised means not quite three percent of links compromised. You can then start doing various improvements on this. You can get each node to 'whisper' – to gradually increase the volume when they respond to a greeting, rather than shouting at full volume, and that improves things. You can then get white nodes to construct multiple paths to each other, in the hope that not all of them will be overheard by black nodes, and that improves things a lot. Dan Cvrček and his colleagues have improved this still further[2] – there was a seminar in the Opera group earlier this week.

The details you can get in the paper. There are all sorts of mechanisms that you can use for reinforcing and refreshing the key security in your cloud of dust – even after deployment, even after the attacks start happening.

---

[2] See `http://www.cl.cam.ac.uk/~dc352/CL_talk2005_wsn.pdf`. Possibly see also Daniel Cvrcek and Petr Svenda, Smart dust security - key infection revisited, International Workshop on Security and Trust Management Milano, 2005; available at `http://www.fit.vutbr.cz/research/view_pub.php?id=7821`.

Other applications? Well one or two of us having been discussing (and Virgil Gligor mentioned yesterday[3]) that a peer-to-peer system might start out with a whole bunch of white nodes, and then black nodes start arriving – perhaps because the Hollywood people put some black nodes in your system, or turned up with court orders and turned ten thousand of your users into disruptive users simply by demanding that they hand over their passwords or go to jail. This is very much like the smart dust model – right? Just like the insects going around turning the white nodes black.

Same with subversive networks: you set up your network of terrorists, and you disperse them all around the world, then you do your 9/11, and some guys say, 'Oh dear, I didn't really sign up to this!' and they go to the FBI. Other people are taken to Guantanamo, and their attitudes are altered. So all of a sudden you have a network in which a percentage of your people have been turned. How do you go about dealing with that – both from the point of view of defence, and from the point of view of attack?

In many real world systems the critical factor is going to be not the cost and effectiveness of initial security bootstrapping, but what you do later for resilience and for recovery.

Now we've been interested in is security economics, because economics often ends up providing the big show stopper. Most of the stuff that breaks in information security doesn't break because Alice uses green encryption instead of red encryption; it breaks because Alice was the person defending the system, whereas Bob was the person who suffered when this security failed.

Now how does the game work for smart dust or for peer-to-peer systems or for terrorist networks? Well it depends on both the initial, and the marginal, costs of attack and defence. The initial key increases the initial cost to both because Alice has got to design her artillery shell so that it can inject an AES key into all the nodes on launch. From Bob's point of view, the initial keying increases his cost because he's then got to design little ants to sink their microprobes into white dust and suck the master key out.

Equilibrium however tends to depend not on your initial costs – that is assuming the markets are in some sense competitive – but on your marginal costs. That's going to mean, on the one hand, your defender efforts, and on the other hand, your attacker resilience.

To see what's going to happen from the point of view of conflict theory, look at Hal Varian's paper in the workshop on Economics and Information Security 2002[4]. Either the defender – Bob – will give up completely, or the attacker – Alice – will have to go all-out to maintain the network. In the latter case, Alice will be continually lobbing over shells of white dust to maintain her network, or else she will be having to devote most of her computational resources to simply

---

[3] These proceedings.

[4] H. Varian, System reliability and free riding. Workshop on Economics and Information Security University of California, Berkeley May 2002; pp. 1-15 in Economics of Information Security, L. J. Camp, S. Lewis, eds. (Kluwer Academic Publishers, 2004), vol. 12 of Advances in Information Security.

keeping the network going, rather than doing useful work. So logically Alice is going to make the investment in resilience rather than bootstrapping. This confirms the intuition that in the long run it's resilience that's going to matter.

Now this brings us to the next question: not how you maintain the data, but how you maintain the code. We know that this can be extraordinarily expensive. Some of us have talked about the world's ATM networks, where a bank protocol upgrade to introduce CVVs, for example, affected perhaps 20,000 financial institutions round the world, so it took many years to roll out, and cost many billions of pounds. And there are horrendous compatibility issues. At present, as we know, the UK chip and PIN system has actually made customers less secure because the various backward-compatibility modes (such as magstripe use in ATMs) interact with the fact that everybody's now using PINs everywhere. Anybody can set up a market stall, get people to swipe cards and PINs, and then can make an ATM card that will work in a cash machine. So the costs of evolving and upgrading a network can be very, very large.

Another issue is the context in which the evolution takes place. Protocols used to evolve socially, and they took hundreds of years to evolve. Nowadays protocols are written by company employees. What are the likely effects of this? Well, in the short term of course, they will promote the interests of that particular corporation, they will enable it to capture markets, lock in aftermarkets, exploit its customers, etc. But how's it going to evolve in the longer term?

There's a philosophical question here, which came out in a discussion that I had with Richard Clayton, Karen Sparck-Jones, George Danezis and Steven Murdoch, a few days ago. Are protocols more like roads, or more like laws, or more like fences, or more like the chemical interfaces, or more like habits? What sort of philosophical model should we have when we contemplate a question such as whether TLS should be upgraded, or whether SSH should be upgraded? Maybe a protocol like SSH is easy to upgrade because it's owned by a company, which can take decisions, but a protocol like TLS is hard? So is this a legislative thing, like changing a law, or is it a private action thing, like a fence, where somebody who owns the land can put up whatever fences he wants? Or is it a mechanical interface? My Peugeot radio has a problem but if I want to change the tape player for a CD player I have to buy it from Peugeot because the mechanical interface has a funny trapezoid rather than a standard rectangle fit.

Economics affect protocol evolution in other ways. We know from history that features get added to a protocol until it breaks. Now why does this happen? Well on the one hand protocols are infrastructure, but they're not regulated by the government; on the other, they tend not to make an owner monopoly profit (except in one or two cases), and so you don't have the right incentives to keep a protocol's design in good shape.

If you're one of the developers who contributes to a protocol, the incentive for you is to add features for your client, and to hell with the adverse effects that this will have on the clients of other people who may very well be your competitors. And so protocol evolution is a classical tragedy of the commons. What do we do about it?

There are a few proprietary exceptions, like the shape of the radio slot in my Peugeot, or the protocol that Hewlett Packard uses to block its printers using non-Hewlett-Packard ink cartridges. But what about protocols that rely on other protocols? I saw an interesting example recently when I tried to open a PayPal account. In order to authenticate me, PayPal wanted to identity of my bank branch, so I said 'NatWest, King's Parade'. It turned out – to cut a long story short – that a couple of weeks ago the NatWest had moved their King's Parade branch to Market Square and they hadn't bothered to tell me, one of their customers. I'm sure you can come up with fancier electronic versions of protocols relying on other protocols, but a real world example perhaps brings the message home.

Now in theory, if you've only got a few parties they can sort it out by contract, but if you've got too many parties you can't do that. PayPal is not really in a position to enter into a contract with each of the world's fifty thousand banks saying: 'if you close or move one of your bank branches then you shall follow the following protocol laid out in this 83 page PDF about how you should duly notify your customers.' Similarly if you're identifying people in Britain on the basis of gas bills, then what sort of regulations do you impose on the gas companies to make sure that they don't issue gas bills to dubious persons who are perhaps illegal immigrants?

So you see there's a number of interesting messes here which spill over from the technical to the policy side of things. What I suggest is wrong about our approach to protocols up to now, is the assumption that authentication is a one-shot game whose purpose is tobootstrap trust. I don't think that will do any more. Maintaining keys within a protocol, and maintaining the protocols themselves by embracing, extending, and so on, is interesting, it's difficult, and it's important.

So what can we do? Well what I've been suggesting here is that firstly we can filch some ideas from social network theory where trust is more of a group reinforcement – bonding people into a particular mode of behaviour – and also from economics which gives us the insights into why protocols get extended until they fail. And we should apply these tools in realistic applications and realistic threat models. And this is just the beginning. Where does it go from here? How do we get a handle on this new complex world of constantly-evolving complex protocols where there's no-one really in charge?

Richard Clayton. You said that protocols get extended till they fail. Perhaps the cause and effect are not that way round. Protocols just fail – they're not very robust things inherently – and that at that point you stop extending them and try and find something else to play with. But if it's a really good design to start off with, then you can keep on extending and adding bits on for a very long time before it actually doesn't work.

Reply. You then push the arguments off to the meta level: who's got the correct incentives to keep the protocol's architecture clean? Because if you allow uncontrolled extension then anything will fail pretty quickly.

Ben Laurie. So how come we've got protocols that work?

Reply. Well we've got lots of protocols that don't work and which people have used quite happily, such as SSL.

Ben Laurie. What do you mean when you say SSL doesn't work?

Reply. Well in a narrow technical sense it works. But in the sense of it doing what people expect to be done when they see a padlock on the browser, it doesn't work at all – as you see from the current spate of phishing attacks.

Ben Laurie. But that's not an extension, that was wrong from the beginning.

Reply. It was perhaps the opposite of an extension because people originally, when they designed X509, thought it was a universal directory service, and they just assumed that everybody would put a cert, that all clients would have certs, and all servers would have certs. Now that didn't happen, so you could see that as a case of a failure where one protocol in the SSL suite depended on another protocol, namely public key infrastructure, which just didn't happen. People said 'All right, let's press ahead with the thing that sort of works, and hope that it will be fixed in time', and then they extended its usage into mass electronic commerce, for which it wasn't particularly suited. So there are many ways you can argue this, but it's still a case of stuff being extended, and relying on other stuff, and breaking.

Ben Laurie. And we seem to have a large number of protocols that work perfectly well like TCP, NGP, SSH, FTP, and BGP.

Richard Clayton. Now look, most of those don't work at all, right, BGP!

Ben Laurie. I didn't say they worked well, I said they worked, they have not failed.

Richard Clayton. No, BGP has been tweaked considerably in order to make it work, and it's heavily damped – i.e. it has lots of pre-set configurations so as to keep it stable. All of the experts would then say that, practically, it isn't stable, and we're just very lucky. They don't know why it works.

Ben Laurie. Well, that does not prove the point. The point is that protocols are supposed to be extended till they fail, and yet I see lots of protocols which have not failed.

Mike Bond. Is working on maintainability of protocols simply playing into the hands of the protocols themselves? You can consider protocols as entities whose purpose, like any other entity, is to persist, and sustain existence. And we need our protocols to ensure a nice stable situation where we can get on with whatever it was we were doing at the time, it's just persisting. The other more cynical view to take is maybe to see all of these things as tools for going away from stability – and that progress is actually driven, not by the desire to allow people to get on with whatever it was they were doing, but by the desire to stop them.

Reply. Well, they're clearly involved in a market context, the IETF protocols versus the ITU protocols, because the IETF ship faster, because the computer industry has a 15 month product cycle while the phone industry has a 15 year product cycle, and that I think is well enough understood. But of course there may be emergent properties as you describe when you consider protocols to be needed.

Tuomas Aura. Protocols can evolve quite fast because they don't depend fully on specification. But there's legacy too: there are some existing methods like passwords for users and SSL certificates for servers, and it seems that no matter what your nice new protocols will define in their version, yes, you can also do SSL certificates for server authentication and passwords for users. This causes a lot of vulnerabilities. If you keep running the old protocols, the new ones break, because you're using the old credentials.

Reply. You could perhaps see the beginnings of a strategy in terms of where parties communicate, they maintain a pool of shared keys, shared secrets, shared randomness, shared history, shared anything. We had a talk from Feng Hao yesterday about how you can extract crypto from shared analogue sites[5], and you have got an extensive theory of pseudorandom number generators. Perhaps if two principals communicate regularly, by means of a number of different protocols, you can define a meta protocol whereby they maintain a pool of shared state that they can update somehow, and thereby get higher quality key material out, which is at least as good as any of the keys they already share. Perhaps you can do this in such a way that it doesn't transmit compromises to any protocols that aren't already compromised, by linking through a hash function. Maybe you can do something like this as a research topic.

Alf Zugenmaier. As you say, we see some research into economics giving you insights, but we need ways to foresee incidents and thus prevent protocols getting extended till they fail. This is actually the research that should get done somehow: what is the incident that happens when we combine two protocols?

Reply. Well there's a technical instrument which enables guys like us to sit down and design a protocol which under certain circumstances won't break, but then there's the higher level process by which this protocol gets sold to Microsoft, and also to Sun, and also to IETF, and so on and so forth. Now history is littered with protocols that might have kind of worked but didn't make it in the market. Think SET – good idea on the face of it, in practice the development got out of control and the thing never got built.

Mike Roe. There are subtleties. For example, suppose someone's protocol has broken someone else's extension of your protocol but doesn't break the original deployment?

Reply. It depends. If you use your key material in a broken protocol then it does – this is the insight of the chosen protocol attack[6]. If you absolutely lock your key material down to a particular instance, in a particular application of a protocol, and you can ensure that any bootstrapping that gets done off that is one-way, then you're probably all right. But we don't have meta rules for doing

---

[5] These proceedings.

[6] J. Kelsey, B. Schneier and D. Wagner. "Protocol Interactions and the Chosen Protocol Attack", LNCS 1361, pp91-104.

that, at least not meta rules that are widely understood by the general developer community.

Mike Roe. OK, so if you've got some key material then people will do more and more slightly different things with that key material until they can't, that seems to be how it goes.

Reply. That's one aspect of it, the extension of crypto transaction sets is another aspect of it. Do we have any things that we can say in general? Now of course it's easy to say in general that if Richard and I want to accumulate high-grade crypto key material then we should not put all our keys into the pot, we should at best take one-way hash functions with appropriate confounders to the key material that we've got, and put that into the shared band in this pot, that's tripos level stuff.

Pekka Nikander. I think we have to make a distinction between two ways that protocols get extended. One is that they get tactically extended, so somebody actually decides something new to the protocol – or a new twist in a way something that's more or less part of the protocol – that extends it. Then there is external extension, where something uses the protocol, or the key material in a different context. So there is a distinction between changing, or extending, the protocol in a tactical sense, and then changing or extending the context where the protocol's used.

Reply. Yes, there is, and protocol failures have occurred in both contexts. Examples of extension: I suppose the fact that in S/MIME you can choose the order of encryption and signature, and SSL, which introduces ciphersuites so that you could have exportability. Certainly there are many protocols used in inappropriate contexts.

Richard Clayton. You've not really said anything about when protocol changes first break your assumptions. I was particularly struck by the example the other week where somebody stole a credit card from the post, and then they needed some other information in order to activate it. So they dropped a note through the person's door, pretending to be the courier company who failed to deliver the card. The person rang the 'courier company' and left their number on an answering machine. The crooks then had the cardholder's phone number, and rang pretending they were about to send out a credit card. I thought that was very neat. The bank probably assumed that people would not leak their phone numbers to card thieves, because lots of people are ex-directory these days. A lot of protocols break that way. There's the assumption that something is secret, like your mother's maiden name and so forth, but once we've set up a database so that we can look up birth certificates on-line, suddenly that information is available. Anybody can play.

Reply. Absolutely, one man's password is another man's name.

Alice and Bob

John Gordon

University of Hertfordshire

Good evening Ladies and Gentlemen[1].

There comes a time when people at a technical conference like this need something more relaxing. A change of pace. A shift of style. To put aside all that work stuff and think of something refreshingly different.

So let's talk about coding theory. There are perhaps some of you here tonight who are not experts in coding theory, but rather have been dragged here kicking and screaming. So I thought it would be a good idea if I gave you a sort of instant, five minute graduate course in coding theory.

Coding theorists are concerned with two things. Firstly and most importantly they are concerned with the private lives of two people called Alice and Bob. In theory papers, whenever a coding theorist wants to describe a transaction between two parties he doesn't call then A and B. No. For some longstanding traditional reason he calls them Alice and Bob.

Now there are hundreds of papers written about Alice and Bob. Over the years Alice and Bob have tried to defraud insurance companies, they've played poker for high stakes by mail, and they've exchanged secret messages over tapped telephones.

If we put together all the little details from here and there, snippets from lots of papers, we get a fascinating picture of their lives. This may be the first time a definitive biography of Alice and Bob has been given.

In papers written by American authors Bob is frequently selling stock to speculators. From the number of stock market deals Bob is involved in we infer that he is probably a stockbroker. However from his concern about eavesdropping he is probably active in some subversive enterprise as well. And from the number of times Alice tries to buy stock from him we infer she is probably a speculator. Alice is also concerned that her financial dealings with Bob are not brought to the attention of her husband. So Bob is a subversive stockbroker and Alice is a two-timing speculator.

But Alice has a number of serious problems. She and Bob only get to talk by telephone or by electronic mail. In the country where they live the telephone service is very expensive. And Alice and Bob are cheapskates. So the first thing Alice must do is MINIMIZE THE COST OF THE PHONE CALL.

The telephone is also very noisy. Often the interference is so bad that Alice and Bob can hardly hear each other. On top of that Alice and Bob have very powerful enemies. One of their enemies is the Tax Authority. Another is the

---

[1] This is part of an after-dinner speech given at the Zurich Seminar, April 1984, by John Gordon, at the invitation of Professor James Massey. It is reproduced here by kind permission of the author.

B. Christianson et al. (Eds.): Security Protocols 2005, LNCS 4631, pp. 344–345, 2007.

Secret Police. This is a pity, since their favorite topics of discussion are tax frauds and overthrowing the government.

These enemies have almost unlimited resources. They always listen in to telephone conversations between Alice and Bob. And these enemies are very sneaky. One of their favorite tricks is to telephone Alice and pretend to be Bob.

Well, you think, so all Alice has to do is listen very carefully to be sure she recognizes Bob's voice. But no. You see Alice has never met Bob. She has no idea what his voice sounds like.

So you see Alice has a whole bunch of problems to face. Oh yes, and there is one more thing I forgot to say - Alice doesn't trust Bob. We don't know why she doesn't trust him, but at some time in the past there has been an incident.

Now most people in Alice's position would give up. Not Alice. She has courage which can only be described as awesome. Against all odds, over a noisy telephone line, tapped by the tax authorities and the secret police, Alice will happily attempt, with someone she doesn't trust, whom she cannot hear clearly, and who is probably someone else, to fiddle her tax returns and to organize a coup d'etat, while at the same time minimizing the cost of the phone call.

A coding theorist is someone who doesn't think Alice is crazy.

Author Index

Lecture Notes in Computer Science

Sublibrary 4: Security and Cryptology

Vol. 4296: M.S. Rhee, B. Lee (Eds.), Information Security and Cryptology – ICISC 2006. XIII, 358 pages. 2006.

Vol. 4284: X. Lai, K. Chen (Eds.), Advances in Cryptology – ASIACRYPT 2006. XIV, 468 pages. 2006.

Vol. 4283: Y.Q. Shi, B. Jeon (Eds.), Digital Watermarking. XII, 474 pages. 2006.

Vol. 4266: H. Yoshiura, K. Sakurai, K. Rannenberg, Y. Murayama, S.-i. Kawamura (Eds.), Advances in Information and Computer Security. XIII, 438 pages. 2006.

Vol. 4258: G. Danezis, P. Golle (Eds.), Privacy Enhancing Technologies. VIII, 431 pages. 2006.

Vol. 4249: L. Goubin, M. Matsui (Eds.), Cryptographic Hardware and Embedded Systems - CHES 2006. XII, 462 pages. 2006.

Vol. 4237: H. Leitold, E.P. Markatos (Eds.), Communications and Multimedia Security. XII, 253 pages. 2006.

Vol. 4236: L. Breveglieri, I. Koren, D. Naccache, J.-P. Seifert (Eds.), Fault Diagnosis and Tolerance in Cryptography. XIII, 253 pages. 2006.

Vol. 4219: D. Zamboni, C. Krügel (Eds.), Recent Advances in Intrusion Detection. XII, 331 pages. 2006.

Vol. 4189: D. Gollmann, J. Meier, A. Sabelfeld (Eds.), Computer Security – ESORICS 2006. XI, 548 pages. 2006.

Vol. 4176: S.K. Katsikas, J. López, M. Backes, S. Gritzalis, B. Preneel (Eds.), Information Security. XIV, 548 pages. 2006.

Vol. 4117: C. Dwork (Ed.), Advances in Cryptology - CRYPTO 2006. XIII, 621 pages. 2006.

Vol. 4116: R. De Prisco, M. Yung (Eds.), Security and Cryptography for Networks. XI, 366 pages. 2006.

Vol. 4107: G. Di Crescenzo, A. Rubin (Eds.), Financial Cryptography and Data Security. XI, 327 pages. 2006.

Vol. 4083: S. Fischer-Hübner, S. Furnell, C. Lambrinoudakis (Eds.), Trust and Privacy in Digital Business. XIII, 243 pages. 2006.

Vol. 4064: R. Büschkes, P. Laskov (Eds.), Detection of Intrusions and Malware & Vulnerability Assessment. X, 195 pages. 2006.

Vol. 4058: L.M. Batten, R. Safavi-Naini (Eds.), Information Security and Privacy. XII, 446 pages. 2006.

Vol. 4047: M.J.B. Robshaw (Ed.), Fast Software Encryption. XI, 434 pages. 2006.

Vol. 4043: A.S. Atzeni, A. Lioy (Eds.), Public Key Infrastructure. XI, 261 pages. 2006.

Vol. 4004: S. Vaudenay (Ed.), Advances in Cryptology - EUROCRYPT 2006. XIV, 613 pages. 2006.

Vol. 3995: G. Müller (Ed.), Emerging Trends in Information and Communication Security. XX, 524 pages. 2006.

Vol. 3989: J. Zhou, M. Yung, F. Bao (Eds.), Applied Cryptography and Network Security. XIV, 488 pages. 2006.

Vol. 3969: Ø. Ytrehus (Ed.), Coding and Cryptography. XI, 443 pages. 2006.

Vol. 3958: M. Yung, Y. Dodis, A. Kiayias, T.G. Malkin (Eds.), Public Key Cryptography - PKC 2006. XIV, 543 pages. 2006.

Vol. 3957: B. Christianson, B. Crispo, J.A. Malcolm, M. Roe (Eds.), Security Protocols. IX, 325 pages. 2006.

Vol. 3956: G. Barthe, B. Grégoire, M. Huisman, J.-L. Lanet (Eds.), Construction and Analysis of Safe, Secure, and Interoperable Smart Devices. IX, 175 pages. 2006.

Vol. 3935: D.H. Won, S. Kim (Eds.), Information Security and Cryptology - ICISC 2005. XIV, 458 pages. 2006.

Vol. 3934: J.A. Clark, R.F. Paige, F.A.C. Polack, P.J. Brooke (Eds.), Security in Pervasive Computing. X, 243 pages. 2006.

Vol. 3928: J. Domingo-Ferrer, J. Posegga, D. Schreckling (Eds.), Smart Card Research and Advanced Applications. XI, 359 pages. 2006.

Vol. 3919: R. Safavi-Naini, M. Yung (Eds.), Digital Rights Management. XI, 357 pages. 2006.

Vol. 3903: K. Chen, R. Deng, X. Lai, J. Zhou (Eds.), Information Security Practice and Experience. XIV, 392 pages. 2006.

Vol. 3897: B. Preneel, S. Tavares (Eds.), Selected Areas in Cryptography. XI, 371 pages. 2006.

Vol. 3876: S. Halevi, T. Rabin (Eds.), Theory of Cryptography. XI, 617 pages. 2006.

Vol. 3866: T. Dimitrakos, F. Martinelli, P.Y.A. Ryan, S. Schneider (Eds.), Formal Aspects in Security and Trust. X, 259 pages. 2006.

Vol. 3860: D. Pointcheval (Ed.), Topics in Cryptology – CT-RSA 2006. XI, 365 pages. 2006.

Vol. 3858: A. Valdes, D. Zamboni (Eds.), Recent Advances in Intrusion Detection. X, 351 pages. 2006.

Vol. 3856: G. Danezis, D. Martin (Eds.), Privacy Enhancing Technologies. VIII, 273 pages. 2006.

Vol. 3786: J.-S. Song, T. Kwon, M. Yung (Eds.), Information Security Applications. XI, 378 pages. 2006.

Vol. 3108: H. Wang, J. Pieprzyk, V. Varadharajan (Eds.), Information Security and Privacy. XII, 494 pages. 2004.

Vol. 2951: M. Naor (Ed.), Theory of Cryptography. XI, 523 pages. 2004.

Vol. 2742: R.N. Wright (Ed.), Financial Cryptography. VIII, 321 pages. 2003.